Virtual Reality ExCursions
WITH **PROGRAMS** IN C

LIMITED WARRANTY AND DISCLAIMER OF LIABILITY

Virtual Reality ExCursions
WITH PROGRAMS IN C

Christopher D. Watkins
Stephen R. Marenka

AP PROFESSIONAL

Boston   San Diego   New York
London   Sydney   Tokyo   Toronto

AP PROFESSIONAL
955 Massachusetts Avenue, Cambridge, MA 02139

An imprint of ACADEMIC PRESS, INC.
A Division of HARCOURT BRACE & COMPANY

United Kingdom Edition published by
ACADEMIC PRESS LIMITED
24–28 Oval Road, London NW1 7DX

ISBN 0-12-737865-0

Printed in the United States of America
94 95 96 97 98 ML 9 8 7 6 5 4 3 2 1

Contents

List of Illustrations

Acknowledgments

The outline for this book was generated by Christopher D. Watkins and Stephen R. Marenka. The technical text and figures were written and created by Christopher D. Watkins, while the vast writing of the general text was done by Stephen R. Marenka. Vincent Mallette of the Georgia Institute of Technology made gross contributions to the human perception chapter of this book, with the research assistance of Alice Merta and Cassandra Jeffries. Christopher D. Watkins is totally responsible for the labour of birth for all of the software found with this book. Some proofing of the manuscript, as well as compilation of profiles for companies and universities involved in virtual reality products and research, was done by Christina N. Noland.

All of the software in this book was written in C using Borland C++ version 3.1. The Borland C++ software was furnished by Borland International, 1800 Green Hills Road, Scotts Valley, CA 95066.

Thanks also to WATCOM of 415 Phillip Street, Ontario, Canada, N2L 3X2 for supplying the WATCOM compiler version 9.5.

Thanks go to director Michael Sinclair of the Georgia Institute of Technology Multimedia Technology Laboratory for supplying images of the Eye Surgery Simulator, of the Motion Interactive System for sports, and of the three-dimensional scanner output.

Thanks go to Paul Kingston and Schelly Weedman of IVEX Corporation for information and images regarding the IVEX Visual System for Flight Simulation. IVEX Corporation designs, manufactures, and markets a series of high-performance visual simulation systems for use in civil and military training markets. Their systems distinguish themselves from others in that the overall reality of the visual scene is greater. This "reality" is primarily achieved using fractual texturing methods and high polygon counts for detail. IVEX Corporation is located at 4355 International Blvd., Norcross, GA 30093.

Thanks go to director James D. Foley, Larry Hodges, and Tom Meyer of the Georgia Institute of Technology College of Computing Graphics, Visualization & Usability (GVU) Center for the remainder of the images found throughout the book and for their contributions regarding virtual reality research.

Thanks go to Thomas Morley of Georgia Institute of Technology for supplying information on mass-spring systems.

Thanks to John Poulton and Linda Houseman of the University of North Carolina at Chapel Hill for their contributions regarding their research into virtual reality.

Thanks go to Ken Welton and Michael Glaser of Lavista Systems, Inc., Tucker, Georgia for supplying equipment necessary for the completion of this book.

Thanks to Jordan Hargrave for supplying us with the BGI graphics drivers found along with the software. The drivers are copyright Jordan Hargrave.

Thanks to Jack Brady of Southeastern Digital Images, Inc. and C/Food Software, Atlanta, for acting as a sounding board for ideas.

Thanks go to Jack Tumblin for his brainstorming regarding three-dimensional computer graphics techniques.

Thanks go to Stephen B. Coy for his help in obtaining information on algorithms for polygon filling and for his brainstorming on three-dimensional computer graphics techniques.

Thanks go to Adam Schiffman of The Graphics Alternative for production of his copyrighted image "silver surfers" found on the front cover of this book. The Graphics Alternative consults for 3D Animation, 2D Imaging, and Video. The Graphics Alternative is located at 190 El Cerrito Plaza #107, EL Cerrito, CA 94530, and TGA can also be contacted by voice at 510-528-1652 or BBS at 510-524-2780.

Thanks go to Mitch Kolbe of 34 W. Orange Street, Tarpon Springs, Florida for providing the photorealistic paintings used as texture maps. Mr. Kolbe has worked on such projects as one of America's largest murals, The Cyclorama, which depicts the Civil War in Atlanta in 1864. Several projects followed the completion of The Cyclorama; these included museum background murals, which required molding, casting, and fiberglass sculpture, as well as work for the U.S. Fish and Wildlife Service, Epcot Center, and Disney World. Since 1985 Mr. Kolbe has been fully dedicated to the creation of fine art oil paintings. He presently resides in the original studio of the famous artist George Innes Jr. in Tarpon Springs, Florida.

Algorithm, Inc. of 3776 Lavista Road, Suite 100A, Atlanta, GA 30084 produces tools for ray tracing, volume rendering, 3-D modeling and VR, animation, image processing, and interactive image warping and morphing. Contact us at the above address or call/fax (404) 634-0920 for more information regarding our products.

And special thanks again go to our parents, wives, and friends for their love and patience with us during this project.

And, as always, much thanks again to the Coca-Cola Company and to the Jolt Cola Company for providing Cola and to Snapple for providing tea to keep us awake long enough to complete this project.

Biographies

Christopher D. Watkins is founder and president of *Algorithm, Inc.*, an Atlanta-based scientific research and engineering company that produces software for medical imaging and visualization, photorealistic rendering, virtual reality, and animation. He is an electrical engineer, an experienced programmer, and coauthor of *Photorealism and Ray Tracing* (M&T Books, 1992) and *Modern Image Processing: Warping, Morphing and Classical Techniques* (Academic Press, 1993). He received his degrees from The Georgia Institute of Technology and is a member of the IEEE and of the ACM/SIGGRAPH.

Stephen R. Marenka is an electrical engineer from the Georgia Institute of Technology, specializing in intelligent control, data reduction techniques, and human-computer interfaces for multiplatform computing (VAX/VMS, Unix, Macintosh, and PC systems). He is working on his MS in electrical engineering control systems. He is also a coauthor of *Modern Image Processing: Warping, Morphing and Classical Techniques* (Academic Press, 1993) and is a member of the IEEE Control Systems and Computer Societies.

It's All in the Name

You will be encountering some unusual words and terms which surround virtual reality research and development, some of which follow.

> display—a device (as a cathode-ray tube) that gives information in visual form in communications

The term display as used in the virtual environments field of research is applied more generally, such as:

> display—a device that gives information in communications

Now we may use the term display in reference to a visual display—a computer screen, an auditory display—a stereo or other sound source, and a haptic display—motion, tactile, or force-feedback equipment.

> haptic—relating to or based on the sense of touch

The term haptic includes all displays that present information to the loosely defined sense of touch, including tactile, texture, force-feedback, motion, and pressure.

Virtual environments research in modern times is often traced to Ivan Sutherland's 1965 paper "The Ultimate Display," presented to the triennial conference of the International Processing Societies. Sutherland described "a program of research in computer graphics which has challenged and guided the field ever since." Sutherland said that one must look at a computer display screen as a window through which one beholds a *virtual world*. "The challenge to computer graphics is to make the window look real, sound real, and the objects act real. Indeed, in the ultimate display, one will not look at that world through a window, but will be immersed in it, will change viewpoint by natural motions of head and body, and will interact directly and naturally with the object in the world, hearing and feeling them, as well as seeing them." Such research has proceeded under a variety of names, including *virtual environments, virtual reality, artificial reality,* and *synthetic experience.* (Fuchs and Fisher)

> virtual—being in effect but not in actual fact

environment—the conditions, circumstances, and influences surrounding and affecting an organism.

reality—of or relating to practical or everyday concerns or activities

Many of the top researchers in the field, including Frederick Brooks at the University of North Carolina in Chapel Hill and Scott Fisher, formerly of NASA Ames Research Center and now of Telepresence Research, prefer the usage of the term *virtual environments* to describe the field. Jaron Lanier, formerly of VPL Research, coined and prefers the term *virtual reality.* Myron Krueger coined and prefers the term *artificial reality,* which refers to a specific subset of research defined in his book *Artificial Reality.*

This book uses the terms virtual environment and virtual reality indiscriminately. Also, we specifically include parallel lines of research which may not be wholly immersive in nature (since very few systems, if any, can totally immerse all of the senses at this point in time anyway).

The term DataGlove is VPL Research's trademark name for a hand-based input device, further defined in the glossary. You will soon encounter other terms which may be unfamiliar to you; please refer to the glossary in the appendix for definitions of these and other important relevant concepts.

Initialization

Welcome to a magical land where anything is possible and the physical laws of the real world no longer apply, the land of virtual reality. In this book we make an excursion into this realm to learn about its history, the defining boundaries of the land, and all the fascinating things happening within its borders. In the first chapter we explore the current applications in the vast field of virtual reality. The second chapter presents a brief history of the field and its founders. Chapter 3 comprises human perception and how it works. We cover some interesting notes and much of the hot debate in the field in Chapter four. The fifth chapter describes many of the complexities involved in implementing virtual environments on real equipment. There is lots of good stuff in the appendix; we highly recommend that you take a look. Enjoy the ride!

If we perceive our role aright, we then see more clearly the proper criterion for success: a toolmaker succeeds as, and only as, the *users* of his tool succeed with his aid. However shining the blade, however jeweled the hilt, however perfect the heft, a sword is tested only by cutting. That swordsmith is successful whose clients die of old age.

—F. Brooks, "Grasping Reality Through Illusion: Interactive Graphics Serving Science"

CHAPTER 1

VIRTUAL REALITY APPLICATIONS

Introduction

Research and development into virtual environment applications can be found in many places, all over the world. This chapter presents a smattering of the applications either commercially available or still under development but demonstrating important possibilities. The fact of the matter is that only recently has the computer power become available to allow virtual environments of reasonable complexity to be built. It remains to be seen whether business and consumers will adopt or discard any of this technology. Some of the major potential applications that may define the field in the future are discussed in the Virtual Considerations chapter.

Applications for virtual environments can be divided into the following major categories: architectural walkthroughs and computer-aided design; augmentation and decision support; telecommunications, interfaces, and remote workplaces; training; scientific exploration; entertainment. Because of the potential for revolution in the medical field, all related virtual environment techniques are presented together. As we explore some of the important

Figure 1.1—In another world (Virtual Research HMDs)

applications for each field in turn, you will notice that many of these fields overlap—in which case the selection of category is quite arbitrary.

Section 1—Architectural Walkthroughs and Computer-Aided Design

The field of computer-aided design ranges from computer-aided drafting, which replaces the T-square, paper, and pencil with a computer, to Computer-Aided Manufacturing, where a computer controls some sort of manufacturing machinery apparatus. These seemingly diverse fields can all be incorporated on the same computer (or several computers working closely together). The design for some product, be it a building, an aircraft, or a computer expansion card, can be created using that computer. Then that very design may be used for quality assurance, design for manufacturing, design for environment, and logistics (to make sure all the parts are readily available, for instance).

Virtual environment techniques can add a great deal to the computer-aided designer's arsenal. Allowing a designer to see a design from all possible angles, and to manipulate it using a hand instead of a keyboard, can greatly aid rapid prototyping and verification of designs before any kind of working drawings are created or large expenses are incurred. Perhaps even more remarkable, the whole design process can be documented on the computer system, allowing future designers and field engineers to have access to the whole system design documentation. With the help of an expert system, a field engineer who had never seen that particular piece of equipment before could have all the information she could need to fix the system.

In one of the following examples, a designer can sit in a tractor, operate all the important controls, and "look around" the design to ensure that the operator will have as much visibility as possible and that all safety issues are addressed. It is surely much less expensive to do several iterations of such a design in a virtual environment than it is to build a prototype tractor in iron.

Architectural walkthroughs can be treated as a well-defined subset of computer-aided design applied to architecture. In any virtual environment, the participant may be allowed to walk around the entire environment, but in buildings the experience is more directly comparable to our everyday experiences. Even in a cartoon-like world, the participant generally avoids walls, columns, and other solid-looking objects and walks through doors, even when the environment allows participants to walk through all solid objects (as most environments do).

Frederick Brooks and the University of North Carolina in Chapel Hill have been pioneering the field of architectural walkthrough. The concept is to model a building in full detail before it is built, indeed before the first real working drawings have been drawn. In this manner changes can easily be made and tested before any significant expense has been incurred. Architects and engineers have long held that they can read blueprints and "see" the building in three dimensions in their head. Although this may be true, the customers rarely have this gift or training. The only traditional ways for them to see a model of the building is by means of architectural renderings or foam, paint, and glue models.

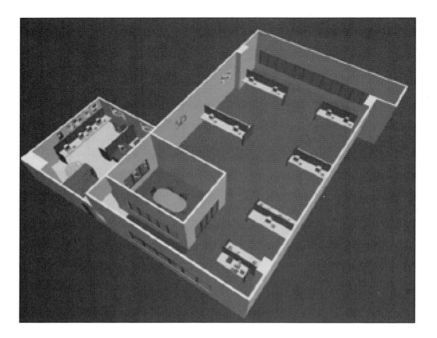

Figure 1.2—Aerial view of the GVU Center lab

Figure 1.3—View of a virtual man in a virtual environment

As their first virtual environment, the UNC team created the lobby of Sitterson Hall, the building to which they would be moving once it was built. The virtual environments team wanted to make some design decisions about the width of the upper lobby. Their experience with this project led them to realize that the complexity of real buildings was an excellent "driving problem" for the creation of virtual environments. It provides real challenges in the complexity and problems of three-dimensional real time interactive computer graphics. Another advantage is that sooner or later the building will be built, and then it can then be compared to the virtual environment model.

The UNC researchers have experimented with many different ways of exploring their virtual environments. The view may be provided by big screen displays or head-mounted displays. They use joysticks; a Polhemus 3-space tracker embedded in half of a pool ball, called the "eyeball"; a steerable treadmill; and even a room-sized virtual environment that incorporates a head-mounted display with a ceiling tracker. (UNC Literature)

The Seattle Port of Authority, in conjunction with the Human Interface Lab in Seattle, Washington, is developing a virtual environment to test proposed expansion plans for the port. Cecil Patterson, the information systems director, feels that there are two major reasons for looking at virtual reality technology. First, there is no substitute for walking around a model in three dimensions to get a feel for how it will do the job. Even though many of the users of the port are from Pacific Rim countries where English is not the native language, it is much harder to have disagreements and misunderstandings about exactly what changes are proposed when all concerned parties can explore the same virtual environment. The second use of the technology is as a "what if?" machine for computer-aided design. Instead of wondering what moving a dock twenty-five feet or half a mile will mean, the operator can pick it up and move it. (Rheingold, VR)

Caterpillar Inc. of Peoria, Illinois is very excited about virtual environments. They are working in conjunction with the National Center for Supercomputing Applications at the University of Illinois in Urbana-Champaign. Earth moving and construction equipment operators need visibility from as many different angles as possible, both for reasons of safety and for ease of operations. Designers sit in a minimalist mock-up cab, wear a head-mounted display, and get the feel of operating the equipment in different configurations. Gear shifts, bucket controls, and pedals are all part of both the mock-up and the virtual environment. Virtual reality tools allow designers to try new configurations, determine which designs are superior, and avoid committing bad designs to iron. Since many of the production runs are small lots, price, safety, and time to market are all significantly enhanced. (Adam, p. 24)

The Boeing Company is working in conjunction with the Human Interface Technology Lab and the University of Washington to develop a new generation of computer-aided design tools to develop large aircraft. The Boeing Company's new 777 airliner is the first ever created without a full-scale physical mock-up and with few conventional working drawings. While VR tools are currently only for experimental use at Boeing, virtual reality support played a key part even though the technology is not capable of displaying the whole design at acceptable frame rates and detail. When you are is trying to envision a complex collection of parts, it is of great use to be able to "stick your head" into the design. (Adam, pp. 26-7 and Peterson, p. 10)

The city of Berlin, now no longer separated, contracted with the German company Art+Com and VPL Research to model the city of Berlin in VPL's Virtual Reality environment. The model will help in planning the reconstruction of the city and many of its buildings. Several buildings are completely modeled, including the national gallery. (Lanier)

A department store's kitchen sales area in Tokyo, Japan has a VPL system. "The salesman takes down the measurements of the kitchen at your house. Then you put on goggles and glove and suddenly you're in a room the size of your kitchen." You can design your kitchen by moving things around the virtual environment until everything is the way you want it. The cabinet doors open and the water faucet works. If you're happy with the design, you sign a form, and the store delivers and installs your new kitchen. Matsushita Electric Works intends to extend this vision to include a complete house, allowing the owner to design and try out the house in cyberspace. (Lanier)

Lockheed Missiles and Space Company of Palo Alto, California and General Dynamics Corporation's Electric Boat Division of Groton, Connecticut under the auspices of the Defense Advanced Research Projects Agency (DARPA), are assessing virtual ship and submarine design. The Seawolf submarine has three times the number of drawings that its predecessors had—and humans are simply unable to keep up with the complexity of such designs. The current contract calls for building virtual environments of sections of a submarine, such as the torpedo room. The eventual goal is to test-fire virtual submarines on virtual seas, which would allow different designs to be evaluated long before any prototypes are built. (Adam, p. 27)

The big three American automobile manufacturers are joining the U.S. Army vehicle center, United Technologies' automotive division, the University

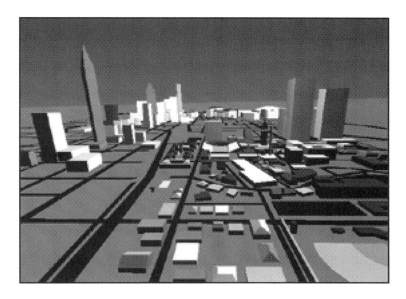

Figure 1.4—View over Georgia Tech Campus and Downtown
Atlanta from the North

Figure 1.5—View over Georgia Tech Campus and the Tower

Figure 1.6—View over Georgia Tech Campus and the Coliseum

of Michigan, Ann Arbor, and many smaller firms to form a consortium for industrial VR. They believe VR will provide the following benefits:

1) virtual prototyping to reduce or eliminate the need for physical mockups
2) engineering simulation of virtual prototypes
3) operational simulation of virtual prototypes—people can sit in a car and see if they like the upholstery
4) virtual simulations of assembly, production, and maintenance to develop optimum strategies and to detect and eliminate potential problems
5) augmented reality to support assembly and maintenance, which will increase effectiveness and decrease training time
6) concurrent engineering communications tools

(Adam, pp. 25-6)

Chrysler is working with IBM's Watson Labs in Hawthorne, New York, to develop virtual cars. Three-dimensional images are displayed on a large front-projection screen using goggles to provide stereo vision. A glove provides such manipulation capabilities as turning the steering wheel.

Lockheed Corporation's Optical Design Group under the auspices of NASA have created a virtual prototype, called Preview (gak—Prevent Real Errors by Virtual Investigation of Engineering Worlds), of the Hubble Space Telescope primary mirror aberration repair equipment, called Costar (Corrective Optics Space Telescope Axial Replacement). That is, NASA had a virtual environment built within which the Hubble Space Telescope and the equipment that was used to fix its main mirror aberrations was built. The virtual prototype quickly found several problems that would not have been found until the physical prototype was built (which would have required the Space Shuttle repair schedule to have been slipped back). One of the problems found probably would not have been detected even with the physical prototype.

The Costar replaced one of the instrument equipment racks on the Hubble. It has several lenses placed on extension arms with which it can correct the image coming from the secondary mirror before the image reaches any of the other instrument packages. The virtual prototype discovered that one of the arms could not be properly extended; it verified an optical collision with the Faint-Object Camera; and most important, it discovered that some of the corrective lenses had stray light reflections of the secondary mirror—a problem that could mask faint objects with a haze of light. Finally, the virtual prototype enabled cameras to be properly positioned and focused to verify that the space hardware would properly fit in an exact instrument bay physical mock-up. The virtual prototype was fantastically successful in these applications. (Hancock, pp. 34 - 39)

The Rockwell International Science Center in Thousand Oaks, California has developed Virtual Reality interfaces for Rockwell products using the Sense8 WorldToolKit. Rockwell believes that "intimate human/computer interfaces" including "stereoscopic head-coupled head-mounted displays, 3D localized audio cues, speech recognition, force-feedback and tactile sensing" are required for the computer-aided design system of the future. Research has been conducted on the following virtual reality interfaces: "(1) the Intelligent Vehicle Highway System (IVHS), a next-generation highway vehicle control system; (2) mobile missile launch Command and Control centers; (3) fighter cockpits; (4) space vehicle crew systems; (5) guided remote robotics systems; and (6) complex structure prototyping and human factors evaluation." (Sense8)

NASA's Marshall Space Flight Center in Huntsville, Alabama has constructed a "low fidelity space station to help pathfind and check out the

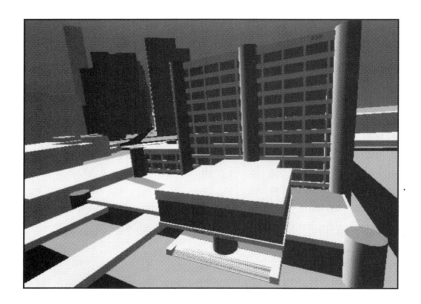

Figure 1.7—View above Georgia State University Urban Life / Law Building and downtown Atlanta

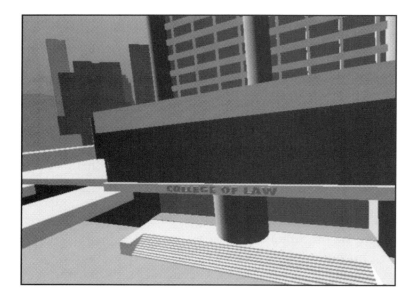

Figure 1.8—View from street of Georgia State University Law Building and downtown Atlanta

system." The virtual environment has been created on a VPL RB2 (Reality Build for 2) system. Among other experiments, the system has been used to "evaluate and assess three different configurations of the space station Crystal Growth Furnace." (VPL & Lanier)

Northrop Corporation in cooperation with SimGraphics Engineering Corporation is redesigning the U.S. Air Force's F-18 fighter. The virtual reality system lets engineers move parts of the airplane around—the parts even "bump" when they collide. Parts can be tested to be sure they fit even before they are committed to physical models. (Hamilton, p. 98)

Section 2—Augmentation and Decision Support

Augmentation, having computers supplement human capabilities, is one of the oldest goals of virtual reality research. Computers and virtual environment techniques can provide operators with physical augmentation, such as "seeing" with radar, and intellectual augmentation, such as financial analysis processing. Augmentation includes the part of computer-aided design that would allow a field engineer access to all of the design information, all of the manuals and reference works, while in the field. The most important concept is that the computer is helping a human perform a function, often one which could not be performed in a timely manner or with the same quality without computer assistance. A decision support system is simply an augmentation system designed to help operators, such as air traffic controllers, make important decisions, usually in a timely manner.

Paul Marshall of Maxus Systems International "helps America's largest mutual fund find secure and profitable markets to invest in. The fund is one of the few that invests in international industries, from Hong Kong to Kuala Lumpur and from paper to communications." A Reuters news feed provides the constantly fluctuating data of the world markets to an analytical program which summarizes the data. Sense8's WorldToolKit software is used to provide a desktop, three-dimensional virtual landscape of multicolored squares which are at varying "heights" and represent different stocks. Rows represent financial markets such as Hong Kong or Tokyo. Columns represent industries such as oil and construction. Textures are used to identify rows and columns. The financial analyst can "fly" over the financial landscape, gaining information about the changing relationships of patterns of the world's stock markets. (Sense 8, Hamilton, p. 99, and Coull, p. 23)

Crystal River Engineering has developed a piece of equipment that provides audio in three dimensions, called the Convolvotron. NASA, in association with the Federal Aviation Administration, is studying use of this system to help aid air traffic controllers. The system has already been tested as part of a collision-avoidance system—pilot responses were sped up by one to two seconds, enough to change a collision into a near miss. (Graff, p. 617)

The Boeing Company is working in conjunction with the Human Interface Technology Lab and the University of Washington on a project which involves the augmentation of factory floor workers. Instead of exploring another (virtual) world, these systems would be superimposed on part of the real world. Several of the applications include virtual manuals that can be displayed next to whatever the worker is doing. Difficult and complex processes which require expensive templates might be simplified with virtual overlays. The overlay would be seen only by the worker, could be customized to the individual physical piece, and would eliminate the problems of manufacturing and aligning a physical template. Augmented realities could include oscilloscope readouts, schematics, or drill-hole locations. (Adam, pp. 26-7 and Peterson, p. 10)

Professor Ronald Pickett of the University of Massachusetts at Lowell has developed a virtual world that looks like grass. The blades of grass may change length, curve, and arc to represent data such as income level, age, and sex. The selection of grass goes back to our genetic makeup and the reflexes our forebears needed for survival; our highly optimized information-gathering systems can be put directly to use with the selection of a proper metaphor (such as grass). (Hamilton, p. 100)

Jim Mitchell was convicted of manslaughter in the shooting death of his brother Artie. The main evidence is a videotape of Artie wielding a broken bottle and Jim shooting down the hall—the unusual part of all of this is that the videotape is a graphical simulation, including bullets of red light. One of the ultimate questions facing the use of virtual reality is, "Even in the best simulations, can reality be manipulated unfairly?" (Hamilton, p. 99)

Section 3—Telecommunications and Virtual Interfaces

Virtual reality techniques may revolutionize the telecommunications industry. No longer will the standard bandwidth of communications be limited to voice only (or keyboard); it will be expanded to include vision and touch. Proper interfaces could allow telecommuters full access to office personnel, meetings, and equipment. Whole new fields of people could work from their homes and/or at a remote, potentially hazardous work site, using cyberspace. A special subset of the field of telecommunications is the field of teleoperation, which includes the use of computers to control machinery placed at a remote area. Telepresence is the use of computers to enable the operator to perform as if he or she were at a remote site. Virtual environment interfaces would allow an operator to use telepresence as part of a teleoperation job. Not only would the operator perform some duty at a remote workplace, but the operator would perform as if her or she were actually there in person, and could "look around" and solve the problems that only the infinitely adaptable human can handle. Few workplaces can be as difficult to reach as those at the molecular level or deep in space.

The United Nations is considering developing a virtual "Trade Point," complete with "a virtual office with working information systems to illustrate the use and value of a real Trade Point." Fifteen pilot Trade Points, which are service bureaus targeted at small businesses and "offering access to a wide range of international commercial information via a formidable array of high technology," are due to be set up throughout Europe. The virtual Trade Point may serve two purposes; as a demonstration environment and as a VR system front end to a live Trade Point database. The Trade Point concept is due to be a showpiece at the UN's major Trade and Development Conference in 1994.

The Virtual Reality Applications Research Team of the Department of Manufacturing, Engineering, and Operations Management at the University of Nottingham is developing three-dimensional graphical browsing aids to hypertext systems. Although hypertext—"databases in which units of information are linked in a nonsequential way—provides an excellent vehicle for intuitive, nonlinear access to information," it is frequently disorienting; users can easily get lost with no way to retrace their steps. The team is working on a hypertext system that incorporates information in both "schematic and spatial terms in three dimensions." (VRR June 1992)

Figure 1.9—One time step in a molecular dynamics simulation. A NaCl cluster is smashing into a Ne surface with temperature mapped to color.

A Telepresence system developed by VPL for Fujita Corporation, a Japanese construction company, will let an operator control a spray-painting robot anywhere in the world. (Hamilton, p. 100)

Molecular Studies

Frederick Brooks and the University of North Carolina (UNC) in Chapel Hill Computer Science Department have long thought that force feedback is very important in the study of virtual environments. The GROPE system, created in 1972, provides interaction with virtual environments using both a force display and a visual display. An Argonne Remote Manipulator (ARM) is interfaced to a dedicated computer to provide manipulation capabilities in the virtual environment; in addition, this system allows the operator to "feel" the virtual environment—the environment "pushes back" at the operator (it is possible to run into a virtual wall). A large screen and goggles provide a three-dimensional real time graphical display of the virtual environment. Many of the other UNC systems described herein use the GROPE system as the basis for their functionality. Trailblazer is being designed as the next generation of this project. (Brooks, 1993)

Frederick Brooks and researchers at the UNC Chapel Hill are working on a virtual environment interface for a scanning tunneling microscope (STM) called a nanomanipulator. "The system approximates presence at the atomic scale, placing the scientist *on* the surface, *in* control, *while* the experiment is happening." The interface uses UNC's existing head-mounted display and GROPE force feedback system. The scientist can "see" the surface of the material at which the microscope is pointed. The tip of the STM probe can be used either to "feel" the surface of the material or to deliver a voltage bias pulse to modify the surface. The system could be used to transform individual atoms to and from the surface of a material. In effect, the scientist could build a custom silicon chip, one atom at a time. (Brooks, 1990)

The SCULPT system at the UNC Chapel Hill allows chemists to perform interactive molecular model manipulation—specifically, it is designed to let chemists interactively deform virtual protein molecules. The molecules continue to obey such physical constraints as bond lengths, bond angles, and dihedral angles. The chemists may specify deformations by attaching virtual springs to particular atoms or groups of atoms and specify the amount and direction in which the spring will pull. The system uses the GROPE ARM to provide force feedback to the chemist. (Brooks, 1993)

The UNC Chapel Hill GROVE system performs interactive volume visualization of electron density maps. The system is powerful enough to perform dynamic clipping of electron density levels and provides near-real time Fourier transformations to calculate the electron density maps from structure factors. (Brooks 1993)

The UNC Chapel Hill computer science team is developing Trailblazer as "a single unified molecular graphics workbench, for viewing, fitting, docking, and folding." This system will eventually incorporate many of the diverse systems implemented at UNC to include the GRIP-75, the GRINCH, R-Space systems, GROVE, SCULPT, VIEW, and GROPE. This will allow a unified system with a unified support base to support quicker prototyping and to facilitate creating new tools and new visualization techniques. (Brooks 1993)

Teleoperation and Telepresence—Remote and Hazardous Workplaces

NASA's Jet Propulsion Laboratory is working on computer-assisted teleoperation with emphasis on space applications, such as servicing and building the space station and satellites. This research includes robotic sensing, planning, and control as well as human factors research. The program includes interactive planning and simulation aids and the human-machine interface necessary to provide programming, command, and status information as well as "kinesthetic position, rate, force-feedback, and shared compliance modes of teleoperation." (Molendi)

The Virtual Environment Vehicle Interface (VEVI) created by NASA Ames, has been successfully interfaced to a Russian Mars rover. VEVI uses StereoGraphics' equipment to provide the three-dimensional view for the operator. Sense8's WorldToolKit rendering library was used to create the images. The operator can control a vehicle even with the time delay of forty minutes required to get an image from Mars and send a command back. VEVI works by creating a world database, which it updates with every received transmission from Mars. The operator then programs the rover to move based on the world database. It should also be noted that the rover has certain intelligent abilities, such as being able to dig itself out of sinking sand. The system would also allow multiple scientists to work together and submit requests at the same time. For example, if a geologist is analyzing soil just recently collected and finds something of interest, she could put in a request for further collection, even while the operator is moving the rover and another scientist is performing a different type of analysis. The whole environment can then be archived so that later scientists can replay the mission and participate as if they were there.

VEVI has also been used to pilot an unstaffed submarine to explore the waters of McMurdo Sound in the Antarctic. This experiment allowed exobiologists to examine "the primitive life that has evolved under the permanently frozen lakes." In addition, researchers were able to learn more about remotely operating vehicles under harsh conditions. (Eisenberg)

The Monterey Bay Aquarium Research Institute in Monterey, California has been "using a remotely operated vehicle to compile a detailed record of the cavernous underwater Monterey Cavern." The system includes a three-dimensional stereoscopic view which provides distinct advantages over two-dimensional views, especially when operating the robot arm to pick up a delicate object off the ocean floor. (Eisenberg)

Figure 1.10—IVEX Corporation Flight Simulator showing cockpit and view

Section 4—Training

Training in virtual environments may not only decrease training costs but also allow high-risk, low-probability situations to be rehearsed at leisure. Pilots and medical staff can rehearse emergency procedures, the military can rehearse wars, and the police can rescue hostages. Everyone can make mistakes without repercussions in a virtual world. Although only a few applications are listed here, the discussion of training in the medical section provides a better feel for how all encompassing virtual environments applications in the field of training could become.

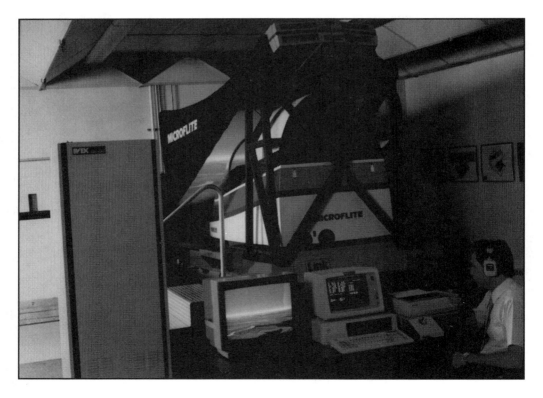

Figure 1.11—IVEX Corporation Flight Simulator showing simulation behind the scenes

Flight simulation provided the first of the modern virtual environments. The Atlanta-based "IVEX Corporation designs, manufactures and markets a series of high-performance visual simulation systems for use in civil and training markets." Although its flight simulators are of comparatively low cost, IVEX is one of only five companies certified by the Federal Aviation Administration to provide level C flight simulators. IVEX systems feature "real time out-of-the-window simulated scenes" of high fidelity and detail which are sufficiently difficult to distinguish from reality. IVEX systems are used "for virtual reality, education, training and entertainment." (IVEX)

Figure 1.12—IVEX Corporation Flight Simulator showing helicopter cockpit setup

The Defense Advanced Projects Research Agency (DARPA) is sponsoring a tank training simulation that runs on SIMNET. SIMNET runs on the MILNET and allows soldiers from all over the world to take part in a simultaneous training exercise. Each tank crew enters a simulator that appears, from the inside, to be an M-1 tank. The viewports display the battlefield and all the controls work just like their real-world counterparts. In one of the simulations you might find yourself part of the 2nd Armored Cavalry during the battle called "73 Easting" of the Persian Gulf War. The soldiers alongside you will probably be sweating and cursing as if it were a real war. Most important, "scores for battlefield acumen improve dramatically after they practice with these video tank crews." (Rheingold and Hamilton, p. 97)

MITRE Corporation and the Electric Power Research Institute are determining whether virtual environments can be built to train fossil-fuel plant operators. Current costs for a conventional training room are U.S. $1 million. (Hamilton, p. 100)

NEC Corporation has developed a virtual reality ski training system. The trainee dons a three-dimensional, wide-field-of-view, head-mounted display; stands on two movable steel plates; and grasps the ski poles. The computer monitors foot position and stance. In addition, a sensor monitors the flow of blood through a finger and estimates the stress (or relaxation) level of the trainee. The system takes all of these inputs into consideration before deciding the difficulty and speed of the simulation presented to the trainee. Future enhancements will include the ability to perform parallel and short swing turns (currently, only snowplow turns are allowed), and body monitoring may include sway, brain wave activity (EEG), skin resistance, electrocardiograms (EKGs), blood pressure, and eye movement. (Dunn, p. 9)

SRI International of Menlo Park, California, has built a virtual environment to train the ground crew that direct aircraft to park. The combination of a head-mounted display and gloves allows a trainee to direct aircraft, even into virtual buildings which cost (virtually) nothing to repair. (Antonoff, p. 85)

Section 5—Scientific Research

New ways to display and share data become available in virtual environments. Scientists can stand in the middle of an experiment with data sprawling around them outward in all directions. Researchers will discover new ways to handle and process information. The field of scientific visualization will be greatly empowered with the addition of virtual reality techniques.

The Electronic Visualization Laboratory of the University of Illinois in Chicago has created an immersive virtual environment without a head-mounted display called the Cave (Cave Automatic Virtual

Environment). The system uses projectors to display a three-dimensional image on three walls and the floor. Participants wear special glasses to see the image in three dimensions. This solution eliminates many of the problems associated with head-mounted displays, such as requiring the computer to recompute the display based on the participant's ever-changing head position, which creates an unpleasant lag between head movement and display update called time lag. Sound cues are also provided with a three-dimensional audio system. "The applications demonstrated have included practical and educational programs, such as molecular biology models, superconductor design, fractal mathematics, weather mapping, and environmental management." One of the Cave's strongest points is that people may work together naturally in a shared virtual environment. (DeFanti, p. 30)

The U.S. Air Force has been developing the Super Cockpit program at Wright-Patterson Air Force Base in Ohio. Thomas Furness (now at the Human Interface Technology Lab in Seattle, Washington) directed both the precursor to this project, called VCASS, and the Super Cockpit program. The system uses a high-resolution head-mounted display (estimated at U.S. $1 million each— just the display) to immerse the pilot in a symbolic representation of the world. The pilot "sees" the horizon and terrain as if it were always a clear day through the use of the airplane's radar. The pilot uses voice commands to perform many of her tasks. Audio cues supplement the display—incoming aircraft can be "heard" coming from the proper direction. Important information such as air speed and compass heading is displayed prominently; information that is not needed is not displayed. The system greatly increases the amount of important information that can be presented to the pilot in a timely manner, while reducing the display of irrelevant information.

The Virtual Reality Applications Research Team of the Department of Manufacturing Engineering and Operations Management at the University of Nottingham is comparing quicker virtual reality systems using collision detection and "traditional labor-intensive mathematical modeling procedures to see whether the VR system can provide comparable accuracy in describing particle behavior" in a simulation of "discrete element flow both through static walled hoppers and rotating elliptical hoppers." (VRR June 1992)

The VIEW (Visualization Impromptu Exploration Workbench) system being developed at the UNC Chapel Hill is "built on a new model of visualization, one which encourages extemporaneous sketching that is data-constrained, but which allows almost infinite flexibility in the geometric, color, surface-treatment, etc. representations used for data features." The system design assumes that for every one insight-producing visualization, many attempts will not be so successful, so backtracking is conveniently implemented. "The VIEW approach is especially suited for studying structures such as molecules, cells, and man-made structures, but it appears extensible to continuous data as well." (Brooks, 1993)

NASA has a virtual wind tunnel where, using a boom-mounted display and a glove, a scientist can "explore the aerodynamic intricacies of air streaming past an airplane in a virtual wind tunnel." (SN: 6/22/91, p. 368 and Peterson, p. 9)

Section 6—Entertainment

Most people will get their first introduction to virtual environments as entertainment. In fact, the broad acceptance or rejection of this technology may hinge on how people accept entertainment in virtual environments. A number of virtual environment entertainments are available with more being announced all the time. A number of virtual environment interfaces will soon be available on the Internet or by dial-up modem.

Carnegie Mellon University has a team of researchers creating the Networked Virtual Art Museum. "The project team will design and construct a multi-cultural art museum articulated through networked virtual reality, and established by a grid of participants, or nodes, located in remote geographical locations. The nodes are interconnected using modem to modem, or high bandwidth tele-communications." The virtual worlds will be constructed with Sense8 WorldToolKit software. "Participants [nodes] will be invited to create additions or galleries, install works, or commission researchers and artists to originate new work for the museum. Further, guest curators will have the opportunity to organize special exhibitions, explore advanced concepts, and formulate the basis for critical theory pertaining to virtual reality and cultural expression." (Sense 8)

W Industries of the United Kingdom has created several "Virtuality" games, including Dactyl Nightmare, Capture the Flag, and Legend Quest. The systems run on 68040 33-MHz Amiga computers and are interconnected via Ethernet. Each unit consists of a small stand, a head-mounted display with built-in sound and position sensors, and a joystick that controls walking and the participant's weapon. The virtual worlds are three-dimensional but cartoon-like, and the illusion suffers from lag; however, consumers are presented with an enjoyable trip into a virtual environment and are generally so engrossed in the "fight" that the quality is of lesser importance. (VRR, July/Aug. 92)

Spectrum Holobyte, a computer games and arcade company in Alameda, California, has announced StarPost—a virtual reality game based on Star Trek: The Next Generation. It promises lightweight head-mounted displays with reasonable resolution (three times that of Dactyl Nightmare). The reality engine will be a Silicon Graphics workstation. The virtual environment will include a transporter to beam down to planets below. A 30,000 square foot facility called the United Federation of Planets: Star Base is planned to be opened in 1994. (Antonoff, p. 125)

Chicago, Illinois is the home of perhaps the largest installed base of virtual reality units, BattleTech. Thirty-two people can sit in separate BattleMech cockpits, each surrounded by controls, a large forward-view screen, and a small satellite-view screen. All of the BattleMechs play against each other, either individually or on teams. A BattleMech is a robo-tank which engages in battles on virtual terrain. Month-long battle leagues, tournaments, and five-hour campaign games can supplement the standard twenty-five minute experience. (VPL)

Greenleaf Medical Systems of Palo Alto, California is using the DataGlove to make pitchers more effective. Four Red Sox pitchers, including Roger Clemens, donned DataGloves and pitched, while an Apple Macintosh recorded speed, hand position, and finger flex, among other variables. Analysis of this data should provide ways to make pitchers more effective. This type of system could also have applications in diagnosing and relieving repetitive-stress injuries and other orthopedic and neurological ills. (Hamilton, p. 98)

Todd Rundgren is developing the concept of virtual performers which stage a show from within a virtual environment. He controls the performance and the performers by wearing a VPL DataSuit. (Kerris)

The Grateful Dead have incorporated virtual environments to help them visualize the band's stage design, and develop graphics for programs and T-shirts, and to be used interactively to control parts of the stage show itself. (Kerris)

The recently released Sega VR includes a head-mounted display selling for U.S. $200 that plugs into the Sega Genesis video game console. Sega has also recently announced a full body input device called the Activator. This will undoubtedly provide the least expensive entry point to the realm of virtual reality. (Antonoff, p. 84 and Dunn, p. 2)

Figure   1.13—Motion Interactive Dive Sequence

Section 7—Medical Applications Using Virtual Reality

The field of virtual reality may have a great impact on the manner in which the medical field works. The applications to the medical field all actually fall under other categories, such as computer-aided design, augmentation, interfaces and remote workplaces, and training. However, a revolution in the field of medicine may be in the making because of the application of virtual environment techniques. It seems appropriate to keep the applications to the medical field together. They may be illustrative of what could happen in other fields as similar introductions of technology take place.

Computer-Aided Designed Treatment

Computer-aided design (CAD) will almost certainly become an important tool in helping surgeons plan operations and in helping physicians design custom-tailored treatments for individual patients. The following examples provide some other possible insights.

Henry Fuchs and the staff of the University of North Carolina (UNC) in Chapel Hill are engaged in a large effort to employ computer graphics and virtual environment techniques to the field of radiation oncology. As part of this research, James Chung is developing a CAD tool to help radiotherapists in making better plans and decisions for treatment. Radiation must pass through healthy tissue on its way to the tumor. Computer graphics are being used to help the design configuration and planning processes so that a minimum of healthy tissue, especially radioactively sensitive tissue, is hurt while the tumor is destroyed. Virtual environment tools are expected to aid the process greatly because the physician will be free to examine the patient naturally at any angle instead of exploring a projection within the limitations imposed by a two-dimensional computer screen. (Brooks, 1990 and Holloway)

The Hines Rehabilitation and Research and Development Center, in cooperation with the Sense8 Corporation, is developing virtual environments to help companies comply with the Americans with Disabilities Act. They are creating a CAD package that will help architects design systems that are equal accessible to both the "physically abled and disabled." The system is designed so that people in wheelchairs can don the ubiquitous head-mounted display and glove and enter the virtual environment to see if things really are well within their reach and spaces are large enough to accommodate wheelchairs easily. This will greatly simplify the current process and in addition give people with disabilities an easier and more concrete way to help architects. (Sense 8)

Virtual Treatments and Rehabilitation

The Phobia Project, at the Georgia Institute of Technology's Graphics, Visualization, and Usability Center under the direction of James Foley and

Figure 1.14—Virtual view from a balcony overlooking a lobby

Figure 1.15—Virtual view from a glass elevator overlooking
Georgia Tech campus

Larry Hodges, is studying using virtual reality graded exposure in the treatment of acrophobia—the fear of high places. As part of the treatment, patients are exposed to a fifty-story virtual glass elevator. (Adam, p. 27 and Ga. Tech GVU)

The Loma Linda University Advanced Technology Center in Loma Linda, California is applying virtual environment techniques to create a Neuro-Rehabilitation Workstation (NRW). The system incorporates pressure sensors, biofeedback, EEG, electromyogram, TekScan sensors, and a BioMuse eye-tracking system with a DataGlove, a Convolvotron, and an advanced visualization UNIX-based workstation. The NRW is being used for diagnosis, diagnostics, and as a therapeutic device for such problems as "Parkinson's disease, Huntington's Chorea, Alzheimer's disease, and physical disorders resulting from severe accidents and birth defects." Another problem faced during rehabilitation is a "patient's lack of motivation." An interactive user interface wherein virtual objects can be manipulated allows patients to get more out of a session by interjecting play. "Additionally, patients who can't pick up certain objects or can't enjoy freedom of movement in the real world can pick up those objects or practice certain motions in the virtual world." (Warner and Molendi)

The Neuro-Motional Rehabilitation System developed at the Ospedale San Raffaele Servizio di Riabilitazione in Milan, Italy is being used to study, diagnose, and rehabilitate patients with neuro-motional problems, such as atassy, which effects stability. The patient may be immersed in a virtual environment, then studied as the environment is changed. The physical laws of the virtual environment need not be the same as those of the real world, which can help in localizing the area of dysfunction at either a perceptual or a motional level. (Molendi)

Rutgers University's College of Engineering of Piscataway, New Jersey, in cooperation with Advanced Robotics Research, Ltd., of Salford, England has integrated the ARRC Teletact Glove with the Rutgers Force Feedback Hand Master. Diagnosis may be performed by having the patient wear the glove and exercise the hand, while the computer records tactile and force pattern information. This provides for better diagnosis than conventional tools such as goniometers and strain gauges. The system may be used for rehabilitation by wearing the glove while performing exercises and grasping virtual objects. The computer-generated force feedback can be individually tailored to the needs of the patient, which improves recovery time. (Molendi)

San Jose State University of San Jose, California and BioControl System of Palo Alto, California have combined the EyeCon and BioMuse systems for "clinical diagnosis, bioelectric research and medical rehabilitation. Using the bioelectric signals generated by the eyes, the muscles and the brain, these controllers provide a direct link from nervous system to computer." For instance, a physician can use the individual eye-tracking abilities of BioMuse to determine the degree of eye misalignment in patients with strabismus. Video game—type exercises can then be devised that may help patients with mild cases avoid surgery. These systems are also being used with EEGs to determine specific cognitive activities, especially in diagnosing sleep disorders. (Molendi)

Georgia Institute of Technology is using active and passive optical targets placed on the joints of the body to capture and analyze human motion data. Tracking targets can be worn on the hand and track both hand and finger movements in a manner similar to a data glove. Targets worn on all articulated parts of the body can be used as a whole-body input device to a virtual environment. The system can be used to improve the understanding and performance of human bodies in sports and rehabilitation. (Sinclair)

Therapy with Digital Puppets

SimGraphics Engineering Corporation in cooperation with Loma Linda Children's Hospital has developed a "digital puppetry" application based on

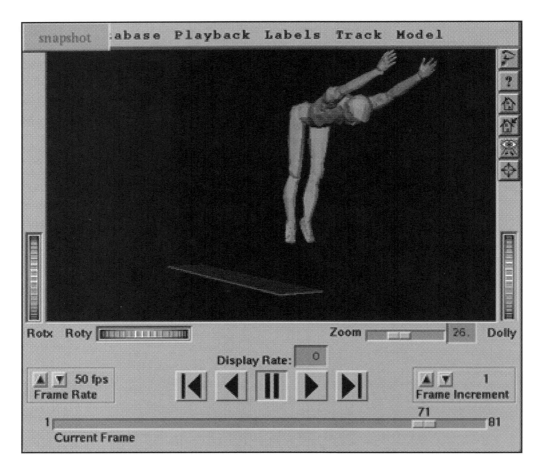

Figure 1.16—Motion Interactive of a Diver

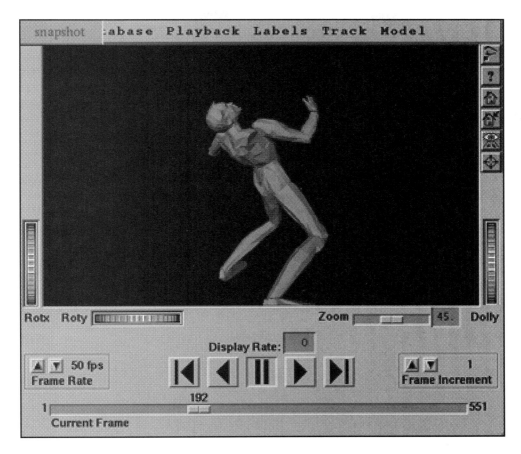

Figure 1.17—Motion Interactive of an Athlete

SimGraphics' Performance Animation System (PAS). This system allows actors to control in real time the computer-animated creatures. An actor's face, body, or hand can be an input device, which will be directly mimicked by the computer-generated image. The operator "wears a specially designed type of face armature called a Waldo that tracks the operator's eyebrows, cheeks, chin, and lip movements." Three-dimensional animated characters may one day be controlled by rehabilitation therapists or educators. "Familiar, friendly and non-threatening computer-generated cartoon characters may help reduce a patient's anxiety about operations and therapy. In these contexts, the characters would converse with patients and explain operation procedures in advance and, possibly, help small children discuss sensitive topics, such as abuse. The system may also help school children, problem patients and children under long-term hospitalization in educational studies and tutorial work." (SimGraphics and VRR Jun. 1992)

Augmentation

The idea of augmentation is to have computers complement human abilities to make humans more able and capable—both physically and intellectually. A medical example of physical augmentation is the use of various imaging techniques such as ultrasound to allow a physician to "see inside" a patient. Another example is the use of computers to perform tasks that a human alone could not do. Intellectual augmentation is the computer presentation of information to allow someone to make better and perhaps more timely decisions. These different types of augmentation often overlap in practice. The physician with X-ray vision is allowed abilities beyond normal human sight which can enable him or her to provide better and more timely diagnosis and treatment.

Helping the Physician

Henry Fuchs and UNC Chapel Hill researchers are trying to connect an ultrasound scanner to a head-mounted display (HMD). The two-dimensional ultrasound image is transformed and processed by a computer. A small camera is mounted on the front of the HMD to provide real time video pictures of the patient. These two images are then composited in real time and displayed to the physician wearing the HMD. The ultrasound images appear stationary in three-space. This gives the physician the effect (for example) of looking "into" a pregnant mother and "seeing" the baby. This could be useful for such diverse activities as watching an amniocentesis probe as it moves within a pregnant mother in relation to the baby in the womb, and seeing arteries that lie near where a surgeon is about to make an incision. (It could also be used by firefighters and would-be rescuers to see inside a burning building.)

The UNC X-Ray Vision project is attempting to take a head-mounted display through which one can see (called a see-through head-mounted display) and superimposing a computer-generated world onto the real world. The computer images might come from ultrasound, computed tomography (CT), magnetic resonance imaging (MRI), or some other imaging technique. Richard

Holloway's research involves superimposing static three-dimensional reconstructions of CT or MRI images onto a real patient. In this manner, a surgeon planning reconstructive surgery can see the real soft tissue and underneath it the three-dimensional bone at the same time. (Stix and Holloway)

Latent Image Development Corporation has developed a StereoSynthesis process to convert two-dimensional images to three-dimensional images algorithmically. It can also combine views of different types of images to create "cybersomatic visualization" of the patient for the physician. Other types of medical applications for StereoSynthesis include the visualization of data such as provided by an EKG in a "more discernible form than paper tracing." (Molendi)

Helping the Handicapped

Greenleaf Medical has developed the Motion Analysis System, which "is a tool for quantitative assessment of upper-extremity function that provides new methods of collecting data and performing analyses for orthopedic surgeons and physical therapists." This system uses the DataSuit to collect its data.

Greenleaf Medical has also developed the Gestural Control System (GCS), which "is an assistive input technology for physically impaired individuals—like those afflicted with cerebral palsy—having limited use of their hands and severe speaking difficulties." GCS in conjunction with a DataGlove allows users "to perform complicated tasks using simple hand gestures." A prototype uses a DataGlove and a Macintosh to control a telephone receptionist's switchboard. Simple hand gestures allow phone calls to be answered and routed, or prerecorded messages to be played. (Molendi & VRR, July/Aug. 92)

Crystal River Engineering has developed a piece of equipment that provides audio in three dimensions, called the Convolvotron. Jack Loomis, a psychologist at the University of California in Santa Barbara, thinks this tool could serve the blind. A computer using information from a Global Positioning System receiver (now inexpensive and pocket-sized) could provide information to the blind using the Convolvotron. Intuitive sounds "placed" in the right direction could provide information such as where the nearest landmark is or the relative location with respect to intersections and streets. (Graff, p. 617)

Sign Language

Stanford University has created a Talking Glove. A custom glove developed by Stanford for this project, the CyberGlove, translates American sign language to voice synthesized speech. The other part of the integrated system translates speech for either an alphanumeric display or a hand-held Braille display. Common words and hand shapes can be associated to speed communications. (Molendi)

Greenleaf Medical has developed GloveTalker. A computer accepts gestural input from a DataGlove, and can translate American Sign Language either directly into voice synthesized speech or into a format suitable for sending over telephones or computer networks. The system may also be configured to interpret custom gestures or the gestures of people capable only of "relatively gross muscle control." (Molendi & VRR, July/Aug. 92)

Artificial Realities Systems, the Department of Computer Science at the Universita' degli Studi di Milano, and the Ente Nazionale Sordomuti are collaborating to build a system called the Sign Language Interface Machine. A person using the Italian sign language and wearing a DataGlove would be able to "talk" to people. A computer would translate the sign language into voice synthesized speech. (Molendi)

The University of Tasmania Computer Science Department, in Hobart, Tasmania, Australia developed the Sign LAnguage RecogniTIon (SLARTI) system to translate Auslan, the Australian sign language, into voice synthesized speech. It is based on an advanced version of the Stanford CyberGlove. (Molendi)

The University of Toronto, Canada has developed a prototype system based on the DataGlove. A handshape made by the user selects from one of sixty-six words which is passed to a voice synthesizer. "It is not based on an actual sign language." (Molendi)

Loma Linda University's Advanced Technology Center uses DataGloves to allow patients who cannot otherwise communicate to make gestures which can be converted to speech. Moving the index finger could be "yes," while moving a pinky could mean "no." An unrecognized gesture causes the computer to cycle through the "gesture space" until the patient hears the auditory feedback. This system would help people who otherwise cannot communicate with their physicians but who have the cognitive capabilities to provide feedback to questions such as "are you feeling pain?" (Warner, p. 21)

Virtual Surgery

Interfaces

One of the first areas in which virtual environment techniques will affect medicine is as a new type of interface. Until the advent of minimally invasive surgical techniques, physicians used a variety of traditional skills that generally included the "look, sound, and feel" of a patient to make diagnosis, to perform surgery, and to determine treatments. However, minimally invasive surgery consists of inserting a catheter which must wind its way through the body to the point of the intended operation. Small cameras and miniature instruments allow the surgeon to guide the system to the point of the intended operation, then perform complex surgery at that point. Unfortunately, few of the conventional surgeon's skills apply to this type of surgery, even though it makes surgery much easier on patients in a variety of ways. Virtual environment interfaces to the system may allow the surgeon to perform surgery in a more conventional and human-friendly manner.

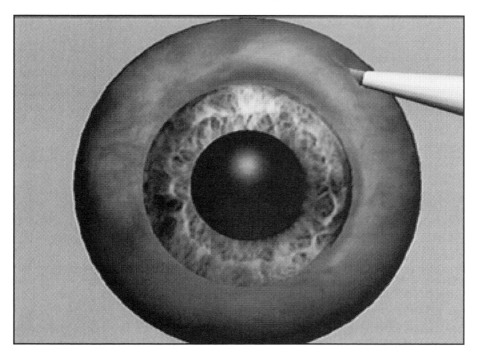

Figure 1.18—Ocular Surgery Simulator

Philip Green at SRI International of Menlo Park, California has developed a Telepresence Surgery System. It "gives to minimally invasive procedures—performed with endoscopes inserted through tiny incisions—the same certainty and dexterity that open surgery affords." Surgeons can operate through a more natural interface at a workstation with all the "motor, visual and sensory responses that they would experience having their heads and hands right inside the patient." A system designed especially for laparoscopic surgery is under development. (Molendi & VRR, May 1992)

The Johannes Gutenberg Universitat Neurochirurgische Klinik in Mainz, Germany, in cooperation with Aesculap AG, has developed a three-dimensional endoscope. The endoscope is designed to allow safe movement inside the "neurological structures of the human brain." Two miniature cameras provide stereo viewing to monitors, which, when viewed using polarized or shutter glasses, allow three-dimensional viewing from the endoscope's point of view. (Molendi)

Dartmouth Hitchcock Medical Center, in conjunction with MIT's Media Lab Computer Graphics and Animation Group, is "trying to develop a patient model of skeletal muscle for surgical simulation systems." This system is intended to capture not only the geometry of the body, as provided by imaging techniques, but also the biomechanics of the body using finite-element modeling techniques which can handle the nonlinear behavior of muscles. In this manner, the simulation would respond in the same ways as a real body would. The surgeon may view this patient model using a head-mounted display and manipulate the virtual patient using a whole-hand input glove. Ultimately the system could be used to "perform microsurgery on nerves or blood vessels, controlled through Virtual Reality techniques at a 'human scale' more comfortable for people." (Molendi)

Surgeons from the Brigham and Women's Hospital in Boston, Massachusetts are working with scientists at General Electric's Research and Development Center in Schenectady, New York. They are taking "pictures" of the brain with a magnetic resonance imaging (MRI) machine. These pictures are two-dimensional "slices" of the brain. A computer combines these two-dimensional slices to form a three-dimensional picture of the brain. With the aid of special goggles, humans can see the brain in three dimensions from any angle. A few keyboard clicks allow the gray matter to be peeled away and the white matter to be seen in a manner never possible before. The viewer can travel "through" any part of the brain and see what it looks like from inside. The eventual goal for this system is to allow a surgeon to "walk through" a "patient's body, threading between organs without disturbing them and performing precision surgery without damaging surrounding tissue." (Naj)

The COMPASS system developed by the Department of Neurosurgery at the Mayo Clinic in Rochester, Minnesota provides the ability to reconstruct tumors defined by CT or MRI sources. The COMPASS is a three-dimensional stereotactic system that interactively utilizes robotic technology and a carbon dioxide laser to perform volumetic tumor resection. The system can also perform stereoscopic digital angiography "for the three-dimensional localization of intracranial blood vessels for interactive surgical planning, simulation and determination of the safest possible approach trajectory to subcortical tumors." The COMPASS system allows "more complete removal of intra-axial tumors, many of which had previously been considered inoperable." (Molendi)

The Department of Neurosurgery at the Istituto Nazionale Neurologico in Milan, Italy has developed a five-joint high-precision tool holder. Using virtual reality techniques, the surgeon may move the tool holder inside a three-dimensional anatomical virtual environment. (Molendi)

Remote Workplaces

The most potentially promising future uses of virtual environment technology are called telediagnosis and teleoperation. Telediagnosis will allow physicians, perhaps experts in large cities or physicians in hospitals, to perform examinations and diagnoses of patients who are in remote, perhaps rural, areas. Certain computer equipment in conjunction with appropriately trained staff present at the site would aid the physician; however, for the most part the concept of telepresence (explained later in greater detail—essentially the physician would "see" and "feel" things just as if he or she were at the remote site) would apply. Teleoperation is a similar concept, except that the entire surgery process would be handled by remote robots directly under control of the surgeon. Please notice that a virtual environment interface would imply that the surgeon need not know the actual location of the patient, whether in a local operating theatre or far away; such details would be innately hidden in any case.

Training

Training in virtual environments promises to decrease the cost of training for medical field workers, while increasing their abilities and preparation. However, the ability to familiarize oneself with and rehearse for a difficult or high-risk operation with data that came directly from a patient will save lives and reduce complications. If the training takes place using the same virtual environment interface as used for surgery, then the physician need not even distinguish between a training session and a real operation.

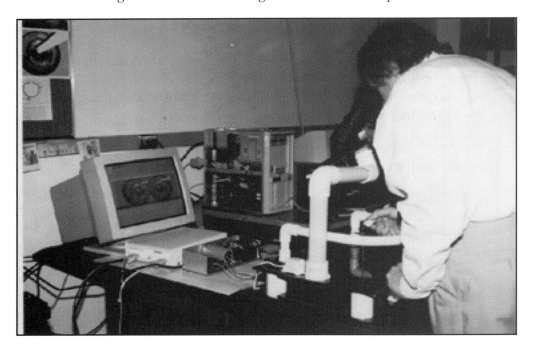

Figure 1.19—Ocular Surgery Simulator

Georgia Institute of Technology in collaboration with the Medical College of Georgia has developed a prototype ocular surgery simulator. This device is capable of creating real time photorealistic three-dimensional stereo images of the anterior ocular structures of the human eye with real time surgical instrument manipulation and elementary tactile feedback. The researchers have developed near-realistic tissue manipulation of the ocular structures with

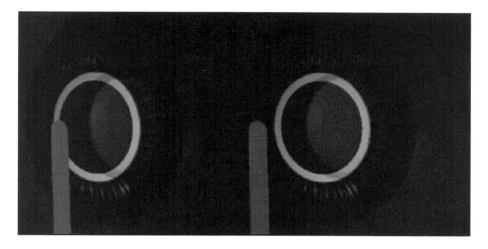

Figure 1.20—Ocular Surgery Simulator: Fusable Stereo Pair, inner features

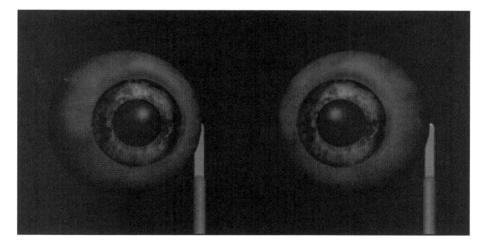

Figure 1.21—Ocular Surgery Simulator: Fusable Stereo Pair, outer features

regard to being cut with a knife and an early simulation for lens phakoemulsification—a process for removing a problem lens.

The display is presented through a stereo eyepiece similar to an operating microscope, with the image created by a Silicon Graphics ONYX computer graphics workstation. The image of the eye's anterior segment structures is of sufficient quality to show blood vessels, the iris and sclera texture, and the transparency of the cornea—the computer-simulated display should not distract the surgeon.

A three-dimensional Polhemus digitizing stylus simulates the surgical instrument in sufficient real time that all interaction appears to be done by the surgeon. The system is currently designed only for one-handed techniques— two-handed techniques are a planned future improvement. The stylus represents two simulated instruments, a scalpel and a phakoemulsifier. The scalpel cuts whenever it encounters tissue. The phakoemulsifier must be activated by pressing a button on the side of the stylus. The tool-tissue interaction algorithms are very realistic and provide reasonable tactile feedback. (Sinclair)

Georgia Institute of Technology in cooperation with the Medical College of Georgia is also simulating catheter insertion and arterial navigation. The physician must feed a long catheter into a patient's heart from its insertion point in an artery in the leg. The physician twists, pulls, and pushes the catheter through the maze of arteries, even while the whole structure moves each time the heart beats. The difficulty is heightened because the physician has only a fluoroscope with which to watch the entire process. This simulator allows the student to practice this technique without risk to a real patient. (Sinclair)

Ixion in Seattle, Washington has developed a surgical simulator for students. This system combines video graphics and endoscopic instruments that incorporate force feedback. The surgery is performed inside a mannequin, which allows the sensors to provide geometric information about the scopes and catheters within a body. (Molendi)

Silas B. Hays Army Hospital, Fort Ord, Monterey, California has developed a Virtual Abdomen in cooperation with Philip Green at SRI International. It contains a "stomach, pancreas, liver, biliary tree and gallbladder as well as a few surgical instruments (scalpel, clamps)." The system uses EyePhones and a DataGlove and provides cartoon-level graphics with no tactile feedback. The simulator is currently a stand-alone teaching aid, but in the future it may be combined with a Green Telepresence Surgery System to allow training and real surgery on the same workstation. This combination would also allow surgeons from different cities to work together on a single patient, perhaps even in a remote or inaccessible environment. (Molendi & VRR, May 1992)

Dr. Richard Satava of the U.S. Army Medical Center at Ford Ord is working with VPL to create a virtual reality surgical simulator. The inside of the abdomen has been created in three dimensions. Certain instruments are available, such as scalpels, clamps, and scissors. Surgeons-in-training will have the opportunity both to "practice surgical operations on a computer simulation" and to have the opportunity "to learn anatomy as never before by 'flying' in the stomach, flying back up into the bile duct, and actually seeing the stomach from behind instead of front. (This will give surgeons a completely new and better understanding that they can apply during surgery.)" (VRR, May 1992)

The University of Washington and the Human Interface Technology Laboratory are cooperating on several projects, including "an anatomy browser based on the Digital Anatomist database," overlaying of computer-generated image and textual data on a see-through head-mounted display, and the simulation of opthalmic surgery, which utilizes a video display and collision detection of instruments with virtual objects. The simulator "will supplement hands-on instruction and promises to improve both medical training and clinical practice, particularly for high-risk low-probability situations." (Molendi)

A dentist in Brooklyn, New York has recently received a patent for a computerized oral surgery simulator. A stylus is passed over the intended patient's teeth and gums, which creates X-ray pictures. A three-dimensional computer simulation yields a "sort of high-resolution topographical map of the mouth's interior" on which the dentist can practice the surgery to be performed. (Edupage)

The Virtual Reality Applications Research Team of the Department of Manufacturing Engineering and Operations Management at the University of Nottingham, working with a local Nottingham school, has developed a system to help teach intellectually handicapped children the Makaton communications scheme. The system provides three-dimensional virtual images, the symbol, the word, and the sign language representation if applicable. Video sequences are planned to allow the children to interact with the system. (VRR June 1992)

Application Notes

This brief tour of the very exciting virtual environments field has shown a number of different applications grouped into several broad categories. It should be clear that virtual environments have the potential to affect most types of work in many diverse ways. The impact of virtual environment tools on the medical field illustrates the powerful potential of this technology. However, in all the excitement it should be remembered that many problems have yet to be conquered, many of which are difficult and any of which can render a large part of the field no longer viable.

The following chapter deals with the development of virtual environments, who the modern "founding fathers" are, and how the field got to its current state. It should also provide some perspective on why hype is so prevalent and why many of the founders are so cautious about proclaiming the wonders of virtual reality.

CHAPTER 2

FROM WHENCE VIRTUAL REALITY—A BRIEF AND INCOMPLETE HISTORY

Introduction

The virtual environments field is quite diverse in many ways—geographically, technically, and philosophically. Although the media have contributed greatly to the hype and hysteria surrounding this field, the field's potential is enormous. However, we must remember that the field is still in its infancy; it has just reached the point of usability and many hurdles exist that must be crossed. To understand further what virtual reality is, it is important to understand its origins. The modern roots of this field are generally traced to an Ivan Sutherland paper published in 1965. However, Sutherland references the work of Edwin Link, which dates to the 1930s. Indeed, if certain historians and paleontologists are correct, the whole concept of virtual environments can be considered quite ancient as our species reckons things.

In this chapter we are going to explore some of the "classical" history of virtual reality. Then we present a brief (incomplete) accounting of the major milestones of virtual environments technology, dating up to the present. A very brief history of the graphic arts is also included to lend perspective and because graphics is such an important part of the virtual environments field.

Figure 2.1—Front view of a virtual Japanese Temple

Section 1—Classical History

In the Oral Tradition, Theater and the Dramatic Arts

According to the theories of paleontologist John Pfeiffer, between 10,000 and 30,000 years ago, most of the human species changed its way of life. Deep in the caves of Lascaux in southern France and other caves along the western Mediterranean are perhaps the first virtual environments of all. Hours of crawling through utterly dark, labyrinthine passageways leads to cave paintings. These paintings take advantage of the natural shapes and outcroppings of rock to give simple hand paintings on the cave walls three-dimensional attributes. Some of the paintings would appear to float in the dark if lighted properly.

It is thought that after hours of fasting, ordeals of pain, and rituals of chanting and drumming, the initiates to the mysteries of toolmaking and crop sowing were led down to the caves individually. There, they were exposed to figures floating in space in front of them; animals and symbols seemed to leap out of the darkness to fill their field of view. It is believed that these places were constructed for the purpose of impressing new ways of thinking on these initiates. While the initiates were in this state of altered consciousness, the ever growing amount of information required to maintain their way of life was imparted to them—information about seed saving, toolmaking, herbal medicine, animal husbandry, and the other bodies of lore that allow humans to live in settlements instead of leading a nomadic life of constant migration.

> One way of preparing people for imprinting has been known for a long time by tribes everywhere, modern as well as prehistoric: bring them into unfamiliar, alien, and unpleasant places, part of the procedure known in recent times as brainwashing. This is designed to erase or undermine his everyday world as completely as possible, which apparently serves as an effective preliminary to making him remember ... (Pfeiffer)

The oldest continuously inhabited human settlements in North America are the northern Arizona mesas of the Hopi, who are direct descendants of the Anastazi people. They have underground initiation chambers called kivas. Although many of their ceremonies are still unknown outside the Pueblo clans, it is known that the technology of planting and harvesting corn is part of the information transferred during an initiation. Corn is an artificial plant deliberately crossbred from a wild corn and a native grass in central Mexico, a process that was accomplished over many generations. The sophisticated agricultural system required for such things was imprinted during the ceremonial cycle held deep in the kivas. Stellar patterns indicate the exact time to plant the corn. Beans must be planted next to the corn to help it fix nitrogen from the soil. The corn stalks provide a trellis on which the beans may climb. In the heat of the summer, squash is planted—its broad leaves help conserve the moisture and help repel pests. It is known that this complicated system was imprinted during rituals in the kivas which included masked figures and painted three-dimensional symbols.

The followers of Dionysus at the roots of Western culture and the devotees of Shiva in northern India shared similar festivals. They stole from their homes in the night to gatherings in the forest, where they would partake of food, wine, and perhaps cannabis. They would dance, sing, and practice their ceremonies and rituals. Often, these meetings would include orgies or ritual cannibalism. In the hills of Greece, these gatherings were often held in natural amphitheaters.

Dionysus was the ancient god of wine. His attributes are that duality which wine may bring, freedom and ecstatic joy, and savage brutality—happiness and madness. The priests of the Dionysian cults were also introduced to the mysteries of their faith in dark chambers which were painted with dioramas.

> There was a metal bowl associated with the initiation which has been mathematically reconstructed. The concavity of the bowl was such that a young man looking in expecting to see his own face, would see instead the face of an old man, or the mask of an old man held up by the candidate. The shock of realization, the death and age within youth, represents an opening of the mind to a logic dimension of its own existence. Not becoming fixed to this particular moment of life, the initiate is awakened to the whole course of life. Out of that there will be associated restructuring as to the sense of it all. This kind of shock would not be experienced if the young man had been told by a friend who had gone through the mystery. That is why it was regarded as criminal to betray anything of the mysteries. Now, if things like this also were associated with a slight hallucinogenic situation in the mind, you can imagine what kind of illumination would come through. (Campbell)

The Greek theater is directly descended from the Dionysian revels. The Dionysian celebration of the death and rebirth of the god and the earth became the tragedies of Aeschylus and the comedies of Aristophanes. The purpose was the same, to stimulate the release of deep emotional and spiritual energies. Aristotle called this the state of catharsis, which implied the purification of the senses and the emotions. Dialog and plot replaced the ritual and frenzy of Dionysian celebration. Carefully crafted simulations of people, with whom the audience could identify, faced difficult decisions and anxieties. The audience was able to gain a new viewpoint on their own world by visiting another, though artificial, world for a short while.

In the Manner of Records and Writing

The oral tradition flourished for most of human history. Written text gradually supplemented the oral tradition and eventually totally supplanted much of the information passed by word of mouth. Speech was probably first aided by sketch maps made by the Egyptians—one of their gods was called the Plan Maker. Modern printing can be dated to A.D. 700 when the Chinese were using woodblock printing. By A.D. 1040 the Chinese had ceramic movable type. The printing press was invented in 1455 by J. Gutenberg. This latest invention meant that books could finally be mass produced. Text, and with it knowledge, was no longer limited to a subset of the population. Individuals could be influenced directly and privately through books.

Among other important discoveries during the 1400s was that made by Florentine artist Giotto, who discovered how to create three-dimensional perspective paintings on a two-dimensional canvas surface .

In 1669, Robert Boyle found that boring, detailed writing directly implied painstaking experimental work to his "community of like-minded gentlemen." His production of the detailed academic paper was so successful that this style of writing is still held in high regard by many scholars and academics.

In 1788, the Scottish painter Robert Barker created the first panorama. He created a painting ten feet tall that formed a circle sixty feet in diameter. The image filled the full field of view of a spectator standing at its center. Later panoramas would include objects subtly placed in the foreground to enhance the depth of the image.

The Beginning of Electronic Communication

The mid-1800s saw the popularization of yet another new technology, photography. In 1833, Wheatstone created the first stereoscopic displays. His pictures could be created in one of two ways. The first way was to take one picture, move the camera over a few inches, then take a second picture. The second way made use of a custom camera with two special lenses that could be used to create the picture. The simple viewer ensured that the left eye saw only the left image and the right eye saw only the right image. The displays became immensely popular. In 1844, David Brewster refined the invention, which led to the well known Viewmasters.

The first public telegraph appeared in 1844. The first transatlantic telegraph was completed in 1866. At the turn of the century there was a great debate about who founded broadcast radio (actually, this war raged until 1943, when the Supreme Court of the United States overturned Marconi's patents in favor of Tesla's prior art and patents; {Cheney, p. 176} even so, Tesla is often forgotten in favor of Marconi). It cannot be disputed that Nikola Tesla foresaw, way ahead of everyone else, that radio would have a great effect on the way people think.

> World Telegraphy constitutes, I believe, in its principle of operation, means employed and capacities of application, a radical and fruitful departure from what has been done heretofore. I have no doubt that it will prove very efficient in enlightening the masses, particularly in still uncivilized countries and less accessible regions, and that it will add materially to general safety, comfort, and convenience, and maintenance of peaceful relations. ... A cheap and simple device, which might be carried in one's pocket may then be set up anywhere on sea or land, and it will record the world's news or such special messages as may be intended for it. Thus the entire earth will be converted into a huge brain, capable of response in every one of its parts. ... it must needs immensely facilitate and cheapen the transmission of intelligence. (Tesla in Cheney p. 178).

Thomas Edison created the Kinetoscope in 1889 to provide a visual accompaniment to his phonograph. The Kinetoscope made use of a continuous loop of film which was animated by turning a crank handle. The arcade version of this machine had a chest-mounted viewer and cost a nickel. Thus, the first motion pictures were born. Edison rejected the notion of projecting these pictures for a large audience. In 1895, Auguste and Louis Lumiere previewed their Cinematographe system for a private audience in Paris. The first motion picture was entitled *La Sortie des Ouvriers de l'Usine Lumière*.

The first years of film were dominated by "technologists and experimenters" (Cook); little thought was given to narrative or dramatic content. In 1896, Melies was filming an omnibus as it left a tunnel when the camera jammed. By the time the camera was fixed, a hearse had replaced the omnibus. When the film was shown, the omnibus seemed to transform into a hearse. Melies had stumbled upon a whole new use for film; one that used a set of rules other than reality for guidance. In 1902, Melies released *A Trip to the Moon*, which defined film as a narrative medium.

The concepts of a camera shot, rapid cuts between events happening simultaneously, and other editing innovations were introduced by D. W. Griffith in *The Birth of a Nation*, which was released in 1915. Many of Griffith's developments are still in use today.

In 1923 sound made its debut in the movies in New York City. *The Jazz Singer,* released in 1927, ushered in the area of "talkies" for good. Two years later, nearly all theaters had added sound capabilities. Also in 1923, the three-color Technicolor process was introduced. Its difficulty and expense limited it to major features. Throughout film history, new technology has been introduced with gimmicks. Over time, the gimmicks that did not contribute to the storytelling, such as three-dimensional effects, were forgotten.

In 1941 regular broadcast television made its debut. The resolution was poorer than that of cinema, but people could buy televisions and take them home. The early 1950s was a pivotal time for the film industry. The Hollywood money people had been resisting change for quite some time. The serious threat of television brought a wave of new experiences to moviegoers— experiences one could not get from television: wider screens, three-dimensional movies, and stereophonic sound.

A man named Fred Waller began experimenting with multiple projector, multiple screen display systems as a way of presenting a wider field of view than films. He obtained an Air Force contract for one of the first flight simulators, which was to have five projectors, three on the bottom and two on top. The cameras were all mounted at slightly different angles and synchronized, as were the projectors. After World War II, Waller decided to try to sell a three-projector version of that system to Hollywood. Waller found a producer named Mike Todd. Their first feature was *This Is Cinerama*, which was a big hit. Although at its peak popularity no more than one hundred theaters ever showed Cinerama, it was credited with bringing people back to the movies in a manner unseen since 1946. It gave the experience of "being there."

Morton Heilig and the Experience Theater

The field of virtual reality was almost created over thirty years ago, but not by the technologists, the engineers, or the computer programmers. Indeed, it could have been the entertainment industry that gave us virtual reality. The man with the vision was Morton Heilig and he was foremost a cinematographer.

Heilig became interested in cinematography as a young man. Soon after, he began to dream of the future and of the possibilities of multisensory experiences. He was drafted the day before the atomic bomb was dropped on Hiroshima and was stationed in postwar Europe. Once his time was served, he took his G.I. Bill money and a couple of Fulbright fellowships to study film making in Rome. After that, he set out as a self-employed documentary maker. In the early 1950s, Heilig began to read about Cinerama, an idea that immediately fascinated him for what it foreshadowed. Heilig read everything he could find about Cinerama in Italy and then decided to go to Broadway to see it himself.

Heilig was entranced by all of these new developments. He began to envision the next step. What would it take to make people believe they were truly part of the experience? Heilig wrote a manifesto calling for Hollywood studios or the government to mount a broad-based research and development effort on sound, peripheral vision, vibration, smell, and wind elements. Since Heilig was an unknown, he found no publisher, and no one listened.

So, Heilig went to Mexico to shoot documentaries. There he met the great Mexican muralist Siqueiros, who introduced him to many other people. Heilig was invited to lecture on his ideas to a group of intellectuals, engineers, and artists who met at Siqueiros' house. In 1955, Heilig published his manifesto in a bilingual Mexican journal named *Espacios*. It included sketches and schematics of his vision of the Experience Theater.

> Celluloid film is a very crude and primitive means of recording light and is already begin replaced by a combination television camera and magnetic tape recorder. Similarly, sound recording on film or plastic records is being replaced by tape recording ... a reel of the cinema of the future being a roll of magnetic tape with a separate track for each sense material. With these problems solved it is easy to imagine the cinema of the future. Open your eyes, listen, smell, and feel—sense the world in all its magnificent colors, depths, sounds, odors and textures—this is the cinema of the future!
>
> The screen will not fill only 5% of your visual field as the local movie screen does, or the mere 7.5% of Wide Screen, or 18% of the "miracle mirror" screen of Cinemascope, or the 25% of Cinerama—but 100%. The screen will curve past the spectator's ears on both sides and beyond his sphere of vision above and below. In all the praise about the marvels of "peripheral vision," no one has paused to state that the human eye has a vertical span of 150 degrees as well as a horizontal one of 180 degrees. The vertical field is difficult, but by no means impossible to provide. ... This 180 degree by 150 degree oval will be

filled with true and not illusory depth. Why? Because as demonstrated above this is another essential element of man's consciousness. Glasses, however, will not be necessary. Electronic and optical means will be devised to create illusory depth without them.

In the same article Heilig notes that human vision tends to be sharp at the center and less focused at the periphery—something that today's VR systems are just beginning to exploit. His article caused quite a stir in Mexico, enough that the minister of education decided to support his project.

The Mexican-sponsored project built a "huge semispherical screen," and designed and built one of the first bug-eye lenses. They took test pictures and displayed them on the screen. Then things fell apart; the minister of education who had been supporting Heilig died in a plane crash. Not longer after that, Mike Todd, the Cinerama producer, died in a separate plane crash. Soon after Heilig's Mexican support crumbled, so he returned to New York.

Without a prototype, he was unable to interest any financial backers. He resolved to build an arcade-sized one-person version to make it obvious to anyone that this was the direction in which to go. Heilig took a job teaching film appreciation and set out to build his system. He found a partner and they started a company named Sensorama. They built the first working prototype, but still no one would back them. They had tried to sell the prototype as a showroom display to Ford and International Harvester. They tried to sell to educators. They also tried to sell to industry. Finally, an arcade owner allowed them to put the machine in an arcade at 52nd and Broadway in New York, but it broke within hours. Even with many months of work, the system was simply too complex for arcade treatment. Eventually, Heilig's partner lost interest.

One night, Heilig received a call from a man who had seen the Sensorama on Broadway—he was interested in discussing it further. The backer turned out to be interested in mass producing Sensoramas. The man's U.S. $50,000, a vending machining company, and an engineer built the second prototype Sensorama.

This Sensorama prototype consisted of a wooden booth that somewhat surrounded the user, who was seated on a motorcycle-like contraption. A nickelodeon-like viewer provided the stereographics. Below the faceplate was a small grill to provide smells to the nose. Two small speakers were positioned near the ears. The seat lurched, wind blew by the face, as the rider, strictly a passenger, took a motorcycle ride through Brooklyn, or a bicycle ride in California. This prototype again failed to win further financing. Heilig's backer finally lost interest.

Heilig did have some successes. He had built a "Stereoscopic Television Apparatus for Individual Use" in 1960. Another patent was granted in 1962 for a "Sensorama Simulator." Heilig's head-mounted display predates the one Ivan Sutherland assembled at MIT, which is generally credited as being the ancestor of today's head-mounted displays.

But for bad luck, Heilig and the entertainment industry might have ushered in the era of virtual reality over thirty years ago. Fortunately, Morton Heilig had other contemporaries who had similar ideas, and some of whom, had better financial backing.

Section 2—The Age of Information Technology and the Dawn of Cyberspace

ARPA and the ARC

J. C. R. Licklider was a professor at the Massachusetts Institute of Technology. He was developing mathematical models to understand how humans hear, a field called psychoacoustics. One day, surrounded by stacks of paper, he began to wonder how research scientists actually spent their time. A brief but thorough search revealed that no time-motion studies, nor any kind of studies, were in existence about this topic. He began recording his own activities during each day. He learned that nearly 85 percent of his time spent "thinking" was actually spent "getting into a position to think, to make a decision, to learn something I needed to know." He thought that perhaps specially designed computers could assume some of the mechanical acts of paper shuffling.

The computers of the day were very large and very expensive. They were kept in special rooms that were maintained at a fixed temperature and humidity. In order for the computer to do anything, a programmer wrote a FORTRAN or COBOL program. These programs were encoded onto stacks of punch cards, many boxes of which would constitute a program, and all of which were fed into the computer. Results were eventually printed out on paper. Sometimes the programmer would not see the results of the program for days or weeks. This was the system called "batch processing." It did not make sense to waste precious computer cycles catering to fancy human-computer interfaces. It was far more cost effective to put things into the computer's terms and then translate back to human terms when the project was done. A "priesthood" of highly skilled people grew into power around these systems. They were well versed in all things computer and understood how to perform these translations just as anyone who is multilingual can understand different languages. They were also very restrictive with their computer secrets and their computer cycles. Thus computers were simply not accessible to many people, including researchers who could greatly benefit from their use. It was tacitly understood that any increases in computer technology would merely allow the creation of larger and more powerful computers, which would remain under the control of the "priesthood."

A radical new concept had recently developed in the use of computers. Aircraft designers were turning lists of numbers into graphic models of how air flows over the surfaces of wings. This process was called "modeling" and is the ancestor of the current field of scientific visualization. Then, in an unprecedented event, Digital Equipment Corporation (DEC) created the PDP-1, the first "minicomputer." This machine was not near as powerful as some of the "mainframes." However, instead of costing millions of dollars, this machine cost hundreds of thousands of dollars. Instead of occupying a large room, it was the size of a large refrigerator. This machine used high-speed paper tape for programming, which allowed programs to do in hours what had once taken days. It gave the hard-core programmers a taste of interactive computing (hours instead of days or weeks). It also allowed a great deal more people to have access to a computer.

Having attained tenure, Licklider went to work consulting with Bolt, Beranek and Newman (BB&N), a company that had a PDP-1. Licklider found that, indeed, it was possible to use computers to build models from experimental data and to help make sense out of the complicated interrelationships of the data. In 1960, Licklider wrote "Man-Computer Symbiosis," in which he predicted that "in not too many years, human brains and computing machines will be coupled together very tightly, and that resulting partnership will think as no human being has ever thought and process data in a way not approached by the information-handling machines we know today."

The creation of the Advanced Research Projects Agency (ARPA) was a direct response to the Soviet's launching of Sputnik on October 4, 1957. ARPA's mandate was to directly fund unconventional ideas in hopes of leapfrogging the Soviets in computer technology. MIT's Lincoln Labs was employed to build the computerized Semi-Automatic Ground Environment (SAGE) to help protect the United States from nuclear attack. Licklider worked on the SAGE project and was thus acquainted with Jack Ruina, director of ARPA. Licklider and his "interactive computing" views were just the kind of thing for which ARPA was looking to lead to an important breakthrough. Licklider convinced Ruina that interactive computing could revolutionize not only the military's command and control structure but also civilian business. In October 1962, Licklider became the director of the Information Processing Techniques Office (IPTO).

Licklider's new job was to raise the state of information processing. He looked all over the country for eager young minds. One of the people he found was a young NASA administrator named Bob Taylor. Taylor had been funding another young man with new and quite similar ideas, Douglas Engelbart.

Douglas Engelbart and Intelligence Augmentation

Douglas Engelbart was driving to work one morning in 1950. He was musing about to what he should devote his life and talents. He had been a naval radar technician during World War II. After the war, he earned a degree in electrical engineering. He had a wife and a challenging profession. In short, he had accomplished at age 35 everything he had set out to achieve in life. His musings led him to a vision of computers and humans collaborating to solve problems.

Today we are accustomed to believing that computers should display things on screens, and having one computer dedicated to one user is far from unusual. However, in 1950 Engelbart seemed the only person who thought such things. Computers were few, large, and very expensive.

When Engelbart first heard about computers, he immediately recalled from his radar technician experience that if a computer could print out the numbers, it could also display them as symbols, graphically. His vision was of computers drawing symbols on the screen and people manipulating knobs and levers in order to look at this information space in different ways. He even imagined a theater-like environment where you could sit with your colleagues and work together, through and with, the computer.

Engelbart quit his job and went to the University of California, where one of the two computers in California was located. Unfortunately, he was unable to convince anybody to waste their precious computer time learning how to help people solve problems. Eventually, he took a job with Stanford Research Institute as an orthodox computer researcher. He wrote the conceptual framework for his vision in his spare time. That framework written during the 1950s and early 60s reads much like a blueprint for our work in the 90s and beyond.

Though nobody was listening to Engelbart then, Sputnik's launch would eventually change all that and make Douglas Engelbart a leader in the personal computer revolution and a founder of what would be the field of virtual reality. When Engelbart was visited in 1964 by an ARPA team, he had his conceptual framework and the complete design for a laboratory to build it. The ARPA team promised him the equipment and the funding to build the system of his writings and of his dreams.

Engelbart decided to name his laboratory the Augmentation Research Center (ARC). He chose the term augmentation to contrast with the term automation, a word much in use at the time. Automation in general describes the means of using computers to replace human labor. Augmentation means using computers to enhance human labor. In 1963, more than a decade before word processors, Engelbart published "A Conceptual Framework for Augmenting Man's Intellect." He thought it would be possible to use a computer and a video display screen to enhance the entire process of writing.

Other inventions at the ARC we now take for granted include the mouse (invented in the 1960s but not commercially feasible until the 1980s). A rudimentary form of hypertext which enabled users to jump from one word or phrase in one part of a document to another related word or phrase elsewhere in that or another document. The use of multiple windows to display text on a screen was also first presented at the ARC, as was the use of text and graphics in the same document.

In 1968, Engelbart gave an amazing demonstration at the Fall Joint Computer Conference. On stage, he had a keyboard, a video display screen, a crude mouse, and an earphone-microphone headset. From an iconic display, he selected a document from which to read. He collapsed the full text document to a single-line descriptive outline format. He used the mouse to cut and paste text from one part of a document to another. Engelbart had built the computer of the future at a time when most people dealt with computers through batch systems with punch cards.

Sketchpad—"The Most Important Program Ever Written"

In 1962, a graduate student named Ivan Sutherland was invited to attend a meeting of the top researchers in computer graphics, even though he was not asked to give a paper. A number of reasons contributed to his invitation: he was a Ph.D. student of Claude Shannon, the father of information theory and someone who did not sponsor ordinary graduate students; Sutherland was creating a graphics program as part of his Ph.D. research; and, ARPA was looking for just this kind of prodigy to lead a major breakthrough.

Toward the end of the meeting, Sutherland asked a question that indicated that this unknown young man might have something to say. He was invited to speak the next day. His slides clearly showed that his dissertation work, named Sketchpad, was far more innovative than any of the work presented thus far; in fact he had leapfrogged their research.

Ted Nelson also saw the implications of Sketchpad. In 1977 in *The Home Computer Revolution,* he wrote in a Chapter titled "The Most Important Computer Program Ever Written":

> You could draw a picture on the screen with the lightpen—and then file the picture away in the computer's memory. You could, indeed, save numerous pictures this way.
>
> You could then combine the pictures, pulling out copies from memory and putting them amongst one another.
>
> For example, you could make a picture of a rabbit and a picture of a rocket, and then put little rabbits all over a large rocket. Or little rockets all over a large rabbit.
>
> The screen on which the picture appeared did not necessarily show all the details; the important thing was that the details were *in* the computer, when you magnified a picture sufficiently, they would come into view.
>
> You could magnify and shrink the picture to a spectacular degree. You could fill a rocket picture with rabbit pictures, then shrink that until all that was visible was a tiny rocket; then you could make copies of that, and dot them all over a large copy of the rabbit picture. So when you expanded the big rabbit till only a small part showed (so it would be the size of a house, if the screen were large enough), then the foot-long rockets on the screen would each have rabbits the size of a dime.
>
> Finally, if you changed the master picture—say, by putting a third ear on the big rabbit—all the copies would change correspondingly.
>
> Thus Sketchpad let you try things out before deciding. Instead of making you position a line in one specific way, it was set up to allow you to try a number of different positions and arrangements, with the ease of moving cut-outs around on a table.
>
> It allowed room for human vagueness and judgment. Instead of forcing the user to divide things into sharp categories, or requiring the data to be precise from the beginning—all those stiff restrictions people say "the computer requires"—it let you slide things around to your

heart's content. You could rearrange till you got what you wanted, no matter for what reason you wanted it.

There had been lightpens and graphical computer screens before, used in the military, but Sketchpad was historic in its simplicity—a simplicity, it must be added, that had been deliberately crafted by cunning intellect—and its lack of involvement with any particular field. Indeed, it lacked any complications normally tangled with what people actually do. It was, in short, an innocent program, showing how easy human work could be if a computer were set up to be really helpful.

As described here, this may not seem very useful, and that had been part of the problem. Sketchpad was a very imaginative, novel program, in which Sutherland invented a lot of new techniques; and it takes imaginative people to see its meaning.

Admittedly the rabbits and rockets are a frivolous example, suited only to a science-fiction convention at Easter. But many other applications are obvious: this would do so much for blueprints, or electronic diagrams, or all the other areas where large and precise drafting is needed. Not that drawings of rabbits, or even transistors, mean the millennium; but that a new way of working and seeing was possible.

The techniques of the computer screen are general and applicable to *every*thing—but only if you can adapt your mind to thinking in terms of computer screens.

It was suddenly very clear to all who watched that computers could be used for far more than data processing. Much of what is said about this program may seem familiar to any of the readers who have watched skilled computer-aided design (CAD) operators or people using the sophisticated desktop drawing programs now available. In fact the entire field of CAD is the direct descendant of this program.

In 1964, Licklider recommended Ivan Sutherland, age 26, for the post of IPTO director. He held the post until the following year, when he passed the job to Bob Taylor, another man in his twenties. Ivan Sutherland was off to MIT to build head-mounted displays.

In 1965, Sutherland published an article called "The Ultimate Display" which challenged the rest of the computer world. This paper is generally credited with the beginning of the field of virtual reality and led us directly to where we are now.

We live in a physical world whose properties we have come to know well through long familiarity. We sense an involvement with this physical world which gives us the ability to predict its properties well. For example, we can predict where objects will fall, how well-known shapes look from other angles, and how much force is required to push objects against friction. We lack corresponding familiarity with the forces on charged particles, forces in non-uniform fields, the effects of nonprojective geometric transformations, and high-inertia, low friction motion. A display connected to a digital computer gives us a chance to gain familiarity with concepts not realizable in the physical world. It is a looking glass into a mathematical wonderland.

The ultimate display would ... be a room within which the computer can control the existence of matter. A chair displayed in such a room would be good enough to sit in. Handcuffs displayed in such a room would be confining, and a bullet displayed in such a room would be fatal. With appropriate programming such a display could literally be the Wonderland in which Alice walked.

(Sutherland, 1965)

Ivan and the Sword of Damocles

In 1966, having just vacated the post of director of IPTO at ARPA, Sutherland had little trouble lining up funding for his next project. ARPA and the Office of Naval Research cosponsored the first head-mounted display (HMD) at MIT's Lincoln Labs. The HMD work continued when Sutherland moved to the University of Utah in 1970. Sutherland was building the tools necessary to fulfill his prophesy espoused in "The Ultimate Display."

The first HMDs were test models and partial systems designed to help solve problems and test key theories. Because the user's head was wrapped in machinery that was suspended from the ceiling, it became known as the "Sword of Damocles." It was suspended from the ceiling because it was very heavy and used a mechanical gaze-tracking system.

The HMD required six interconnected systems to generate the first wire-frame virtual worlds: a general-purpose computer, a clipping divider, a matrix multiplier, a vector generator, a headset, and a head position sensor. The general-purpose computer was the TX-2, which was new back in the early 1960s and was also the computer on which Sketchpad ran. It provided the world model to the rest of the system. The clipping divider was a dedicated computer that handled the tasks of hidden-line removal and the projection of a three-dimensional object onto a two-dimensional display screen. The matrix multiplier was another special-purpose computer that was dedicated to transforming the lines (vectors) of the virtual three-dimensional object as the viewpoint of the HMD changed. The vector generator actually handled drawing the vectors (lines) on the display screen.

The headset included the display screens, which were 6-inch-long, $^{13}/_{16}$-inch-diameter CRTs mounted near the temples. The displays from these CRTs were bounced through lenses and mirrors to project a virtual image 14 inches in front of the user. The image appeared to overlie the physical world. "Thus displayed material can be made either to hang disembodied in space or to coincide with maps, desk tops, walls, or the keys of a typewriter," wrote Sutherland in 1968. The first displays were actually capable of displaying 3000 lines at 30 frames a second (respectable even by today's standards). This did not afford stereoscopic graphics; Sutherland decided that true stereo vision could wait. In order to get a three-dimensional display, the binocular display showed the same image to each eye but the image was shifted (translated), in much the same manner as our own eyes work. Each eye sees the same scene, shifted to one side just a little. (For proof, hold a finger out in front of you, and close one eye, and then the other; the finger will shift back and forth.) This HMD had a 40-degree field of view, which is better than the 4- to 6-degree field of television but not near the 300 by 150 degree field of view afforded by some systems today.

The head position sensor was a mechanical system. It consisted of a pair of telescoping tubes that slid freely along their common axis, which was fastened by universal joints to the headset and to tracks in the ceiling. Like many systems at the time, it was more accurate and much simpler than its digital equivalent. (They had also experimented with ultrasonic position sensing.) The user was free to move, turn around, tilt his or her head up or down up to 40 degrees. In all, the user had an area 6 feet in diameter and 3 feet in height in which to move around.

The first virtual object was a cube approximately two inches on a side, an object of light floating before the wearer of the HMD. It was first viewed on January 1, 1970 by Daniel Vickers, a University of Utah student who was responsible for integrating and writing the software that connected the separate systems. Another early object was a molecular model of cyclohexane.

Later experiments at the University of Utah used a DEC PDP-10 to supply the virtual world. A square virtual room was constructed in which the boundaries were painted in light and the walls were marked N (North), S (South), E (East), W (West), C (Ceiling), and F (Floor).

A pistol grip–-shaped wand with four buttons, a slide switch, and a small dial was a later addition to the system. The magic wand was used to create and interact with objects in the virtual world. By pointing at a wall chart and pushing a button, the wand could cause objects to appear, disappear, shrink, stretch, rotate, fuse together, or fall apart. The incantations of a participant wearing the HMD and using the wand to interact with a world only he or she could see led the wand to be called the "sorcerer's apprentice."

ARPAnet and the Internet

Electronic computer networks of every kind must trace their origins to ARPAnet. The ARPAnet was designed to allow the scattered members of ARPA to share data and exchange messages. The Mansfield Amendment essentially restricted the ARPAnet to use by the military only. The ARPAnet split into the Internet and the MILNET. The Internet is a worldwide interconnection of computers for scientific and research use. It is also one of the premier information and communications sources in the world (more about this later). The MILNET handles the U.S. military's communications requirements and supports SIMNET, a system that allows tank simulators all over the world to "play war games" together.

The Ethernet was created by Alan Kay and company at Xerox Palo Alto Research Center (PARC). The whole idea was taken from ARPAnet, but designed for computers that were closer together where higher-speed connections could be used.

The Mansfield Amendment, drafted during the height of the Vietnam War, effectively prevented ARPA from funding non-weapons-related research. About this time Bob Taylor, who had become the IPTO director in 1965, moved to the new Xerox PARC facility. He started to assemble the best of the researchers who had worked on the scattered ARPA programs.

Xerox PARC

A company named Xerox had been exploiting the technology called photocopying which IBM had abandoned in the 1950s. In 1970 a new leader named Peter McColough came to Xerox. The company was worried about the talk of a "paperless office" and decided to redefine itself as an information company. It set up an interdisciplinary research laboratory called the Palo Alto Research Center (PARC) near the Stanford University campus. They were given the funds and the mandate to create "the architecture of information for the future," as the president of Xerox called it.

What with the Mansfield Amendment and the new vagaries of military funding during the Vietnam era, many of the former ARPA researchers were available to the PARC. Bob Taylor, the former IPTO director at ARPA, was hired to assemble a team. Among the ARPA researchers who came to the PARC was Alan Kay, who became chief scientist.

Kay had been at the University of Utah, had studied Sutherland's Sketchpad source code, and had seen Sutherland and Evans leading the way in computer graphics. He had been working on Sutherland's project to find ways to display information on an ever changing interactive computer display.

Kay derives his inspiration from Marshall McLuhan, Seymour Papert, and Ivan Sutherland. McLuhan led him to think of the computer as a medium rather than a tool. The ideas of Papert showed him that computer languages could be thinking tools, that graphical communication can be a powerful means of human-computer interaction, and that children can and should be able to use computers. Ivan Sutherland's Sketchpad showed him that computers could be used as interactive tools. Kay led the way away from the command line interface that all interactive computers used to a new type of computer and computer interface.

This new machine used a direct manipulation interface, first described by Engelbart and first shown by Sutherland, and was called the Altos. It displayed all of the computers resources graphically on the screen. The PARC team also had some new technology at their disposal. They used "bit-mapped graphics," a system in which for every element of the graphic display (pixel) there exists a piece of computer memory that exactly describes it, to depict these resources using the concept of metaphors and small pictures called icons. For example, a simulated painter's palette, created by Kay in 1972, enabled the user to "paint" pictures on the computer screen. They invented a whole metaphorical world. The computer operator had a desk on which could be found a filing cabinet complete with folders and files and a trashcan in which to dispose of these things. The mouse, brought along with the ARC researchers, in conjunction with a pointer on the screen was used to show the operator's current position in this world. The mouse-and-pointer combination also allowed the operator to manipulate the object icons found in the environment.

Howard Rheingold recalls his 1982 encounter with the Alto:

At first, it seemed strange. I typed on a keyboard, just as I would type on a regular word processor. But instead of memorizing different alphabetic codes to mark, copy, move, and delete blocks of text, I moved the mouse on the desktop while I watched the cursor move and characters and words and paragraphs highlight on the screen. The "desktop metaphor" that turned files and filing cabinets, electronic mailboxes and digital trashcans, into graphic symbols on the computer screen was a primitive "virtual world" that let me put my thinking tools right here in front of me, where I could see them. By clicking the mouse on the right "icons," I could send my document across the laboratory, to my partner's electronic mailbox, and send an automatic copy to the editor of a scientific journal halfway across the continent. The screen acted as a visual cache for my short-term memory, the way placing documents and file folders on a physical desktop serves as a visual reminder.

About this time, the outside world saw the introduction of the first microcomputers. Xerox decided to invest in the leading company of the microcomputer revolution. In 1979, Xerox bought 100,000 shares in Apple Computer but in exchange had to allow Apple access to the PARC's research.

Peter McColough left the company, and competition from the Japanese gave Xerox too much about which to think. Xerox management decided not to turn the Alto into a marketable product. Apple's cofounder and representative, Steve Jobs, found the Alto while touring the PARC facility. And thus the course of computer history would be changed.

In 1982 came the Lisa. Although itself not very successful, it was a breakthrough and the prototype of the very popular and successful Apple Macintosh. It also heralded the introduction of other much more recent graphical user interfaces (GUIs) such as Microsoft Windows and MIT's X-Windows (often found on UNIX machines along with Motif). Xerox is even developing a new GUI which features a three-dimensional look with rooms, doors, and pockets in which to carry your tools as you wander from room to room.

Myron Krueger and Responsive Environments

In April 1969, GLOWFLOW opened to the public at the Memorial Union Gallery of the University of Wisconsin at Madison. GLOWFLOW used networks of tubes filled with phosphorescent colored fluids, hidden minicomputers, and sound synthesizers to produce a new type of art form. GLOWFLOW was a computer-controlled light and sound environment that responded to human attention and behavior. Hidden lights would illuminate phosphorescent particles in the glass tubes to created different light effects in the otherwise dark room. Pressure-sensitive plates embedded in the floor enabled the audience to control the performance, although they were unaware of exactly how.

In 1983, Myron Krueger wrote about GLOWFLOW:

People had rather amazing reactions to the environment. Communities would form among strangers. Games, clapping, and chanting would arise spontaneously. The room seemed to have moods, sometimes being deathly silent, sometimes raucous and boisterous. Individuals would invent roles for themselves. One woman stood by the entrance and kissed each man coming in while he was still disoriented by the darkness. Others would act as guides explaining what phosphors were and what the computer was doing. In many ways the people in the room seemed primitive, exploring an environment they did not understand, trying to fit into what they knew and expected. Since the GLOWFLOW publicity mentioned this responsiveness, many people were prepared to experience it and would leave convinced that the room had responded to them in ways that it simply had not. The birth of such superstitions was continually observed in a sophisticated university public.

Krueger had been part of the team of artists who created GLOWFLOW. The artists who had recruited him wanted to maintain a contemplative quality to the place, but Krueger wanted to experiment with the strong human emotions created by the "responsive environment."

Kruegar's METAPLAY debuted in May 1970. It was sponsored by the National Science Foundation and the University of Wisconsin's Computer Science Department. This presentation included 800 pressure-sensitive switches, video cameras, rear projected video screens, and computer graphics. Digital Equipment Corporation (DEC) lent him their latest minicomputer, a PDP-12.

One wall of the METAPLAY room was an 8 by 10 foot rear-projected video screen. A video camera and projector were hidden behind the screen. In the control room, a drawing tablet allowed the facilitator to create computer graphics on an Adage Graphic Display Computer, one of the first special-purpose computer systems. A video camera aimed at the Adage display was mixed with live video feed from the METAPLAY room under the facilitator's control.

Krueger began things by drawing an outline of light over a participant's hand. When the participant moved her hand, Krueger quickly drew another outline. The participant then took her finger and started to draw with it. Krueger responded by drawing wherever the "magic finger" went. The audience found that they could pass the "finger" from person to person by touching fingers together. Something not envisioned by the creator but possible within the system manifested itself through the interaction.

During the exhibition, a transmission problem with the pressure switches arose. While discussing the problem on the phone with the operator in the gallery, Krueger hit upon a better way to communicate. They moved a camera to transmit the picture displayed on the PDP-12 in the galley to the computer center. A video camera relayed the graphics computer display back to the gallery. Both signals could be seen by both operators. They could point to signals from either computer while they were talking, definitely a breakthrough in communications.

Kruegar's next work was PHYCHIC SPACE, which featured a maze for the participants to move through. But the maze could not be completed and attempts to step over the boundaries resulted in the boundaries stretching or bending out of the way. This and other games of ideas were played out in the "psychic space" hidden in the darkened room and created by experimentation.

VIDEOPLACE debuted in October 1975 at the Milwaukee Art Center. It was designed to be an open-ended laboratory that would evolve over the years. VIDEOPLACE moved to the University of Connecticut in the late 1970s. The concept of VIDEOPLACE is that of a world in which full physical participation is possible. This concept was the basis for Kruegar's 1974 doctoral dissertation, "Computer Controlled Responsive Environments," later published as *Artificial Reality* (Addison-Wesley, 1983), in which he also coined the term artificial reality.

VIDEOPLACE is a dark room with a real time silhouette image of the participant displayed on a large video projection screen in the room. The computer analyzes the participant's motion and responds accordingly. Over 30 interactions are possible within VIDEOPLACE. The participant can draw on the screen without operator intervention by holding up one finger. Closing the hand ceases the drawing. An open hand can erase the drawing.

A graphical creature named CRITTER lives in VIDEOPLACE. CRITTER will chase your image. If you offer it a hand, it will climb up your silhouette. If it reaches the top of your head, it will dance a celebratory jig. If you then offer it your hand, it will climb out onto it. With a little coaxing, CRITTER will dangle from your finger. Any sharp movement with the hand will splat CRITTER on the ground, but it will shortly be resurrected somewhere else on the screen. If you trap CRITTER between your hands, CRITTER will try desperately to escape. Failing that, he will explode to re-form elsewhere later.

Although many of the interactions depict the participant full size, some shrink the participant. These reduced-scale participants can fly around the area, jump from graphic objects, and fall under moon gravity. The participant could even form a chorus line with other previous images of herself. A second person can also play and even be at a different scale. Generally, the larger person is displayed as a pair of hands. The smaller person could swing from the second person's finger, or be moved around by the larger person.

> VIDEOPLACE is a deliberately informal and playful arena for exploration of the human interface. However, because we do a great deal of development, we have a number of tools we can operate standing within the VIDEOPLACE environment. Being able to stand while working is a valuable addition to the inventory of user interface options. Overcoming the sedentary tyranny of existing systems is one of VIDEOPLACE's ongoing goals.
> (Krueger, p. 420)

Krueger has also started a VIDEODESK experiment. A camera overlooks the clear surface of a desk. In one of the most dramatic demonstrations, the operator uses hand motions to create quickly a multicolor, three-dimensional solid object. The whole thing is displayed on the screen as it is built.

Krueger believes that at the center of every VR system is a human experience, including the experience of being in an unnatural or remote world. Attention is the instrument wielded by the artist, "Response is the medium," for virtual reality art. VR art must be fundamentally interactive.

In a time when many are considering donning gloves, suits, and helmets to enter another world, Krueger is creating a responsive world, an artificial reality, that leaves the participant unencumbered and able to move in more natural ways. Krueger believes that "human interface research will branch in two directions. One fork will have the objective of completing an artificial reality technology that includes force and tactile feedback, using whatever intrusive and encumbering means that are necessary. The other fork will pursue an interface that merges seamlessly with the rest of our environment." (Krueger, p. 420)

MIT's Arch-Mac and the Media Lab

In 1970, Nicholas Negroponte outlined how he wanted to combine the presentation capabilities of cinema and the information manipulation capabilities of computers. He thought that the fusion of digital computers, audio, video, broadcast, and networks would evolve into an integrated "media technology," what Alan Kay called a "metamedium." Negroponte and coresearcher Richard Bolt led MIT's Architecture Machine Group, with strong backing from ARPA, down this new road.

The Arch-Mac group had their eyes on the next breakthroughs and the future possibilities. They used voice commands, eye trackers, and holographic film. The group consisted of researchers from the cognitive sciences and the computer sciences and their research featured ideas from the theater and cinema and the latest telecommunications technologies. This group has never been enamored of the gear often associated with VR research; they think the image of people moving unencumbered is the "sexier" one. Many of the research areas pioneered at Arch-Mac can be seen in use today.

Bolt has long stressed that gaze direction is very important in human communications, and not inconsequentially, many of the Arch-Mac and Media Lab systems make use of gaze trackers. One such area of research used three-dimensional displays and techniques for transmitting facial expressions and gaze direction for telecommunications. The system envisioned showed animated faces whose gaze and major features moved in synchrony with their conversational partner's face.

In 1976, Negroponte and Bolt began work on a project they called "spatial data management." The idea was to turn the computer into an office, a virtual office. The display became a metaphorical desktop complete with diary, telephone, an in-box, and other such tools. This concept was pursued to discover new ways of placing the user within a virtual office. This process led them to create the Media Room—a "room-sized personal computer where the whole body [is] the cursor-director and your voice the keyboard," (Brand, the Media Lab, p. 139). The computer operator sat in a chair at the center of a room whose walls were computer displays. The operator could point at an object on the screen and say "put that ..." and then point to the object's desired location and say "there." Motion sensors and gaze trackers would determine which object was to be moved, and to where, and the object was moved automatically.

The Media Room was used to derive other important concepts. One of the most important concepts, pioneered during the late 1970s, was that the data stored in computers could be displayed in some sort of visual form and somehow explored by physical navigation through "data space." This concept led to the prototype of "Dataland" and to the field now known as scientific visualization. The operator could sit in the Media Room and *fly* through the two-dimensional representation of three-dimensional data. This was also part of the Spatial Data Management System, a system for visually navigating through databases which was implemented in the Media Room.

The World of Windows system continues to influence VR research. Large windows of information could be opened on wall-sized screens which are under eye tracking control. The screen can show text, photographs, full motion video, etc. The windows can be fed by live data feeds from satellites, news wires, or videodisk databases.

Other researchers extended Kenneth Knowlton's work at Bell Labs during the 1970s. Knowlton developed a virtual desktop workspace for the use of telephone operators. The operator's keyboard configurations were complex and changed often. Knowlton placed a half-silvered mirror in such a way that the image from the mirror would overlie the blank physical keyboard. A computer display was aligned with the keyboard in the mirror. The operator could view in the mirror whatever keyboard configuration was required at the time.

In the 1980s, Scott Fisher and Christopher Schmandt used similar techniques to build a virtual three-dimensional environment into which one could reach and move things around. The ability to manipulate the environment added a vital component to the otherwise look-but-don't-touch environment that was common before gloves came into common use.

The Aspen Movie Map and Surrogate Travel

The Aspen Movie Map was created by Andrew Lippman, Scott Fisher, and others at the Arch-Mac. The concept was simply to show a movie of the town of Aspen, Colorado, with the caveat that the viewer could point at the screen and thus determine the direction, literally, that the movie would take. One of the most important points of this project is that it began the idea of a personal simulator, where the operator felt immersed in an alternate reality and had some control over that reality.

Imagery of the town of Aspen was shot with a special camera system mounted on top of a car. Every street and corner of the town was shot. These pictures were combined with pictures from cranes, airplanes, and helicopters. Even the insides of many buildings were shot. All of these images were combined to let the operator be surrounded with front-, side-, and back-looking imagery without a head-mounted display of any type. The operator could decide what road to drive down, what corners to explore, and which buildings to enter. The entire thing was controlled by gestures from the operator. If a house looked interesting, text information further describing the house could be displayed above the screen. The operator could even move forward or backward in time to see the house in different seasons. All of the data for the system was kept on videodisks.

Scott Fisher's masters degree thesis in media technology was a combination of videodisk image storage and three-dimensional display to create virtual space probes. Two videodisks contained pairs of images taken 65 millimeters apart, the average distance that separates the human eyes. A specially designed pair of goggles used shutters to alternate showing one eye its picture and then the other eye its picture at very high speeds. The operator's position was determined by the same magnetic tracking device used in the "Put That There" experiment. The computer automatically retrieved the appropriate pair of images and displayed them in the goggles.

The mid-1980s saw a transition from the Arch-Mac to the Media Lab, newly founded by Negroponte. "Our charter is to invent and creatively exploit new media for human well-being and individual satisfaction" (The Media Lab 5th Anniversary, 1990). Their focus is on what media technology might become in the future. To further that end, they build prototypes for demonstration. Indeed, their in-house slogan is "Demo or Die." Today the Media Lab is still working on some VR-related research. They have created autonomous computer characters that inhabit virtual worlds and devices the can transmit human tactile and kinesthetic senses.

> [Negroponte's] view of the future of desktop computing ... is one where the bezel becomes a proscenium and agents are embodied to any degree of literalness you may desire. In the longer term, as holography prevails, little people will walk across your desk (if you have one) dispatched to do what they know how.
>
> The picture is simple. The stage is set with characters of your own choice or creation whose scripts are drawn from the play of your life. Their expressiveness, character, and propensity to speak out are driven

by an event (external) and a style (yours). If you want your agents to wear bow ties, they will. If you prefer talking to parallelpipeds, fine. (Negroponte, p. 352)

Atari Research

Nolan Brushnell was an engineer for Ampex, a recording equipment and tape manufacturer. He decided to attempt to build coin-operated computer games. Although his first effort was unsuccessful, his second was a huge success. It was a game based on Ping-Pong called Pong. Brushnell left Ampex and started his own company to sell the game, Atari. In 1976, Warner Communications bought Atari.

In the early 1980s, when video games were creating huge sums of cash and the personal computer revolution was beginning, the Atari managers aspired to turn computer games into something more. They envisioned computer games as a new medium which could perhaps rival television and film. To that end, they hired Alan Kay to assemble a team of researchers. This team was given the mandate to dream up the entertainment and education media of the future and was given a budget to do so.

The Atari crew included many researchers with PARC and Arch-Mac roots. Scott Fisher, Michael Naimak, and Kristina Hooper also had recently worked on the Aspen Movie Map. Eric Hulteen had been an important part of the "Put That There" experiment. Thomas Zimmerman, Brenda Laurel, and Susan Brennan were Atari Research members.

Warren Robinett also joined the Atari Research team. Robinett had been told that the classic computer game Adventure would never fit in the space the Atari home game computers had. Robinett created the game anyway, complete with graphics that the original had lacked, it was a big seller for Atari. Robinett also created Rocky's Boots, a game that taught Boolean logic to kids while they played an adventure game.

Jaron Lanier was another member of team. He had created an Atari game called Moondust and had earned a great deal of money from it. Lanier was creating a programming language that was fundamentally symbolic instead of cryptic text.

The Atari Research team was supposed to be building the system of the future. They decided from the outset to take their time and develop an extensive conceptual framework on which to hang their research. This was a computer interface that was more than just what could be seen on a small screen; it would be an interface into which people could walk and of which people could become a part. This was the computer-generated responsive environment that Ivan Sutherland had predicted. Scott Fisher was looking toward the HMD approach. Many of the others preferred the Media Lab approach, which left operators unencumbered.

Unfortunately, the video game boom did not last, and Atari Research was dissolved. The conceptual framework and the people who developed it survived and moved elsewhere, many to Apple and many to the NASA Ames Human Factors Lab.

NASA Ames Human Factors Research Division

Michael McGreevey was seeking a Ph.D. in the interdisciplinary field of cognitive engineering. He was a graduate student of Stephen Ellis at the University of California at Berkeley. McGreevey was interested in both the psychological and technological aspects of three-dimensional and immersive displays. In 1981, McGreevey, with encouragement from Ellis, began a research program involving "spatial perception and advanced displays" at NASA Ames.

McGreevey had been following the pioneering work of Sutherland and the state-of-the-art VCASS system of Thomas Furness and the Air Force. In 1984, Scott Fisher was invited to talk at NASA about stereoscopic head-mounted displays. Ellis and McGreevey thought that it was a natural technology for the visual perception experiments they wanted to explore. McGreevey put forth a proposal to build a prototype head-mounted display system. He was granted U.S. $10,000.

McGreevey contacted Thomas Furness, who directed the U.S. Air Force's VCASS system at Wright-Patterson Air Force Base in Ohio. Furness' quote for the helmet part of the system alone was U.S. $1 million, clearly outside McGreevey's budget.

With the help of a hardware contractor named James Humphries at Sterling General, McGreevey discovered that the new technology of liquid crystal displays (LCDs) could replace the portable televisions that were the most expensive parts of the VCASS system. The LCD televisions could display only 10,000 (100 x 100) picture elements, in comparison to the millions of the Air Force version, but it was affordable. The LCDs were mounted in a motorcycle helmet with a special visor attachment. Additional optics were added in front of the displays to focus and expand the images so that they could be viewed easily. The system was called the Virtual Visual Environment Display (VIVED) and it cost a mere U.S. $2000.

In order to test the new system, they needed to create independent left and right eye images, called stereo pairs. Since they did not have a computer, they mounted two video cameras side by side. To create the stereo pairs for their first production, they wheeled the cameras around the Human Factors Lab, through the offices of the division, and out into the hanger where the XV-15 Tilt Rotor aircraft was being developed. The people who viewed this film agreed that they had a real sense of "being there."

McGreevey and Amy Wu, his support programmer, proceeded to develop the computer system necessary to drive their new display. They used an Evans and Sutherland Picture System 2 graphics computer to create the stereo, wide-angle, perspective images on two 19-inch monitors. Two video cameras were mounted facing the 19- inch displays to drive the HMD. A Polhemus head tracking sensor was mounted on top of the HMD. The position and orientation of the operator's head were communicated from the sensor to a PDP-11/40.

Their first virtual environment consisted of data from one of McGreevey's earlier projects. He had been studying air traffic control issues. The wearer of the HMD appeared to be standing on a computer-generated grid that appeared to stretch out to the horizon. Three-dimensional wire-frame aircraft were suspended in the air. Users could view the aircraft from any angle. McGreevey had a steady stream of visitors from academia, industry, and the military as word of his accomplishments got out.

In 1985, NASA hired Scott Fisher, at which time Michael McGreevey went to Washington, D.C. for a two-year training assignment. Fisher brought with him the conceptual framework that the Atari Research group had devised. Fisher wanted to extend the original system into a general-purpose test bed that could be used for visualization tools, surgical simulators, telerobotics, virtual workstations, and other research interests. While Fisher built the system, McGreevey made sure there was money with which to build.

The VIVED HMD totally obscured the real world, so keyboards and buttons were obsolete. Fisher bought an off-the-shelf voice recognition package. Simple voice commands greatly extended the types of things the operator could do. A voice synthesis package was also added; a robotic voice would echo your command back to you after it had been processed.

Fisher began searching for contractors who could build a three-dimensional audio system. Dr. Elizabeth Wenzel, Dr. Frederick Wightman of the University of Wisconsin, and Scott Foster of Crystal River Engineering devised just such a system. The device is called a Convolvotron and works by mathematically modeling a specific human signal processing function. The model is called the Head Related Transfer Function, and it accounts for how our ears transform the sound signal as it is passing through the air near our head. An average person can generally pick out several conversations in a large crowd of people and can also tell the direction from which a conversation is coming. The Convolvotron adds this ability to the NASA system. The operator can hear up to four different conversations or radio tunes without the conversations or tunes becoming entangled.

Fisher also wanted to start experimenting with tactile feedback (output) devices. He wanted a way to manipulate objects in his virtual world. Fisher started negotiating with VPL Research for a glove-based input device for the system. VPL Research contractors Thomas Zimmerman and Jaron Lanier created and patented just such a glove. The glove not only provided a way for users to interact with the virtual world but also greatly enhanced the virtual experience. Seeing your hand moving in a virtual world, even if it's a stick hand, gives you a perceptual anchor to that world.

Warren Robinett joined the NASA team in 1986 and started to write the application code that tied the system together. He was constrained by the inexpensive equipment; even so, he created dramatic demonstrations featuring stick figure and wire-frame creations of architectural structures, hemoglobin molecules, the space shuttle, and even turbulence flow patterns. Douglas Kerr also joined the team and became responsible for system software.

By 1988 McGreevey had returned from the East Coast and resumed control. VIVED was changed to VIEW, Virtual Interface Environment Workstation. Kerr succeeded Robinett when he left NASA and ported the software to a Hewlett Packard 9000 workstation that could draw worlds with shaded surfaces instead of wire-frames. Scott Fisher left NASA in 1990 to begin a business with Brenda Laurel at Telepresence Research.

NASA had a number of reasons for pursuing this research. Telerobotics, or remotely operated robots, might be the easiest, or indeed the only, way to build and maintain a space station. The sheer volume of information with which astronauts have to deal is also a problem. A virtual world might be one way to deal with all that information. It might allow three-dimensional menus operated by gesture and voice which include three-dimensional sound cues to aid in the navigation of this data space.

NASA's system proved that a "low-cost" virtual reality system could be built. It established a commercial contractor syndicate that could supply many of the components off the shelf. The NASA system also became the first to incorporate an HMD and a glove into one system.

Jaron Lanier and VPL

Jaron Lanier has become virtually a figure of myth and legend. He is "a large, shaggy bear of a man, with his brown hair falling naturally around his bearded face like Jamaican-style dreadlocks" (Sherry Posnick-Goodman, Peninsula). And as Marvin Minsky puts it, "He is one of the few computer scientists who looks at a larger picture."

Lanier learned the art of programming at the height of the video game boom. He created his own games for Atari. One of his games, Moondust, made enough money that he could quit his job and pursue his other interests.

Thomas Zimmerman had an undergraduate degree from MIT and he loved to build things. He realized that perhaps the most significant part of the human body for gestural input to a music synthesizer was the hand. Anyway, he wanted to be able to play air guitar, literally. He bought an old work glove and some miscellaneous electrical parts and tubing. Zimmerman used thin, bendable plastic tubes to conduct light, similar to but not the same as the mechanism of fiberoptics. At one end of each tube was an inexpensive electronic light, at the other end an electronic photosensor. Each tube traversed a finger, over the knuckle and down the back of the hand. When the tube was bent, a measurable amount of light failed to pass through. The amount of light passing through corresponded to the bend in the finger. It was not terribly accurate, but it worked. He applied for and received U.S. Patent No. 4,542,291.

Zimmerman went to work at Atari Research while awaiting his patent. He met Jaron Lanier and Scott Fisher, among others. In 1983, Lanier and Zimmerman attended a meeting of computerized musicians (people who used personal computers with their electronic synthesizers), where Lanier spoke. Lanier discovered that Zimmerman had invented a glove-based input device to a computer. Lanier had long been creating a programming language that used images and sounds to replace cryptic text, and he needed just such a device.

One of Lanier's passions was to create a programming language that used images and sounds instead of cryptic text. He called this language "Mandala," and later it was known as "Grasp" and "Embrace." This visual programming language made extensive use of the glove. A 1984 *Scientific American* cover shows a mockup of Mandala, complete with a musical staff, chirping birds, kangaroos, and melting ice cubes. The article alludes to the origin of the name of his company. When the editors asked the name of his company, he replied "VPL Research, Inc." because he didn't want to tell them that he had no name as yet.

That same year VPL Research was founded and Scott Fisher of NASA came to call. Lanier and Zimmerman had made a deal which assigned Zimmerman's patent to the company and made Zimmerman a part owner and founder of VPL Research. Jean-Jacques Grimaud joined VPL as president, while Lanier remained CEO. Grimaud brought a conservative business approach and a management background to VPL which served as counterpoint to Lanier's eclectic style. All of this is very important when you are trying to sell a U.S. $250,000 system to a conservative company.

Marvin and Margaret Minsky were VPL's first investors after Lanier's Moondust money ran out. Margaret Minsky was responsible for telling Lanier to contact Scott Fisher of NASA. Thompson Avionics also became a major VPL financial backer.

Zimmerman went to work on the next version of the glove. At Lanier's behest the new glove included a Polhemus sensor to determine glove position and orientation. The new glove also incorporated fiberoptics, which were invented by Young Harvill. The software which made the glove useful to a computer was written by Charles Blanchard, Young Harvill, and Steven Bryson.

In 1986, VPL Research delivered the glove to NASA for the VIVED system. Since NASA's work is all in the public domain, VPL was well positioned to make the items commercially. In 1988, VPL created the field of complete virtual reality systems. A new improved head-mounted display based on the NASA design was dubbed EyePhones. It included Scott Foster's Convolvotron to created three-dimensional sound.

VPL combined two Silicon Graphics workstations and an Apple Macintosh computer with EyePhones and the DataGlove to create the Reality Built for Two, or RB2, system. VPL became a booming business by selling EyePhones and DataGloves to lab researchers and garage inventors who were creating their own virtual worlds.

The Macintosh was responsible for defining the virtual worlds which the Silicon Graphics machines rendered. Young Harvill created a Macintosh program called Swivel 3-D, a tool for creating and modeling three-dimensional worlds and objects. It is one of the most popular three-dimensional modeling Mac tools. Chuck Blanchard created another Macintosh program called Body Electric. Body Electric controls the dynamics of the three-dimensional worlds. A rendering program called Isaac, which runs on the Silicon Graphics machines, takes the Swivel 3-D and Body Electric data and displays the final images.

To create a virtual world, you would start with Swivel 3-D and create whatever objects you wanted to inhabit that world. For instance, if you wanted a spinning banana, you would use Swivel 3-D to create the banana. Body Electric would be used to define how the banana was to spin and what would happen to the banana when the DataGlove touched it. Body Electric would control the whole process, including the Silicon Graphics machines, as the simulation runs. If you donned the EyePhones, a slowly rotating banana would appear before you, floating in space. You could use the DataGlove to reach out and grab that banana. With a little more programming, you could even peel it.

RB2 also presented a new kind of ability: two people could inhabit a virtual world at the same time and interact with each other. One of the first demonstrations involved two people represented as lobsters to each other.

In 1987, VPL introduced the DataSuit. This is a full-body version of the DataGlove with a network of sensors to provide information on 50 degrees of freedom of the body including the orientation of the knees, neck, ankles, and wrists.

Another VPL venture was the ill-fated Mattel PowerGlove. In 1987, Abrams-Gentile Entertainment, AGE, offered VPL access to the toy market. The PowerGlove was an input device for the popular Nintendo video game. Royalties were shared between VPL, AGE, and Mattel. Although the PowerGlove did not have the accuracy of the DataGlove, it did sell for under U.S. $100. Unfortunately, the PowerGlove is no longer available commercially.

VPL has finally done what Morton Heilig set out to do many years ago; they have made virtual reality, a term coined by Lanier, a commercial business. They were the first company to offer the products of immersive virtual reality for sale off the shelf to anybody who wished to purchase them.

In mid-1992, Lanier removed himself from day-to-day operations. A new president was brought in to help manage the company. In December 1992

Thompson CSF, VPL's largest creditor, seized the company's patents, which were being held as collateral for U.S. 1 million in loans. VPL had failed to repay the loans and had run out of cash. Management, backed by Thompson, fired the entire staff, including Jaron Lanier.

"Despite demand for its systems, VPL suffered from poor management, the failure to satisfy orders on time and disorganized research," claimed Jean-Jacques Grimaud, CEO of VPL. "Attempts to find fresh financial backing have also been unsuccessful" (Atlanta Journal and Constitution, Monday, Dec. 7, 1992, B1).

Lanier has recently started a new company. It would be imprudent to think he won't be heard from again.

Frederick Brooks and UNC Chapel Hill

The Department of Computer Science at the University of North Carolina in Chapel Hill has been quietly working on virtual reality—related research since the 1960s. Frederick Brooks directs the efforts at the facility. He has been joined by many capable researchers including Henry Fuchs, Stephen Pizer, and until recently Warren Robinett. Unlike many other institutions, UNC has used tactile force feedback since the beginning.

Brooks directed the team that developed the IBM 360 series operating system, undoubtedly the greatest programming feat of its time. He is also the author of *The Mythical Man-Month*, a very important book in computer culture. In that book he attempted to discredit the still prevalent notion that a man-month can be applied to software programming. He demonstrated that doubling the man-months of a project three months behind schedule by doubling the number of programmers will in effect guarantee that the project will become at least six months behind schedule, a notion with which most programmers agree.

Brooks and Intelligence Amplification

Frederick Brooks espouses a concept called intelligence amplification, a concept very similar to Engelbart's intelligence augmentation. Brooks sees three areas in which human minds are more powerful than any computer yet designed. "The first of these is pattern recognition, whether visual or aural. Computer

Scientists don't even have good ways of approximating the pattern recognition power a one-week-old baby uses to recognize its mother's face from an angle and with lighting it has never seen before." The second area is in what Brooks calls evaluations. "Every time you go to the supermarket, you're performing the kind of evaluations that the computer algorithms we have today can only roughly approximate." The third area is in "the overall sense of context that enables us to recall, at the appropriate moment, something that was read in an obscure journal twenty years previously, in reference to a completely different subject, that we suddenly see to be meaningful."

Brooks also sees three areas in which computers are more capable than humans. These are the "evaluations of computations, storing massive amounts of data, and remembering things without forgetting." Brooks' ideal system would couple the human strengths with the computer strengths. The hardest part is building such a system. When designing the interface to such a system, you end up where Sutherland did in 1965 with his paper entitled "The Ultimate Display."

Brooks also believes in a "driving problem" philosophy. Technology advances best if a real application is used, if the problem is chosen carefully, and if good collaborators can keep everybody honest. This can be seen by the careful selection of driving problems that both push computer science and solve real problems of value.

In 1965, Brooks attended a conference where Ivan Sutherland spoke about "The Ultimate Display." Brooks became excited about the possibilities and committed himself to research that allows people, in Sutherland's words, "to gain familiarity with concepts not realizable in the physical world." In 1969, Brooks acquired a special graphics computer from IBM. He also had a very capable and experienced graduate student, William Wright. With these two things, Brooks went to the UNC provost and asked (only half in jest), "Who on this faculty most deserves to have his intelligence amplified?" He explained that he was looking for a collaborator who had a problem with a high geometric content, because to start with you might as well deal directly in three-space as in some abstract space. His problem should also be too hard to do by machine algorithm alone, too hard to do by human insight alone, and one that required a great deal of calculation.

The provost provided a long list of candidates, "including astronomers who were studying galactic structure, geologists who were looking at the oil-bearing cavities under the ground, molecular chemists, architects who were designing low-cost housing and wanted real time interactive cost estimating because if they move a brick it's multiplied by 100 because they're making a hundred units. Highway safety people were concerned about driving simulators. Geographers were worried about city planners who were worried about what happens to the rainwater as you progressively pave over Greensboro."

Brooks knew Jan Hermans, one of the protein chemists, from working with him on scientific programming. Hermans was game, so they picked the molecular structure of life molecules in nucleic acids as their first driving problem. In 1971, Wright and Hermans designed the GRIP-71 system.

The GROPE-I system was also finished in 1971 by another graduate student of Brooks, James Batter. This initial exploration was to build a two-dimensional system for continuous force fields. These were radical simplifications, but a reasonable place to start. The system had a small knob attached to a movable platform. The platform could be positioned with a horizontal plane two inches square. Potentiometers were used to measure forces in X and Y, while servomotors were used to exert forces in X and Y. The system was connected to a computer with a display which provided force magnitude and direction information to the operator.

Molecular Docking

Brooks wrote, "If watching imaginary objects move and alter as one manipulates them endows them with a kind of real existence, and if this process yields more power for understanding and designing imaginary objects, can we build yet more powerful tools by using more sense?" In 1972, Brooks and his students set about combining force-reflection feedback with interactive computer graphics. Raymond Goertz who had designed the Argonne remote manipulators (ARMs) for Argonne National Laboratories, arranged for them to receive a pair of orphaned ARMs. The ARM was a master-slave system that enabled humans behind a lead shield to manipulate radioactive substances by using machines that mimicked what they did with their own hands. The team substituted the computer for the slave part of the ARM.

Brooks and P. Kilpatrick undertook the next phase of the GROPE system; they hoped to build a full 6-D system, three degrees of rotation and three of translation. The GROPE-II system allowed seven virtual children's blocks to be manipulated by tongs on a table in a wire-frame virtual environment. Audible clicks could be added whenever collisions between blocks, table, or tongs occurred. The system successfully represented hard forces, but could not handle more than seven blocks and provided only three degrees of translation. Unfortunately, the problem was beyond the scope of the computing power they had available at that time. They retired the GROPE-II system, awaiting an increase of one hundred times in computing power.

In 1986, the mothballed project was brought out again. This time the VAX computer power was sufficient and the molecular docking system was taken on by Ming Ouh-Young to produce the GROPE-III system. This systems works approximately twice as well as the next best system used to dock molecules. However, it is important to remember that the purpose for Brooks is not numbers, it is computing insight. The driving problem is a means to an end.

Howard Rheingold had this to say when he tried out the system:

Floating in space in front of the screen at eye level was a computer-generated visual model of the receptor site within the human protein dihydrofolate reductase. The protein looked like a lumpy, airy, sculpture made of clouds of blue and red points aggregated into the shape of beach balls and tennis balls melded together. It seemed to be about two feet across, looked to be a little more than an arm's length away from me, and appeared to float in midair. The colored sphere-clouds were clumped, folded and twisted into a geometrically complex pocket—the docking site. Think of it as similar to the kind of three-dimensional puzzle found inside a lock; the proper key opens a door by "solving" the lock.

Between the protein model and my hand floated a smaller molecule model in the form of thin yellow lines, like glowing, rigid wires, representing the angles between the atoms of a synthetic molecule, methotrexate—the "key" candidate. These were not just computer graphic representations of molecules, but multidimensional simulations of those molecules, including all the measures that chemists use to describe molecular behavior—visible bonds could only stretch so far, and when the two molecules were brought together, neighboring atoms attracted or repelled one another according to the physical rules governing the electromagnetic forces at the molecular level. The cloud-solids and stick figures were just two of many possible representations of the modeled entities. There were invisible but palpable representations, as well. When I tried to push the models together by exerting force on the ARM, the force I felt in reaction was an analog of the way the physical molecules would behave if pushed together in physical space.

The grip enabled me to use arm and hand movements to manipulate the models in relation to one another. The more I used the grip to rotate the models that floated in midair, the more three-dimensional they seem. My job was to use the ARM grip to maneuver the 3D puzzle pieces together close enough, in precise spatial relationship, to bond together—a successful dock. If a chemical can be found that makes such a fit on the protein shape found on a tumor cell or a pathogenic bacterium, then it is a potentially medically useful compound.

A consolidation of many of the different tools developed for molecular studies is currently under way. The new project is called Trailblazer. Trailblazer is to bring "a unified support base that will radically reduce the effort at building new prototype visualization tools, for each tool will have data structures and many classes of graphics, interaction, molecular computation, and geometric functions already built, tested, and available." (Brooks, 1993)

The Architectural Walkthrough

In 1985 another driving problem was taken on by Brooks and his UNC team, the architectural walkthrough. Brooks says, "it has the tremendous advantage that sooner or later the building gets built and you can compare the real and the virtual worlds and see how far away you are from realism." Another strength of this problem is that although many architects claim they have no trouble visualizing three-dimensional buildings from floor plans and elevations, the clients most certainly do have trouble. The building can be debugged before any of the working drawings have even been begun, when it is still very inexpensive to make changes to the building plans.

For example, the building that houses the team is Sitterson Hall. During its planning stages, the VR researchers converted the architects' plans into a full-scale three-dimensional model in cyberspace. When the people who were going to spend their time in the building walked through the model, they found a partition in one particular hallway that gave them a cramped feeling. The architects refused to believe any such thing until they walked through the three-dimensional model themselves. The partition was moved. Now there is a room in Sitterson Hall where, by donning goggles and walking on a treadmill (turning the handlebars to change directions), one can stroll through the very same three-dimensional model, complete with the offending partition.

They have found that current technology head-mounted displays often provide low resolution and a relatively limited field of view. So in addition to the head-mounted displays they have a four by six foot rear projection display.

The big screen display is translucent and preserves polarization for stereo viewing. Since it is fairly natural to constrain the direction of motion to be the direction of gaze, the big screen display works well with the treadmill.

They have a nonmotorized exercise treadmill fitted with bicycle handlebars and sensors to determine steering direction and treadmill rotation. The treadmill may be used with either a head-mounted display or a big screen display. This allows the user to "walk" through the virtual environment and experience the scale of the space. Its primary disadvantage is that the treadmill is fairly stiff, so users wear out walking through large buildings. This system is also too slow for a rapid survey of a large building.

Another direction of research is the room-sized ceiling tracker. Special cameras mounted on a head-mounted display track beacons on the ceiling of a special ten by twelve foot room to determine position. The user walks around the virtual environment, always aware of the physical limitations of the room because of a red band at eye level that demarks the real room.

Different combinations of joysticks and three-dimensional position trackers have been used to allow the user to fly through the architectural models. Monoaural sound cues have been added to contribute to the realism. Day- and nighttime lighting and even lighting provided by a fire can be simulated. The current system provides for 32 different types of textures such as woodgrains, acoustic ceiling tiles, linoleum, wallpaper, and brick. Current analysis leads them to want one hundred twenty-eight total different textures. They feel that textures contribute to the effect far more than an additional one thousand or even twenty thousand polygons/second update rate.

Medical Imaging and Three-Dimensional Interactive Graphics

Medical imaging is another driving problem being worked on at UNC. Several projects have been undertaken including Radiation Treatment Planning, See-Through Ultrasound, and X-Ray Vision.

A large effort is under way to apply computer graphics techniques to the field of radiation oncology. As part of this research, James Chung is developing a CAD tool to help radiotherapists in making better plans for treatment. Radiation must pass through healthy tissue on its way to a tumor. Computer graphics are being used to help the design configuration and planning processes so that a minimum of healthy tissue, especially radioactively sensitive tissue, is hurt while the tumor is destroyed. Virtual environment tools are expected to greatly aid the process because the physician is free to examine the patient naturally at all angles instead of on a two-dimensional screen. (Stix and Holloway)

Another current project is to connect an ultrasound scanner to a conventional head-mounted display. The two-dimensional ultrasound image is transformed and processed by the computer. A small camera mounted on the front of the HMD provides real time video of the patient. These two images are composited in real time and displayed to the physician on the HMD. The ultrasound images appear stationary in three-space. This gives the physician the effect of (for example) looking "into" a pregnant mother and "seeing" the baby. This could be useful for such diverse activities as watching an amniocentesis probe as it moves within a pregnant mother relative to the baby, seeing arteries that lie near where a surgeon is about to make an incision, and seeing inside a burning building.

The X-Ray Vision project is attempting to take a head-mounted display through which one can see and superimpose the computer-generated world onto the real world. The computer images might come from ultrasound, computed tomography (CT), magnetic resonance imaging (MRI), or some other imaging technique. Richard Holloway's research involves superimposing static three-dimensional reconstructions of CT or MRI images onto a real patient. In this manner, a surgeon planning reconstructive surgery can see the real soft tissue and underneath it the three-dimensional bone at the same time.

Brooks, Fuchs, and the UNC research team are working on many other projects as well. They are interfacing a scanning-tunneling microscope to the GROPE system; such a system could allow a scientist to "build" a silicon chip one atom at a time. They are working on scientific visualization tools to help provide researchers insight into their work. They have also built some of the fastest computers in the world. It takes a great deal of computer power to drive any reasonable virtual environment.

More History Related to VR

Actually, the military history of virtual reality is inextricably intertwined with the civilian history. Most of the major advances made in the field, and indeed in computers in general, were made with government contracts. ARPA (later the name was changed to DARPA, then recently back to ARPA) was an important military entity. They funded Engelbart's ARC, Sutherland at MIT, and the University of Utah. The Arch-Mac had strong ARPA funding. All of this was the basis for PARC and NASA Ames. This section will be devoted to filling in some of the missing pieces, not already discussed, that the military supplied to the field of virtual reality.

Flight Simulation

The danger of flying airplanes has been obvious from nearly the dawn of the industry. The first flight accident happened a scant five years after the Wright brothers' first flight at Kitty Hawk. The accident happened at a flight trial for the American War Department. Orville Wright was seriously injured; his copilot was killed. Designs for flight simulators were first patented in 1910.

Edwin Link was born into a family that built mechanical musical instruments. Edward Link, Edwin's father, had founded the Link Piano and Organ Company of Binghamton, New York. He had also received his first patent for an enhancement technique for the player piano. This device used a series of pneumatic switches to play the piano's keys. The switches were activated by a series of holes punched in a ribbon of paper. The system was an impressive demonstration of the power of pneumatics and of automation.

Edwin Link used the pneumatic technology he had learned in the music business to attempt to reproduce the aircraft movements of flight. In 1929, Link received his first patent and was selling trainers to the government. His trainer had no instrumentation; it was simply a cockpit mounted on a base that rolled, pitched, and yawed in response to the simple controls provided to the pilot. This first trainer had wings and a tail, all in miniature, to provide recognition features to both student and instructor.

The player piano technology was responsible for trainers as late as 1943. The Silloth Trainer was an example from one of Link's competitors, Aeolian (who manufactured the Pianola brand piano player). This trainer was superior to the others of its time because it could imitate multiple types of airplanes. It also generated certain in-flight phenomena such as cockpit noise. Still, these systems only *imitated* flight. To truly *simulate* flight, the equations that translated the aircraft's flight controls into simulated motion would have to, in turn, be consistently reflected on the aircraft's gauges.

In the 1930s Vannevar Bush encountered problems in computing and predicting electric power flow. The U.S. power system was becoming increasingly interconnected and distributed. Bush designed and built a mechanical computer, which he called a "differential analyzer." It used a roomful of cogs and rods to compute and generate a plot of the particular differential equations he needed to solve. Differential equations can describe very complex behavior, but they can be very hard or impossible to solve exactly by hand. They may be approximately solved numerically, however. Bush proved that such a system could be built.

World War II was forcing the development of technologies that would allow flight trainers to progress from imitation to simulation. The military needed to determine ballistics tables faster and more accurately. These tables were used by a gunner or bomber to determine the force and direction to apply to a long-range projectile to allow for missile weight, atmospheric conditions and phenomena. The Army also wanted to be able to calculate many of the solutions for a wide range of problems. The U.S. Army's Aberdeen Proving Ground was responsible for the work load. By 1944, they were receiving an average of six requests a day. A single, sixty-second trajectory could be solved by hand in about twenty hours. A machine like Bush's differential analyzer would cut that time to fifteen minutes. A new development at the University of Pennsylvania promised to calculate a trajectory in thirty seconds, faster than real time. The Electronic Numerical Integrator and Computer (ENIAC) was commissioned to do the job. The designers also pointed out that the ENIAC could solve other types of problems as well.

Also in 1944, Jay W. Forrester at MIT's Servomechanisms Lab led a project to build an "airplane stability control analyzer." The project's goal was to use the same electronic, digital technology that created the ENIAC to build a generalized flight trainer. A member of the team, Robert R. Everett, promised that "putting wind tunnel data into the trainer would cause it to fly like an airplane not yet built." The project was dubbed Whirlwind. It was finished for testing in 1949 and completely operational in 1951, just in time for the U.S. Navy's funding to run out. The new funding would have to come from the Air Force, which was interested in the system for air defense purposes.

The researchers who built Whirlwind learned some entirely unexpected things. In late 1948 and early 1949, while playing with the oscilloscopes that were used to display system information, they noticed that certain computer instructions would cause certain patterns on the oscilloscope displays. They even managed to create a game including a dot, called the "ball," which could be made to fall through a "hole" in the "floor" by adjusting some of the input variables. The dynamics of a real ball could be reproduced using just the pure math. They had developed the first interactive computer display, as well as the first computer game.

One of the early Whirlwind testing programs displayed the states of the system's memory devices on the oscilloscope as a series of dots. The researchers wanted to know which dot represented which particular memory tube. So, they built a "light gun" from a tube and a light-sensitive detector. When it was hooked up to the system and pointed at the oscilloscope it was able to identify the associated vacuum tube. This was the first lightpen and the first interactive graphics tool.

The U.S. Navy was funding another effort at the University of Pennsylvania with the ENIAC developers. Their job was to develop a real time simulation system to model aerodynamics. The project was called the Universal Digital Operational Flight Trainer (UDOFT) and it was successful in this quest even as Whirlwind was not.

The 1960s saw the commercial development of a flight simulation computer when Link released the Mark I. The system allowed the pilot to manipulate the controls, which responded according to the rules of aerodynamics. The simulator included landscape seen through the cockpit window, wind, and engine noise. The pilot's instruments and the force feedback on the controls all responded accordingly.

Evans and Sutherland

While working on head-mounted displays, Sutherland realized that computers could generate the images for flight simulators instead of cameras. Sutherland and David Evans teamed up in 1968 to form *Evans and Sutherland* and to develop electronic scene generators.

The old system of constructing scale models for the scenes used paint, foam, and glue. Any three-dimensional object can be recreated on a computer with points and lines; the object is said to be digitized. The view of the object may be transformed with a series of calculations. It has long been known that the closer to reality the simulation is, the more use it is. The problem with this is that "realism" involves a great number of calculations. These calculations have to be done quickly enough that the scene can be rendered before it is already out of date. Every computer has a limit on what complexity can be achieved in what time. If the rendering is too slow, no amount of detail will make the system appear real. In fact, it can cause the operator to experience "simulator sickness," a feeling very much akin to motion sickness, which is described elsewhere.

Military HMDs

The military began experimenting with head-mounted displays in 1979. The idea was to reduce expense and the size of the system by projecting the whole thing directly into the pilot's eyes. One of the first of these systems was produced by McDonnell Douglas and was called VITAL. It used an electromechanical head tracker to determine head orientation and gaze. It had two monochromatic cathode ray tubes mounted in the helmet next to the pilot's ears. The CRTs projected the image onto beam splitters in front of the pilot's eyes. VITAL allowed the user to view and manipulate the mechanical controls in the cockpit while simultaneously viewing the world painted by the computers on the CRTs. Problems with the bulky helmet and the unnaturalness of looking through beam splitters limited its acceptance.

In the 1970s, for the first time, the capabilities of advanced fighter aircraft began to exceed that of the humans who flew them. The F-15 had nine different buttons on the control stick, seven more on the throttle, and a bewildering array of gauges, switches, and dials. Worse, in the midst of the stress and confusion of battle, perhaps even as they begin to black out from the high-G turns, pilots must choose the correct sequence of manipulations.

Thomas Furness III had a background in creating visual displays for the military dating back to 1966. He had some ideas on how to manage the deluge of information provided to pilots. He succeeded in securing funding for a prototype system to be developed at Wright-Patterson Air Force Base in Ohio. The Visually Coupled Airborne Systems Simulator (VCASS) was demonstrated in 1982. Test pilots wore the Darth Vader helmet and sat in a cockpit mockup.

VCASS included a Polhemus tracking sensor to determine position, orientation, and gaze direction in six degrees of freedom. It had one-inch-diameter CRTs that accepted images with two thousand scan lines, four times what a television uses. It totally immersed the pilot in its symbolic world, a world which was created to streamline the information to be presented to the pilot. The world was symbolic for the same reasons we use a map and not a photograph to determine where we are going.

The Air Force saw promise in VCASS and funded its second phase, called Super Cockpit. Thompson, in an *Air & Space* article, described what the future Super Cockpit pilot might see:

> When he climbed into his F-16SC, the young fighter jock of 1998 simply plugged in his helmet and flipped down his visor to activate his Super Cockpit system. The virtual world he saw exactly mimicked the world outside. Salient terrain features were outlined and rendered in three dimensions by two tiny cathode ray tubes focused at his personal viewing distance. Using voice commands, the pilot told the associate to start the engine and run through the checklist ...
>
> Once he was airborne, solid clouds obscured everything outside the canopy. But inside the helmet, the pilot "saw" the horizon and terrain clearly, as if it were a clear day. His compass heading was displayed as a large band of numbers on the horizon line, his projected flight path a shimmering highway leading out toward infinity.
>
> A faint whine above and behind him told the pilot even before the associate announced it that his "enemy" ... was closing in ...

Furness found a new way to combat the information overload that advanced fighter pilots face. He manufactured a symbolic virtual world that presents the important information from the fighter's instruments and sensors while filtering out the irrelevant. He incorporated voice and sound cues to simplify the many tasks the pilot has to perform. Radar and sensors become the pilot's eyes and ears; his words command his fighter to perform.

So What's the History of VR?

The story of virtual reality is the story of communication. The first artificially created worlds were paintings created in caverns. Initiates, already placed in an altered state, were exposed to this world under the careful control of the keepers of the mysteries. Much of what was taught was for the sole purpose of maintaining the complicated lifestyle of the farmer. The worshippers of Dionysus and Shiva also had similar ceremonies for similar reasons, as did the Hopi on another continent. The Greek theater is a direct descendant of those ceremonies. The Greeks experimented with creating different worlds and exposing their audiences to different thoughts.

Then came text and especially the printing press. Writing allowed much of the human oral tradition to be written down. In this manner, authors could carefully craft an artificial world and have it experienced directly by the reader. Information and knowledge could be passed privately, even between people who had never, and would never, meet face to face.

Electronic communications entered the scene. People could be allowed to be passive as they were wrapped into the plot, story, and experience. People from all over the world suddenly found themselves closer together. People in the United States could watch people in Great Britain or Russia and even feel a vicarious part of their world.

Hence we reach information technology and cyberspace. People can now directly experience and manipulate worlds that do not even obey the laws of our physical world. Indeed, it is conceivable that anything that one can dream could be constructed as or in a virtual environment. But, today's virtual environments have just crossed the boundary of true usability. In the next chapter, we try to explain exactly what today's researchers are up against and why virtual environments that fool all the senses have yet to be or, indeed, may never be built.

3

FROM THE POINT OF VIEW

Introduction

This chapter is dedicated to shedding some understanding into the nature of the human senses, how they work, and how they can be fooled. To build any type of virtual environments system, the creator must understand not only the strengths and limitations of the system, but especially the strengths and limitations of the system's users, humans.

> If the energy of a pea falling one inch could be completely converted into light, it would provide a faint glimmer for every man, woman, and child who ever lived.[1]

---

[1] This is from the Time-Life book, *Vision*. The number of people in question—"the population of Heaven and Hell"—is about 100 billion.

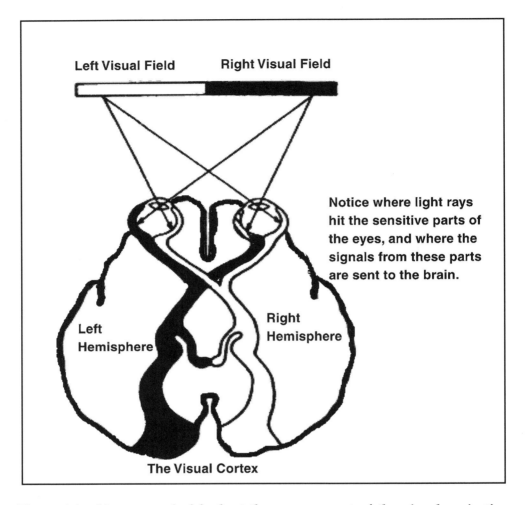

Figure 3.1—"An anatomical look at the arrangement of the visual projection system in humans. Information from each visual half-field is projected directly to the visual cortex of the contralateral hemisphere."

Section 1—Of Sight

As I sit typing this, I'm seeing things through the best pair of eyes in the world—mine.

Well, not mine personally—I'm 20/200 without glasses—but human eyes in general. Human eyes are the best all-around eyes on the planet. The legendary hawk[2] has better acuity, the harbor seal has greater dark sensitivity, certain fish can distinguish finer color shades, cats can perceive tinier motions—but only human eyes can resolve a penny at 215 feet,[3] see 10,000,000 colors,[4] trigger on a single photon,[5] go tele and pick out the Andromeda Galaxy,[6] then go micro and watch a fly wash its face. This gives us human beings a wonderful intimacy with the world. If any animal was meant to enjoy virtual reality, it is the human being.

Practically all animals have eyes; no plants do. Animals are nearly as cleanly separated from plants by the presence of eyes as by motility itself. Indeed, the very origin of eyes is thought to lie in the demands of motility: early swimming life forms developed visual pads to enable them to swim toward the light and away from shadows (hovering predators blocking the light). This theory also neatly explains the crossover of the visual fields[7] in the two sides of the brain: to swim *toward* the light you wiggle your fin on the *opposite* side of your body.

---

[2] A hawk can read a newspaper headline at $1/4$ mile—that is, if a hawk could read.

[3] The standard 1 minute-of-arc resolution. Stirling Moss, the race driver, could read the fine print of a newspaper across a room *(Playboy,* Sept. 1965, p. 241), and a number of people can see the moons of Jupiter and the phases of Venus with their naked eyes.

[4] "The most accurate photoelectric spectrophotometers possess a precision probably only 40 percent as good as this." *The Guinness Book of Records 1993,* ed. by Peter Matthews (New York: Bantam Books, 1993), p. 161. The *Guinness* book also gives the 10,000,000 figure, which agrees with experiments performed years ago at the Walt Disney Studios.

[5] This is another way of saying that under optimum conditions, the human eye has a D.Q.E. (detective quantum efficiency) of 100%.

[6] The Andromeda Galaxy, at about 2 million light-years, is the most distant object visible to the naked eye.

[7] Contrary to popular belief, the right visual field is not entirely located in the left brain, nor vice-versa. The eye is hemianoptic: both *right-halves* of the visual fields map into the *left* brain, and both *left-halves* map into the *right* brain. This means that people with severe injuries to the right hemisphere have scotomata (blind spots) in both left halves of their visual fields, <u>but</u> still have O.K. vision in the right halves. There is probably a survival value in this—if the whole left visual field were knocked out, you could be "blindsided" by an attacker on that side, whereas the split fields still give us warning. *(Science,* 24 Sept 1993, p. 1755, in a review of the book *Hemispheric Asymmetry).*

There are many mysteries about human visual perception. One of the biggest is this: the eye has no shutter, or scanning raster,[8] yet the world is not a blur. When we walk down the street, the buildings seem quite stationary. We do not perceive them as a bundle of streaks on our retina, which in fact they are.[9] Best explanation: the eye is in no sense a camera, neither still nor video. The eye is an image-processing system backed up by the greatest image processor of them all, the human brain. Millions of years ago, all the animals that saw the landscape as a blur died. (*"Mama! What's that blur?"* CHOMP!) Those that lived demanded that their brains come up with what amounted to computer programs for stabilizing the scenery. In developing these programs, which the brain did magnificently,[10] the brain was not hampered by any adherence to Euclidean geometry—on the retina, parallel lines can, and frequently do, converge. The brain allows the eye to operate on a profoundly nonmetric geometry, the better to get on with its business of deconvoluting a dynamic image stream so as to pass on invariant features to higher cortical centers for advanced processing (*"Mama—that blur is a banded krait with a neurotoxic venom, fatal in 3 seconds. Mama, why aren't you answering?"*)

Let's ride a photon that caught my eye recently and learn something about the visual system. This particular photon left the surface of the star *VV Cephei A* 2500 years ago. At that time the Greeks thought that the eyes emitted light, or emanations of some kind, and these eye-rays collided with object-rays given off by bodies out in 3-space; the result was vision. With a theory like this, who needs science?[11] While this lunacy held sway, the little photon traveled on for 2000 years; Leonardo da Vinci endorsed the Greek theory, and added some fancies of his own. As late as 1893 so great a light-wight as Tesla affirmed that the eyes of Helmholtz and others could emit light, enabling them to see in total

---

[8] I am aware that the eye has an approximately 30 Hz refreshment rate, but in spite of this does not behave like a movie camera cranked at 30 frames per second. For example, the human eye does not see stroboscopic effects in rolling wagon wheels, which have plagued the movies from the beginning.

[9] "Visual Motion Perception"—by Gunnar Johansson, *Scientific American*, June 1975, pp. 76 ff.

[10] As is well known, the brain writes in "C" (that is, Cortex).

[11] 13% of nine-year-olds think that nothing need reach the eye for you to see something (*The Physics Teacher*, Nov. 1970, p. 447).

darkness (only the gifted had this ability; the rest of us stumbled around in, uh, darkness).[12]

But enough of the errors of the past; thanks to a legion of brilliant men and women we know today what really happens. That little photon went through the wretchedly astigmatic lens of my eye and delivered its energy $h\upsilon$ to my retina, driving the system through a photochemical cycle and pumping protons against an electrochemical gradient, beginning a photoisomerization process that is complete in *half a trillionth* of a second,[13] and enabling me to exclaim "Look! There's *VV Cephei A*!"

What happens between the completion of the photoisomerization process and "Look!"? A lot. Signals pass from the retina, where some preliminary processing has already been done,[14] along the optic nerve (said to be the densest information channel in the universe), to the lateral geniculate body, deep in the brain. From there, the information stream is dispatched, curiously, all the way to the rear of the brain, farthest from the eyes, to the striate cortex. The striate cortex calls on its good buddies, the inferior temporal cortex and the posterior parietal cortex, for advanced processing, in which an object is broken up into different attributes, not necessarily the ones Aristotle would have thought of. For example, edges are analyzed independently of overall shape, and spots of color are handled differently from widespread color—this constitutes the "object" pathway. Position, with respect to visual landmarks, is assessed separately in its own "spatial" pathway. In a fantastic division of labor, platoons of individual neurons are slavishly flagged for certain object properties, and no others.[15] (It appalls me to think that there may be

---

[12] "Helmholtz...was able to *see*, in total darkness, the movement of his arm by the light of his own eyes. ...It is very likely that the luminosity of the eyes is associated with uncommon activity of the brain.... It is fluorescence of brain action, as it were." Originally printed in *Scientific American*, Oct. 1893; reprinted in *Scientific American*, Oct. 1993, p. 12.

[13] "Protein Catalysis of the Retinal Subpicosecond Photoisomerization in the Primary Process of Bacteriorhodopsin Photosynthesis" by Li Song, M. A. El-Sayed, and J. K. Lanyi, *Science*, 13 Aug 1993, p. 892.

[14] Not surprising, since the retina is developmentally an outgrowth of the brain; it is as though the brain put out a part of itself to enlarge its cyberspace kingdom: McGraw-Hill *Encyclopedia of Science and Technology*, latest edition, article "Eye (vertebrate)", p. 585 and p. 590.

[15] This material is adapted from the brilliant article by Mishkin and Appenzeller in the *Scientific American* for June 1987, mainly p. 83.

thousands of neurons in my brain waiting for years to pounce on puce, to inform me that that color has finally been encountered.) It seems incredible to break up a percept in this way for analysis, and it's plain that the vulnerability of the brain to a rich variety of (so-called optical) illusions is largely due to this strange-attribute processing. The other side of that coin, of course, is the tremendous efficiency of the brain, working massively parallel,[16] to recognize a pattern from almost no information. These two sides—susceptibility to illusion and ability to operate on near-zero data—make the brain such a wonderful client for virtual reality.

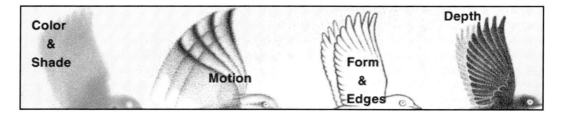

Figure 3.2—The impression of a flying bird is built up in the brain from color, motion, form, and depth

> The eye, whilst it makes us see and perceive all other things, takes no notice of itself.
>
> —John Locke, *Essay Concerning Human Understanding*

Alexander Pope said that the proper study of mankind is man, yet as regards the visual system man's study of man has been remarkably tardy and ill-informed. As many as one person in eight is color-blind,[17] and this must have been true for at least the last ten thousand years, yet nobody recognized

---

[16] Possibly *10 trillion calculations per second*: *Discover* magazine, Nov. 1992, p. 104; see also *Science*, 13 Sept. 1991, p. 1290.

[17] "Anomalously color-equipped," as we PC folk say. The actual percentage varies with the group sampled; Czechoslovaks have the most color-handicap, and Fijians and Brazilian Indians the least.

the problem until 1794, when John Dalton (who suffered from the condition) found that he could not distinguish certain colored chemicals, though other people could.[18] Mind you, differences in color perception had been noted prior to Dalton: they were ascribed to witchcraft.

However, as regards the blind spot, which we all have, no one seems to have suspected a thing until 1660, when Edmé Mariotte discovered it. Mariotte was well-versed in the anatomy of the eye, and he deliberately set out "to make therefore the Rayes of an Object to fall upon the Optick Nerve of my Eye, and to find the consequence thereof...."[19] The consequence thereof was that the Object disappeared, if the other eye was covered. Don't be bashful; try it now:

Cover the left eye (don't squint it closed, cover it). Then look at the white cross with the right eye. Move the page closer and farther away. There will be a distance where the black disk disappears and is replaced by white. Had the background been slanted lines, the disk would have been filled in by slanted lines, at the same angle.[20]

This blind spot, which you have now located and which you may never have seen before in your life, can cover the area of 75 to 100 full moons.[21]

This discovery of the blind spot by Mariotte was considered "spectacular" and swept Europe. Charles II of England was much taken with the effect and required his courtiers to participate in a demonstration to see "how they would

---

[18] *Eye and Brain*—by R. L. Gregory (New York: McGraw-Hill Book Company, 1966), p. 126.

[19] *Philosophical Transactions of the Royal Society of London*, Vol. 3, p. 668 (1668). This is the Royal Society's English translation of a letter from Mariotte, describing work purportedly done eight years earlier.

[20] "The reason the surface area corresponding to the blind spot can look black or white or colored or striped or checkered or slanted is that it *cannot* appear to be a hole or gap in the surface. To see a hole or gap requires stimulus information, and that is just what the blind spot cannot [provide]. 'Filling in' is a misnomer, therefore, since there never was a phenomenal hole in the world to be filled in." *The Senses Considered as Perceptual Systems*—by James J. Gibson (Boston: Houghton Mifflin Company, 1966), p. 263.

[21] *The World of Perception*—by Kai Von Fieandt (Homewood, IL Dorsey Press, 1966), p. 36.

Figure 3.3—Filling in the blind spot with a pattern—close your left eye, stare at the cross, and slowly move the page closer and farther until you notice the disk filled in by slanted lines

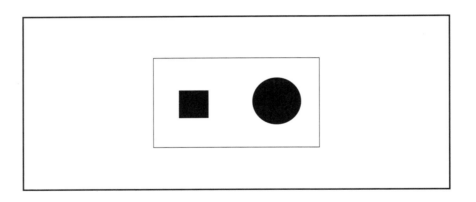

Figure 3.4—Filling the blind spot with background

look with their heads off!"[22] Ironically, in spite of his anatomical expertise, Mariotte believed that the retina was insensitive to light; in his opinion a

---

[22] *The Human Senses*—by Frank A. Geldard (New York: John Wiley & Sons, Inc., 1953), p. 9. The "filling-in" process (footnote 14) does not extend to the human head!.

layer called the choroid was the seat of vision.[23] Fortunately, the astronomer Kepler had already proved (1604) that the retina is essential to vision.[24] As for Mariotte, he remained in the public eye by igniting gunpowder with a giant lens made of ice[25] (don't ask me why).

Incidentally, little, preyed-upon animals like mice have tiny blind spots[26]—possibly a big blind spot might hide a predator when looking around corners.

* * *

In a day when a single command to a computer can produce the most startling transformations, it seems unbelievable that there was ever any problem about the image on the back of the eye being upside down. Yet the great philosopher Bishop Berkeley spoke of the "mighty difficulty" posed by the inverted image.[27] So reluctant were people to believe that the image was inverted that a man named Scheiner in 1625 had to slaughter an ox, remove the eye, strip the rear of it down to the retina, and actually show the upside-down world through the semitransparent membrane of the still-intact eye.[28] To this day, there are parents who believe that babies initially see things upside down, but "learn through experience to allow for the inversion."[29] A religious magazine gushes, "What a blessing for us that the Designer of the eye also instructed the brain on how to turn these images the right way up!"[30] Of course, it's completely immaterial how the information is arrayed on the retina—it's

---

[23] *History of Psychology*—by Otto Klemm (Scribners, 1914), p. 321. Also see the "letter to Pecquet," in 1668, translated and quoted in *Readings in the History of Psychology*—comp. & ed. by Wayne Dennis (New York: Appleton-Century-Crofts, Inc., 1948), p. 43.

[24] *Eye and Brain*—by R. L. Gregory (New York: McGraw-Hill Book Company, 1966), p. 45.

[25] *New Catholic Encyclopedia*—(New York: McGraw-Hill Book Company, 1967), Vol. 9, p. 228.

[26] *The Vertebrate Eye and Its Adaptive Radiation*—by Gordon Lynn Walls (New York: Hafner Publishing Company, 1963), p. 179.

[27] *A New Theory of Vision* [1709]—by George Berkeley, § LXXXVIII.

[28] *Eye and Brain*—by R. L. Gregory (New York: McGraw-Hill Book Company, 1966), p. 45.

[29] *Experiments in Seeing*—by Harry Asher (New York: Fawcett World Library, 1966), p. 49.

[30] *Awake!* magazine, July 22, 1971, p. 16.

all just grist for the brain's mill. Admittedly, once a particular arrangement is hard-wired by a million years of evolution, any change will be noticed; but people wearing upside-down goggles adjust in a few days to a few weeks.[31] Incidentally, you can very easily prove that the brain has an inversion program: in a dark room, place a powerful flashlight against the center of your forehead. The light will go through your skin and bone and illuminate the top nasal sides of your retinas. But you will see the red glow on the bottom temporal sides. And while you're at it, you may as well see your retina, in all its rivered glory: exchange your big flashlight for a penlight, and wave the glowing penlight back and forth in the corner of your open eye, still in a darkened room. (The trick is to keep it at the side and not look at it directly; also, blue cellophane over the bulb may help.) With each wave of the penlight, you should see a momentary flash of a huge, scarred, alien planet—your retina, covered with a thicket of nerves and blood vessels. One of the ironies of evolution is that the retina of vertebrates has ended up with the light-sensitive cells *on the bottom,* overlain by its own life-support system. Our clear, unmarred view of the world is due to the same insidious brain mechanisms that wash away our blind spots.

Another self-discovery experiment: make a pinhole in a large piece of aluminum foil. Go outside and view the sky through the pinhole. (Don't look at the sun; just the sky.) You are seeing your pupil. Don't believe it? Drench the other eye with strong sky light while still looking at the sky through the pinhole. *You will see the pinhole patch expand and contract—in sympathy with your illuminated pupil.* There's an interesting little time delay.

This is as good a place as any to mention another belief about the retina: that it retains the image of the last thing seen before death. Actually, it may even be true, if the eye can be obtained quickly and treated with a fixative. In the 1880s a German researcher named Kuhne removed an eye from a just-executed criminal, sliced it open, and treated the retina with alum.[32] He obtained an image, but an unrecognizable one—possibly blurred by tears, according to one speculation. To my knowledge, nobody has repeated this experiment.

> Those born blind dream of touch, sound, smell.[33]

---

[31] Such experiments were done as long ago as 1895! "Vision and Touch"—by Irvin Rock and Charles S. Harris, *Scientific American,* May 1967, p. 96.

[32] *Scientific American,* August 1950, pp. 32 ff.

[33] *Reader's Digest,* March 1972, p. 94.

Figure 3.5—Beauty is in the pupil of the beholder: pupil shapes in vertebrates

For hundreds of years scientists "knew in their bones" that there had to be three types of color receptors in the eye to account for color vision, but only very recently has there been objective evidence of this, from microspectrophotometry of excised retinas and reflection densitometry of living eyes.[34] In fact, the spectral responsivities of these three kinds of photoreceptors—the cones—are now well known. These cones are conventionally referred to as red, green, and blue, but they don't all peak in those colors, and they overlap in their responses, especially the "red" and "green." The overlap is necessary to enable us to distinguish related colors—because it is the *ratios* of the excitations that the brain looks at. This is a powerful stratagem, but lays the eye open to a special vulnerability—that the same "color," for example a certain green, might be built up of different spectral components. (This was known all the way

---

[34] *Physics Today*, Dec. 1992, p. 25.

back to Newton's time.[35]) These look-alike colors are called metamers; different to a spectrophotometer, they are identical to the eye. The up side of metamers is that they facilitate color matching: without the availability of metameric matches, color production and reproduction techniques—printing, photography, television—would be almost impossible.

Roughly 8% of people have some anomaly in color perception.[36] But the really interesting thing is the 92% who are "normal." What's interesting is that the 92% agree on colors to within a fraction of a percent. This is unprecedented for the human senses, which tend to follow a Gaussian distribution of sensitivity and agreement. This seems to argue that color perception in the unflawed is under some special kind of control, perhaps digital.

When I was a kid, all the other kids wondered if people saw the same colors and if we have the same names for them: was the "red" that Ricky saw the same as the "red" that Mikey saw? I knew that Ricky's and Mikey's reds were the same, and the same as mine, because of the sameness of our bodies, and the paucity of methods with which nature addresses these problems. (No, I didn't really use the word "paucity" when I was eight years old.) However, if you doubt this, you can make a little experiment in color matching. You have a Ricky and Mikey inside your head—your two eyes. Look at a book of wallpaper swatches or color tiles with first one eye, then the other. You'll be amazed at how similar the two appearances are.

Still, people do have color anomalies, especially men (at least an order of magnitude more color anomalies in men than in women).[37] Most people with a color handicap gradually become aware of it. One sufferer wrote, "My friend was raving about the rainbow again. There it was, the same old dirty dishrag of colors that it had always been. What was the matter with these idiots?" When it dawns on color-deficient people that the handicap is theirs, they often go into denial. They will go to elaborate lengths to keep from being found out, and will avoid situations in which it's necessary to identify colors. (Occasionally color-deficient people get into trouble when they make strenuous

---

[35] Newton may well have been the first to recognize metamers, but contrary to popular belief he was not the first to decompose white light into a rainbow with a prism: he bought his prism at a fair, so that he could try "the celebrated phenomenon of the Colours.".

[36] See footnote 17.

[37] It's a so-called sex-linked recessive; women have to get a double dose to be a sufferer rather than just a carrier.

efforts to get into a car whose color, by bad luck, is metameric to that of their own.)

A great deal is now known about the details of color deficiency. Basically, color-deficient people either lack a family of cones outright, or one of their families has a crippled spectral response. (It is not certain whether there are any human monochromats—people with no color vision at all; most animals, including dogs and cats, are now known to have substantial color vision.[38]) When the color vision of normal people is plotted as a solid in 3-space,[39] the color vision of deficient people maps into surfaces or lines, which means in practice that they have millions more metamers vis-à-vis normal vision. There is no treatment, though there are strategies to make daily life less trying.

It is possible to lose color vision, due to accident or disease. Back in horse-and-buggy days, the kick of a horse sometimes resulted in loss of color vision (not to worry if a mule kicked you—that resulted in blindness or death).

Once in a while, a color-deficient person has an advantage over normal individuals. The art of camouflage strives to paint fortifications, gun emplacements, etc. with colors which are metameric to innocent grass or trees. Such camouflage colors may not, however, be metameric to a color-"handicapped" person. There are several cases of color-blind observers being used to unmask camouflage; in particular, there was a famous color-blind chaplain in Vietnam who was ferried all over the country, because he could spot camouflaged Viet Cong emplacements with a single glance.[40] It would seem that appropriate programming of the color channels of a video camera could reproduce this ability, not that I am trying to do color-deficient people

---

[38] "See Spot See Blue: Curb that dogma! canines are *not* colorblind"—*Scientific American*, Jan. 1990, pp. 20-21. According to this new work at the University of California, dogs definitely, and most mammals probably, have at least two-color vision. According to the *Guinness Book of Records* for the last several years, human monochromats are "very rare."

[39] "Color vision, of all psychophysical phenomena, has perhaps the most elegant scientific formulation. The color manifold can be represented as a closed three dimensional space with reference to three arbitrary primaries. ...All theorems of projective geometry for closed spaces can be made to apply." Jozef Cohen and Donald Gordon, *Psychological Bulletin*, March 1949, p. 97.

[40] I cannot lay my hands on this reference, but the chaplain was written up in *Time* Magazine in the early 1970s.

out of a job.[41] (Another way to defeat camouflage is to take aerial stereo photos with several hundred feet of baseline separation; military installations tend to literally "stick out."[42])

Let's return to a discussion of color vision in putatively normal people. It's apparent that standard three-gun video is an efficient way of feeding the color system of human beings. We might ask, can red, green, and blue channels produce, or reproduce, all colors? The short answer is, pretty close. On the standard horseshoe-shaped chromaticity diagram, any given three colors can match all the colors within the triangle marked out by the points representing those colors. Red, green, and blue (say, 650, 520, and 436 nanometers) are chosen as "primaries" because they make a triangle that encloses the largest possible area—that is, the most colors. The only colors that cannot be matched by a well-chosen R-G-B are "selvage" colors near the periphery of the horseshoe.[43]

But wait. There is one more reservation here. There is more to color than color, so to speak. Our perception of color is also conditioned by the *surface which is invested with that color*. Imagine a blue shawl crumpled on a table-top. It's all "the same color"—but our eye sees differences in the appearance of different parts. It's not just due to differences in luminance, or the nap of the fabric. There is a family of colors which can be appreciated only as surface colors; brown is an example. Brown is actually a form of yellow; or to put it another way, brown is to yellow as gray is to white. Try the following experiment: imagine a Kodachrome slide of a man wearing brown pants. Project it on a screen. Now cut a hole in the screen where the image of the brown pants

---

[41] There is at least one science-fiction story in which the world is saved by color-blindness; a color-blind woman fails to notice that invading aliens are blue, and they're so delighted by her tact in not commenting on their bright cerulean hue that they decide not to destroy earth.

[42] *Scientific American*, Feb. 1965, p. 38.

[43] In fairness, I would have to admit that these "selvage" colors do include many of the most vivid and pure spectral colors [*Colour: Why the World Isn't Grey*—by Hazel Rossotti (Princeton, NJ: Princeton University Press, 1983), p. 154]—however, these colors cannot be fully reproduced by present-day printing or video techniques in any case, so the failure is not a fatal criticism of the 3-primary system. If these colors must be matched within the framework of the CIE chromaticity diagram, "negative" amounts of a primary can be added—in practice, it works like this: if you fail to match (say) a vivid spectral yellow with red and green, add a little blue *to the yellow*; this is equivalent to adding a negative amount of blue to the primary mix (Rossotti, p. 154).

is showing, and let that light fall on another screen behind the main screen. Look at this light in isolation; it will be a dull yellow. Brown, like olive and a few other colors, gets its effect from the luminance of the surround.

A far more common visual defect than color-blindness is nearsightedness, myopia. Literally hundreds of millions of people are nearsighted. If you are one of those sufferers, however, take heart—most tests show that the myopic have higher I.Q.'s and higher socioeconomic standing than the perfect-sighted. (Sorry—just putting on glasses will not automatically raise your I.Q.—forget it) Though not all authorities agree, it is pretty certain that the cause of most nearsightedness is now known. Not for nothing do most (young) people have 20/20 vision. The architecture of the eye is under feedback control. When the eye is the right size for perfect visual acuity, it stops growing. How does it know? Cells toward the periphery of the retina are programmed to sense a high contrast (high sharpness) situation, and say, Enough is enough. But if you read all day and don't get outside where the big trees are, with their big contrasty outlines, those cells will never get the nudge, and your eye will never stop growing (until it runs into the bony socket of your skull), and you won't be able to see Rock City on a barn, let alone a penny at 215 feet, and your retina will be all thinned and stretched out, and prone to detachment—but maybe you will be able to pay for an operation, with your high socioeconomic status. Seriously, classic myopia is a disease of civilization; few if any Eskimos were ever found to be nearsighted until they went to school and became literate; then there were Eskimos who couldn't tell a whale from a walrus (though they could locate them in a dictionary). Since you can't experiment on human beings to check out this new notion of nearsightedness, freshly hatched chicks were made to wear fuzzy filters, and sure enough their eyes grew out of control and developed the typical myopic geometry.[44]

Bad as our eyes can sometimes be (I should know[45]), we usually accept the judgment of our eyes over, say, the sense of touch. Experiments have been performed that show that vision is totally dominant over touch. "If a subject looks at his hand through a prism, so that the hand appears to be several inches to the right of where it really is, he soon comes to believe the hand is

---

[44] And shortly thereafter, moved into palatial condos. *Scientific American, Oct. 1987, p. 36.*

[45] When I was called up to see if I was fit to serve in the Vietnam War, the eye examiner, who'd taken note of my thick glasses, asked "How many fingers am I holding up?" To which I replied, "Go ahead; hold your hand up" (he already was). They declared that I would be a menace with a rifle, and sent me back home.

where it appears to be."[46] In more sophisticated tests, people were asked to sketch a block which they were allowed to handle, while viewing it through a reducing lens; they almost invariably drew it small, matching the visual appearance. Few subjects even remarked on the conflict of information from hand and eye; they had a "unitary" impression. Encouraged to handle a straight rod viewed through a curvy lens, subjects reported not only that the rod was curved, it "felt curved." This phenomenon has been termed "visual capture," and means that most input in a VR environment probably should be visual. So strongly does vision, like a bully of the senses, enforce its rendition of a subject, that after a sufficiently long disagreement between vision and touch, "there is a change in the sense of touch itself."[47] In any case, the "old philosopher's" belief that touch could educate vision is *clearly* wrong.

There is hardly a visual property which is not influenced by its surroundings; this is called the adjacency principle. The classic science-museum demonstration is the pair of identical gray squares, one bounded by white and the other bounded by black: observers never fail to pronounce the white-bounded square darker than the black-bounded one; then you turn a crank and juxtapose the two squares seamlessly, proving their identity. The same thing can foul up your color judgments; an aqua can go to green or blue depending on the surround. It is less well known that judgment of motion is similarly vulnerable: a light moving horizontally in a dark room is seen to bob—if a bobbing light is nearby.[48] Likewise, your stereo vision can be fooled by neighboring objects that are at preconceived distances. There are two ways of viewing (love these visual metaphors!) these effects. Gestalt psychologists would say that evolution has chosen an "adjacency function" to organize visual stimuli: the perceptual world "would tend to be too fragmented if the adjacency function were too steep; it would tend to be too undifferentiated if the function were too shallow."[49] Another way to look at adjacency is in terms of sampling strategy: our sampling algorithms baseline themselves largely in the surroundings of the object being inspected; in older terms, our sensory judgments are more relative than absolute. The sampling concept, however, has the advantage that it can explain many properties of the visual system. Almost surely, for example, sampling explains

---

[46] *Scientific American*, May 1967, p. 96.

[47] *Scientific American*, May 1967, p. 104.

[48] "The Adjacency Principle in Visual Perception"—by Walter C. Gogel, *Scientific American*, May 1978, p. 126.

[49] Gogel, p. 139.

"hyperacuity": there are at least five visual tasks where human subjects can perform better than the spacing between their individual photoreceptors should permit![50] In modern terms, "...appropriately encoded 'snapshots' of the world appear to allow the synthesis of computational mechanisms effectively equivalent to vision algorithms for tasks ranging from hyperacuity to object recognition."[51]

It is well known that some people can detect microwaves with their unaided human body; they hear crackling sounds apparently due to differential heating of tissues (don't stick your head in the microwave oven to check this out!). Less well known is that for years a few people have been able to "see" X-rays. They perceive them usually as blue flashes. This is made more plausible by the fact that in deep space Apollo 14 and other astronauts saw flashes of light in their eyes, explained by NASA as due to cosmic rays making direct impacts on the retina or optic nerve.[52]

Most animals have two eyes, but the visual fields do not always overlap. If they do overlap substantially, as in human beings, they have the possibility of binocular vision: the slightly different shape and angle of the same object seen in the two visual fields enable us to locate that object in 3-space (out to about 100 feet, farther under ideal conditions). It is apparent that the visual channels could be fed artificially with different perspectives, to produce the sensation of 3-D, but the experiment seems not to have been done until 1832, when Sir Charles Wheatstone invented the stereoscope. By 1858 stereoscopic pictures had been taken of everything, including the moon.[53] The vogue for stereo pictures reached a height in the 1860s, but by the twentieth century most stereoscopes had been relegated to Granny's attic. However, in the early 1950s a craze arose for 3-D movies. Although Edwin Land had demonstrated stereo

---

[50] The tasks are vernier alignment, 3-point alignment, bisection, curvature detection, and interval comparison. They are all illustrated in Fig. 1 of "Fast Perceptual Learning in Visual Hyperacuity"—by Tomaso Poggio, Manfred Fahle, and Shimon Edelman, *Science*, 15 May 1992.

[51] Poggio et al, p. 1020.

[52] "Cosmic Rays in the Eyes," *Awake!* Magazine, May 8, 1971.

[53] No spacecraft were involved; pictures of the moon were taken 5 months apart from a single observatory, to take advantage of the moon's libration, the natural rocking of the moon in its gravitational cradle, to get the different stereo views (*American Journal of Physics*, April 1972, p. 538).

movies with polarizing glasses in 1936,[54] the first commercial 3-D movies were shown with red and green projectors, and the audience wore glasses with red and green cellophane lenses—this is called the anaglyphic method for achieving 3-D. To this day, some comic books are sold with stories printed in red and green (or magenta and cyan) inks; the viewing glasses are supplied with the book. By the time of such 3-D movie blockbusters as Vincent Price's *House of Wax* (1953), polarized projectors and glasses were universal. (My first experiments with polarized light were done with lenses stripped from these old glasses.) Within less than a decade the 3-D movie fad had fizzled; although Alfred Hitchcock's *The Birds* was originally made in 3-D in 1963, it has rarely been shown in that format.[55]

Holograms have now revived interest in 3-D display, but 99.99% of our daily vicarious visual presentation is still tendered in two dimensions. Yet stereo vision is very important in our assessment of how real something is, and this should always be borne in mind in the design of VR systems. A simple example: experiments have shown that babies recognize a rattle and reach for it—when a picture of it is shown stereoscopically.[56] Only many months later will they reach for the same toy shown in flat photos.[57] Indeed, many pre-literate peoples fail to respond at all to flat photos; perspective rendering is lost on them; they esteem sculpture only. (A famous exception: a missionary in an airplane showered a cannibal tribe with photos of himself, by way of introduction; when he landed they not only recognized him, they ate him. He had a little too much VR for his own good.)

Binocular vision can be impaired by stress, something that should be kept in mind when building VR simulators for training people to cope with real-world emergencies. In the naval battle of Jutland in World War I, the British rangefinders—essential for aiming the big battleship guns—were old

---

[54] *The Encyclopedia of Photography*, ed. by Willard D. Morgan (New York: Greystone Press, 1974), p. 3532.

[55] I'm told there is a Florida theme park which has obtained the stereo version and shows it in that format. It's also worth mentioning that as late as 1961 a Warner Bros. movie, *The Mask*, had 3-D dream sequences—in the old red-and-green anaglyph system! [*The Encyclopedia of Photography* ed. by Willard Morgan (New York: Greystone Press, 1974), p. 132].

[56] How a stereo picture is shown to a baby I do not know. *The Encyclopedia of Photography* ed. by Willard D. Morgan (New York: Greystone Press, 1974), p. 3528

[57] Ibid.

mechanical clunkers that matched two images with a crank. The Germans had state-of-the-art Zeiss rangefinders based on optical enhancement of the gunners' natural stereo vision, fed into a "heads-up" display. But when the shells started falling, the German gunners lost their stereo perception, and were helpless. The Brits, likewise terrified, still had the wits to crank their horribly antiquated coincidence rangefinders, and scored hit after hit. (In any case, about 2% of the otherwise-normally-sighted are "stereo blind"; for unknown reasons they cannot achieve stereo fusion in artificial situations.[58])

If you have mastered the trick of fusing adjacent stereo images without glasses, you can make simple stereograms in which print seems to float, just by bumping a line of type in otherwise identical text:

<table>
<tr><td>X</td><td>X</td></tr>
</table>

The danger of virtual reality: A dog had got a piece of meat and was carrying it home in his mouth to eat. As he went by a brook he happened to look down and saw his own shadow reflected in the water beneath. Thinking it was another dog with another piece of meat, he snapped at the shadow in the water, but as he opened his mouth the piece of meat fell into the brook and was never seen again. —Aesop's *Fables*	.The danger of virtual reality: A dog had got a piece of meat and .was carrying it home in his mouth to eat. As he went by a brook he .happened to look down and saw his own shadow reflected in the .water beneath. Thinking it was another dog with another piece of .meat, he snapped at the shadow in the water, but as he opened his .mouth the piece of meat fell into the brook and was never seen .again. —Aesop's *Fables*

<table>
<tr><td>X</td><td>X</td></tr>
</table>

Everyone old enough to remember the change-over from "hi-fi" to "stereo" knows the enjoyment provided by binaural listening (though we did have to endure hearing interminable tennis games played through our friends' newfangled music systems). Our two ears enable us to locate sounds, with certain reservations—we can generally only locate sounds in a horizontal plane, and we have trouble with pure tones. We do best with clicks and the like, localizing

---

[58] *Scientific American*, July 1981, p. 152.

them in azimuth to within 4 degrees[59] under ideal conditions. We're fairly helpless to tell whether a sound comes from above or below, unlike the barn owl, which has the right ear pointed up and the left down, to produce a differential signal for localization in elevation[60] (we don't fly, so we don't need this ability so much; I wonder if Superman's ears point up and down). Basically, human beings localize sounds with a complex blend of mechanisms, the mix of which varies according to the sound spectrum and duration. The crudest ingredient is just whether the sound is louder in one ear than another; much more subtle is the relative arrival time; more subtle yet is the phase difference (the equivalent of a hundred-thousandth of a second may be perceptible[61])—the brain relies on a cocktail of these to enable us to say, "I think it came from over there." Having more space between our ears—bigger heads—would be of advantage; audio locators have been constructed with big horns fitting on the ears to extend our acoustic baseline. It is for this reason that grasshoppers have their ears on their legs instead of on their tiny pointy heads[62] (it'll never catch on).

One very important side benefit of stereo hearing is "the cocktail-party effect." Most of us can "tune in" on a particular conversation in a crowded room— if we have normal stereo hearing. Present us with the highest-fi *mono* recording of the party, and we can no longer do this. Well-made binaural recordings, delivered to our ears by headphones, enable us to recover much of this ability.

> Only our eyes can categorize the color of objects; spectrophotometers cannot.—Edwin H. Land

No treatment of virtual reality would be complete without an account of that most virtual of all reality systems, the Land theory of color. In 1959 a

---

[59] *Physics, with Applications in Life Sciences*—by G. K. Strother (Boston: Houghton Mifflin Company, 1977), p. 154.

[60] "The Hearing of the Barn Owl"—by E.ric I. Knudsen, *Scientific American*, Dec. 1981, p. 113. Just think—if Dealey Plaza had been full of intelligent barn owls on November 22, 1963, we might not be in doubt about where the shots came from: "Two shots from the Book Depository, three shots from the grassy knoll, and one fool popping a paper bag."

[61] *Acoustics of Music*—by Wilmer Bartholomew (Englewood Cliffs, NJ: Prentice-Hall, 1960), p. 214.

[62] Bartholomew, p. 215.

businessman, Edwin H. Land, the founder of the Polaroid Corporation, stunned the world of professional scientists with a simple demonstration which seemed to produce color where there should be none.[63] Land had photographed a richly colored still life—on black-and-white film. Actually, he had photographed it twice: once through a red filter (the "long" record) and once through a green filter (the "short" record). The long and short records—black-and-white transparencies—were projected on a screen and superimposed. The trick: the black-and-white transparency made through the red filter was projected through a red filter. But no filter whatsoever was used for the other transparency, which was projected raw in white light. According to conventional color theory, nothing should be produced on the screen but pink—that is what red and white make. However, observers claimed to see the still life in near-full-color glory.

To this day the effect has not been fully explained to everyone's complete satisfaction. Indeed, some reputable optics scientists think the Land effect is uncertain and suspect. Land died believing that his "retinex" (retina and cortex) theory, a complex scheme for encoding color independent of light flux, accounted for the basics of the maddening phenomenon. Nearly twenty years after the original demonstration, Land elaborated the theory and added a number of refinements.[64] There are two things which should be kept in mind, however. First, the effect cannot be photographed, at least not in any simple-minded way. The purported color encoding, if it exists, is lost on three-layer color film. (Regular color mixing—for example, white from red, green, and blue—can be photographed.) Second, not all observers agree on the colors seen; some people don't see any colors at all. Some years ago, when I arranged a public demonstration of the Land effect, there were so many disagreements about color that the audience practically came to blows. When an Air Force doctor demonstrated the effect at the San Antonio air base, there was no disagreement—because the commanding officer ordered everyone to see

---

[63] *Scientific American*, May 1959, pp. 84 ff. I give no credence to the suggestion that theatrical lighting directors had been familiar with the effect prior to Land's discovery, from their simultaneous use of red and white spotlights in certain displays. The red and turquoise shadows seen in these displays are plainly after-effect phenomena. *Colour: Why the World Isn't Grey*—by Hazel Rossotti (Princeton, NJ: Princeton University Press, 1983), pp. 140-141.

[64] *Scientific American*, Dec. 1977, pp. 108 ff.

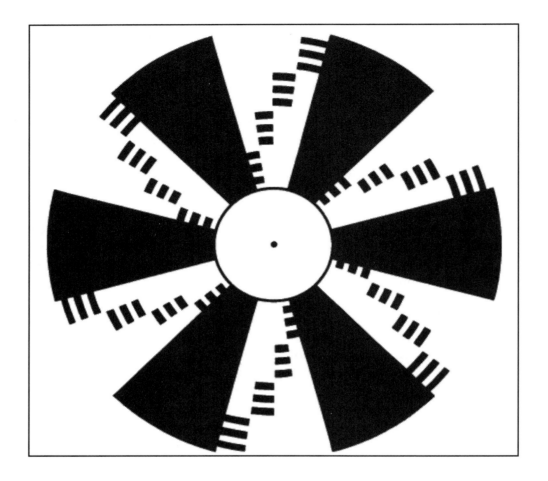

**Figure 3.6—Roger Hayward's pattern for a
Prevost-Fechner-Benham disk**

the same colors![65] Still, whatever the ultimate status of this ingenious discovery, it is a wonderful example of how subjective and personal color is, a fact that will have to be taken into account in any virtual reality presentation.

The most famous subjective color effect has the rather unwieldy name Prévost-Fechner-Benham. A black-and-white disk is rotated, and pale colors are seen along the trailing edges.

---

[65] Personal communication, Dr. Thomas Schermerhorn, M.D., Nov. 16, 1993.

If you have a phonograph turntable, try copying and spinning this disk at 45 rpm, then 78 and 33. Most people will see colors, but not necessarily the same hues under the same conditions. The accepted explanation today revolves around (heh, heh) differential fatigue of color receptors. It is analogous to the way a color monitor, displaying white, will flash brightly in some color when suddenly switched off. Any imbalance in the time response of our "white balance" will show up as a predominance of some color. Possibly the most fascinating thing about P-F-B is that it has been independently discovered no fewer than 13 times, most recently by the behaviorist B. F. Skinner, who wrote, "So far as I am aware, no comparable effect has been reported."[66] (He wrote this in 1932, when the phenomenon was over 100 years old and had been written about by dozens of investigators.) The original discovery was by a French monk, Benedict Prévost, who in 1826 observed "a heavenly light on his fingers"[67] when he waved his hands about in the cloisters. A dozen years later Gustav Fechner rediscovered the colors and did extensive experiments. After rediscoveries by David Brewster and others, Charles E. Benham in England capitalized on the effect, made it into a child's top, and sold it commercially, appropriately enough through the Newton toy company.[68] Surprisingly, some people can see colors in a P-F-B disk when it is illuminated by sodium light,[69] which of course contains no other colors.

Geometrical—what for many years were called "optical"—illusions can be divided into two broad classes: those that involve motion and those that do not (though both are rich sources about the functioning of the brain). Probably the most famous static illusion is the Necker or reversing cube, which goes back to the 1830s. Figure 3.7 is a cute variation.

Children especially are disturbed by Necker cubes; they feel that an object should be "one way or another." A subtle illusion built on a Necker object is Thiéry's figure.

According to whether the figure is viewed "concavely" or "convexly," the shaded region comes out as paint—or a shadow. A very simple static illusion figure is this one, the Gibson after-effect:

---

[66] *Psychological Bulletin*, March 1949, p. 124.

[67] *The Oxford Companion to the Mind*, ed. by Richard L. Gregory with the assistance of O. L. Zangwill (Oxford & New York: Oxford University P.ress 1987), p. 79.

[68] *Nature*, Nov. 29, 1894, pp. 113-114.

[69] *Nature*, Dec. 27, 1894, p. 200.

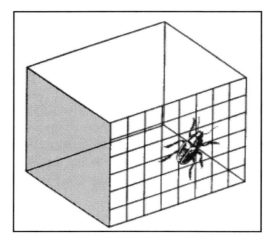

Figure 3.7—The Necker cube

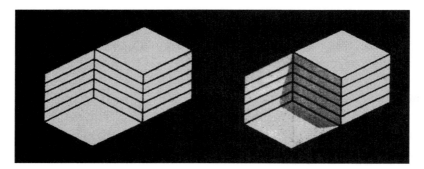

Figure 3.8—Thiéry's figure

Figure 3.9—The Gibson after-effect

Stare at the left-hand line intently; then switch your gaze to the straight line on the right—it will appear to bulge.

One of the most important illusions for the success of VR is the supplied image from illusory contours:

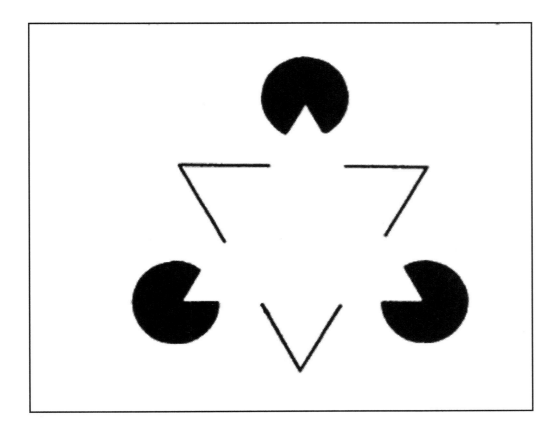

Figure 3.10—Here about 80% of the white triangle <u>is not present</u>, but is synthesized in toto by the brain, and appears as convincing, if not more so, than the line triangle, which is 80% explicitly drawn.

The brain has the ability to take exactly the same contours and see them as very different images or constructs, depending on what it is tricked into choosing as the *figure* and the *ground*:

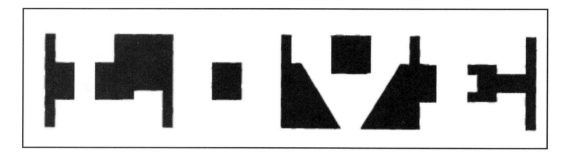

Figure 3.11—What do you see?

These and other geometrical illusions—so convincing and maddening to us—are not always perceived by people who live in "nonorthogonal" worlds. Zulus live in rounded huts with rounded doors, plow fields in curves, and in fact have no word for "square" in their language[70]—and they aren't very susceptible to these classic visual illusions.[71] Cultural background and previous visual experience will have to be borne in mind when designing VR systems.

A famous motion illusion is the Pulfrich pendulum, first described by Carl Pulfrich in Germany in 1922. Arrange a pendulum with a conspicuous bob (a tennis ball on a string) swinging several feet away across your field of view; look at it with both eyes, one covered with the lens from a pair of sunglasses.[72] "The bob will appear to swing in an elliptical orbit! ...The depth illusion is so strong that if a large object is held behind the path of the bob, the bob actually seems to pass through it like a ghost."[73] The standard explanation is that dark-adapted nerves don't transmit impulses as fast as nerves that have all

---

[70] *Scientific American*, May 1970, p. 124.

[71] Ibid.

[72] Professional researchers use filters of 5% to 25% transmission. "Stereopsis, Visual Latency, and Three-dimensional Moving Pictures"—by J. T. Enright, *American Scientist*, Sept-Oct. 1970, p. 539.

[73] *Scientific American*, May 1970, p. 126.

the light they want; the difference amounts to tens of milliseconds.[74] (As for poor old Pulfrich, he was blind in one eye and couldn't see his own illusion![75]) In 1970 J. T. Enright generalized the Pulfrich effect and pointed out that pilots and drivers could have disastrous accidents, due to misestimation of velocities, whenever one eye receives much more or less light than the other.[76] Astronauts, because of the harsh contrast effects in space, might be particularly susceptible to Pulfrich-Enright calamities.

What you might call a frame-of-reference illusion can be done with pencil and paper, and your head. Or rather your forehead. Hold a slip of paper against your forehead and—Quick! without thinking—sign your name. Most people produce what is technically called a perverted signature; look at it in a mirror and it reads right.

Figure 3.12—"perverted signature"

Although Aristotle described the "waterfall" illusion in the fourth century B.C.[77] (in which a few minutes watching a waterfall causes the scenery to move up), for thousands of years people had the attitude that "seeing is believing," and were reluctant to admit that their eyesight could play tricks on them (though Mariotte of blind-spot fame was an early writer on optical illusions, which he called "fausses apparences"[78]). In the 1850s it was noticed that a

---

[74] *Scientific American*, March 1978, p. 142.

[75] Ibid.

[76] *Science Digest*, Nov. 1970, pp. 15-17.

[77] *National Geographic*, Nov. 1992, p. 38.

[78] *Nouvelle Biographie Générale*, ed. M. le Dr Hoefer (Paris: Firmin Didot Frères, Fils et Cie, 1863), Vol. 33, p. 806.

star, on which you had intently fixed your attention, would sometimes dart about in a mysterious way.[79] Obviously psychological (observers didn't all see it at the same time), the effect was at first attributed to irregularities in the atmosphere, a kind of super-twinkling—so loath were people to admit that their eyes (and brain) lied big-time.[80] There is a simple way to get some idea of how big the twinkle-pads in the atmosphere are. Arrange a post five or six feet away, in your field of vision but not blocking it, and look at a bright star with your eyes focused at the distance of the post. You will of course see two images of the star—but they will not twinkle in unison.[81] This is a proof that some, at least, of the atmospheric irregularities are no bigger than three inches!

The glow of the cat's eye is not an illusion. Cats, and many other animals (but not human beings), have a special layer in the back of their eyes called the *tapetum lucidum*. This layer is powerfully reflective, especially on-axis, like the retro-reflector beads in road signs. All the old books say that the tapetum helps the animal see in dim light, by giving the retina a second chance at intercepting a photon. In the late 1980's it was realized that this "explanation" was inadequate; a retina as dark as possible would be better.[82] Which leaves the cat with eyes that are now as mysterious as they are beautiful!

Section 2—Of Sound

Practically every one of the human senses is subject to illusions. Who has not, as a kid, carefully dried an ice cube and applied it to the back of someone's neck? The victim jumps—and complains of being burned. Roll a marble between the index and middle fingers, with the fingers already crossed. Most people feel two marbles. Approach a block of "hops" (for beermaking) with the nose held

---

[79] *Light and Colour in the Open Air*—by M. Minnaert (New York: Dover reprint, 1954), p. 142.

[80] Not fully explained today, the so-called autokinetic effect is definitely perceptual. See any introductory book on psychology or perception.

[81] *Physical Optics* by R. W. Wood (New York: 1905), p. 76.

[82] A local newspaper fielded an inquiry from a reader about the glow of animal eyes; however, they dodged the matter of the *reason* for this special structure. Atlanta *Journal-Constitution*, Nov. 24, 1993, p. A2.

close, then retreat. The hops changes odor. Eat a perfectly good tomato while looking at a rotten one, and see if your enjoyment is not spoiled. The fact is, though, that I had to think hard to come up with these examples of touch, taste, and smell illusions—they are not a rich subject compared to the illusions of sight. However, sound, and music in particular, sustains a number of illusions. Here is an easy sound illusion you can show yourself. Have a blindfolded person sit in a chair. Walk around the person while clicking two spoons together. Ask the subject to say when you are directly behind, judging just by the sound. Most people estimate correctly to within 10 degrees. (A barn owl could nail it to within $1\text{-}^1/_2$ degrees.[83]) Now have the subject place a cardboard tube tightly over one ear (the core from a roll of paper towels does fine). This time the spoons will be several feet off to one side when they are judged to be behind. The ear and brain have equalized the *path length*—which now includes the channel through the tube.

If phase-controlled oscillators are available, a simple but surprising property of the ear can be demonstrated. Feed an oscilloscope and a loudspeaker with several sine waves. View their superposition on the scope. It will be some weird waveform, and you will be hearing some weird sound. Now drastically alter just the phase relations of the waves. The scope trace will change drastically. But the sound will not change (except transiently, as you are twiddling the knobs). The ear does a Fourier analysis of the incoming sound, in terms of both amplitude and phase—but only on a fast time frame. The ear is deaf to the phase relations of the component waves *if* they change in a time longer than a few milliseconds.[84] This makes sense; the chief use of the ear's phase sensitivity is as a part of its program for localization of sound direction, and the ability to "remember" phase relations over more than a dozen cycles of a wave train would be useless. ("Five minutes ago, Fred, you made an out-of-phase remark to me, and I'd like you to apologize.")

There are many musical illusions. A very simple one was popularized by Bell Labs: a musical tone rises in pitch in 12 steps. After the 12th rise, there is a pause, and the tone drops a whole octave. Hardly anyone notices.[85] Here are

---

[83] *Scientific American*, Dec. 1981, p. 123.

[84] Personal communication, Dr. Eugene Patronis, Nov. 16, 1993. Also see "The Fourier Transform"—by Ronald N. Bracewell, *Scientific American*, June 1989, pp. 86-95.

[85] *Journal of the Acoustical Society of America*, Dec. 1964, pp. 2346-2353.

some more complicated musical (or pure tone) illusions:[86] Present an alternating sequence of 400 and 800 Hz tones to both ears simultaneously through headphones; when one ear receives the high tone, the other receives the low tone. Practically nobody hears a chord under these conditions; most listeners report only a single tone that shifts from one ear to the other. "In other words, the listener alternately heard the high tone in one ear and the low tone in the other."[87] Curiously, right-handed subjects heard the high tone in their right ear and the low tone in the left, even when the headphones were reversed; even more curiously, lefties had no preferred ear for either tone.

A tonal illusion that seems contradictory to expectation is the following: Present very rapid sequences of tones to listeners and ask them to rank the tones in order of pitch; it's easy when the tones are *close together*, almost impossible when they're far apart in pitch. This would have a bearing on the way melodies are perceived in music. It also helps to explain why it is nearly impossible to figure out one of Yngwie J. Malmsteen's guitar leads.

An illusion sometimes called the phantom tone is achieved by having two loudspeakers (preferably in an echo-free room), one emitting a low tone, the other a high. A listener turns gradually toward the low-frequency speaker and finally hears "a single tone of constant pitch that [seems] to be coming from both speakers"[88]; turn 180 degrees and the tones switch, the speaker that is in fact emitting the low tone now seems to be reproducing the high!

A simpler phantom tone illusion can be heard in a train station, or the like, that has multiple loudspeakers broadcasting the same message. Fix your attention on a particular speaker while you are listening to a broadcast, then walk toward another speaker. The sound will stay "fixed" for the longest time in the speaker you are looking at, finally jerking back to the closer source.

Years ago I was at the Aberdeen Proving Grounds in Maryland, where they have a large, high-quality anechoic chamber. You enter through something like a submarine air lock, then sit down on thin wire mesh. Above, below, and on all sides of you are very efficient sound absorbers. You scream, and hear almost nothing. They watch you through a little peephole the whole time, because some people freak out when they get so little return from their voice. But if you keep your sanity, after a couple of minutes you hear a very faint hiss.

---

[86] These are summarized from the beautiful article by Diana Deutsch in *Scientific American*, Oct. 1975, pp. 92-104.

[87] *Scientific American*, Oct. 1975, p. 92.

[88] Deutsch, p. 95.

Opinion is divided on whether this is the sound of air molecules bombarding your eardrum (calculations show we're about 3 db shy of having that sensitivity), or the sound of turbulence in blood flow. But you are definitely hearing noise in your auditory sensory channel. And maybe it is the air, calculations to the contrary—it's known that the ear can detect a sound which moves the eardrum less than the diameter of a hydrogen atom!

Section 3—On Haptics

While we're on the subject of the ear, we may as well talk about a nonauditory but very important function of our sound organ.

Balance

This is a good time to talk about how animals balance. I am perhaps not the best authority on this subject, since, along with my 20/200 vision, my sense of balance has been compared to that of "a drunken cow"; still, I will do my best.

There are two aspects to balance. One is the "ensemble of maneuvers" that one makes, from a physics standpoint, to "keep" one's balance, on a narrow perch. This properly belongs to gymnastics. The other aspect, more relevant to VR systems, is what's going on inside the body, from a physiological standpoint, to monitor orientation and maintain balance.

When the anatomist Antonio Scarpa located the semicircular canals of the inner ear in 1772, he had no idea he had found the seat of balance. Yet he had. The tip-off was that there were three canals—one each for "roll, pitch, and yaw," as pilots say. Today we know that there is more to balance than just this famous triune organ; the otolith receptors (little stones that are also in the inner ear) must certainly be mentioned, and the eyes and muscles all contribute to a "multimodal" system of balance.[89] Briefly, we have sensors for detecting

---

[89] For example, see *Exercise Physiology*—by Scott K. Powers and Edward T. Howley (Dubuque, IA: Wm. C. Brown Publishers, 1990), pp. 139-141. The term "multimodal" for

two kinds of disturbance to the body: angular accelerations (such as nodding your head) and linear accelerations (such as scratching off at a stoplight). The semicircular canals handle the "a.a.'s" and the otoliths detect the "l.a.'s."[90] (This is much the way that inertial guidance systems in airplanes and missiles divvy up the job of navigation between gyros and accelerometers.)

The otoliths also detect the direction and strength of gravity, so we know when we're upside-down or falling. Falling, the failure of balance, is one of humans' very few instinctive fears;[91] yet some people find the sensation delicious, as in sky-diving or bungee-cord jumping.

Another failure of balance is motion sickness, which results (according to the traditional theory) when our inner ears don't "hear" what our eyes see:[92] you're in your stateroom cabin while the ship is tossing wildly in the storm, but your eyes see normalcy; this makes you sick. Astronauts experience "zero-G" sickness in space, probably for a similar reason: their inner ears are screaming *You're falling, falling, falling*, but nothing's happening. Curiously, world-class gymnasts are much more susceptible to zero-G sickness than average subjects; the trained gymnasts have learned "to make precise use of gravity," and when gravity goes screwy they're more afflicted than stumblebums like me.[93]

A recent development that foreshadows the future—or one future—of VR is the cochlear implant. People with "sensorineural" deafness, in which the functioning of the cochlea, the inner sanctum of hearing, is impaired, can receive an electronic implant which transmits impulses from a microphone directly to the auditory nerve. Conversation cannot be distinguished, but volume and rhythm of sound are preserved; improvements in multiband implants promise almost-normal—perhaps supernormal—hearing to the nerve-deaf. It is but a step from that to imagining VR parlors of the future in which signals representing a VR environment are piped directly to the appropriate

---

this system is from "The Vestibular Apparatus"—by Donald E. Parker, *Scientific American*, Nov. 1980, p. 118.

[90] My treatment here and elsewhere is based on "The Vestibular Apparatus"—by Donald E. Parker, *Scientific American*, Nov. 1980, pp. 118-135.

[91] Traditionally, the other one is fear of loud noises, but some anthropologists add the fear of snakes, and even the fear of knives.

[92] "The Vestibular Apparatus"—by Donald E. Parker, *Scientific American*, Nov. 1980, pp. 132 and 135.

[93] "Spatial Orientation Problems During and After Spaceflight," *USRA* [Universities Space Research Association] *Quarterly*, Summer 1992, p. 2.

nerves, or even brain centers (à la *Brainstorm*). The chief holdup at present is the unknown encoding that the brain and its nerves use for signal transmission; intercepts from nerve channels show a scratchy babel of signals that is definitely not analog, yet not digital as we know it. Part of the puzzle, as always, is the heavy parallelism and division of labor to which the brain is addicted; sounds are broken up into frequency bands, a flying bird is seen as color and movement, heat and cold have separate sensors,[94] all this neural storm going simultaneously into different patches of the cortex for teraflop processing.

Perception

The tremendous impact of human perception of the design of virtual environment systems cannot be underestimated. For instance, many of the cues virtual reality systems depend on are culture dependent, will we require other cultures to learn our way of "looking" at things? Would that even work? The area of human perception is a complex and an important area of research, one which cannot be ignored by virtual environments researchers, but one to which we do not have all the answers.

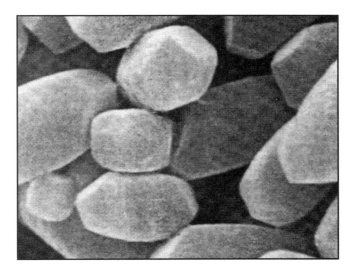

Figure 3.13—The ototconia crystals

[94] Your fingertip has about 13 cold sensors and 65 hot sensors.

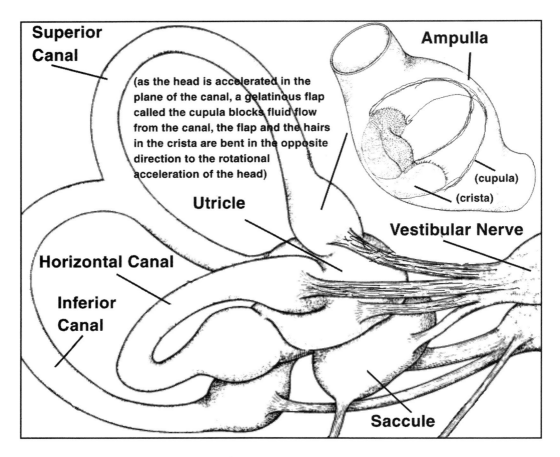

Superior Canal

(as the head is accelerated in the plane of the canal, a gelatinous flap called the cupula blocks fluid flow from the canal, the flap and the hairs in the crista are bent in the opposite direction to the rotational acceleration of the head)

Ampulla

(cupula)

(crista)

Utricle

Horizontal Canal

Inferior Canal

Vestibular Nerve

Saccule

Figure 3.14—The vestibular apparatus and the semi-circular canal

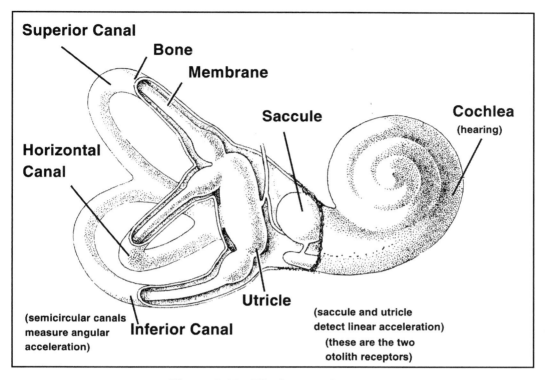

Figure 3.15—The human inner ear

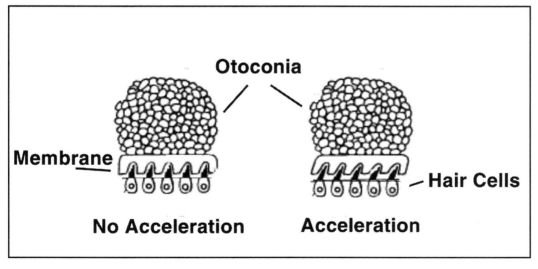

Figure 3.16—Hair bundle displacement

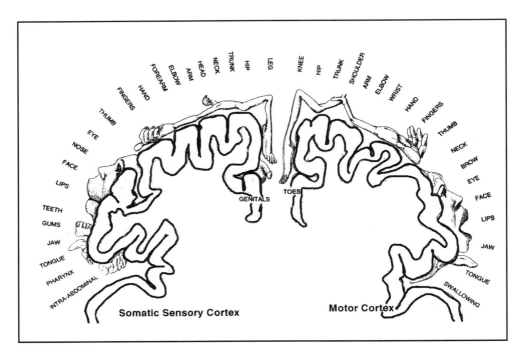

Figure 3.17—Here is a modern update, for motor and sensory cortex, of the famous "homunculi" diagrams of Wilder Penfield and others

CHAPTER 4

VIRTUAL CONSIDERATIONS (AND OTHER RELIGIOUS ISSUES)

Introduction

This chapter consists of the authors' ruminations on the field of virtual reality, its potential futures, and some of the hot debates in the field. Much of this chapter is devoted to opinions—some the authors', some those of researchers in the field. For the most part the differences should be obvious. Please remember that this is an immature field whose future is far from certain.

Section 1—Desktop versus Immersion (What's the View?)

Although we have presented desktop versions of virtual reality as if they were on a par with immersive systems, many researchers would consider this to be a grave error; they believe that only immersive systems should be considered as virtual reality systems. Others believe that the manner in which one views or manipulates a virtual world is less important than the actual ability to do so. No matter which side you are on, the debate still rages and both sides have their points. This section will provide some of those points and cover some of the gray areas between the total-immersion virtual environments and the desktop approaches to virtual environment interfaces.

Figure 4.1—Stereo VR Glasses at work

The World through a Window

Computer graphics is one of the driving forces in the creation of virtual environments. In a manner of speaking, all computer displays provide a window into a virtual world of some sort. Programmers inhabit a virtual world of abstract software control constructs; financial analysts buried in their spreadsheets also inhabit virtual worlds. Computer graphics is currently making large strides in the creation of photorealistic images. Current rendering techniques include ray tracing, texture mapping, and radiosity. Other research directions include animation and real time interactive graphics generation. All of these techniques can and will be used in virtual environment systems to make them appear more "realistic"—closer to the physical world.

Virtual environments displayed on (through) computer monitors can be displayed in three dimensions using special goggles which work with high-frequency monitors. An older form of projecting three dimensions on a computer display is called "two and a half dimensions." It borrows from realistic art techniques, which include skewing angles and lines to fool the human sense of perspective. These and other techniques are discussed in detail earlier in this book and are the basis for the software included with this book.

The world-in-a-window approach to virtual environments has two large advantages; computer graphics monitors are ubiquitous and inexpensive, especially compared to other forms of virtual environment displays. Other strengths include relatively high resolution, no encumbrance (you bear none of the weight of the display), and entering and leaving the virtual environment are quick and easy. The largest disadvantage is that if you turn your head, you don't see the environment any more—it is a window onto another world—so the interface tends to be less intuitive. Comprehensive computer simulations and many scientific visualization tools will remain on computer monitors, as will much of the leading research in computer graphics which is also driving the graphical displays used in virtual environments. At this point the tools to build virtual environments are intended predominantly for use from outside the environment and even those tools are relatively immature.

Boom-Mounted Displays

An interesting mix between the world-through-a-window approach and the totally immersive approach to virtual environments is provided by the boom-mounted display. This display typically incorporates a three-dimensional sound system, position-sensing equipment, and a binocular three-dimensional high-resolution immersive display, all mounted on a boom to allow multiple degrees of viewing freedom. The operator looks into the virtual environment and may change the viewing angle by changing the direction in which the boom display is pointing. On the downside, viewing is restricted to the directions and angles of the boom's movement, a free hand is required to change viewing direction, and the displays can be somewhat expensive. On the upside, image resolution is on par with that of most monitors and easily superior to that of most head-mounted displays (excepting the multimillion-dollar U.S. Air Force ones). The operator also need not bear the weight of the system on the head and shoulders. The operator can also enter and leave the world just by moving his or her head; one's hair need not even get mussed and many persons can easily share such a display.

Immersion in a Room

Immersion in a virtual environment need not require a head-mounted display of any type. Several room-sized virtual environment displays exist, such as the Media Room at Massachusetts Institute of Technology's Media Lab and the Cave created by the Electronic Visualization Laboratory of the University of Illinois in Chicago. Such systems feature high-resolution large-screen displays that can occupy one or more walls, the ceiling, and/or the floor. Three-dimensional sound systems are typically built into these rooms, although the sound cues are usually valid only near the center of the room. The participants generally must wear simple goggles that handle the decoding of the stereo pairs received from the large screens to present the virtual environment in three dimensions. Several persons can easily walk around and through any type of model (often real time interactive simulations) so displayed. Unfortunately, such systems come with a high price tag and are not usually very portable. Many researchers believe that the future of virtual reality lies in this direction, one which requires little or no encumbering equipment—certainly this is one of the "sexier" ways to enter a virtual environment.

Gloves and Goggles

Virtual environments featuring head-mounted displays (HMDs) and hand position input gloves are the center of most of the hype surrounding the field. A head-mounted display is one of the most natural ways to "look around" a virtual environment. To change your view of the virtual environment, you turn your head—nothing could be more intuitive. Three-dimensional sound cues are always available because, where such systems exist, they may be built directly into the helmet. When this is combined with a force-feedback glove, you can reach out your hand to "touch" a virtual wall. Gloves can be used with any of the other systems, but they are nearly required when using an HMD. When you are wearing an HMD, a keyboard is not an optional input device, unless it's a virtual keyboard. Voice recognition systems are also very important for handling voice commands.

On the downside, most of the current systems are limited by low-resolution displays and display update lag, and HMDs are heavy enough to cause fatigue and can be difficult to put on, adjust, and take off. In addition, the tactile and force-feedback displays are generally rudimentary. In fact, most virtual environments have yet to include any type of haptic display. However, these systems support one of the most natural interfaces with a computer possible today, and that above all else is why they are so exciting. It is important to remember that the technology has just reached usability and may still be considered to be in its infancy.

Section 2—Future Possibilities

This section will present some of the future possibilities inferred from the current research directions, debates, and applications of virtual reality. It is divided into the major areas, as seen by the authors, of virtual environment applications and research.

Architectural Walkthroughs and Computer-Aided Design

Architectural walkthroughs and computer-aided design are among the most natural research fields to build and test useful virtual environments. Both applications require work in three dimensions, which will generally lead to a three-dimensional physical equivalent being built. This provides an excellent opportunity to test the system for both realism and usefulness in design. Another interesting possibility being experimented with in labs is computer-aided design within a virtual environment. Researchers enter a virtual environment, which supplies all the tools necessary to build a virtual environment. Instead of drawing on a computer screen or programming, the operator would enter the virtual environment to create and manipulate objects such as walls and wheels. Construction could become more akin to manufacturing in the real world than to drawing on a computer.

Virtual reality interfaces to computers will undoubtedly become more popular for certain applications. Computer-aided design can always use a technology that allows the designer a better and more complete simulation experience of the design. A virtual environment can let a tractor designer or a space station designer sit in, walk around, and "kick the tires" on a design before the cost of design and working drawings is incurred.

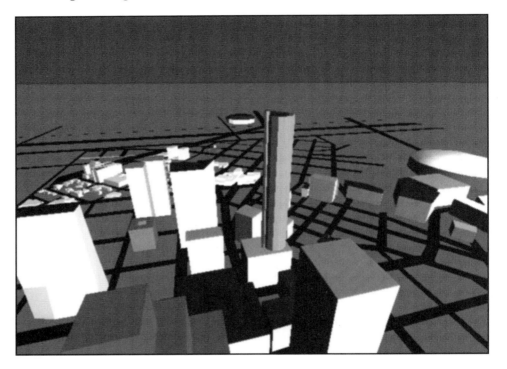

Figure 4.2—View of downtown Atlanta over Peachtree Plaza

Augmentation

The idea of human augmentation has been with virtual reality from the beginning. Now it may see commercial implementation before many other forms of virtual environments. Most forms of augmentation are less graphically intensive than fully immersive systems, which makes them less expensive and much easier to implement.

Some of the first systems will be used to augment assembly line workers and field engineers. Templates are often used to overlie complex assembly line processes. A virtual template could be projected onto the physical world using special goggles. In this manner, the templates do not have to be drawn on the material, thereby avoiding stretching, warping, or alignment problems that usually result. This would also facilitate rapid changes in template or material design; the latest template comes from the computer on which it was designed, avoiding a configuration management problem.

Field and office workers will also soon benefit from virtual environment research. Imagine wearing a small set of goggles which allows you to view your reference material in cyberspace off to the side of your work. Dictionaries, encyclopedias, reference books, schematics, and recipes, all can be laid out where you can see them, yet not take up any physical desk space. Furthermore, a voice command or gesture can open one of these references to the page or section you seek. On top of that, full-motion video and sound cues would fit into this scenario easily as the technology becomes available. You could watch a television that no one else can see and that seems to be the size of a wall. You could have all the information on your computer available to you wherever you went—without carrying even a laptop computer (when things get small enough and the networking becomes more available).

Another form of virtual environment is providing new ways of looking at data and filtering out unneeded data to aid in timely decision making. Looking at data modeled in three dimensions by "flying" around and through the data can give whole new perspectives on the interrelationships of the data. Such systems already provide decision support for stock analysts, who can fly through the data and fly up to and around an anomalous stock or group of stocks to get a better understanding of what is happening. Virtual environments are also providing decision support for the next generation of experimental interfaces to fighter aircraft. The "Super Cockpit" project is a way of providing only relevant data to the pilot and thereby filtering out the rest of the information supplied by the system. In this manner, a pilot need not be overwhelmed by the torrent of data coming from the myriad of gauges, dials, and switches.

Augmenting the Handicapped

Soon augmentation may become an enabling technology for the handicapped—they may be able to participate in life in ways only imagined before. With the aid of virtual environment techniques, the handicapped will soon be able to deal with everyone else on a mostly even footing. Gloves are being adapted to translate gestures to speech; eye-tracking devices are being used to translate eye movement into gestures or to enact commands. All of these examples require computers and virtual reality gear of some sort. Handicapped people are entering cyberspace to help architects and engineers design more accommodating areas for handicapped access. Perhaps the most important contribution will be made when handicapped people enter cyberspace and simple gestures, movements, or voice commands can be translated into cyberspace actions. Nobody in cyberspace will be handicapped!

Telecommunications

One of the largest potential beneficiaries of the advances made and projected in virtual environments may be the field of telecommunications. Already the telephone industry is attempting to establish the videophone as a serious enhancement of the telephone. Virtual environment technologies would go even further in enlarging the communications bandwidth available. Virtual environments will affect not only interpersonal communications but also virtual meetings and remote and hazardous workplaces in general.

Researchers around the world are working on ways to enhance long-distance communications and the next generation of the telephone. An integral display screen will provide an animated representation of your caller, complete with major features, moving in synchrony with your caller or real time video feeds. Then, not only voice cues but also shrugs, facial expressions, and other important aspects of body language will be available to transmit information. All of us wince, smile, frown, and wave our hands while speaking on the telephone, even though no one can see, which suggests that our different modes of communication are tightly coupled. Other researchers would like to see you don goggles and gloves to reach out and "touch" someone. Such systems would provide virtual reality interfaces to the phone system. Establishing a call could be like floating in a virtual sea, swimming or flying toward the person to whom you wish to speak. Such interfaces could enable access to libraries and other information sources and even workplaces, all from the comfort of your own home.

Virtual environments may revolutionize the workplace. Today conference calling is a common way for people who are geographically distant to communicate. Soon, participants at meetings in cyberspace may be from around the world. Scheduling a meeting place of appropriate size, or any meeting place, will no longer be a hassle. Traffic will also not be a problem. The number of telecommuters is growing every year. Instead of having to come into the office once in a while to touch base with officemates or attend a meeting, they could "suit up" and participate from home. In fact, for a great number of jobs now inappropriate for telecommuting it could become the standard. Physicians could practice techniques and procedures with their entire staff from home. Indeed, the way current technology is heading, they could even do the procedures from home.

Remote and Hazardous Workplaces

Current methods for exploring remote and/or hazardous areas fall in two general categories—send a human into the environment wearing suitable protection or send some sort of mechanical contraption, usually controlled by a human, into the environment.

The former method provides far more flexibility; in general, a human on the scene can gather more information and do so much more quickly. Humans are also extraordinarily good at coping with unplanned situations or predicaments. Unfortunately, the intense cold of outer space or the ocean deep and the radioactivity of a nuclear reactor are not safe places for humans, nor can they be endured long. Particularly in the radioactive-type inhospitable environments, even the best protection available may not afford enough time to handle the job, with the result that people act heroically and die.

The second method is to send a human-controlled or -aided robot into the environment. Some of these robots are quite intelligent and can handle most situations without human intervention (witness the many exploration satellites). However, communications can be difficult and most contingencies must be planned for in advance; otherwise the robot may not be able to reach its objective at all. Often, the human-machine interface is poor at best.

A virtual environment interface can allow the human part to move comfortably in ways humans are used to moving and translate those movements into directions the robot can understand, thus making the best use of each part of the partnership. In the case of minimally invasive medical procedures, the virtual environment interface is expected to allow physicians to work in a manner to which they are accustomed, yet with miniature tools that no human could otherwise handle.

Computer Interfaces

Virtual reality as an interface to a computer is a major research topic. Physicians will soon be benefiting from virtual environment interfaces to their work. Minimally invasive surgical techniques need a more intuitive interface, one that will allow a surgeon to use the haptic as well as graphic and audio cues learned in school and through experience. Other fields such as radiation beam planning and reconstructive surgery will greatly benefit from the ability to superimpose images from sensors such as computed tomography (CT), magnetic resonance imaging (MRI), and ultrasound devices onto patients. Virtual reality can not only provide a more personal and intelligent interface, it can also point out potential interface improvements of a more conventional type. What follows concerns some of the hot topics and what they might mean.

The Metamedium

Computers are coming to be regarded as more than simply tools, instruments for storing and manipulating data which will show up somewhere on paper. Computers are more often producing and facilitating communications without print or any other media. In short, computers are becoming a medium for communication. This new medium may be multimodal, "incorporating text, voice, music, graphics, video, and animation." It can produce real time interactions or store interactions for future replay.

Perhaps even more important, the medium is inherently "soft"; it relies only on improvements in software design and methodology. The hardware on which it is based is no longer the limiting factor. Software is inherently easier to manipulate than hardware, so obsolete forms can be more easily replaced. A hardware medium form such as television or radio is very difficult to change as technology advances; witness the difficulties in defining a high-definition television (HDTV) standard. This means that the exploitation of this new medium need not depend on the marketeers, but rather "the design space may be *deliberately* explored." For these reasons, computers should be considered a metamedium. (Oren)

Agents and Animation

People have long dreamed of creating companions, whether through witchcraft and wizardry or through high technology. We want teachers, helpers, confidants, playmates, or friends. The underlying theme remains the same; we personify many of the complex things which we regularly encounter, such as ships, storms, and computers. We often say that certain computer tools or applications "behave" in certain ways, they have predispositions. A computer program, known as an agent, can make use of this metaphor to serve humans in the computer domain.

> An interface agent can be defined as a character, enacted by the computer, who acts on behalf of the user in a virtual (computer-based) environment. Interface agents draw their strength from the naturalness of the living-organism metaphor in terms of both cognitive accessibility and communication style. Their usefulness can range from managing mundane tasks like scheduling, to handling customized information searches that combine both filtering and the production (or retrieval) of alternative representations, to providing companionship, advice, and help throughout the spectrum of known and yet-to-be-invented interactive contexts. (Laurel, "Interface Agents," p. 356)

When you are exploring a virtual environment, an agent might be available to help you when you are lost, or it might provide information about the environment (such as about the art and its artist at an on-line art show). Different agents would perform different actions at which they were proficient. They could even appear in a manner suggestive of their function, such as an accountant agent wearing a bow tie or an engineering design agent with a pocket protector and slide rule. Agents show a great deal of promise in helping us navigate in and make sense of information space and other virtual environments. (Laurel, "Interface Agents")

Training

Virtual environments research seems destined to revolutionize the manner in which training is performed. High-risk, low-probability techniques and otherwise hazardous encounters may be rehearsed numerous times at leisure. Operators can be exposed to types of situations that were never before possible and adapt the necessary skills to cope. Improved training techniques will help skiers, pitchers, policemen, and surgeons alike. Simulation and training are also candidates for virtual environments. Aircraft pilots, air traffic controllers, truck drivers, medical staff, and even car drivers can get experience in the safety of a virtual environment, yet develop the reflexes necessary to survive in the real world. In addition, experience with unusual, potentially fatal situations may be rehearsed safely at leisure and on a regular basis.

Scientific Exploration

Scientific exploration will benefit from first-person experiences in remote environments, and scientists will have better tools to explore their abstract domains. Complex models and simulations may be produced, then walked around and through even while they are being computed and updated. The exploration of abstract domains will certainly lend itself to virtual environments, provided that the equipment and software are easy enough to use that scientists may concern themselves with science and not the mastery of yet another field—a problem with conventional computers and their interfaces. A virtual environment can be the ultimate way to explore a theory—as it is working and from inside.

Entertainment

The entertainment industry has already brought virtual environments to consumers. As the hardware and software improve, new entertainments that are more personal, more interactive, and less encumbering will appear. First-person experiences and groups of people sharing an environment will certainly dominate, at least until software complexity allows virtual players to play on an equal footing with human players.

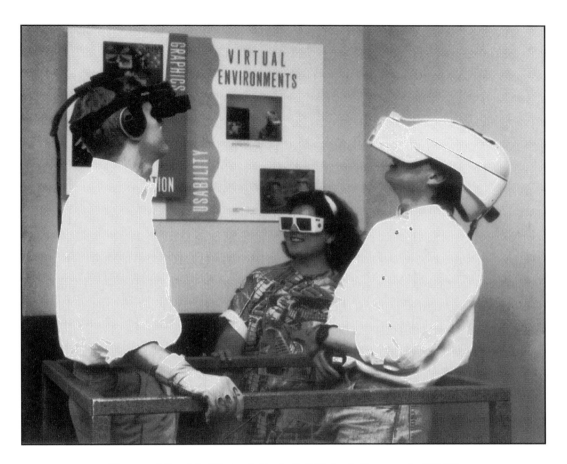

Figure 4.3—"A Virtual Party" (Virtual Research HMD
and a Cyberglove Data Glove)

Section 3—Virtual Reality and Society

As virtual environments become more accessible to the population they will begin to affect society, probably in ways yet to be imagined, certainly in ways yet to be understood. In certain respects, virtual environments have already begun to affect society. A large group of people already have access to one another over the huge network known as the Internet and other bulletin board and on-line services. These people are restricted to communicating by keyboard and display screen, yet are already exploring the effects of virtual environments when they allow people to interact in new ways. The relationships of people who are unsure of each other's social (and even sexual) identity is just one of the areas currently being explored which will certainly be seen in virtual environments (where people can be lobsters if they want). Virtual communities of people who are friends, enemies, and merely acquaintances, yet have never "met one another face to face," have already emerged. The issue of law enforcement on this network and in cyberspace is also a subject of great contention.

The Internet (and the Matrix)

A vast network interconnects the United States and stretches across the world. It is generally referred to as the Internet, the matrix, or simply the net. The Internet is a large collection of networked systems used by businesses, universities, educators, and computer people from all over the world. The system was originally developed for research and educational use, and for the most part these are still its main uses. Around the Internet have sprung up many smaller networks and bulletin boards connected both to the Internet backbone and to each other. The system is truly global, with nodes as far away as Australia. A more recent name for the net derives from William Gibson's *Neuromancer*, the matrix. The matrix is described in cyberspace terms but, simply put, it is all of the networks networked together all over the world. However, it has become far more than even that: the Internet had developed its own societies, news, even "virtual communities." People interact with each other, develop friendships, make enemies, and share information. These people have developed complex relationships and have never met each other physically face to face.

The net has interests for everybody. There are on-line art exhibitions (for those with the appropriate hardware), news groups, discussions, information sources, and games. If it can be done on a computer, it can be found on the net. Several efforts are under way to allow network access to virtual environments—to be explored from your own home.

Virtual Identities

One of the things most people do sooner or later on the net is try on a new identity. In fact, many of the people you will meet go by made-up names. Names can hide, or suggest, identities, sex, and personality. Since none of these things are immediately obvious (pretty much everybody communicates by text only), it is easy to "switch sexes," represent yourself as someone else (which is not highly thought of), or simply remain an enigma. Having everybody interact through text-based communications is a great leveler of the playing field. You are ugly only if you act ugly.

Figure 4.4—Three-dimensional Scanner Image

Virtual environments will increase the bandwidth of communication and hence the types of communications possible; however, there is no guarantee that all men are men or women are women (of course, these days you don't have much of a guarantee with which to start). In fact, one of the early Reality Built for 2 demonstrations (VPL Research) featured both participants represented as lobsters. You are free of the constraints of humanity (I guess). How such freedom will affect society and personal interaction is still a subject of hot debate. It seems we have launched a grand experiment, and we are the guinea pigs.

Virtual Community

People from all over the world sit in isolation, yet are communicating with one another via keyboards and computer displays. Although this form of communication is somewhat limited compared to the mannerisms humans use in face-to-face communications, it is more than enough to form relationships with other people, some of whom may be thousands of miles away. Soon, you form groups of friends with similar interests and meet people with totally differently likes. You even meet some people with whom you would rather have no contact whatsoever. In short, a community of sorts forms wherever people meet, whether to discuss computers, music, or art or "shoot the bull" around the "water cooler." These sorts of communities have formed on the net too. The term virtual community has come to mean the large number of people all over the world who communicate with each other, often on a daily basis, and many of whom have never met physically in the real world.

The net itself began as a means of sharing information between greatly physically separated research sites. Many academic and technologically forward companies have worked together sharing information, time, and interests on the net. These virtual communities have become a grand uncontrolled social experiment. Perhaps one day, people will go to their cubicles, interface with their computers (however), and go to work, play, fall in love, and grieve all without physical contact with other people. However, it is equally possible that these virtual communities and the virtual society that they form will not be viable by themselves. Humans are physical animals, after all, and we may indeed require physical contact for our mental health.

All of these thoughts have been and are being explored by both the pioneers of the net and the newcomers in a joint partnership. Determining what the future holds for virtual societies of people on-line will be a process of discovery. (Rheingold V. C.)

NetLaw

The matrix (read cyberspace network) that currently exists is composed of the Internet, all of its multitudinous gateways and interconnections, and all the wide-area networks, local-area networks, and bulletin board systems that are, or soon will be, interconnected to form a worldwide maze of computer networks. On these networks exist many virtual communities, including friends and enemies many of whom will never meet each other in the physical world. Furthermore, this society is currently restricted to communicating through a single channel—the keyboard and computer screen. Even as technology evolves and people can communicate through virtual interactions, how people choose to portray themselves is still a matter left unresolved.

It is clear that new rules of etiquette will have to be fashioned for a virtual society to be viable. To complicate matters, people who have little computer literacy are now gaining access to the system—when they encounter problems similar to those encountered in the real world, they expect the same rules or laws to apply. In many cases, those who enforce "real world" laws are ignorant of computer technology in general and the matrix in particular.

> ... one can imagine the government's problem. This is all pretty magical
> stuff to them. If I were trying to terminate the operations of a witch coven,
> I'd probably seize everything in sight. How would I tell the ordinary
> household brooms from the getaway vehicles?
> (John Perry Barlow - as quoted in Cockayne)

So, if indeed the matrix is incapable of policing itself—which seems likely given its increasingly pervasive nature and human beings' track record on policing themselves—some sort of netlaw will have to be established and some sort of netpolice who understand both netlaw and the matrix will have to be created. To make matters more complex, at present it is unclear who has jurisdiction when persons violate laws in other countries over the net.

Perhaps the worst current example of what happens when what would be netlaws are handled by the current law and judicial process is the United States Secret Service and Operation Sundevil. The Secret Service seized computer equipment from alleged criminals and brought these suspects before the courts to face charges by AT&T, Sprint, and American Express, among others. These actions nearly bankrupted a company that was never under investigation, cost thousands of taxpayer dollars and man-hours, and resulted in the entire matrix community turning on the Secret Service and the judicial process.

Although it is unclear what, if any, form netlaw and netlaw enforcement will take, it is clear that the current judicial process is inadequate and does not apply well. Certainly those responsible for netlaw enforcement will have to learn more about computers and the matrix of networks that interconnect this world. (Cockayne)

Section 4—Wireheads—Living in a Virtual Environment

Certainly many of us wonder if people will ever live in virtual environments, spending most or all of their waking life in worlds other than the physical. At this point no one knows; the technology is young and immature and has just reached the boundary of usability. Still, this question should be considered because it could have a profound effect on our society.

Living in Virtual Environments

For a moment, let's go out into the ether beyond reality into fiction. It is conceivable that some day people will crawl into their virtual reality couches, plug themselves into an alternate world, and never leave. The couch would have to supply the needs of the body, but machines are already capable of such things. Perhaps the connection for the machine would be directly into the nervous system. The computer handles all stimuli for your body; it sets your emotions however it's programmed to and ignores all physical requests. You are part of the computer. Your thoughts lead your exploration of worlds beyond the physical.

Why would people ever consider such a thing as living their lives in a virtual environment? Well, severely handicapped people could ignore the limitations of their physical bodies forever. Virtual environments might also be the ultimate fantasy experience—why go to the movies when you can experience one firsthand?

Of course, this speculation raises another question—what if someone else controls the computer? How will you know if you are still plugged into the computer? Will you even care?

VR as the Ultimate Drug

Another of the most asked questions about virtual reality, and one of those least likely to be answered by the founders is about virtual reality as the ultimate drug (such questions are considered to trivialize the research). Some people will tell you that you can always pull the plug (sure, you can always stop smoking crack whenever you want, right?).

It is conceivable that the worlds you encounter will be so incredible that you don't ever want to leave. If the computer is supplying enough stimuli, you might get addicted to it—the physical world would always seem more mundane and unappealing. Or perhaps our earlier speculations apply and the world is so realistic with someone else at the controls—how will you know if it's the real physical world or a virtual one? And again, will you even care?

Reality Check

Flights of fancy are not uncommon in this field. Dreamers, artists, writers, mathematicians, and engineers are all attracted to the possibilities of virtual environments. The first fact in this world is that so far **anything** is possible, and a virtual environment need not obey physical laws. The second fact is that virtual reality is a very new discipline. Worlds are generally low-resolution, are slow to update, and generally resemble cartoons. The longest anyone spends in a virtual environment is on the order of an hour, and that's a long time. Psychological and physical sickness issues will have to be dealt with, as will many difficult or perhaps insurmountable problems in building virtual environments that can truly fool someone. Smell and taste have hardly even been considered. Haptic displays are still in their infancy compared to graphical and audio displays. There is a long way to go, and there is no telling what will happen (or can happen) along that road.

Section 5—Teledildonics (Cybersex) and Home Entertainment

Okay, the title is a little provocative—then again, so is the subject. First, it must be said that most of the leaders of the virtual environments field do not like to discuss this subject; it trivializes the field and gives people the wrong ideas (just like VR—the Ultimate Drug), and anyway only so much can be said on the topic. Invariably, one of the first questions most people pose when they begin to think about the possibilities for virtual reality and meeting people in other worlds, and yes, touching other people, is can people have sex in virtual environments? The answer is why not?

Some of the facts in favor of the future for teledildonics (a term coined by Ted Nelson) are as follows: sex has been central to human society as far back as we have recorded history (as Robert Heinlein put it, if as much study was spent on space exploration as on the woman's breast, we'd be running hot dog stands on the moon by now); the phone sex business is burgeoning (so to speak); sex topic–related bulletin boards, CD-ROMs, and interactive on-line discussions already exist and are doing big business; simple tactile feedback devices for the hands already exist and, as sad as it may sound, how difficult do you think it will be to make one finger puppet instead of five? I hope you see my point.

The facts against virtual sex are as follows: it is still glorified masturbation; since any virtual body part could in theory be mapped to any physical body part, exactly who or what partner you are pleasuring, and exactly how, is quite undefined (not a pretty thought); the technology is a long way from anything beyond coarse and simple tactile responses (might as well grunt on the phone). However, most of these complaints are technology related; anything can happen and probably will.

Section 6—Simulator Sickness

Virtual reality systems appear to be especially susceptible to a phenomenon long apparent in flight simulators—simulator sickness. Operators and passengers of both simple and high-quality simulations may experience motion sickness-like symptoms severe enough to cause operator performance problems or safety hazards. Symptoms commonly include eye strain, vertigo, headache, nausea, and general discomfort. In some cases aftereffects, sudden disorientation, and even flashbacks have been reported several hours after exposure to the simulation.

The causes of simulator sickness appear to be as varied as its manifestations among different people. A trivial case of simulator sickness is when a simulator portrays a "real" event that would be enough to make you sick; i.e., a 10 G turn may cause you to black out. Sensory conflict appears to be one of the major causes of simulator sickness. Delays and uncoordinated simulator displays (e.g., visual and motion) are often related to simulator sickness. Visual delay appears to be more important than motion delay, however any significant departure from reality is enough to cause trouble. Even simulators that have no motion base can cause sickness.

Simulator sickness is one of the most important hurdles facing the use of virtual reality systems. It already limits the time an operator may spend in a simulation and in severe cases it can undermine the utility of the simulator altogether. Faster and higher quality hardware and software will help in many cases however, the causes and cures for simulator sickness are still not fully understood. (Sinclair)

Section 7—The Contributions of Science Fiction

Science fiction is responsible for pointing out the possibilities of the future, in many cases with great accuracy. Virtual environments are in no way an exception. Such things have been written about throughout the age of science fiction. A recent culture called cyberpunk has emerged wherein virtual environments are a predominant theme.

The Classics

Many of the strides currently being made with virtual environments were predicted decades ago by science fiction's visionaries. Some examples of this follow. Robert Heinlein introduced "waldoes" before the United States entered World War II. These devices resembled a glove and acted as a master glove for another slave glove of perhaps a different size and in a different place. These gloves provided complete tactile and force feedback when appropriate. Arthur C. Clarke described "personalized television safaris" on which the operator could explore remote environments from the safety of his or her home. Aldous Huxley in *Brave New World* described the follow-on to movies called "feelies"—the "All-Super-Singing, Synthetic Talking, Coloured, Stereoscopic Feely." Ray Bradbury's story "The Veldt" described a sentient simulation which started as a psychological experiment and ended up reading the thoughts of children to provide a form of entertainment in an African veldt. Another Ray Bradbury story, "The Happiness Machine," describes a technology that allows people to live

their fantasies but ends up making them unhappy when they have to return to their normal drab, unaugmented existence.
(Rheingold VR p. 53, 140 & Fisher p. 427)

Cyberpunks

Science fiction spawned a new form and movement during the mid-1980s that bore repercussions far outside its field. The 1982 movie *Blade Runner*—an unlikely adaptation of the Philip K. Dick book *Do Androids Dream of Electric Sheep*— combined with the 1984 book *Neuromancer* written by William Gibson to become the defining points of what became to be known as cyberpunk.

The people who inhabited these grim, gritty worlds lived on the street, were products of the street. Yet, they led their lives with a certain morbid, fatalistic optimism. Technology totally pervaded these worlds, but it was neither celebrated nor despised; it was simply ubiquitous—a "combination of high-tech and low life" (Maddox). And a central theme, as Gibson so eloquently puts it, is that "the street has its own uses for technology." Gibson's world is also the place where the term "cyberspace" was first given meaning (coined).

A Texas writer named Bruce Sterling, who was a friend of William Gibson, was the publisher of a fanzine called *Cheap Truth* which featured "guerrilla raids" on science fiction. Its principal contribution was that many people, writers and such, became aware of each other. "Gardner Dozois committed the fateful act of referring to this group of very loosely-affiliated fold as 'cyberpunks'." Sterling "picked up the label so casually attached by Dozois and used it as the focal point for his own concerns."

Before too long the media were applying the term cyberpunk to everything from kids with modems who committed computer crimes to people that wear black, listen to tech-pop, read *Mondo 2000*, and drink "smart drinks." The term cyberpunk had appeared in *People*, the *Wall Street Journal*, on MTV, and in the *Communications of the American Society for Computing Machinery*.

Authors such as Sterling (*Schismatrix* and *Islands in the Net*), Pat Cadigan, John Shirley, and Rudy Rucker added to and expanded the world of cyberpunk fiction. Both good and bad imitators also set out to cash in on cyberspace and cyberpunks.

As it turns out, the particular movement that was cyberpunk has already changed. It has branched beyond it sources and mutated in so many different ways that it is no longer recognizable as such. But its influences have been felt, and not just in the world of science fiction. (Maddox & Cobb)

Final Considerations

The promise of virtual reality is the same as the lure of magicians, sorcerers, knights, dragons, and fairies. A virtual world need not obey the laws of the physical world. Indeed, it is conceivable that anything that one can dream could be constructed as or in a virtual environment. Indeed, much of the literature on virtual reality is the extrapolation and dreams for what might be. If you read it in a book that had no claim to fact, you'd call it Science Fiction. The reality of the field called virtual reality is something else entirely. Perhaps one day, anything will be possible. But today's virtual environments have just crossed the boundary of true usability. The researchers are striving hard just to handle the basics of moving, exploring, and manipulating a virtual world. Some of the simpler and more obvious virtual worlds and augmentation equipment are now becoming available for limited commercial use.

We have attempted to present a great deal of the information that surrounds and defines the field of virtual reality. We have seen a great number of potential applications, explored the history, and delved into how the human senses work. Finally, we shall show the complexity of the software used to create virtual environments.

CHAPTER 5

TECHNICAL CONSIDERATIONS FOR VIRTUAL REALITY SYSTEMS

Section 1—The Concept of a Virtual Reality System

In the previous parts of this book, we discussed some of the more practical applications of virtual reality (VR) technologies, applications that present virtual reality as a class of technologies for the means of intelligent human interface with computers. We began our excursion into virtual reality with a look at what virtual reality technologies can do for us. Then we journeyed to learn about some of the history of the field, and we even took a look at the evolution of the technologies that comprise the field.

After our more commercially oriented sojourn, we became scientists with studies in human perception and how understanding of perception has importance for the design of both desktop and immersion VR systems.

Finally, we traveled to see the field in a very philosophical light, in order to understand some of the potential social ramifications of its existence.

Now it is time for us to pull away from the subjective and scientific and delve into the black-and-white engineering side of it all, where a basic desktop virtual reality system is realized.

Many say that this is the boring "cold and dry" part. The engineering can be as enjoyable as the pure science. The engineering is really not so cold and dry, given a basic mathematics and engineering background and given that the product that is realized can be much fun with which to work or play.

The issues of geometry, matrix algebra, and trigonometry that we will briefly cover in this section are no more complex than those taught in high school. The concepts of computer graphics that we will cover are basic:

- Polygon projection from the 3-D polygonal world to the 2-D screen (through which we see the likeness of the world)
- Sorting polygons from farthest to nearest for display (like an oil painter painting a scene layer by layer)
- Clipping polygons that fall behind us or partially off the sides of the computer display
- Shading and texturing polygons in order to create a realistic appearance (including mapping pictures onto polygons—like a picture of good ole uncle Bob mounted on a wall)
- Hidden surface removal for removing those nasty polygons that are on the far sides of objects that are in our view

Even mathematically intensive subjects like interactions with objects (dynamics and kinematics) are briefly covered from a useful viewpoint.

Well—enough chatter; let us start our journey into the technical aspects of virtual reality with a conceptual discussion of how all of the technologies work together to produce the effect. Do not worry if you do not catch all of it now, it will be repeated at the end of this part, after you have been introduced to all of the integral concepts in reasonable detail.

A Brief, Yet Premature Overview of a VR system

Imagine that you are in an airplane. You have a window at the front of the cockpit which allows you to see the world primarily in front of you. You know that the world outside is made of three-dimensional objects like trees, mountains, and houses, but if you had never been outside to experience these objects up close, the seemingly two-dimensional image that you see through the window of your airplane would be all that you know. Make your computer screen this airplane window.

Now imagine that the surfaces of all of those three-dimensional objects in your world are made up of tiny polygonal patches like triangles and rectangles. That very simple house in your view (you are still imagining things, right?), for instance, could be made of four rectangles for walls, two rectangles for a roof, two triangles to fill in the ends of the roof, and assorted rectangles for windows and doors (Figure 5.1). That tree next to the house could be made of a group of rectangles and triangles—rectangles to construct cylinders for the trunk and limbs and triangles for leaves. The more polygons you have, the more detail possible in your objects.

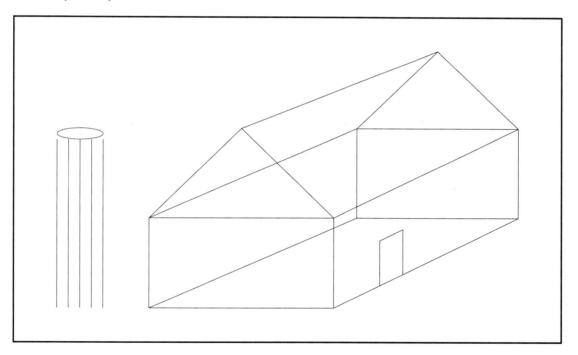

Figure 5.1—House and Tree Constructed from Polygons

Okay, now try to visualize how your very complex three-dimensional world might look if it were made only of triangles and rectangles, pretty flat and without a lot of detail, eh? Well now think about coloring, shading, and texturing those polygons. Maybe our objects are rough, like roadways, so they diffuse light;

thus they do not look very shiny. Maybe our objects are smooth, like freshly waxed cars, and light reflects specularly off of them; you know they are very shiny. Or maybe our objects are marble columns that make up the front of the governor's mansion. The surfaces of our objects and their interaction with light can be simulated with mathematics. Remember that our objects are constructed from polygons, so we apply these mathematical rules to each individual polygon. We now have objects that have varying shade across their surfaces based on where the lights are, where your eyes are, and what material the polygon is "made" from.

Well, by now you may be getting a feel for where I am headed. We have a three-dimensional world whose objects are constructed from shaded polygons, and we have a computer display that acts like a window into that world. Much like the airplane's cockpit window with the real three-dimensional world of real objects, our computer display can assume any position and orientation in our virtual three-dimensional world of polygonal objects. What you see through the cockpit window of your airplane is a projection of the three-dimensional world onto that two-dimensional cockpit window. You can now make the extension that we can perform perspective projection on all of those three-dimensional polygons that make up our objects in our virtual world, onto the two-dimensional computer display, and there we have it, a "rendering" of our virtual world.

Okay, the next thought; we can move our "window" around in space, just like the airplane cockpit window, repositioning it and reorienting it as time goes by. So, yes, we are now flying.

This is how it all works; you orient and position the viewer (the person sitting in front of the computer display) relative to the screen and relative to the three-dimensional polygonal-object world. You project all of those polygons from three dimensions into two dimensions with geometric perspective and display them on the computer display. You take input from your control devices (keyboard, mouse, joystick, yoke, pedals, wheel, etc.), and you reorient and reposition the viewer based on the status of those controls.

Repeat the above process over and over, and if you have mathematics that accurately physically model the way the viewer would move, bounce, and crash based on input from controls, then you have the beginnings of a simulator. Give each eye an independent perspective view of the three-dimensional scene, and you now have stereo vision; you are one step closer to immersion. Add tactile feedback to the controls so that they feel real (i.e., virtual knife cutting virtual tissue, or the resistance felt when turning a steering wheel), add sound (the person being operated on is screaming about the rising cost of health care), and maybe add smell, and you have an immersion virtual reality simulator.

By now, you have some idea about how it all works together. Let us look at each part of a virtual reality system in some detail, primarily the mathematics and algorithms for a computer graphics engine. A good graphics engine is the basis for any VR system, and such an engine would be used to generate the images seen on your visual displays in "real time."

Most of the following explanations use source code for examples. For those needing some support or reference regarding the C programming language (that does include us—te he he), there is an appendix touching on the C language and some of our programming conventions.

Section 2—The Mathematics of Three-dimensional Computer Graphics (Geometry, Matrix Algebra, and Trigonometry)

Given some conceptual understanding and a little knowledge of the C programming language, let's begin our discussions on computer graphics with a review of the basic tools required. These tools include routines that perform special mathematical functions related to geometry and trigonometry which are commonly performed through matrix algebra.

Most of the functions in this chapter are used to manipulate two- and three-dimensional vectors using the basic techniques of linear algebra. Vectors are used to describe all of the geometry of the three-dimensional world including both the positions and orientations of all objects, the viewer, and light sources. The routines described here provide both an efficient and an eloquent means of manipulating vectors to perform such functions of rotation, scaling, and translation of objects, viewing, and light intensity calculations.

Three types of routines are found in the mathematics module: numerical, vector, and matrix functions. The numerical functions are single-valued functions that take as input a single number and compute some function of that number. Functions like sine and cosine fall into this category. This module also contains the definitions of common mathematical constants such as π and e.

The vector and matrix functions create and manipulate vectors. For our purposes, a vector is a collection of numbers (normally 2 or 3) that represents either a point on the plane (X,Y) or in 3-D space (X,Y,Z). Vectors are also used to define directions, such as in what direction a surface is facing. All of the standard vector operations such as the vector dot and cross products can be found here. Since we will often need to transform vectors (such as in rotating an object), several transformation routines are provided. Vectors are transformed by multiplication of the vector coordinates by a single three-by-three or four-by-four matrix. One of the most convenient aspects of vector transformations is that each type of three-dimensional transformation can be represented by one four-by-four matrix and that these individual matrices may be multiplied together to produce a single matrix that represents all of the desired transformation operations: rotation, scaling, and translation. Transformations such as these will allow us to construct complex objects from primitive polygonal objects like triangles and parallelograms and place them into our virtual world.

So let us first take a look at some of the data types in our modules. Then we will examine the functions and macros found in the mathematics modules and afterward examine some of their uses. This section can be used like a reference guide for three-dimensional computer graphics. Note that program modules for these functions are listed at the end of this chapter.

A Discussion on Data Types and Structures

In order to make our job easier and our code easier to understand and maintain, we use many type definitions and structures. The following section explains the usefulness and functionality of each data type.

General Types

Data type	Use
alg_byte	unsigned char
alg_word	unsigned int
alg_dword	unsigned long
alg_char	char
alg_int	int

alg_long	long
alg_float	double (normally float, but we need the precision)
alg_double	double
alg_boolean	ALG_TRUE or ALG_FALSE
alg_palette_type	256-color palette

Point and Vector Types

Data type	Use
alg_matrix_2x2_type	describes a 2 x 2 matrix
alg_matrix_3x3_type	describes a 3 x 3 matrix
alg_matrix_4x4_type	describes a 4 x 4 matrix
alg_point_2D_int_type	describes a single Cartesian point (used to store a 2-D integer point)
alg_point_2D_type	describes a single Cartesian point (used to store a 2-D point)
alg_point_3D_int_type	describes a single Cartesian point (used to store a 3-D integer point)
alg_point_3D_type	describes a single Cartesian point (used to store a 3-D point)

`alg_point_4D_int_type`	describes a single Cartesian point (used to store a 4-D integer point)
`alg_point_4D_type`	describes a single Cartesian point (used to store a 4-D point)
`alg_vertex_3D_type`	describes a single Cartesian point in local coordinates, world-transformed coordinates, and viewer-transformed coordinates (used to store a set of 3-D points)

Polygon Types

`alg_horz_line_type`	describes the beginning and ending *x* coordinates of a single horizontalline (used for polygon filling)
`alg_horz_line_list_type`	describes num_horz_lines horizontal lines, all assumed to be on contiguous scan lines starting at y_start and proceeding downward (used to describe a scan-converted polygon to the low-level hardware-dependent drawing code in Alg_Scrn.c)
`alg_polygon_3D_bounding_box_type`	describes a bounding box for a three-dimensional polygon (used for calculation of polygon center and for cuboid bounding)

```
alg_viewport_clipped_polygon_2D_type        describes a polygon
                                            that has been prepared for
                                            viewport display

alg_z_clipped_polygon_3D_type describes a polygon that has
                                been clipped with the   front of
                                the view volume in order to
                                remove that part of the polygon
                                which falls behind the viewer

alg_polygon_3D_type                         describes a polygon

alg_polygon_2D_display_list_type        describes a list of
                                        polygons for display
```

Three-dimensional Graphics World Types

```
alg_object_3D_type              describes an object in the
                                three-dimensional world

alg_world_3D_type               describes the three-dimensional
                                world

alg_viewer_3D_type              describes the viewer in the
                                three-dimensional world
```

Control Types

```
alg_controls_type               describes the controls of an
                                airplane for intuitive control
                                of the viewer
```

Okay, now that we have seen the type definitions for our mathematics modules, let's see a quick example of their use. Below you will find the identity matrices being defined.

```
// 3x3 identity matrix

alg_matrix_3x3_type          alg_identity_matrix_3x3 =

                             {{  { 1.0, 0.0, 0.0 },
                                 { 0.0, 1.0, 0.0 },
                                 { 0.0, 0.0, 1.0 } }};

// 4x4 identity matrix

alg_matrix_4x4_type          alg_identity_matrix_4x4 =

                             {{  { 1.0, 0.0, 0.0, 0.0 },
                                 { 0.0, 1.0, 0.0, 0.0 },
                                 { 0.0, 0.0, 1.0, 0.0 },
                                 { 0.0, 0.0, 0.0, 1.0 } }};
```

It is now time for us to take a look at the functions and macros that make up our mathematics library. The next section will be followed by a discussion of the theory and the uses of the functions..

Basic Mathematics Functions and Macros

The mathematics modules contains some handy numerical conversion functions as listed below:

Function	Description
ALG_ABS(x)	absolute value
ALG_RAD(x)	converts degrees to radians
ALG_DEG(x)	converts radians to degrees
ALG_COS(x)	cosine (rad)
ALG_SINE(x)	sine (rad)
ALG_COSD(x)	cosine (deg)

`ALG_SIND(x)`	sine (deg)
`ALG_FLOOR(x)`	floor
`ALG_CEILING(x)`	ceiling
`ALG_ROUND(x)`	round
`ALG_TRUNC(x)`	truncate fractional part
`ALG_FRAC(x)`	fractional part
`ALG_SQR(x)`	number squared
`ALG_SQRT(x)`	square root
`ALG_CUBE(x)`	number cubed
`ALG_LN(x)`	natural logarithm
`ALG_LOG(x)`	base 10 logarithm
`ALG_EXP10(x)`	10 raised to power
`ALG_SIGN(x)`	-1 if negative 0 if 0 1 if positive

Comparison Functions and Macros

These functions are used for determining which of a set of numbers is the largest or smallest.

Function	Description
`ALG_MIN(x,y)`	maximum of two numbers
`ALG_MIN3(x,y)`	maximum of three numbers

`ALG_MIN4(x,y)`	maximum of four numbers
`ALG_MAX(x,y)`	maximum of two numbers
`ALG_MAX3(x,y)`	maximum of three numbers
`ALG_MAX4(x,y)`	maximum of four numbers

Swapping Functions and Macros

These functions are used for swapping numbers.

Function	Description
`ALG_SWAP(x,y)`	swaps two numbers

Power Functions

These are functions for raising a number to a power.

Function	Description
`ALG_POWER(x,y)`	raises float base x to integer exponent y
`ALG_INT_POWER(x,y)`	raises integer base x to integer exponent y

Pseudo-Random Number Generation Functions

These functions are used for pseudo-random number generation.

Function	Description
`ALG_RANDOM_SEED(x)`	initialize pseudo-random number generator

```
ALG_RAND(x)                         floating point pseudo-random
                                    number

ALG_RAND_INT(x)                     integer pseudo-random number
```

Two-dimensional Vector Functions and Macros

These are the two-dimensional vector functions. Note that uppercase letters represent scalar numbers and that lowercase letters represent vectors. Values are passed into the functions at the beginning of the argument list and returned at the end.

Function	Description
ALG_VEC2_MAKE(A,B,v)	makes a vector **v**=(A, B)
ALG_VEC2_COMPONENTS(v, A, B)	returns components of vector **v**
ALG_VEC2_AVERAGE(a,b,v)	returns average of vector components
ALG_VEC2_NEGATE(v)	returns vector with opposite signed components
ALG_VEC2_NEGATE2(a,v)	same as negate, except returns in another vector
ALG_VEC2_DOT(a,b)	vector dot product
ALG_VEC2_LENGTH(v)	length of vector
ALG_VEC2_NORMALIZE(v)	normalizes a vector
ALG_VEC2_MINIMUM(a,b,v)	returns a vector whose components represent the minimum values of two other vectors' respective components

`ALG_VEC2_MAXIMUM(a,b,v)`	returns a vector whose components represent the maximum values of two other vectors' respective components
`ALG_VEC2_COMPARE(a,b,same)`	compares the components of two vectors and returns true if all components match in the two
`ALG_VEC2_COPY(a,b)`	copy vector **a** to vector **b**
`ALG_VEC2_ADD(a,b,v)`	adds two vectors **v**=**a**+**b**
`ALG_VEC2_SUB(a,b,v)`	subtracts one vector from another **v**=**a**-**b**
`ALG_VEC2_LIN_COMB(A,a,B,b,v)`	linear combination **v**=A**a**+B**b**
`ALG_VEC2_SCAL_MULT(A,a,v)`	scalar multiply a vector **v**=A**a**
`ALG_VEC2_ADD_SCAL_MULT(A,a,b,v)`	add scalar multiple to a vector **v**=A**a**+**b**
`ALG_VEC2_MUL(a,b,v)`	multiply two vectors **v**=**ab**
`ALG_VEC2_DETERMINANT(a,b,t)`	returns determinant of matrix produced when vector is "cross" multiplied $\mathbf{t}=\mathbf{a_x}^*\mathbf{b_y}-\mathbf{a_y}^*\mathbf{b_x}$
`ALG_VEC2_ZERO(v)`	zeros a vector
`ALG_VEC2_PRINT(msg, v)`	prints a message and a vector

Three-dimensional Vector Functions and Macros

These are the three-dimensional vector functions. Note that uppercase letters represent scalar numbers and that lowercase letters represent vectors. Values are

passed into the functions at the beginning of the argument list and returned at the
end.

Function	Description
ALG_VEC3_MAKE(A,B,C,v)	makes a vector **v**=(A,B,C)
ALG_VEC3_COMPONENTS(v, A, B,C)	returns components of vector **v**
ALG_VEC3_AVERAGE(a,b,v)	returns average of vector components
ALG_VEC3_NEGATE(v)	returns vector with opposite signed components
ALG_VEC3_NEGATE2(a,v)	same as negate, except returns in another vector
ALG_VEC3_DOT(a,b)	vector dot product
ALG_VEC3_LENGTH(v)	length of vector
ALG_VEC3_NORMALIZE(v)	normalizes a vector
ALG_VEC3_MINIMUM(a,b,v)	returns a vector whose components represent the minimum values of two other vectors' respective components
ALG_VEC3_MAXIMUM(a,b,v)	returns a vector whose components represent the maximum values of two other vectors' respective components
ALG_VEC3_COMPARE(a,b,same)	compares the components of two vectors and returns true if all components match in the two
ALG_VEC3_COPY(a,b)	copy vector **a** to vector **b**

`ALG_VEC3_ADD(a,b,v)`	adds two vectors $\mathbf{v}=\mathbf{a}+\mathbf{b}$
`ALG_VEC3_SUB(a,b,v)`	subtracts one vector from another $\mathbf{v}=\mathbf{a}-\mathbf{b}$
`ALG_VEC3_LIN_COMB(A,a,B,b,v)`	linear combination $\mathbf{v}=A\mathbf{a}+B\mathbf{b}$
`ALG_VEC3_SCAL_MULT(A,a,v)`	scalar multiply a vector $\mathbf{v}=A\mathbf{a}$
`ALG_VEC3_ADD_SCAL_MULT(A,a,b,v)`	add scalar multiple to a vector $\mathbf{v}=A\mathbf{a}+\mathbf{b}$
`ALG_VEC3_MUL(a,b,v)`	multiply two vectors $\mathbf{v}=\mathbf{ab}$
`ALG_VEC3_CROSS(a,b,t)`	returns determinant of matrix produced when vector is "cross" multiplied $\mathbf{t}=\mathbf{a_x}*\mathbf{b_y}-\mathbf{a_y}*\mathbf{b_x}$
`ALG_VEC3_ZERO(v)`	zeros a vector
`ALG_VEC3_PRINT(msg, v)`	prints a message and a vector

3 x 3 Matrix Functions for Two-Dimensional Manipulations

These are the three-by-three matrix functions required for the manipulation of two-dimensional vectors. Note that matrices are represented by **m** and vectors by **v**.

Function	Description
`alg_copy_3x3_matrix(m,m1)`	copy **m1** into **m**
`alg_multiply_3x3_matirx(m,m1,m2)`	**m = m1 * m2**
`alg_zero_3x3_matrix(m)`	zero the matrix components

```
alg_identity_3x3_matrix(m)      m = identity matrix

alg_scale_3x3_matrix(v,m)       make scale matrix and multiply m
                                (m = scale * m)

alg_rotate_3x3_matrix(theta,m)      make rotate matrix and
                                multiply m (m = rotate * m)

alg_translate_3x3_matrix(v,m) make translate matrix and
                                multiply m (m = translate * m)

alg_transform_3x3_matrix(v,m,v1)    transform a vector v = v1
                                * m
```

4 x 4 Matrix Functions for Three-Dimensional Manipulations

These are the four-by-four matrix functions required for the manipulation of three-dimensional vectors. Note that matrices are represented by **m** and vectors by **v**.

```
Function                        Description

alg_copy_4x4_matrix(m,m1)       copy m1 into m

alg_multiply_4x4_matirx(m,m1,m2)    m = m1 * m2

alg_zero_4x4_matrix(m)          zero the matrix components

alg_identity_4x4_matrix(m)      m = identity matrix

alg_scale_4x4_matrix(v,m)       make scale matrix and multiply m
                                (m = scale * m)

alg_rotate_4x4_matrix(v,m)      make rotate matrix and multiply
                                m (m = rotate * m)
```

```
alg_translate_4x4_matrix(v,m)  make translate matrix and
                               multiply m (m = translate * m)

alg_transform_4x4_matrix(v,m,v1)      transform a vector v = v1
                            * m
```

Some of these routines can be easily expressed in terms of C code instead of using our routines (i.e., *N*=N* is the same as *N=Sqr(N)*). We have provided these routines so that the code will be more readable by people considering conversion of the software to other languages.

How the Functions Work

This section will be of interest to those interested in the theory behind the workings of our library, The single-valued functions are covered, as well as the affine transformations of objects.

Functions Involving Radians and Degrees

These functions are very useful when it comes to manipulating data based on angles. Much of the software in the book requires these routines for proper calculation of lighting and viewing vectors and for positioning objects. Most of the time, we need to manipulate angles represented as radians (2π radians = 360 degrees). However, we often want to be able to enter and express angles as degrees, as that is more intuitive to many of us. These routines provide for easily converting between the two. The functions make use of the ALG_DEG_TO_RAD and ALG_RAD_TO_DEG constants. Examples of their usage can be seen in the ALG_COSD and ALG_SIND functions. ALG_DEG and ALG_RAD are functions used to do the conversions.

See Figure 5.2, which shows the correspondence of radian measure to degree measure.

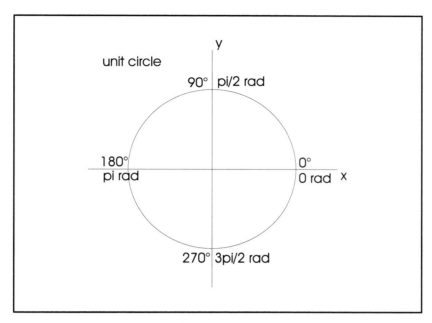

Figure 5.2—Degrees versus Radians

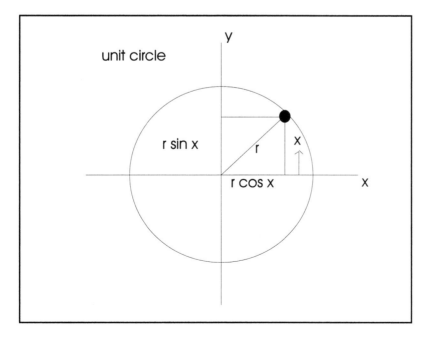

Figure 5.3—Co sine and Sine Vectors

The ALG_COSD and ALG_SIND Functions

These functions make use of the C math library trigonometry functions cos (cosine) and sin (sine), as well as our own degrees-to-radians conversion functions. They perform the same function as the C math library functions except that they take their argument as an angle expressed in degrees. As you might have guessed from Figure 5.2, these functions walk you around the periphery of a circle as the angle in their argument is increased. See Figure 5.3 to see how these functions relate to a circle of radius r.

The ALG_POWER and ALG_POWER_INT Functions

These functions have two arguments, a base value and an integer exponent. They return the value of raising the base to the exponent, i.e., base $^\wedge$ exponent. Essentially, base is multiplied by itself an exponent number of times. If the exponent is equal to zero, the function returns a value of 1, since any number raised to the power of zero is 1. Otherwise, the variable power is initialized to 1 and a loop from 1 to the value of the exponent begins. Power is multiplied by base each iteration of the loop. After the loop has ended, the value in power is returned.

ALG_POWER_INT is the same as ALG_POWER except that the base is an integer. ALG_POWER_INT is a recursive function which raises an integer value to an integer power. Recursion implies that a function calls itself. Like the ALG_POWER function, if the exponent is equal to zero, the value of one is returned. Otherwise, the exponent is decremented and the function calls itself. Once the exponent is zero through successive calls to itself, the value of one is returned to the previous call. One is then multiplied by base and returned to the next previous call and so on until the highest level is reached. The power of the integer is returned.

The ALG_LOG Function

This function finds the base 10 logarithm of a number. Using the C log function, it gets the natural logarithm of the number and then divides this value by the constant Ln10 (the natural logarithm of 10). The real-valued result is then returned.

The ALG_EXP10 Function

This function finds the value of 10.0 raised to the power of a floating point number. First, the value passed to the function is multiplied by the constant Ln10. Then using the C exp function, we calculate the natural logarithm of the new value. The result of this operation is returned.

The ALG_SIGN Function

This function is used to find the sign of a number. A value of -1 is returned if the number is less than zero, 0 if the number is equal to zero, and 1 if the number is greater than zero.

The ALG_MIN, ALG_MIN3, ALG_MIN4, ALG_MAX, ALG_MAX3, ALG_MAX4 Functions

These functions are used to determine the minimum value of 2, 3, and 4 numbers, respectively, and the maximum value of 2, 3, and 4 numbers, respectively. The minimum and maximum routines are useful for finding the boundaries of an object (often referred to as the extent of the object or the bounding box or cuboid). By running through the list of points that make up an object (such as vertices of polygon sides of the object) and computing the maximum and minimum points found so far, you can determine the maximum and minimum values for each dimension. For example, a three-dimensional object requires three tests for each vertex of the object. A bounding box can then be defined by two points: the minimum value in each of X, Y, and Z and the maximum value in each. We will see more of this when bound a polygon to obtain its distance from the viewer.

Vector and Matrix Functions

In this next section, we will be looking at the vector and matrix types used extensively throughout most computer graphics applications. This set of modules will allow us to move objects around in space, orient the viewer with the virtual world, prepare projection of polygons onto a two-dimensional display, and perform most standard vector operations.

In order to facilitate this, we have defined several new variable types. The alg_point_3D_type variable type contains three floating point numbers (x,y,z) representing the components of a three-dimensional vector. In accordance with the normal mathematical notation for vectors, we will also refer to the 3 standard unit vectors (vectors of length 1) **i**, **j**, and **k**. These are simply vectors that point along the positive X, Y, and Z axes. They are defined as:

i $(1, 0, 0)$
j $(0, 1, 0)$
k $(0, 0, 1)$

and may be manipulated as any other vector. Any vector **v** (x,y,z) may be represented as the sum of the vectors **i**, **j**, **k**:

$$\mathbf{v} = x\mathbf{i} + y\mathbf{j} + z\mathbf{k}$$

This is useful in understanding some of the other vector operations such as rotation and scaling.

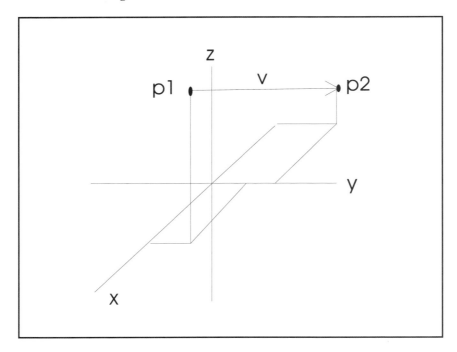

Figure 5.4—Vectors in the 3-D Cartesian Coordinate System

Examine Figure 5.4. This figure shows a three-dimensional vector that begins at point p1 and terminates at point p2. Notice that points p1 and p2 are three-dimensional points, having x, y, and z components.

Finally, the alg_matrix_4x4_type type represents a four-by-four component matrix of floating point values. We will use this type to express all of our vector transformation functions as explained later.

The ALG_VEC2_MAKE and ALG_VEC3_MAKE Functions

These functions are used for the actual creation of vectors. The ALG_VEC3_MAKE function takes three floating point numbers (A,B,C) and stores them into the alg_point_3D_type type (**v**) that it creates. The ALG_VEC2_MAKE function does the same except that it stores two into an alg_point_2D_type. This is a very useful and easy means of working with vectors.

The ALG_VEC2_COMPONENTS and ALG_VEC3_COMPONENTS Functions

The ALG_VEC3_COMPONENTS function extracts the three values stored in an alg_point_3D_type (**v**), and places them into three separate variables (A,B,C). ALG_VEC2_COMPONENTS performs similarly with two components.

The ALG_VEC2_AVERAGE and ALG_VEC3_AVERAGE Functions

These functions add two vectors together and then divide each component by 2.

The ALG_VEC2_NEGATE and ALG_VEC3_NEGATE Functions

These functions negate the components of a given vector by changing the sign of each component. These functions effectively reverse the direction of a vector, making it point in the opposite direction.

The ALG_VEC2_DOT and ALG_VEC3_DOT Functions

This routine computes one of the singularly most useful geometric functions of two vectors, namely, finding their dot product. The dot product of two vectors **A** and **B** is defined as

```
ALG_VEC3_DOT(A,B) = ALG_VEC3_LENGTH(A) *
            ALG_VEC3_LENGTH(B) * cos(theta)
```

where ALG_VEC3_LENGTH computes the magnitude, or length, of the vector and theta is the angle between the two vectors. This is the same as simply multiplying each component of **A** by the corresponding components in **B** and summing all of the products together. The value of the dot product is

$$\mathbf{A} \cdot \mathbf{B} = ab \cos x \qquad\qquad \textbf{(5-1)}$$

VecDot is the number returned, a and b are the magnitude of vectors **A** and **B**, and x is the angle between the two vectors.

This function has a number of interesting and useful properties :

- If VecDot = 0, then the vectors are perpendicular to each other.
- If VecDot = VecLen(A) * VecLen(B), then the two vectors lie along exactly the same direction.
- If VecDot = -VecLen(A) * VecLen(B), then the two vectors point in exactly opposite directions.

Examine Figure 5.5. Here we are taking the dot product of **v1** with **v2**. Notice the angle between the two vectors.

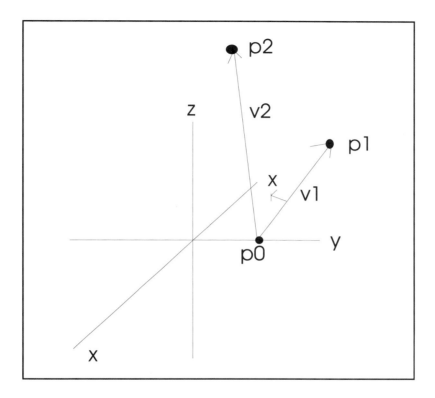

Figure 5.5—The Vector Dot Product

One important use of this function in computer graphics is to determine whether or not we are facing a particular polygon of an object. If the surface normal of the polygon (the surface normal is the direction the surface is facing) is dotted with the viewing direction and the resulting number is negative, then we can see the polygon, since the vectors are pointing opposite to each other (the polygon is pointing in our general direction). If the resulting number is positive, then the vectors are pointing in the same general direction and we cannot see the polygon (it is turned away from us).

ALG_VEC2_DOT functions similarly to ALG_VEC3_DOT, except it deals with 2-D vectors.

The ALG_VEC2_LENGTH and ALG_VEC3_LENGTH Functions

This function finds the magnitude or length of a vector. It is basically just a three-dimensional extension of the Pythagorean theorem. The length is the square root of the sum of the squares of the component values, i.e.,

$$\texttt{ALG\_VEC2\_LENGTH(v)} \; = \; \texttt{sqrt}(x^2 \; + \; y^2)$$

$$\texttt{ALG\_VEC3\_LENGTH(v)} \; = \; \texttt{sqrt}(x^2 \; + \; y^2 \; + \; z^2)$$

This function may also be used to find the distance between two points in three-dimensional space. The vector would contain the differences between each component of the two desired points.

The ALG_VEC2_NORMALIZE and ALG_VEC3_NORMALIZE Functions

A normalized vector is one that has the same direction as a given vector but has unit length or magnitude (length = 1). This can be seen in Figure 5.6, where **v2** is the normalization of **v1**, pointing in the same direction, but with length 1. This is needed quite often, for example, in the computation of the surface normal for a polygon described above. The ALG_VEC3_CROSS function computes a vector pointing in the right direction but the shading model needs a vector of unit length. ALG_VEC3_NORMALIZE fills this need by normalizing the vector, thus giving it unit length.

The first thing this routine does is find the length of the vector passed to it. Next it checks to see if the length is zero and, if it is, prints an error message and exits. The reason for this is that a vector with a length of zero has no direction and therefore cannot be normalized. Once we've determined that our vector is usable, we find the inverse distance by computing $1.0/\text{length}$. Next we multiply each component in the vector by the inverse distance, giving us our normalized vector.

ALG_VEC2_NORMALIZE functions similarly to ALG_VEC3_NORMALIZE, except it deals with 2-D vectors.

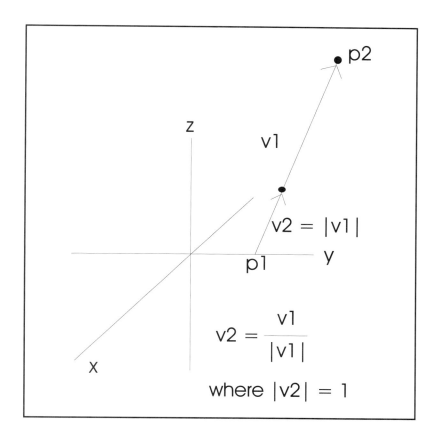

Figure 5.6—Vector Normalization

The **ALG_VEC2_MINIMUM** and **ALG_VEC3_MINIMUM** Functions

The ALG_VEC3_MINIMUM function returns a vector whose components represent the minimum values of two other vectors' respective components. ALG_VEC2_MINIMUM functions similarly to ALG_VEC3_MINIMUM, except it deals with 2-D vectors.

The **ALG_VEC2_MAXIMUM** and **ALG_VEC3_MAXIMUM** Functions

The ALG_VEC3_MAXIMUM function returns a vector whose components represent the maximum values of two other vectors' respective components. ALG_VEC2_MAXIMUM functions similarly to ALG_VEC3_MAXIMUM, except it deals with 2-D vectors.

The ALG_VEC2_COMPARE and ALG_VEC3_COMPARE Functions

These functions compare one vector with another vector, component by component. A value of ALG_TRUE is returned if the respective components match.

The ALG_VEC2_COPY and ALG_VEC3_COPY Functions

These functions simply copy the components of one vector into another vector. Please make note that the vectors you pass to this function (and several others in this module) perform their operations in place, meaning that they modify the vector passed to it. This means that if you need to save your original vector, pass a temporary vector to this function and use the ALG_VEC2_COPY or ALG_VEC3_COPY functions to store the new values into your destination vector.

The ALG_VEC2_ADD and ALG_VEC3_ADD Functions

The functions ALG_VEC2_ADD and ALG_VEC3_ADD perform the operations of addition where the vector components are added. Examine Figure 5.7 to see vector addition. Notice here that vector **v2** slides up to the end of vector **v1** when added.

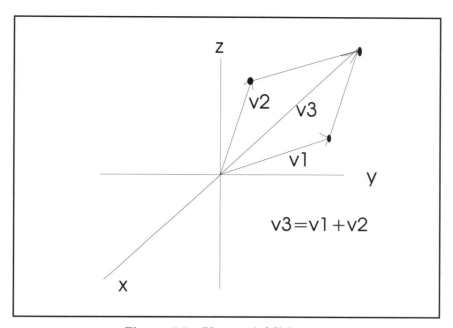

Figure 5.7—Vector Addition

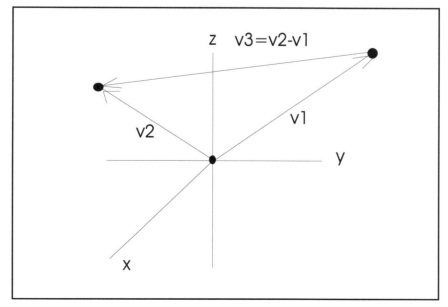

Figure 5.8—Vector Subtraction

The ALG_VEC2_SUB and ALG_VEC3_SUB Functions

The functions ALG_VEC2_SUB and ALG_VEC3_SUB perform the operations of subtraction where the vector components are subtracted. See Figure 5.8 to visualize vector subtraction. Notice that the subtracted vector **v3** points to **v2**, since **v3** = **v2** - **v1**.

The ALG_VEC2_LIN_COMB and ALG_VEC3_LIN_COMB Functions

These functions compute linear combinations of two vectors and place the result into a third.

Four variables are passed, two numbers and three vectors (A, B, **a**, **b** and **v** respectively). The components of **a** are multiplied by A and the components of **b** are multiplied by B. The results are added and stored into the vector **v**. The operation is

$$\mathbf{v} = A\mathbf{a} + B\mathbf{b} \quad \textbf{(5-2)}$$

Note that ALG_VEC3_ADD is equivalent to ALG_VEC3_LIN_COMB(1.0, a, 1.0, b, v) and ALG_VEC3_SUB is equivalent to ALG_VEC3_LIN_COMB(1.0, a, -1.0, b, v).

ALG_VEC2_LIN_COMB functions similarly to ALG_VEC3_LIN_COMB, except it deals with 2-D vectors.

The ALG_VEC2_SCAL_MULT and ALG_VEC3_SCAL_MULT Functions

These functions scale a vector by multiplying each component of the passed vector by a given number and storing the result into a new vector. This operation keeps the vector direction the same but changes its length. Examine Figure 5.9. There you will see that multiplying vector **v1** by 2 yields a vector twice as long.

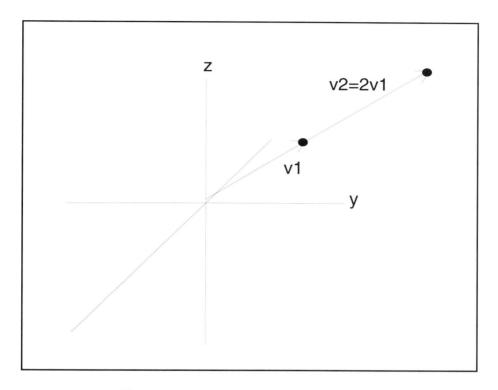

Figure 5.9—Vector Scalar Multiplication

ALG_VEC3_ADD_SCAL_MULT Functions

This function is a convenience function combining several operations into one call. It performs a ALG_VEC3_ADD on the input vectors **a** and **b**, followed by an ALG_VEC3_SCAL_MULT using the argument **a**. The result is stored in **v**. The ALG_VEC2_ADD_SCAL_MULT and The operation is

$$\mathbf{v} = A\mathbf{a} + \mathbf{b} \tag{5-3}$$

The ALG_VEC2_MUL and ALG_VEC3_MUL Functions

These functions accept a number and three vectors as input (A, **a**, **b** and **v** respectively). The components of vector **a** are multiplied by the components of vector **b** and the resulting vector is then multiplied by A. The results are stored in the vector **v**.

$$\mathbf{v} = A\mathbf{ab} \qquad\qquad (5\text{-}4)$$

The ALG_VEC2_DETERMINANT Function

This routine computes the determinant of a matrix whose elements are the two vectors as rows. The scalar value that is returned is equal to

$$\text{scalar} = a_x\, b_y - a_y\, b_x \qquad\qquad (5\text{-}5)$$

The ALG_VEC3_CROSS Function

This routine is probably second most useful tool in computer graphics. It finds the cross product of two vectors. The cross-product generates a third vector that is perpendicular to the plane defined by the first two vectors. The vector cross-product has a length of

$$\mathbf{v} = \mathbf{a} \otimes \mathbf{b} = AB \sin x \qquad\qquad (5\text{-}6)$$

where **a** and **b** are vectors. *A* and *B* are the magnitudes of the two vectors and *x* is the angle between them. ALG_VEC3_CROSS is the resulting vector. The two argument vectors define a plane (if they are not the same vector). ALG_VEC3_CROSS is therefore very useful in determining the surface normal for an object polygon. For example, we can take two of the edges of a polygon as vectors, compute their cross-product, and have a vector representing the direction the polygon face (surface normal). Subsequently, this surface normal is used in the shading of the facet lying in that plane. The vector cross-product is computed as follows

$$\mathbf{v} = \mathbf{a} \otimes \mathbf{b} = (\ (a_y\, b_z - a_z\, b_y),$$
$$(a_z\, b_x - a_x\, b_z),$$
$$(a_x\, b_y - a_y\, b_x)\ ) \qquad (5\text{-}7)$$

Note that the directions **i**, **j**, and **k** refer to the *x*-, *y*-, and *z*- axes, respectively. As a simple example, note that **k** is the cross-product of **i** and **j**. Also note that the order of the two vectors is important. ALG_VEC3_CROSS(v2, v1) is a vector pointing in the exact opposite direction (180 degrees) from ALG_VEC3_CROSS(v1, v2).

Examine Figure 5.10. Here we notice that vector **v** is the cross-product of **v1** and **v2**, and that this vector **v** is perpendicular to the plane defined by vectors **v1** and **v2**.

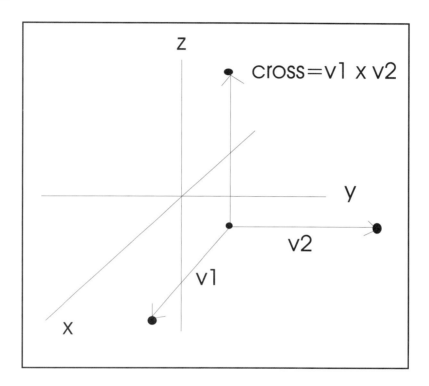

Figure 5.10—The Vector Cross Product

The ALG_VEC2_ZERO and ALG_VEC3_ZERO Functions

The ALG_VEC2_ZERO and ALG_VEC3_ZERO functions simply set all components of a vector to zero.

Affine Transformation Routines

This is the heart of all of our geometric manipulations of vectors. The affine transformation provides a means for concisely expressing all of the graphics transformations we need to perform on objects including translation (moving th object in space), scaling (changing the size of the object), and rotation (changing an object's orientation).

It is natural to wonder why we use a four-by-four matrix when all of our vectors are three-dimensional. The answer is that we wish to incorporate translation into our single matrix transformation. The first column of the four-by-four matrix then represents the translation of the vector using standard matrix multiplication:

$$
\begin{array}{l}
b0 \\
b1 \\
b2 \\
b3
\end{array}
\quad = \quad
\begin{array}{llll}
m00 & m01 & m02 & m03 \\
m10 & m11 & m12 & m13 \\
m20 & m21 & m22 & m23 \\
m30 & m31 & m32 & m33
\end{array}
\quad * \quad
\begin{array}{l}
a0 \\
a1 \\
a2 \\
a3
\end{array}
\qquad \textbf{(5-8)}
$$

where in most of our use, $a0 = 1.0$, and $(a1,a2,a3)$ represents our three-dimensional input vector. In addition, $m00 = 1.0$ and $m01 = m02 = m03 = 0.0$ for most matrices, so that $b0$ will also be equal to 1.0 after the transformation.

The routines in this section create matrices for scaling, rotation, and translation, combine these matrices into a single transformation matrix, and perform various mathematical operations using these matrices. All of the matrix operations use the alg_matrix_4x4_type.

Note that we also have a set of 3x3 matrix routines. Those are not described here, as we will not use them for any of the software found with this book.

The alg_copy_4x4_matrix Function

This function simply copies a given matrix into another matrix.

The alg_multiply_4x4_matrix Function

This function performs the multiplication of two four-by-four real number matrices, effectively combining two separate transformations into one. By chaining all of our transformations together, we produce the single composite transformation that represents all of our rotations, scalings, and translations for each axis.

A composite transformation is generated by first setting it equal to the identity matrix (all 1.0 in the diagonal components, 0.0 everywhere else). We then compute each transformation that we need (rotation, scaling, translation) separately and combine it with the composite matrix using the alg_multiply_4x4_matrix as we go along. The net result will be a matrix that represents all of the transformation operations, which may then be applied to our points and/or vectors as needed. It is important to note that the order of matrix composition is crucial. A different order of multiplication can produce entirely different and unexpected results.

Since each object in a scene may be moved separately, we will potentially need different composite matrices for each object (called local transformation matrices). As we will see, all of these are generated using the same procedure.

The alg_zero_4x4_matrix Function

This function zeros out all of the components in a given matrix.

The alg_identity_4x4_matrix Function

This function loads a given matrix with the identity matrix. It is called an identity matrix, because it leaves a vector unchanged when applied as a transformation.

The alg_scale_4x4_matrix Function

This function creates a scaling matrix to scale each component of a vector. The matrix is first set to the identity matrix; then the diagonal elements are set to the three scaling parameters passed to the procedure and a 1.0 in the first position. The origin of a three-dimensional vector will not be changed by this transformation, only the scale of the vector. If all three scale factors are the same, the result will be the same as using ALG_VEC3_SCAL_MULT, leaving the direction unchanged. If they are different, then both the direction and length of the vector may change. The scaling matrix is

$$\mathbf{S} = \begin{bmatrix} x & 0 & 0 & 0 \\ 0 & y & 0 & 0 \\ 0 & 0 & z & 0 \\ 0 & 0 & 0 & 1 \end{bmatrix}$$

(5-9)

The alg_rotate_4x4_matrix Function

This function creates the matrix to rotate a vector in space about the X, Y, and Z axes. The function first sets the matrix to the identity matrix. Then the cosine and sine of the three angles are placed into certain matrix components, depending on the axis chosen.

The matrix for rotation about the X-axis is

$$\mathbf{Rx} = \begin{bmatrix} 1 & 0 & 0 & 0 \\ 0 & \cos X & \sin X & 0 \\ 0 & -\sin X & -\cos X & 0 \\ 0 & 0 & 0 & 1 \end{bmatrix}$$

(5-10)

The matrix for rotation about the Y-axis is

$$\mathbf{Ry} = \begin{bmatrix} \cos Y & 0 & -\sin Y & 0 \\ 0 & 1 & 0 & 0 \\ \sin Y & 0 & \cos Y & 0 \\ 0 & 0 & 0 & 1 \end{bmatrix}$$

(5-11)

The matrix for rotation about the Z-axis is

$$\mathbf{Rz} = \begin{matrix} \cos Z & \sin Z & 0 & 0 \\ -\sin Z & \cos Z & 0 & 0 \\ 0 & 0 & 1 & 0 \\ 0 & 0 & 0 & 1 \end{matrix}$$

(5-12)

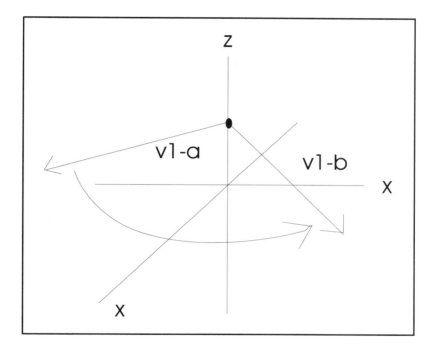

Figure 5.11—Vector Rotation about the Z-axis

The alg_translate_4x4_matrix Function

This function creates the linear translation matrix to translate a vector to a new location in space (Figure 5.12). This matrix starts as the identity matrix consisting of a diagonal of ones. Then we set the last components of the first three rows to the negative of the three translation parameters passed to the function. This results in the following matrix

$$\mathbf{T} = \begin{matrix} 1 & 0 & 0 & -x \\ 0 & 1 & 0 & -y \\ 0 & 0 & 1 & -z \\ 0 & 0 & 0 & 1 \end{matrix}$$

(5-13)

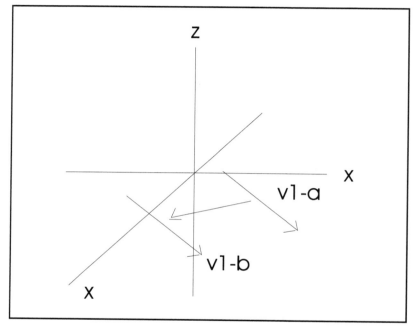

Figure 5.12—Vector (Point) Translation

Note that technically only points can be manipulated in this manner, since a vector is always assumed to have reference to the origin—but for this purpose, points and vectors are interchangeable.

The alg_transform_4x4_matrix Function

This function performs the multiplication of a three-dimensional vector by a four-by-four matrix. The resulting vector will be the one corresponding to the various transformations represented by the passed matrix.

This function is our fundamental vector transformation function. It multiplies the components of a vector by the components of a 16-component composite alg_matrix_4x4_type matrix using the standard mathematical definition. As stated above, this function allows us to transform a vector by rotating, scaling, and translating it in one operation.

Examination of the transform function will show that the fourth component of our vector is assumed to be 1. We do this because we do not need the fourth component (for our work here).

Pseudo-Random Number Generation

These routines create pseudo-random numbers via the power residue sequence approach for positive pseudo-random number generation. By pseudo-random, we mean that the sequence only appears to be random and can be regenerated exactly by passing the same "seed" value to the routine on initialization. In addition, the sequence is only approximately uniformly distributed in the interval 0.0—1.0.

The pseudo-random number generator starts by initialization with an arbitrary floating-point number, referred to as a seed value. New numbers are generated by multiplying a constant (sigma) with the seed value and returning the fractional part, thus guaranteeing that the result is between 0 and 1. Every time the routine is called, a new number in the sequence is generated based on the previous value and, indirectly, the seed. Therefore, it guarantees that any sequence can always be regenerated, if you know the seed. For instance, if your fractal program using the pseudo-random number generator generates an image that you like, you can regenerate the same image with just the knowledge of the seed value.

The ALG_RANDOM_SEED FunctionThis function initializes the random number generator with a real number. old_seed is set to the passed seed value. ALG_RANDOM_SEED must be called for usage of both the ALG_RAND and ALG_RAND_INT functions. Any time the same value is passed to ALG_RANDOM_SEED, the same sequence will be generated by ALG_RAND and ALG_RAND_INT.

The ALG_RAND Function

This function returns a positive real-type random number between 0.0 and 1.0. old_rand takes on the fractional part of old_rand times the constant sigma. old_rand is then the returned value. Note that ALG_RANDOM_SEED must be called prior to any use of ALG_RAND.

The ALG_RAND_INT Function

This function returns a positive integer-type pseudo-random number from an alg_word-type range argument, i.e., a value from 0–(range-1). We simply get the next value from ALG_RAND, which is always in the range 0.0–1.0, multiply this by range, and return ALG_TRUNC of the result.

On to the Program Listings

Now that we have examined some of the basic matrix and vector geometry for computer graphics and seen some of the data structures that we will use, let's carry our focus to the polygon primitive as it applies to a graphics system.

PROGRAM LISTINGS:

```
/*

  +------------------------------------------------------------------------+
  |                                                                        |
  |                        Virtual Reality ExCursions                      |
  |                                                                        |
  |            by Christopher D. Watkins and Stephen R. Marenka            |
  |                                                                        |
  |                   Copyright 1994 : Academic Press, Inc.                |
  |                                                                        |
  |------------------------------------------------------------------------|
  |                                                                        |
  |                              ALG_DEFS.H                                |
  |------------------------------------------------------------------------|
```

```
    |                                                                    |
    |                        Software Issues                            |
    |                                                                    |
    |           Copyright 1987-1994 ALGORITHM, Incorporated.            |
    |                                                                    |
    |      ALL RIGHTS RESERVED. This software is Published, but is NOT   |
    |   Public Domain and remains the property of ALGORITHM, Incorporated and |
    |           Christopher D. Watkins. This software may not be        |
    |   reproduced or integrated into other packages without the prior written |
    |           consent of Christopher D. Watkins. Licensing is possible. |
    |                                                                    |
    +--------------------------------------------------------------------+
*/

    #ifndef     FILE
            #include    <stdio.h>
    #endif


    #ifndef     SEEK_SET
            #define   SEEK_SET    0
    #endif


    #ifndef __ALG_DEFS__
    #define __ALG_DEFS__


    /*

        +----------------------------------------------------------------+
        |                        math constants                          |
        +----------------------------------------------------------------+
    */


    #define     ALG_PI          (M_PI)
    #define     ALG_DEG_TO_RAD  (1.74532925199433e-002)
    #define     ALG_RAD_TO_DEG  (5.72957795130823e+001)
    #define     ALG_LN10        (2.30258509299405e+000)
    #define     ALG_INV_LN10    (0.43429448190325e+000)
```

```
/*

   +----------------------------------------------------------------+
   |                   math precision-error constants               |
   +----------------------------------------------------------------+

*/


#define ALG_ZERO              (1.7e-03)
#define ALG_INFINITY          (1.0e+20)


#define    ALG_SMALL          (1.0e-05)
#define    ALG_LARGE          (1.0e+05)


/*

   +----------------------------------------------------------------+
   |                    single-valued functions                     |
   +----------------------------------------------------------------+

*/


#define    ALG_ABS(x)         ( ((x) < 0) ? (-(x)) : (x) )


#define    ALG_RAD(x)         ( (x) * ALG_DEG_TO_RAD )
#define    ALG_DEG(x)         ( (x) * ALG_RAD_TO_DEG )


#define    ALG_COS(x)         ( cos( (x) ) )
#define    ALG_SIN(x)         ( sin( (x) ) )
#define    ALG_COSD(x)        ( cos( ALG_RAD( (x) ) ) )
#define    ALG_SIND(x)        ( sin( ALG_RAD( (x) ) ) )


#define    ALG_NINT(x)        ( (alg_long)((x) >= 0.0) ? ((x) + 0.5) : ((x)
                              - 0.5)) )
#define    ALG_NINTPOS(x)     ( (alg_long)((x) + 0.5) )
#define    ALG_FLOOR(x)       ( (x) > 0 ? (alg_int)(x) : -(alg_int)(x) )
#define    ALG_CEILING(x)     ( (x) == (alg_int)(x) ? (x) : (x) > 0 ?
                              (1+(alg_int)(x)) : \ -(1+(alg_int)(-x) )
#define    ALG_ROUND(x)       ( (alg_int)(x) + 0.5 )
#define    ALG_ROUND_2(x)     ( (x) > 0 ? (alg_int)((x) + 0.5) :
                              -(alg_int)(0.5 - (x)) )
#define    ALG_TRUNC(x)       ( (alg_int)(x) )
#define    ALG_FRAC(x)        ( (x) - (alg_double)( (alg_int)(x) ) )
```

```
#define    ALG_SQR(x)              ( (x) * (x) )
#define    ALG_SQRT(x)             ( sqrt( (x) ) )


#define    ALG_LN(x)               ( log( (x) ) )
#define    ALG_LOG(x)              ( ALG_LN( (x) ) * ALG_INV_LN10 )
#define    ALG_EXP10(x)            ( exp( (x) * ALG_LN10 )  )


#define ALG_SIGN(x)                     \
{                                       \
      if (x < 0)                        \
              return(-1);               \
      else                              \
      {                                 \
            if (x > 0)                  \
                    return(1);          \
            else                        \
                    return(0);          \
      }                                 \
}


/*
   +------------------------------------------------------------------+
   |                     comparison functions                         |
   +------------------------------------------------------------------+
*/


#define    ALG_MIN(x, y)               ( ((x) < (y)) ? (x) : (y) )
#define    ALG_MAX(x, y)               ( ((x) < (y)) ? (y) : (x) )
#define    ALG_MIN3(x, y, z)           ( ALG_MIN( ALG_MIN(x, y), z) )
#define    ALG_MAX3(x, y, z)           ( ALG_MAX( ALG_MAX(x, y), z) )
#define    ALG_MIN4(x, y, z, w)        ( ALG_MIN( ALG_MIN3(x, y, z), w) )
#define    ALG_MAX4(x, y, z, w)        ( ALG_MAX( ALG_MAX3(x, y, z), w) )


/*
   +------------------------------------------------------------------+
   |                       swapping routines                          |
   +------------------------------------------------------------------+
*/
```

```c
//          swaps contents of a and b
//          requires variable 'temp'
#define ALG_SWAP(a, b)                    \
{                                   \
          temp = (a);         \
          (a) = (b);          \
          (b) = temp;         \
}


/*
    +-----------------------------------------------------------------------+
    |                         type definitions                              |
    +-----------------------------------------------------------------------+
*/

typedef    unsigned char      alg_byte;
typedef    unsigned int       alg_word;
typedef    unsigned long      alg_dword;
typedef    char               alg_char;
typedef    int                alg_int;
typedef    long               alg_long;
typedef    double /* float */alg_float;
typedef    double             alg_double;
typedef    enum {ALG_FALSE, ALG_TRUE}        alg_boolean;
typedef    alg_byte           alg_palette_type[256][3];


/*
    +-----------------------------------------------------------------------+
    |           type definitions for points/vectors and matrices            |
    +-----------------------------------------------------------------------+
*/

// describes a 2x2 matrix
typedef struct
{
      alg_float      mat[2][2];
}
alg_matrix_2x2_type;
```

```
// describes a 3x3 matrix
typedef struct
{
        alg_float       mat[3][3];
}
alg_matrix_3x3_type;

// describes a 4x4 matrix
typedef struct
{
        alg_float       mat[4][4];
}
alg_matrix_4x4_type;

// describes a single Cartesian point (used to store a 2D integer point)
typedef struct
{
        alg_int                 x;      // x coordinate
        alg_int                 y;      // y coordinate
}
alg_point_2D_int_type;

// describes a single Cartesian point (used to store a 2D point)
typedef struct
{
        alg_float       x;      // x coordinate
        alg_float       y;      // y coordinate
}
alg_point_2D_type;

// describes a single Cartesian point (used to store a 3D integer point)
typedef struct
{
        alg_int                 x;      // x coordinate
        alg_int                 y;      // y coordinate
        alg_int                 z;      // z coordinate
}
alg_point_3D_int_type;
```

```
// describes a single Cartesian point (used to store a 3D point)
typedef struct
{
      alg_float      x;      // x coordinate
      alg_float      y;      // y coordinate
      alg_float      z;      // z coordinate
}
alg_point_3D_type;


// describes a single Cartesian point (used to store a 4D integer point)
typedef struct
{
      alg_int                x;      // x coordinate
      alg_int                y;      // y coordinate
      alg_int                z;      // z coordinate
      alg_int                w;      // w coordinate
}
alg_point_4D_int_type;


// describes a single Cartesian point (used to store a 4D point)
typedef struct
{
      alg_float      x;      // x coordinate
      alg_float      y;      // y coordinate
      alg_float      z;      // z coordinate
      alg_float      w;      // w coordinate
}
alg_point_4D_type;


// describes a single Cartesian point in local coordinates, and viewer
//      transformed coordinates (used to store a set of 3D points)
typedef struct
{
      alg_point_3D_type      local;        // local coordinate
      alg_point_3D_type      viewer;       // viewer transformed world
coordinate
}
alg_vertex_3D_type;
```

```
/*

   +---------------------------------------------------------------+
   |                   type definitions for polygons              |
   +---------------------------------------------------------------+
*/


// describes the beginning and ending x coordinates of a single
//      horizontal line (used for polygon filling)
typedef struct
{
     alg_int    x_start;    // x coordinate of leftmost pixel in line
     alg_int    x_end;      // x coordinate of rightmost pixel in line
}
alg_horz_line_type;


// describes num_horz_lines horizontal lines, all assumed to be on
//      contiguous scan lines starting at y_start and proceeding
//      downward (used to describe a scan-converted polygon to the
//      low-level hardware-dependent drawing code in Alg_Scrn.C)
typedef struct
{
     alg_word  num_horz_lines; // # of horizontal lines
     alg_int   y_start;        // y coordinate of top-most line
     alg_horz_line_type  *horz_line_list_ptr;   // pointer to list of
                                                 // horizontal lines
}
alg_horz_line_list_type;


// describes a bounding box for a three-dimensional polygon
//      (used for cuboid bounding to aid in binary space partitioning)
typedef struct
{
     alg_point_3D_type    minimum;
     alg_point_3D_type    maximum;
}
alg_polygon_3D_bounding_box_type;
```

```
// describes a polygon that has been prepared for viewport display
typedef struct
{
        alg_byte               color;
        alg_word               texture;
        alg_word               num_viewport_clipped_vertices;
        // scratch pad for vertices in order to save
        //     memory allocation overhead at run-time
        alg_point_2D_int_type              viewport_clipped_vertex[10];
}
alg_viewport_clipped_polygon_2D_type;


// describes a polygon that has been clipped with the front of the view
//     volume in order to remove that part of the polygon which falls
//     behind the viewer
typedef struct
{
        alg_byte               color;
        alg_word               texture;
        alg_word               num_z_clipped_vertices;
        // scratch pad for vertices in order to save
        //     memory allocation overhead at run-time
        alg_point_3D_type     z_clipped_vertex[10];
}
alg_z_clipped_polygon_3D_type;


// describes a polygon
typedef struct
{
        alg_byte               color;
        alg_word               texture;
        alg_word               num_vertices;
        alg_vertex_3D_type     **vertex;
        alg_float              viewer_to_polygon_distance;
}
alg_polygon_3D_type;
```

```
// descibes a list of 3D polygons for potential display
typedef struct
{
        alg_word                num_polygons;
        alg_polygon_3D_type    *polygon;
}
alg_polygon_3D_display_list_type;


/*

    +------------------------------------------------------------------+
    |           type definitions for three-dimensional graphics        |
    +------------------------------------------------------------------+
*/


// describes an object in the three-dimensional world
typedef struct
{
        // (if we moved our object, we must recompute transformation)
        alg_boolean             invalid_local_transformation_matrix;
        alg_matrix_4x4_type     local_transformation_matrix;
        alg_point_3D_type       scale;
        alg_point_3D_type       rotate;
        // origin in world coordinates
        alg_point_3D_type       translate;
        alg_word                num_vertices;
        alg_vertex_3D_type     *vertex;
        alg_word                num_polygons;
        alg_polygon_3D_type    *polygon;
}
alg_object_3D_type;


// describes the three-dimensional world
typedef struct
{
        alg_word                num_objects;
        alg_object_3D_type     *object;
        alg_byte                background_color;
}
alg_world_3D_type;
```

```
// describes the viewer in the three-dimensional world
typedef struct
{
        alg_matrix_4x4_type    viewer_transformation_matrix;
        alg_point_3D_type      translate;
        alg_point_3D_type      rotate;
        alg_float              perspective_plane_distance;
}
alg_viewer_3D_type;




/*

   +--------------------------------------------------------------------+
   |                    type definitions for controls                   |
   +--------------------------------------------------------------------+

*/



// describes the controls of an airplane for intuitive control of the
//      viewer
typedef struct
{
        alg_boolean            aileron_left_down;
        alg_boolean            aileron_right_down;

        alg_float              aileron_position;
        alg_float              max_aileron_position;
        alg_float              delta_aileron_position;
        alg_float              aileron_dampening;

        alg_boolean            elevator_up;
        alg_boolean            elevator_down;

        alg_float              elevator_position;
        alg_float              max_elevator_position;
        alg_float              delta_elevator_position;
        alg_float              elevator_dampening;

        alg_boolean            rudder_left;
```

```
        alg_boolean              rudder_right;

        alg_float                rudder_position;
        alg_float                max_rudder_position;
        alg_float                delta_rudder_position;
        alg_float                rudder_dampening;

        alg_boolean              throttle_inc;
        alg_boolean              throttle_dec;

        alg_float                throttle_position;
        alg_float                max_throttle_position;
        alg_float                delta_throttle_position;
        alg_float                throttle_dampening;

        alg_boolean              halt_translations;
        alg_boolean              halt_rotations;
    }
    alg_controls_type;

    #endif // __ALG_DEFS__


/*

    +---------------------------------------------------------------------------+
    |                                                                           |
    |                       Virtual Reality ExCursions                          |
    |                                                                           |
    |            by Christopher D. Watkins and Stephen R. Marenka               |
    |                                                                           |
    |                   Copyright 1994 : Academic Press, Inc.                   |
    |                                                                           |
    |---------------------------------------------------------------------------|
    |                               ALG_MATH.C                                  |
    |---------------------------------------------------------------------------|
    |                                                                           |
    |                             Software Issues                               |
    |                                                                           |
    |              Copyright 1987-1994 ALGORITHM, Incorporated.                 |
    |                                                                           |
```

```c
//      system includes
#include <stdio.h>
#include <stdlib.h>
#include <math.h>

//      ALGORITHM, Inc. includes
#include "Alg_Defs.H"
#include "Alg_Math.H"

/*
  +----------------------------------------------------------------------+
  |              micellaneous single-valued functions                    |
  +----------------------------------------------------------------------+
*/

alg_float ALG_POWER( alg_float base, alg_int exponent )
{
        alg_float     power = 1.0;
        alg_int               t;

        if (exponent != 0)
                for (t=0; t<exponent; t++)
                        power *= base;
        return( power );
}

alg_int ALG_INT_POWER( alg_int base, alg_int exponent )
{
        if (exponent == 0)
                return( 1 );
```

```
        else
                return( base * ALG_INT_POWER( base, exponent-1 ) );
}


#ifdef __BORLANDC__


/*

    +------------------------------------------------------------------+
    |                pseudo-random number generator functions          |
    +------------------------------------------------------------------+
*/

static alg_double    old_rand;
static alg_float     sigma = 422.1976;

void ALG_RANDOM_SEED( alg_float random_seed )
{
        old_rand = random_seed;
}


alg_int ALG_RAND_INT( alg_word range )
{
        old_rand = ALG_FRAC( sigma * old_rand );
        return( ALG_TRUNC( old_rand * (float)range ) );
}


alg_float ALG_RAND( void )
{
        old_rand = ALG_FRAC( sigma * old_rand );

        return( old_rand );
}


#endif
```

```
/*

  +--------------------------------------------------------------------+
  |                                                                    |
  |                      Virtual Reality ExCursions                    |
  |                                                                    |
  |            by Christopher D. Watkins and Stephen R. Marenka        |
  |                                                                    |
  |                 Copyright 1994 : Academic Press, Inc.              |
  |                                                                    |
  |--------------------------------------------------------------------|
  |                             ALG_MATX.C                             |
  |--------------------------------------------------------------------|
  |                                                                    |
  |                          Software Issues                           |
  |                                                                    |
  |             Copyright 1987-1994 ALGORITHM, Incorporated.           |
  |                                                                    |
  |     ALL RIGHTS RESERVED. This software is Published, but is NOT    |
  |  Public Domain and remains the property of ALGORITHM, Incorporated and |
  |          Christopher D. Watkins. This software may not be         |
  | reproduced or integrated into other packages without the prior written |
  |         consent of Christopher D. Watkins. Licensing is possible. |
  |                                                                    |
  +--------------------------------------------------------------------+

*/


    //      Algorithm, Inc. includes
    #include        "Alg_Defs.H"
    #include        "Alg_Matx.H"

    //      3x3 identity matrix
    alg_matrix_3x3_type   alg_identity_matrix_3x3 =
    {
            { { 1.0, 0.0, 0.0 },
              { 0.0, 1.0, 0.0 },
              { 0.0, 0.0, 1.0 } }
    };
```

```
//      4x4 identity matrix
alg_matrix_4x4_type   alg_identity_matrix_4x4 =
{
        { { 1.0, 0.0, 0.0, 0.0 },
          { 0.0, 1.0, 0.0, 0.0 },
          { 0.0, 0.0, 1.0, 0.0 },
          { 0.0, 0.0, 0.0, 1.0 } }
};


/*

    +---------------------------------------------------------------------+
    |                                                                     |
    |                     Virtual Reality ExCursions                      |
    |                                                                     |
    |          by Christopher D. Watkins and Stephen R. Marenka           |
    |                                                                     |
    |                 Copyright 1994 : Academic Press, Inc.               |
    |                                                                     |
    |---------------------------------------------------------------------|
    |                             ALG_MATX.H                              |
    |---------------------------------------------------------------------|
    |                                                                     |
    |                           Software Issues                           |
    |                                                                     |
    |              Copyright 1987-1994 ALGORITHM, Incorporated.           |
    |                                                                     |
    |       ALL RIGHTS RESERVED. This software is Published, but is NOT   |
    |   Public Domain and remains the property of ALGORITHM, Incorporated and |
    |          Christopher D. Watkins. This software may not be           |
    |  reproduced or integrated into other packages without the prior written |
    |          consent of Christopher D. Watkins. Licensing is possible.  |
    |                                                                     |
    +---------------------------------------------------------------------+

*/


    #ifndef __ALG_MATX__
    #define __ALG_MATX__
```

```
/*

   +------------------------------------------------------------------+
   |                   two-dimensional vector functions               |
   +------------------------------------------------------------------+
*/
#define ALG_VEC2_MAKE(A, B, v)          \
        (v).x = (A);                    \
        (v).y = (B)


#define ALG_VEC2_COMPONENTS(v, A, B)        \
        (A) = (v).x;                        \
        (B) = (v).y


#define ALG_VEC2_AVERAGE(a, b, v)           \
        (v).x = (((a).x + (b).x) / 2.0);    \
        (v).y = (((a).y + (b).y) / 2.0)


#define ALG_VEC2_NEGATE(v)    \
        (v).x = (-(v).x);     \
        (v).y = (-(v).y)


#define ALG_VEC2_NEGATE2(a, v)        \
        (v).x = (-(a).x);             \
        (v).y = (-(a).y)


#define ALG_VEC2_DOT(a, b)    \
        ( (a).x * (b).x +     \
          (a).y * (b).y )


#define ALG_VEC2_LENGTH(v)    \
        ( sqrt(ALG_VEC2_DOT(v, v)) )


#define ALG_VEC2_NORMALIZE(v)                               \
{                                                           \
        alg_double normlen = ALG_VEC2_LENGTH(v);    \
                                                            \
        if (normlen == 0.0)                         \
                printf("zero-length vector");       \
                                                            \
```

```
        (v).x = (v).x / normlen;                \
        (v).y = (v).y / normlen;                \
}


#define ALG_VEC2_MINIMUM(a, b, v)           \
{                                               \
        if ((a).x < (b).x)                      \
                (v).x = (a).x;                  \
        else                                    \
                (v).x = (b).x;                  \
        if ((a).y < (b).y)                      \
                (v).y = (a).y;                  \
        else                                    \
                (v).y = (b).y;                  \
}


#define ALG_VEC2_MAXIMUM(a, b, v)           \
{                                               \
        if ((a).x > (b).x)                      \
                (v).x = (a).x;                  \
        else                                    \
                (v).x = (b).x;                  \
        if ((a).y > (b).y)                      \
                (v).y = (a).y;                  \
        else                                    \
                (v).y = (b).y;                  \
}


#define ALG_VEC2_COMPARE(a, b, same)        \
{                                               \
        if (( (a).x == (b).x ) &&               \
            ( (a).y == (b).y ) )                \
                same = ALG_TRUE;                \
        else                                    \
                same = ALG_FALSE;               \
}
```

```
#define ALG_VEC2_COPY(a, b)                        \
        (b).x = (a).x;                             \
        (b).y = (a).y

#define ALG_VEC2_ADD(a, b, v)                      \
        (v).x = (a).x + (b).x;                     \
        (v).y = (a).y + (b).y

#define ALG_VEC2_SUB(a, b, v)                      \
        (v).x = (a).x - (b).x;                     \
        (v).y = (a).y - (b).y

#define ALG_VEC2_LIN_COMB(A, a, B, b, v)   \
        (v).x = (A) * (a).x + (B) * (b).x;  \
        (v).y = (A) * (a).y + (B) * (b).y

#define ALG_VEC2_SCAL_MULT(A, a, v)                \
        (v).x = (A) * (a).x;                       \
        (v).y = (A) * (a).y

#define ALG_VEC2_ADD_SCAL_MULT(A, a, b, v) \
        (v).x = (A) * (a).x + (b).x;               \
        (v).y = (A) * (a).y + (b).y

#define ALG_VEC2_MUL(a, b, v)                      \
        (v).x = (a).x * (b).x;                     \
        (v).y = (a).y * (b).y

#define ALG_VEC2_DETERMINANT(a, b, t)      \
        ( (t)(a).x * (b).y - (t)(a).y * (b).x )

#define ALG_VEC2_ZERO(v)                           \
        (v).x = 0.0;                               \
        (v).y = 0.0

#define ALG_VEC2_PRINT(msg, v)                       \
        fprintf( stderr, "%s: %g %g\n", msg,     \
        (v).x, (v).y )
```

```
/*

   +-----------------------------------------------------------------+
   |                three-dimensional vector functions               |
   +-----------------------------------------------------------------+
*/

#define ALG_VEC3_MAKE(A, B, C, v)             \
        (v).x = (A);                          \
        (v).y = (B);                          \
        (v).z = (C)


#define ALG_VEC3_COMPONENTS(v, A, B, C)       \
        (A) = (v).x;                          \
        (B) = (v).y;                          \
        (C) = (v).z


#define ALG_VEC3_AVERAGE(a, b, v)             \
        (v).x = (((a).x + (b).x) / 2.0);      \
        (v).y = (((a).y + (b).y) / 2.0);      \
        (v).z = (((a).z + (b).z) / 2.0)


#define ALG_VEC3_NEGATE(v)                    \
        (v).x = (-(v).x);                     \
        (v).y = (-(v).y);                     \
        (v).z = (-(v).z)


#define ALG_VEC3_NEGATE2(a, v)                \
        (v).x = (-(a).x);                     \
        (v).y = (-(a).y);                     \
        (v).z = (-(a).z)


#define ALG_VEC3_DOT(a, b)                    \
        ( (a).x * (b).x +                     \
          (a).y * (b).y +                     \
          (a).z * (b).z )


#define ALG_VEC3_LENGTH(v)                    \
        ( sqrt(ALG_VEC3_DOT(v, v)) )
```

```
#define ALG_VEC3_NORMALIZE(v)                            \
{                                                        \
        alg_double normlen = ALG_VEC3_LENGTH(v);     \
                                                         \
        if (normlen == 0.0)                          \
                printf("zero-length vector");         \
                                                         \
        (v).x = (v).x / normlen;                     \
        (v).y = (v).y / normlen;                     \
        (v).z = (v).z / normlen;                     \
}


#define ALG_VEC3_MINIMUM(a, b, v)                \
{                                                \
        if ((a).x < (b).x)                       \
                (v).x = (a).x;                   \
        else                                     \
                (v).x = (b).x;                   \
        if ((a).y < (b).y)                       \
                (v).y = (a).y;                   \
        else                                     \
                (v).y = (b).y;                   \
        if ((a).z < (b).z)                       \
                (v).z = (a).z;                   \
        else                                     \
                (v).z = (b).z;                   \
}


#define ALG_VEC3_MAXIMUM(a, b, v)                \
{                                                \
        if ((a).x > (b).x)                       \
                (v).x = (a).x;                   \
        else                                     \
                (v).x = (b).x;                   \
        if ((a).y > (b).y)                       \
                (v).y = (a).y;                   \
        else                                     \
                (v).y = (b).y;                   \
        if ((a).z > (b).z)                       \
```

```
                        (v).z  =  (a).z;                   \
            else                                           \
                        (v).z  =  (b).z;                   \
    }


    #define ALG_VEC3_COMPARE(a,  b,  same)             \
    {                                                  \
            if (( (a).x  ==  (b).x  ) &&               \
                ( (a).y  ==  (b).y  ) &&               \
                ( (a).z  ==  (b).z  ) )                \
                    same  =  ALG_TRUE;                 \
            else                                       \
                    same  =  ALG_FALSE;                \
    }


    #define ALG_VEC3_COPY(a,  b)             \
            (b).x  =  (a).x;                 \
            (b).y  =  (a).y;                 \
            (b).z  =  (a).z


    #define ALG_VEC3_ADD(a,  b,  v)          \
            (v).x  =  (a).x  +  (b).x;       \
            (v).y  =  (a).y  +  (b).y;       \
            (v).z  =  (a).z  +  (b).z


    #define ALG_VEC3_SUB(a,  b,  v)          \
            (v).x  =  (a).x  -  (b).x;       \
            (v).y  =  (a).y  -  (b).y;       \
            (v).z  =  (a).z  -  (b).z


    #define ALG_VEC3_LIN_COMB(A,  a,  B,  b,  v)    \
            (v).x  =  (A)  *  (a).x  +  (B)  *  (b).x;  \
            (v).y  =  (A)  *  (a).y  +  (B)  *  (b).y;  \
            (v).z  =  (A)  *  (a).z  +  (B)  *  (b).z


    #define ALG_VEC3_SCAL_MULT(A,  a,  v)            \
            (v).x  =  (A)  *  (a).x;                 \
            (v).y  =  (A)  *  (a).y;                 \
            (v).z  =  (A)  *  (a).z
```

```c
#define ALG_VEC3_ADD_SCAL_MULT(A, a, b, v) \
        (v).x = (A) * (a).x + (b).x;        \
        (v).y = (A) * (a).y + (b).y;        \
        (v).z = (A) * (a).z + (b).z


#define ALG_VEC3_MUL(a, b, v)               \
        (v).x = (a).x * (b).x;              \
        (v).y = (a).y * (b).y;              \
        (v).z = (a).z * (b).z


#define ALG_VEC3_CROSS(a, b, v)                     \
        (v).x = (a).y * (b).z - (a).z * (b).y;      \
        (v).y = (a).z * (b).x - (a).x * (b).z;      \
        (v).z = (a).x * (b).y - (a).y * (b).x


#define ALG_VEC3_ZERO(v)            \
        (v).x = 0.0;                \
        (v).y = 0.0;                \
        (v).z = 0.0


#define ALG_VEC3_PRINT(msg, v)                      \
        fprintf( stderr, "%s: %g %g %g\n", msg,     \
        (v).x, (v).y, (v).z )


/*

    +------------------------------------------------------------------+
    |        3x3 matrix functions for two-dimensional manipulations    |
    +------------------------------------------------------------------+
*/
//      the identity matrix in Alg_Matx.C
extern alg_matrix_3x3_type   alg_identity_matrix_3x3;


//      copy a matrix
//              matrix = matrix1
#define         alg_copy_3x3_matrix( matrix, matrix1 )              \
{                                                                   \
        memcpy( &matrix, &matrix1, sizeof( alg_matrix_3x3_type ) ); \
}
```

```
//      multiply matrices
//              matrix = matrix1 * matrix2
#define         alg_multiply_3x3_matrix( matrix, matrix1, matrix2 ) \
{                                                                   \
        alg_byte        row, col;                                   \
        for (row=0; row<3; row++)                                   \
                for (col=0; col<3; col++)                           \
                        matrix.mat[row][col] =                      \
                        ( (matrix1.mat[row][0] * matrix2.mat[0][col]) +\
                          (matrix1.mat[row][1] * matrix2.mat[1][col]) +\
                          (matrix1.mat[row][2] * matrix2.mat[2][col]) );\
}


//      create a zero matrix
//              matrix = 0
#define         alg_zero_3x3_matrix( matrix )                       \
{                                                                   \
        memset( &matrix, 0, sizeof( alg_matrix_3x3_type ) );        \
}


//      create an identity matrix
//              matrix = identity
#define         alg_identity_3x3_matrix( matrix )          \
{                                                          \
        matrix = alg_identity_matrix_3x3;                  \
}


//      create a scale matrix where
//              1) vector holds (x,y) scaling factors to produce a
//                      scaling matrix
//              2) matrix = scale_matrix * matrix
#define         alg_scale_3x3_matrix( vector, matrix )             \
{                                                                  \
        alg_matrix_3x3_type   scale_matrix = alg_identity_matrix_3x3; \
        alg_matrix_3x3_type   matrix1;                             \
                                                                   \
        scale_matrix.mat[0][0] = vector.x;                         \
        scale_matrix.mat[1][1] = vector.y;                         \
                                                                   \
```

```
        alg_multiply_3x3_matrix( matrix1, scale_matrix, matrix ); \
        alg_copy_3x3_matrix( matrix, matrix1 );                   \
}


//      create a rotate matrix where
//              1) scalar holds (theta) rotation factor to produce a
//                     rotation matrix
//              2) matrix = rotation_matrix * matrix
#define alg_rotate_3x3_matrix( scalar_theta, matrix )             \
{                                                                 \
        alg_matrix_3x3_type   rotation_matrix = alg_identity_matrix_3x3;\
        alg_matrix_3x3_type   matrix1;                            \
                                                                  \
        alg_float             COS_THETA = ALG_COS(scalar_theta);  \
        alg_float             SIN_THETA = ALG_SIN(scalar_theta);  \
                                                                  \
        rotation_matrix.mat[0][0] =  COS_THETA;                   \
        rotation_matrix.mat[0][1] = -SIN_THETA;                   \
        rotation_matrix.mat[1][0] =  SIN_THETA;                   \
        rotation_matrix.mat[1][1] =  COS_THETA;                   \
                                                                  \
        alg_multiply_3x3_matrix( matrix1, rotation_matrix, matrix ); \
        alg_copy_3x3_matrix( matrix, matrix1 );                   \
}


//      create a translate matrix where
//              1) vector holds (x,y) translation factors to produce a
//                     translation matrix
//              2) matrix = translate_matrix * matrix
#define        alg_translate_3x3_matrix( vector, matrix )         \
{                                                                 \
        alg_matrix_3x3_type   translate_matrix =                  \
               alg_identity_matrix_3x3;                           \
        alg_matrix_3x3_type   matrix1;                            \
                                                                  \
        translate_matrix.mat[0][2] = -vector.x;                   \
        translate_matrix.mat[1][2] = -vector.y;                   \
                                                                  \
        alg_multiply_3x3_matrix( matrix1, translate_matrix, matrix ); \
```

```
        alg_copy_3x3_matrix( matrix, matrix1 );                    \
}


//      multiply a vector by a matrix
//              vector = vector1 * matrix
#define alg_transform_3x3_matrix( vector, matrix, vector1 )        \
{                                                                  \
        vector.x =      matrix.mat[0][0] * vector1.x +             \
                        matrix.mat[0][1] * vector1.y +             \
                        matrix.mat[0][2];                          \
        vector.y =      matrix.mat[1][0] * vector1.x +             \
                        matrix.mat[1][1] * vector1.y +             \
                        matrix.mat[1][2];                          \
}


/*

    +----------------------------------------------------------------+
    |   4x4 matrix functions for three-dimensional manipulations     |
    +----------------------------------------------------------------+
*/


//      the identity matrix in Alg_Matx.C
extern alg_matrix_4x4_type   alg_identity_matrix_4x4;


//      copy a matrix
//              matrix = matrix1
#define      alg_copy_4x4_matrix( matrix, matrix1 )                \
{                                                                  \
        memcpy( &matrix, &matrix1, sizeof( alg_matrix_4x4_type ) ); \
}


//      multiply matrices
//              matrix = matrix1 * matrix2
#define      alg_multiply_4x4_matrix( matrix, matrix1, matrix2 ) \
{                                                                  \
        alg_byte      row, col;                                    \
                                                                   \
        for (row=0; row<4; row++)                                  \
                for (col=0; col<4; col++)                          \
```

```
                        matrix.mat[row][col] =                           \
                            ( (matrix1.mat[row][0]  *                     \
                                    matrix2.mat[0][col]) +                \
                                (matrix1.mat[row][1]  *                   \
                                    matrix2.mat[1][col]) +                \
                                (matrix1.mat[row][2]  *                   \
                            matrix2.mat[2][col]) +                        \
                                (matrix1.mat[row][3]  *                   \
                            matrix2.mat[3][col]) );                       \
}


//      create a zero matrix
//              matrix = 0
#define alg_zero_4x4_matrix( matrix )                                     \
{                                                                        \
      memset( &matrix, 0, sizeof( alg_matrix_4x4_type ) );              \
}


//      create an identity matrix
//              matrix = identity
#define alg_identity_4x4_matrix( matrix )                                \
{                                                                        \
      matrix = alg_identity_matrix_4x4;                                  \
}


//      create a scale matrix where
//              1) vector holds (x,y,z) scaling factors to produce a
//                  scaling matrix
//              2) matrix = scale_matrix * matrix
#define      alg_scale_4x4_matrix( vector, matrix )                      \
{                                                                        \
      alg_matrix_4x4_type   scale_matrix =                               \
              alg_identity_matrix_4x4;                                   \
      alg_matrix_4x4_type   matrix1;                                     \
                                                                         \
      scale_matrix.mat[0][0] = vector.x;                                 \
      scale_matrix.mat[1][1] = vector.y;                                 \
      scale_matrix.mat[2][2] = vector.z;                                 \
                                                                         \
```

```
            alg_multiply_4x4_matrix( matrix1, scale_matrix, matrix ) \
            alg_copy_4x4_matrix( matrix, matrix1 );                  \
}


//      create a rotate matrix where
//              1) vector holds (x,y,z) rotation factors to produce a
//                      rotation matrix
//              2) matrix = rotation_matrix * matrix
//              3) rotation_code defines order of rotations
#define        VIEWER_ROTATION      0
#define        MOTION_ROTATION      1
#define        OBJECT_ROTATION      2
#define        STRAIGHT_ROTATION    3
#define  alg_rotate_4x4_matrix( vector, matrix, rotation_code )  \
{                                                                \
        alg_matrix_4x4_type   x_rotation_matrix =                \
              alg_identity_matrix_4x4;                           \
        alg_matrix_4x4_type   y_rotation_matrix =                \
              alg_identity_matrix_4x4;                           \
        alg_matrix_4x4_type   z_rotation_matrix =                \
              alg_identity_matrix_4x4;                           \
        alg_matrix_4x4_type   matrix1;                           \
        alg_matrix_4x4_type   matrix2;                           \
                                                                 \
        alg_float             COS_X = ALG_COS(vector.x);         \
        alg_float             SIN_X = ALG_SIN(vector.x);         \
        alg_float             COS_Y = ALG_COS(vector.y);         \
        alg_float             SIN_Y = ALG_SIN(vector.y);         \
        alg_float             COS_Z = ALG_COS(vector.z);         \
        alg_float             SIN_Z = ALG_SIN(vector.z);         \
                                                                 \
        x_rotation_matrix.mat[1][1] =  COS_X;                    \
        x_rotation_matrix.mat[1][2] =  SIN_X;                    \
        x_rotation_matrix.mat[2][1] = -SIN_X;                    \
        x_rotation_matrix.mat[2][2] =  COS_X;                    \
                                                                 \
        y_rotation_matrix.mat[0][0] =  COS_Y;                    \
        y_rotation_matrix.mat[0][2] = -SIN_Y;                    \
        y_rotation_matrix.mat[2][0] =  SIN_Y;                    \
```

```
    y_rotation_matrix.mat[2][2] =  COS_Y;                        \
                                                                 \
    z_rotation_matrix.mat[0][0] =  COS_Z;                        \
    z_rotation_matrix.mat[0][1] =  SIN_Z;                        \
    z_rotation_matrix.mat[1][0] = -SIN_Z;                        \
    z_rotation_matrix.mat[1][1] =  COS_Z;                        \
                                                                 \
    switch (rotation_code)                                       \
    {                                                            \
        case VIEWER_ROTATION:                                    \
                alg_multiply_4x4_matrix( matrix1,                \
                    y_rotation_matrix, matrix  );                \
                alg_multiply_4x4_matrix( matrix2,                \
                    x_rotation_matrix, matrix1 );                \
                alg_multiply_4x4_matrix(  matrix,                \
                    z_rotation_matrix, matrix2 );                \
        break;                                                   \
        case MOTION_ROTATION:                                    \
                alg_multiply_4x4_matrix( matrix1,                \
                    z_rotation_matrix, matrix  );                \
                alg_multiply_4x4_matrix( matrix2,                \
                    x_rotation_matrix, matrix1 );                \
                alg_multiply_4x4_matrix(  matrix,                \
                     y_rotation_matrix, matrix2 );               \
        break;                                                   \
        case OBJECT_ROTATION:                                    \
                alg_multiply_4x4_matrix( matrix1,                \
                    y_rotation_matrix, matrix  );                \
                alg_multiply_4x4_matrix( matrix2,                \
                    x_rotation_matrix, matrix1 );                \
                alg_multiply_4x4_matrix(  matrix,                \
                    z_rotation_matrix, matrix2 );                \
        break;                                                   \
        case STRAIGHT_ROTATION:                                  \
                alg_multiply_4x4_matrix( matrix1,                \
                    x_rotation_matrix, matrix  );                \
                alg_multiply_4x4_matrix( matrix2,                \
                    y_rotation_matrix, matrix1 );                \
                alg_multiply_4x4_matrix(  matrix,                \
```

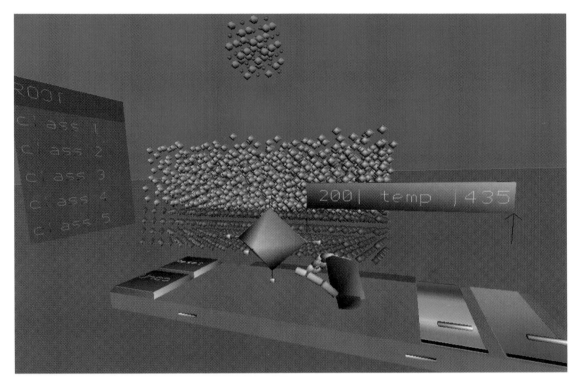

Data1. Interaction with a three-dimensional visualization of molecular data. Data is classified by types, and here the user chooses the type associated with a NaCl cluster.

Data credtis: David Luedtke/Uzi Landman. Photo Credits: Ron van Teylingen/Bill Ribarsky. GVULab Project: SV, Georgia Tech.

Olytorch. Georgia Tech's 1996 Atlanta Torch Carrier used in City Demonstration.

3-D Model Credit: Kleizer-Walczak. Photo credit: Michael Sinclair/Frank Witz. Multimedia Technology Lab Project, Georgia Tech.

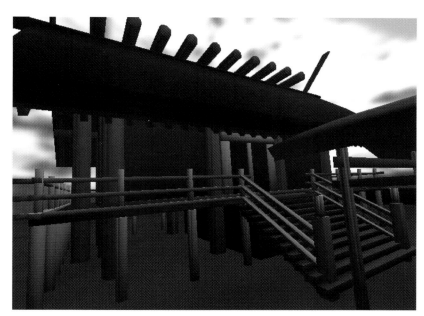

Shrine2. Side View of a Japanese Temple. 1991 Competition Winner—Lucas Santosa, College of Architecture, Imagine Group.

Photo Credits: Thomas Meyer/Lucas Santosa/Tolek Lesniewski. GVU Lab Project: DVE, Georgia Tech.

Hmd. HMD, Data Glove, and Elevator (worn by Thomas Meyer)

Photo Credits: Thomas Meyer/Rob Kooper. GVU Lab Project: ICV, Georgia Tech.

Ivex1. IVEX Corporation Flight Simulator. Image showing light points on runway.

Ivex2. IVEX Corporation Flight Simulator. Image showing light points and fog on runway.

Ivex4. IVEX Corporation Flight Simulator. Image showing 3-D models of buildings in scene.

Ivex7. IVEX Corporation Flight Simulator. Image showing tank simulation.

Ivex10. IVEX Corporation Flight Simulator. Image showing incredible textured mountains and terrain.

Balcony1. View from a balcony.

Photo Credits: Rob Kooper/Larry Hodges. GVU Lab Project: Phobia, Georgia Tech.

Bridge1. View from a bridge over a river.

Photo Credits: Rob Kooper/Larry Hodges. GVU Lab Project: Phobia, Georgia Tech.

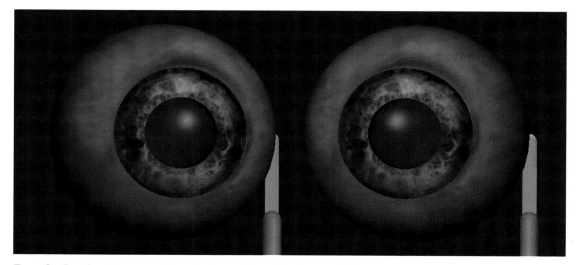

Eyes2. Ocular Surgery Simulator—Fusable Stereo Pair.

In conjunction with the Medical College of Georgia. Photo Credit: Michael Sinclair. Multimedia Technology Lab Project, Georgia Tech.

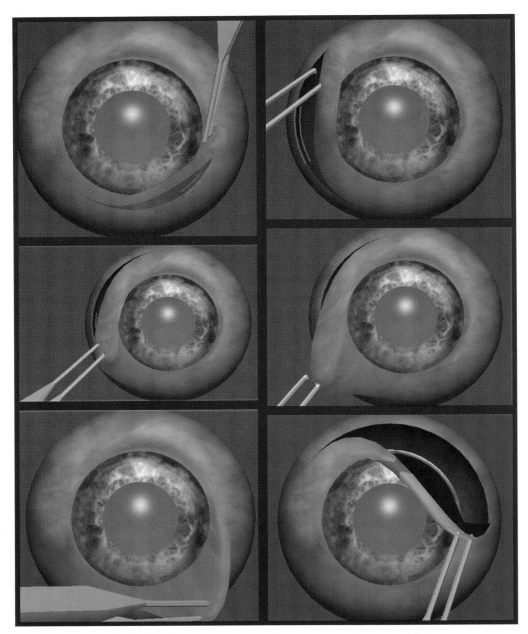

Eyes. Georgia Tech/MCG Eye Surgery Simulation, October 1993.

In conjunction with the Medical College of Georgia. Photo Credit: Michael Sinclair. Multimedia Technology Lab Project, Georgia Tech.

```
                                z_rotation_matrix, matrix2 );         \
                break;                                                 \
        }                                                              \
}


//      create a translate matrix where
//              1) vector holds (x,y,z) translation factors to produce a
translation matrix
//              2) matrix = translate_matrix * matrix
#define        alg_translate_4x4_matrix( vector, matrix )             \
{                                                                     \
        alg_matrix_4x4_type   translate_matrix =                      \
                alg_identity_matrix_4x4;                              \
        alg_matrix_4x4_type   matrix1;                                \
                                                                      \
        translate_matrix.mat[0][3] = -vector.x;                       \
        translate_matrix.mat[1][3] = -vector.y;                       \
        translate_matrix.mat[2][3] = -vector.z;                       \
                                                                      \
        alg_multiply_4x4_matrix( matrix1, translate_matrix, matrix ); \
        alg_copy_4x4_matrix( matrix, matrix1 );                       \
}


//      multiply a vector by a matrix
//              vector = vector1 * matrix
#define    alg_transform_4x4_matrix( vector, matrix, vector1 )    \
{                                                                 \
        vector.x =      matrix.mat[0][0] * vector1.x +            \
                        matrix.mat[0][1] * vector1.y +            \
                        matrix.mat[0][2] * vector1.z +            \
                        matrix.mat[0][3];                         \
        vector.y =      matrix.mat[1][0] * vector1.x +            \
                        matrix.mat[1][1] * vector1.y +            \
                        matrix.mat[1][2] * vector1.z +            \
                        matrix.mat[1][3];                         \
        vector.z =      matrix.mat[2][0] * vector1.x +            \
                        matrix.mat[2][1] * vector1.y +            \
                        matrix.mat[2][2] * vector1.z +            \
                        matrix.mat[2][3];                         \
```

```
}

#endif  //  __ALG_MATX__
```

Section 3—Database Hierarchy and Bubba

This chapter is a discussion of databases for three-dimensional computer graphics. The basic layout for a virtual reality graphics system and database hierarchy are discussed here. Contribution was made to this chapter from Bill Tolhurst's insert into *Photorealism and Ray Tracing*, by Christopher D. Watkins, Stephen B. Coy, and Mark Finlay.

World Order

As with most things, humans desire order, usually hierarchical order. Computer graphics is no different. In order to make it easy for someone to use your graphics engine, you must organize it in such a fashion that they have easy access to sections of the database at different levels, as one transformation may affect only one object in the world (like a spinning top), while another may affect all of the objects in the world (like the viewer turning his head). But you should not make the user deal with the details of the database, unless the user desires to do so.

You can look at a virtual world database as if it were constructed of building blocks. Some sets of blocks may be built up into houses, while others may be built up into cars. One can make copies of the houses and cars and place them anywhere in the world. This is called *instancing* an object. Instancing is a kind of mathematical cookie cutter.

So now, you see that your virtual world is made of building blocks called objects. Well, those objects must be made of something too; like most of the earth, plant life, and organisms are made of carbon, hydrogen, oxygen and nitrogen. And yes, the objects are made of something, and we call these building blocks polygons (triangles and rectangles). Based on how you put your polygons together, you can build almost any object. Much like positioning and orienting objects in your world, you position and orient individual polygons for your object. Picture a soccer ball and the dyocaetriacontahedral mesh of patches that make up its surface.

Okay, you may ask how one defines a polygon. Polygons are defined by two- or three-dimensional coordinates called vertices. See Figure 5.13 for an illustration of polygons existing in two-dimensional and three-dimensional worlds.

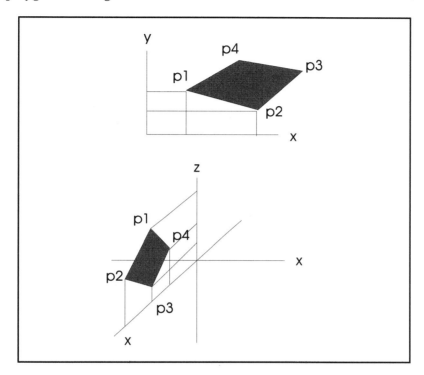

Figure 5.13—2-D and 3-D Coordinate Systems with Polygons

To summarize things, worlds have objects that are made of polygons constructed from vertices. One more time:

our virtual
       world contains
              objects that are constructed from
                     polygons that are defined by
                         vertices

Up until this point, we have blithely assumed that the creation and definition of your three-dimensional environment were a piece of cake. It is as if the world environment specification were the easy part and polygon rendering of the world the hard part. In fact, the opposite is true. The rendering proceeds with only your input as to where to look and an occasional interaction that you might have with an object. Initially positioning objects, setting surface characteristics, and especially building complex models requires extensive use of your mathematical and artistic skills and your time.

Like any other renderer, ours requires complex and fully specified databases with which to interact. This requirement has spawned the creation of companies whose sole products are accurate, detailed databases of everything from the human skeletal structure to helicopters. Other organizations thrive on creating the tools that are used to create, modify, and manage these databases. A trip to your local software dealer would net you at least half a dozen database building products ranging in price (and complexity) from less than $30 to more than $3000.

In the sections that follow, important features of database creation tools are discussed, as well as the importance of a hierarchical approach to creating databases. We also show how affine transformations are applied to take the same basic primitives and scale, rotate, and translate them to make new ones.

The Features of an Ideal Database Modeler

An effective database modeler must provide the user with several key features if it is to be of any commercial value.

Primitive Support and Manipulation

Although it is possible to define an entire world from a least common denominator means such as a list of vertices, it would be extraordinarily difficult and tedious. The modeler should provide a straightforward means for creating elements of the world from collections of predefined graphic elements or "primitives." Typically this creation process is based upon several cardinal primitives such as polygons (that we spoke of earlier), spheres, etc. These primitives should be able to be scaled, rotated, translated, and characterized (e.g., assigned a color, a texture, and other physical properties).

Object Support and Manipulation

In a world of even moderate complexity, manipulating individual primitives is still a daunting task, as there may be anywhere from dozens to thousands of them in the world. In addition, primitives rarely exist on their own, but are collected together to form descriptions of more real-world things like chairs, desks, and cars. Such a collection of primitives is commonly called the "object" that we spoke of earlier.

Manipulating recognizable objects rather than abstract geometric primitives is a much more natural activity for humans (how many times have you heard someone say "Could you move those 143 vertex-common polyhedra closer to the sofa?"). A good modeler must provide means for creating, editing, and placing objects within a world.

The ability to define objects is also integral in creating hierarchical databases, the virtues of which are detailed in the next section.

Database View Update in Human-Tolerable Time

Another key feature that the modeler must provide is a view of the database under construction so that it can be reviewed as it is being built. The fidelity of this view must be traded off against the speed with which the view can be generated. A modeler that produces images nearly identical to that of the renderer but takes as long to generate would be of little use. You'd just as soon use the renderer directly. On the other hand, if the result of your work is displayed in "real time" within the modeler, but the image the renderer produces looks nothing like your previews (e.g., segments of objects are not properly connected, objects are misplaced, etc.), then the modeler is equally useless.

A typical compromise is to provide a 3-D "wire-frame" view of the database from within the modeler. This wire-frame representation of the database is formed by using lines and arcs to create an accurate outline of the objects in view. The resulting image is similar to a Tinkertoy rendition of the objects: sides and endpoints are visible, but the rest of the object is not. The wire-frame view provides a means for checking the construction and placement geometry of objects. It also yields interactive display update rates, since far fewer pixels have to be processed and displayed than would be the case for a more complete view. With this responsiveness the user can quickly see the results of a change in viewing position or an object parameter.

Another approach is the one that our polygon renderer allows us to take, and that is to produce flat shaded objects with which you can interact. This will, of course, have a slower update rate, and things will be a little sluggish, but it is a nice compromise between having just ugly lines and arcs on the screen interactively and a beautiful, yet noninteractive image.

Free Movement through the Database

Most of us find it useful when building a model of something to examine both the item being modeled and the model itself from a number of perspectives. Blueprints for a construction site often include a plan view, which is drawn as if the site were being seen from above, as well as elevation views, drawn from a ground-level perspective.

The capability to move freely throughout the database and evaluate it from several points of view is analogous to multiple views provided in blueprints. In worlds of even moderate complexity, some objects may be partially or completely obscured from view by others. It may be necessary to "zoom in" to an area for greater level-of-detail examination. In addition, relative scale and placement between objects change with eyepoint position. 3-D models typically need to be viewed from several perspectives to ensure proper placement.

Hiding Gory Details of the Database

Another useful feature of a modeler is that it effectively removes the requirement to know anything about the details of the database file format. When you are artistically inspired to produce the graphics equivalent of the Mona Lisa, you'd rather not have to worry about trivialities such as whether polygon vertices are delimited by parentheses or curly braces as in an ASCII world definition file. The modeler is programmed with knowledge of such details and performs the formatting automatically. Those of us with less than stellar typing technique benefit greatly from this feature.

The Importance of Hierarchy in Database Construction

As we mentioned at the beginning of the chapter, the construction of the database describing the world and its elements is the most time-consuming part of the task of producing computer graphics. As a result, you typically want to avoid "reinventing the wheel," which in the following case can be taken both figuratively and literally.

Suppose you are creating a world which includes an automobile, perhaps a brand new Hommina-Pow-Zoom VQZ-5000/LE-X-VR. You'll need to include the four wheels in your world description (Huh? No, no. The Mag-Lev version is the /LE-M). Being the stickler for detail and glutton for punishment that you are, you take hundreds of accurate measurements from a neighbor's /LE-X-VR (you spend your extra pesos on much less expensive and more intellectually sound things like graphics books) and after a time have created the ultimate model of a wheel.

Now you certainly wouldn't expect to have to go through this arduous process again and again (and again) to create four separate wheels from scratch. Rather, you would like to create four copies of your original wheel model within the world. In other words, you would place four "instances" of a wheel "object" at appropriate places within the world. The instancing approach establishes the means for building a database hierarchy. If collections of objects can themselves be objects, then the mechanism exists to support a hierarchy with a practically unlimited number of levels.

You obtain several benefits by approaching your database efforts in a hierarchical fashion, and it is interesting to note that they are similar to the benefits provided through following classic structured programming techniques (so someone told us). These benefits can be summarized as (there will be a test on this!):

Reuse, flexibility, locality, extensibility, and efficiency.

Reuse

As in the preceding example, objects can be used repeatedly within the same world or across several worlds.

Flexibility

Since each instance of an object is a separate entity within the world, each can be independently scaled, rotated, translated, textured, etc.

Locality and Extensibility

What if, after all your modeling work, it turns out that the manufacturer of the /LE-X-VR has recalled them all to be refitted with a different style of wheel (something about them flying off the car at sustained speeds over 40 MPH—you know, I really hate it when that happens). The new wheel has a different hub construction. After gathering new measurement data, you alter the wheel object database to reflect the design changes. Not only will all your future models be corrected, but since all the models you have done in the past used instances of the wheel object rather than hard-coded descriptions of the wheel, all of your /LE-X-VR renderings and visualizations will be correct the next time they are visualized. In this way you have taken advantage of the localized nature of the data describing the wheel.

Now consider that the manufacturer offers a special hub cover as an option. You couldn't change the standard wheel model, since a given vehicle may or may not have the hub cover. You could, however, make a different model based on the standard wheel which includes the hub cover. Or better yet, you could simply model the hub cover as its own object, then create a higher-level object which contains the standard wheel and the hub cover. In either case you have extended the applicability of your wheel model.

Efficiency

Once an object has been modeled and "debugged," your time can be more effectively spent on creating new objects and on the process of integrating objects into new worlds.

There are further benefits of this approach when you want to interact with a given object. For example, if we decide to drive our virtual car using our automobile, we'll need the wheels to rotate to provide the illusion of motion. This is a simple matter when the wheels are separate objects, but would be very difficult if the description of each wheel was integral with the rest of the automobile model.

A Virtual Reality Modeler

So far, we have talked a lot about databases and hierarchy. Now let's take a quick look at what makes up a basic virtual reality world modeler and visualizer.

Materials Factory

All objects are made of something. This module defines what the materials are and their physical properties (e.g., intrinsic color, surface texture, deformability, reflectivity).

Laws of Nature Maker

It seems that a world not only has objects but also has universal rules for object-object interactions and object-world environment interactions. This module helps define those rules.

Object Builder

This is a tool for creating object descriptions and databases. It deals with paradigms for object construction/description, including the facet/vertex list like the one we used, and others like an approach that better handles active (e.g., light source) as well as passive objects. Here we also define object mechanics.

World Builder

This is a tool for defining the extent and contents of the virtual world. It allows you to place objects within the world and establish "initial conditions," since you expect that objects will be manipulated in time. Of interest is a means for defining what happens at the "edge" of the world: reflected world? truncated world? This would include an interactive rate viewer, since manipulation of objects within the world will occur at real time rates.

Stimulus/Response Linker

Links a certain stimulus from the environment to a particular action based on object mechanics perviously defined.

Involver

The interactive rate viewer.

Bubba's Database Hierarchy: Primitives, Objects, and Worlds

First of all, let us introduce you to Bubba. Yes, our interactive, desktop virtual reality visualizer's name is Bubba. We called it Bubba because it has the basic functionality of a VR system, without all of the bells and whistles to confuse you about its functionality.

Now that we have to this point extolled the virtues of hierarchical database construction, let's look at how this approach is supported within Bubba. Bubba supports a database hierarchy consisting of primitives, objects, and worlds. Five types of primitives are recognized by Bubba: the polygon, the rectangular prism, the sphere, the ring, and the cone. As many of each type of primitive as desired can be used to create objects, or primitives may be used by themselves. Objects are collections of primitives and/or other objects, with each object definition stored in a separate object file. By convention, an object file has .VRO as its file extension. A world specifies parameters such as the viewer position within the world, lighting types and placement, etc. The world also includes references to objects which make up the world, specifying their placement, orientation, and other characteristics for each instance of the object. This information is stored in a world file. By convention, a world file has .VR as its file extension.

Quick Review of Bubba's Graphics Primitives

Bubba is lucky to recognize the following graphics primitives:

The Polygon Primitive

The polygon primitive uses three or more planar vertices which define a convex surface. Polygons require parameters detailing the number of vertices and world space X,Y,Z positions of each vertex.

The Rectangular Prism Primitive

This primitive is actually constructed from six four-vertex polygon primitives. It is defined by two three-dimensional points at the extents. This primitive may also be called a cuboid. Its untransformed shape is a cube. It can be scaled along any dimension in order to make it into a prism.

The Sphere Primitive

You've seen a sphere? Well, this makes one. Parameters giving the center in world space X, Y, Z and the radius are required.

The Ring Primitive

The ring creates washer and disk shapes (a disk is a ring with an inner radius of zero). A ring is described by parameters specifying its center, surface normal, and minimum and maximum radius.

The Cone Primitive

The cone primitive creates conic and cylindrical shapes (a cylinder is a cone which has the same radius at both ends). Cones do not have end caps. Parameters specify the centers of the opening at either end in world space X, Y, Z and the radii of the openings. A zero radius at one end produces a pointed cone.

Section 4—Filling Polygons and Anti-Alising

In this section we discuss the basic issue of filling polygons and the more advanced issue of anti-aliasing those polygons. Though our software does not perform anti-aliasing operations due to computational limitations, it is a topic of great importance to computer graphics and the generation of photorealistic images.

As described in the last section, polygons are used to construct objects. Polygons can have the size of a screen pixel and thus represent a point, or they can have many vertices and describe some complex 3-D surface. That makes the polygon a very versatile primitive.

The Polygon

Simply stated, a polygon is a shape formed from lines placed end to end, where the end of the last line touches the beginning of the first line. Drawing just these lines on your computer display would constitute a wire-frame version of whatever object you are displaying using polygons. For our purposes, we will fill in our polygons, since we want to make solid objects. A color-filled polygon is one that has all of the pixels colored that are inside of the closed loop of lines that make up the polygon.

Polygons come in three classes—*convex*, *nonconvex*, and *complex*. See Figure 5.14 for illustration.

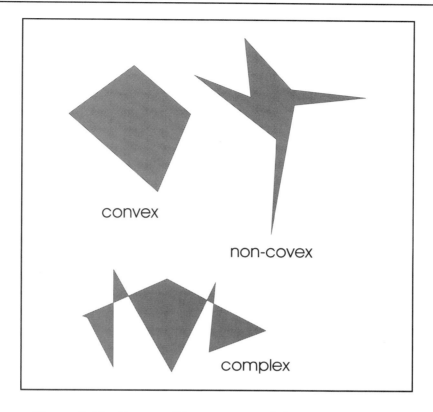

Figure 5.14—Convex, Nonconvex, and Complex Polygons

Our Polygon Definitions

Convex polygons are the type that our polygon renderer Bubba can handle. A convex polygon for our purposes is one for which any line horizontally drawn through the polygon will cross the left edge only once and the right edge only once (excluding any horizontal or zero-length edges of the polygon). Simply stated, neither the left edge nor the right edge of a convex polygon will ever reverse direction from up to down, or down to up. The left and right edges cannot cross each other (though they may touch). This makes for a polygon that can be quickly and easily color-filled.

Nonconvex polygons can have edges that go in any direction, as long as those edges never cross. This makes the color-filling process slower and more complicated, but it is still manageable.

Complex polygons have no limitations as to where the edges can go. Since edges can overlap in a complex polygon, this makes the interesting problem of figuring out which interior parts of the polygon to color-fill.

We use convex polygons because we need performance. The computation cost of nonconvex polygons and especially complex polygons is so high that we could not make a renderer with a suitable screen update rate with them. All objects can be constructed from convex polygons, so we are not limited here.

Color Filling the Convex Polygon

The fundamental principle of filling a polygon on a raster display is the decomposition of a polygon into an array of horizontal lines. We must draw a horizontal line for each raster display scan line (horizontal row of pixels) within the polygon. We will call this process rasterization of the polygon. Rasterization of convex polygons is simply done by starting at the top of the polygon and following down the left and right edges—one scan line (vertical pixel) at a time, filling in the area between the two edges on each scan line, until the bottom of the polygon is reached. Note that this approach is valid only for convex polygons.

Okay, so scan converting polygons is a bed of roses, right? Not true. There are a couple of concerns that make it a bit of work.

The first concern is not so bad; it is the efficiency of polygon rasterization. It is hard to develop efficient code that simultaneously follows two edges from the top of the polygon down and fills in the pixels between them. A simple solution is to decouple the computation of the horizontal lines (the scan conversion of the polygon into a horizontal line list) from the actual drawing of those horizontal lines. This has the advantage of separating what should be device-independent routines like the horizontal line list computations from the device-dependent horizontal line display.

The second concern exists because we want our polygons to fit close together. Our objects are created from clusters of adjacent polygons. If we use some standard line drawing routine to compute the polygon edges, we will get points that fall outside the polygon. This occurs because a line is a one-dimensional creature, and we merely approximate the actual line with our computer display by coloring pixels nearest to the actual line on either side of it.

Well, you might see where we are headed; the key word is "adjacent." We need adjacent polygons, and if we are placing points that fall on either side of the actual line, when we place a second polygon adjacent to an already drawn one, the second will overwrite the first, possibly making an unacceptable image. Please note that standard line drawing routines can be useful when polygons do not overlap, especially when they do not overlap and you want to add borders (different colored edges) to your polygons. And as you may have guessed, that leads us to an algorithm for adjacent polygon drawing.

Drawing Adjacent Polygons

To start, any edge-following or tracing algorithm must select only pixels that are inside the polygon—none of that pixel on either side of the line stuff. This equates to shifting a standard line drawing routine to the left or to the right by one-half pixel, always toward the interior of the polygon.

That leaves us with two cases, points that are exactly on the boundary and points that lie on vertices. For those two cases, we draw these points only once. To do that, we stipulate that points located exactly on nonhorizontal edges are drawn only if the interior of the polygon is to the right. That means that left edges are drawn and right edges are not. Points that are located exactly on horizontal edges are drawn only if the interior of the polygon is below them. That means that horizontal top edges are drawn and horizontal bottom edges are not. A vertex is drawn only if all lines ending at that vertex meet the other two conditions; therefore, no right or bottom edges end at that vertex.

All polygon edges, excluding flat tops and bottoms, will be considered edges. The left edge is the line that starts from the top of the polygon and tends to the left. The right edge is the line that starts from the top of the polygon and tends to the right.

Following these rules guarantees that a pixel of the first polygon will not be overwritten by a pixel of the adjacent second polygon. So we now have an algorithm to implement.

The Polygon Filling Routine

The function *alg_draw_convex_polygon_to_screen_buffer* is our polygon filling routine. It expects a list of vertices that describe a convex polygon. The last vertex is assumed to be the first vertex. The function creates the horizontal line list described above and passes it to the *alg_draw_horz_line_list_to_screen_buffer* for drawing into a screen buffer.

alg_draw_convex_polygon_to_screen_buffer starts by finding the top and the bottom of the given polygon. It then figures from the top point the ends of the top edge.

If the two ends are at different locations, the top is flat. It the top is flat, it will be easy to find the starting vertices and directions through the vertex list for the left and right edges. Also, the top scan line of the polygon should be drawn without the rightmost pixel colored. This is because only the rightmost pixel of a horizontal edge that makes up the top scan line can be part of a right edge.

If the two ends are at the same location, the top is not flat, it is pointed, and the top scan line is not drawn. It is part of the right edge by our rules. When the top is not flat, it is difficult to determine in which direction through the vertex list the left and right edges go, as both edges start at the same (top) vertex. To solve this problem, we compare the slopes of the two edges.

Now that we know where the left edge starts in the vertex list, we can perform our scan conversion of the left edge of the polygon from top to bottom, producing the starting x positions for our horizontal line list. Note that the nearest x coordinate on or to the right (interior of the polygon) is chosen. This avoids drawing a vertex twice and avoids drawing the bottom scan line. Note that the first scan line of our polygon is not drawn if the top is not flat.

Now that we have a list of scan-converted left points for our horizontal lines, we must produce the corresponding list of right points. This is very similar to computation of the left list, except that every edge in the right edge is moved one pixel to the left before scan conversion. This gives us the nearest point to the left of the edge but not on the edge.

Well, now that we know how to make convex polygons and have some idea about how the polygon filling code works, let us take a look at a very useful concept called anti-aliasing.

Image Quality and Spatial Aliasing

The bane of computer graphics are the many and sundry aliasing problems Aliasing is defined in engineering as the erroneous appearance of low-frequency signals resulting from insufficient sampling of a high-frequency signal. The high-frequency signal then masquerades (or aliases) as a low-frequency signal in the sampled data. The most common form (though by no means the only one) in computer graphics is the "jaggies" or "stair-step" edges of scanned polygons. The problem results from the fact that the screen represents a finite sampling, the pixels, of an infinitely high spatial frequency signal, an edge or a texture pattern. When we create the scan-converted polygons described above, we are sampling. It is not hard to see how, in the absence of any other techniques, simply color filling a polygon will frequently fractionally miss edges. This becomes most apparent in any kind of motion like a virtual walk-through, in which the aliasing problems become very distracting along object edges. The problem is also evident when texture patterns are used. As the objects move into the distance, the pattern is sampled less and less frequently, resulting in sampling errors.

Some of the more common graphics aliasing artifacts are shown in images where a bright line is drawn on a computer display against a dark background. The "jaggies" are everywhere. Other common images that show off aliasing artifacts are the checker pattern to the horizon and the zone plate to the horizon.

Let us explore the problem of aliasing further and see how various anti-aliasing techniques can help minimize the artifacts.

Anti-Aliasing

As mentioned above, aliasing problems result when a high-frequency signal is sampled at too low a sampling rate. With a regular sampling pattern, these high-frequency signals appear as low-frequency ones, or beat frequencies. One of the worst case tests of any anti-aliasing schemes is the checkerboard texture (alternating black and white) projected on a flat plane. As the pattern goes off into the horizon, the frequency of the checkerboard gets higher and higher (black and white squares appear closer) due to the perspective. Eventually, the spacing is smaller than adjacent screen pixels, and, voila!, you have aliasing problems. The regular sampling scheme will create new patterns in the image that look almost unrelated to the checkerboard spacing. It turns out that the human eye is very sensitive to such sampling artifacts and we generally find such images objectionable.

Given that some sort of adaptive supersampling must be used to combat the aliasing artifacts, the trick now is to apply the supersampling only on pixels that intersect object edges or are in areas of high contrast, such as in a spotlight or a textured area, thus adaptive. If half of the final image is covered by the background or by a large smooth object, then half of the computing time has been wasted on regions that did not need it.

First, note that for the most part, adjacent screen pixels will intersect the same polygons of objects, just at slightly different positions. Second, only the areas of high contrast exhibit noticeable aliasing problems. We therefore wish to concentrate on these areas, and not on large areas of smooth changes or on the background. The job then becomes the detection of edges and/or high-contrast transitions such as in the checkerboard pattern. This leads us to adaptive anti-aliasing. The renderer decides how to smear (locally average colors) the image by comparing colors of adjacent pixels to see if they are within some user-defined threshold value (or alternatively, that they both intersect the background).

Now that we know what aliasing is and have been very briefly introduced to a method for performing anti-aliasing, let us look at the problem of aliasing when we are moving and/or the objects in our world are moving.

Motion Anti-Aliasing

Wagon Wheels and Temporal Aliasing

Moving the viewer and moving objects within a world introduce yet another potential problem into our imagery, namely that of temporal aliasing. Just as spatial aliasing causes problems in the quality of imagery, temporal aliasing can produce equivalent problems in a scene in motion. The basic situation is the same as in rendering the scene; we are sampling the motion at discrete points in time and at a finite rate. If the motion is too rapid, it will be sampled incorrectly and odd artifacts result. The classic case of this is watching the wagon wheel spokes in old cowboy movies. Movies record a scene at 24 frames per second (each frame is chopped for 48-fps display). When the wheels are rapidly turning, the camera undersamples the rotation and motion appears awkward, such as appearing to rotate backward. The same effect can occur with any type of motion where changes occur more rapidly than the frame rate can effectively sample.

Motion Blur

The wagon wheel problem can be solved, at least partially, by the temporal equivalent of anti-aliasing. The technique is also commonly referred to as motion blur. A motion-blurred wagon wheel will appear as a blur rather than individual spokes. As with all things, you have traded off the aliasing artifacts for lower resolution in time. You can no longer discern quite as fine and rapid a motion as you can in the non-motion-blurred case. However, it usually does not matter, since you can't trust the result in the non-anti-aliased image (wheel turning backward???).

Textures and Aliasing

We said that anti-aliasing is important when using texture mapping. The problem gets worse in a scene with motion. The reason, of course, is that now the actual texture map–-pixel intersections vary slightly from image to image in the motion. Any aliasing problems will be compounded and appear as the "crawlies" or random dot motion in the texture. Motion blur is an effect method for reducing the crawlies.

Progressive Refinement

And a final note on efficiency of anti-alising motion-filled virtual reality renderings. A technique called progressive refinement says that you can hold off on anti-aliasing the image until the motion stops. This way you can use all of those compute cycles to deal with motion, image update rates, and worry about the "jaggies" and "crawlies" only when the image on the computer display is still (the viewer is not moving, or the objects in the scene are still).

PROGRAM LISTINGS:

```
/*

       +---------------------------------------------------------------------+
       |                                                                     |
       |                     Virtual Reality ExCursions                      |
       |                                                                     |
       |          by Christopher D. Watkins and Stephen R. Marenka           |
       |                                                                     |
       |               Copyright 1994 : Academic Press, Inc.                 |
       |                                                                     |
       |---------------------------------------------------------------------|
       |                           ALG_POLY.C                                |
```

```
|--------------------------------------------------------------------|
|                                                                    |
|                        Software Issues                             |
|                                                                    |
|             Copyright 1987-1994 ALGORITHM, Incorporated.           |
|                                                                    |
|        ALL RIGHTS RESERVED.   This software is Published, but is NOT  |
|    Public Domain and remains the property of ALGORITHM, Incorporated and |
|             Christopher D. Watkins.   This software may not be       |
|   reproduced or integrated into other packages without the prior written |
|             consent of Christopher D. Watkins.   Licensing is possible. |
|                                                                    |
+--------------------------------------------------------------------+
*/


//      system includes
#include       <math.h>
#include       <alloc.h>


//      Algorithm, Inc. includes
#include       "Alg_Mem.H"
#include       "Alg_Defs.H"
#include       "Alg_Matx.H"
#include       "Alg_Scrn.H"
#include       "Alg_3D.H"


/*

    +------------------------------------------------------------------+
    |                  convex polygon filling routine                  |
    +------------------------------------------------------------------+


    CONVEX means that every horizontal line drawn through the polygon at
        any point will cross exactly two active edges (horizontal
        lines and zero-length edges are not considered active edges)
        and that the right and left edges never cross.

    See Dr. Dobb's Journal, February and March 1991, for the excellent
        articles "The Polygon Primeval" and "Fast Convex Polygons"
        written by Michael Abrash.  This code is based on some of the
```

```
       code found in the February "The Polygon Primeval" article.  I
       highly recommend obtaining copies of these articles, if you need
       high polygon display rates, or if you just want to learn more
       about polygon generation beyond convex polygons (i.e.,
       overlapping complex polygons).
*/



// used to advance index by one vertex forward or backward with wrap
#define FORWARD          1
#define BACKWARD        -1

#define INDEX_FORWARD(index)     index = (index + FORWARD) % num_vertices
#define INDEX_BACKWARD(index)  index = (index + BACKWARD + \
        num_vertices) % num_vertices


/*

    +------------------------------------------------------------------+
    |                    scan convert polygon edge                     |
    +------------------------------------------------------------------+
*/

// scan converts a polygon edge from (x1,y1) to (x2,y2).  (x2, y2) is '
//      not scan converted in order to avoid overlapping the end of one
//      line with the start of the next. This also causes the bottom
//      scan line of the polygon not to be drawn.  If skip_first is
//      equal to ALG_TRUE, the point at (x1,y1) is not drawn.  For each
//      scan line, the pixel closest to the right of the scanned line is
//      chosen.
static void scan_convert_polygon_edge( alg_point_2D_int_type     p1,
                                       alg_point_2D_int_type     p2,
                                       alg_boolean               set_x_start,
                                       alg_boolean               skip_first,
                                       alg_horz_line_type   **edge_point_ptr
)
{
        alg_point_3D_int_type    line_length;
        alg_int                  y;
        alg_float                inverse_slope;
```

```
        alg_horz_line_type    *working_edge_point_ptr;


// for right-edge scan-conversion, the x coordinates are adjusted
//      one to the left, effectively causing scan conversion of the
//      nearest points to the left of but not exactly on the edge
        if (!set_x_start)
        {
                p1.x -= 1;
                p2.x -= 1;
        }


// calculate edge x and y lengths and the inverse slope of the line
        ALG_VEC2_SUB( p2, p1, line_length );
        // check for horizontal lines
        if ( line_length.y <= 0 )
                return;
        inverse_slope = (alg_float)line_length.x / line_length.y;


// store the x coordinate of the pixel closest to the right of the
//      edge for each y coordinate between y1 and y2, not
//       including y2.  Also do not include y1 if skip_first = ALG_TRUE.

        working_edge_point_ptr = *edge_point_ptr;
        for (y=p1.y+skip_first; y<p2.y; y++)
        {
                // store the x coordinate into the appropriate edge list
                if (set_x_start)
                        working_edge_point_ptr->x_start = p1.x +
                                (alg_int)( ceil((y-p1.y) * inverse_slope));
                else
                        working_edge_point_ptr->x_end   = p1.x +
                                (alg_int)( ceil((y-p1.y) * inverse_slope));
                working_edge_point_ptr++;
        }

        // advance calling function's pointer
        *edge_point_ptr = working_edge_point_ptr;
}
```

```
/*

   +----------------------------------------------------------------+
   |       fills a convex viewport-clipped polygon with flat color  |
   +----------------------------------------------------------------+
*/


void alg_draw_convex_polygon_to_screen_buffer(
      alg_viewport_clipped_polygon_2D_type *viewport_clipped_polygon )
{
      alg_word        vertex_number;

      alg_word        minimum_index_left;
      alg_word        minimum_index_right;
      alg_word        maximum_index;

      alg_word        next_index;
      alg_word        current_index;
      alg_word        previous_index;

      alg_boolean     skip_first;

      alg_int         minimum_point_y, maximum_point_y;

      alg_boolean     flat_top;

      alg_int         left_edge_direction;

      alg_point_2D_int_type        next_line_length;
      alg_point_2D_int_type        previous_line_length;
      alg_long        determinant;

      alg_horz_line_type           *edge_point_ptr;
      alg_horz_line_list_type      working_horz_line_list;

      alg_int         temp;  // for ALG_SWAP

      alg_word        num_vertices = viewport_clipped_polygon->
            num_viewport_clipped_vertices;
      alg_point_2D_int_type        *vertex_ptr =
```

```
            viewport_clipped_polygon-> viewport_clipped_vertex;


// cannot process null polygons
if (num_vertices == 0)
      return;


// scan the list to find the top and the bottom of the polygon


minimum_index_left = 0;
maximum_index      = 0;
minimum_point_y = vertex_ptr[minimum_index_left].y;
maximum_point_y = vertex_ptr[maximum_index].y;
for (vertex_number=1; vertex_number<num_vertices;
      vertex_number++)
{
      if (vertex_ptr[vertex_number].y < minimum_point_y)
      {
            // top
            minimum_index_left = vertex_number;
            minimum_point_y =
                  vertex_ptr[minimum_index_left].y;
      }
      else
      {
            if (vertex_ptr[vertex_number].y > maximum_point_y)
            {
                  // bottom
                  maximum_index = vertex_number;
                  maximum_point_y =
                        vertex_ptr[maximum_index].y;
            }
      }
}


// no zero-height polygons allowed
if (minimum_point_y == maximum_point_y)
      return;


// scan in ascending order to find the last top-edge vertex
```

```
minimum_index_right = minimum_index_left;
while (vertex_ptr[minimum_index_right].y == minimum_point_y)
        INDEX_FORWARD( minimum_index_right );
// back up one to last top-edge vertex
INDEX_BACKWARD( minimum_index_right );

// scan in descending order to find the first top-edge vertex
while (vertex_ptr[minimum_index_left].y == minimum_point_y)
        INDEX_BACKWARD( minimum_index_left );
// back up one to first top-edge vertex
INDEX_FORWARD( minimum_index_left );

// determine directions in the vertex list for the left and
//      right edges, starting from the top vertex

// assume that the left edge runs down through the vertex list
left_edge_direction = BACKWARD;
flat_top = (vertex_ptr[minimum_index_left].x !=
        vertex_ptr[minimum_index_right].x) ? ALG_TRUE :
        ALG_FALSE;
// if the top is flat, figure which end is leftmost
if (flat_top)
{
        if (vertex_ptr[minimum_index_left].x >
                vertex_ptr[minimum_index_right].x)
        {
                // left edge runs up through vertex list
                left_edge_direction = FORWARD;
                // swap indices so that minimum_index_left points
                //      to the start of the left edge, similarly
                //      for minimum_index_right
                ALG_SWAP( minimum_index_left,
                        minimum_index_right);
        }
}
else
{
        // for the two edges pointing down from the top vertex,
        //      point to the downward ends
```

```
            next_index = minimum_index_right;
            INDEX_FORWARD( next_index );
            previous_index = minimum_index_left;
            INDEX_BACKWARD( previous_index );

            // calculate x and y lengths from the top vertex to the
            //      end of the first line down each edge; use lengths
            //      to compare slopes and determine which line is
            //      leftmost
            ALG_VEC2_SUB( vertex_ptr[next_index],
                    vertex_ptr[minimum_index_left], next_line_length);
            ALG_VEC2_SUB( vertex_ptr[previous_index],
                    vertex_ptr[minimum_index_left],
                        previous_line_length );

            determinant = ALG_VEC2_DETERMINANT( next_line_length,
                    previous_line_length, alg_long );

            if ( determinant < 0L )
            {
                    // left edge runs up through vertex list
                    left_edge_direction = FORWARD;
                    // swap indices so that minimum_index_left points
                    //      to the start of the left edge, similarly
                    //      for minimum_index_right
                    ALG_SWAP( minimum_index_left,
                            minimum_index_right);
            }
    }


    // compute the number of scan lines in the polygon, skipping the
    //      bottom edge.  Skip the top vertex also, if the top is not
    //      flat, because the top vertex in that case has a right
    //      edge component.  Set the top scan line to draw, which is
    //      likewise the second line of the polygon unless the top is
    //      flat
    working_horz_line_list.num_horz_lines = maximum_point_y -
            minimum_point_y-1 + flat_top;
```

```
        // return if nothing to draw
        if (working_horz_line_list.num_horz_lines <= 0)
                return;


        working_horz_line_list.y_start = minimum_point_y+1 - flat_top;


        // allocate memory for the line list we will generate
        working_horz_line_list.horz_line_list_ptr = ALG_MALLOC(
                            working_horz_line_list.num_horz_lines,
alg_horz_line_type );
        if ( working_horz_line_list.horz_line_list_ptr == NULL )
                return;


        // scan the left edge and store the boundary points in the list


        // skip the first point of the first line unless the top is
        //     flat, if the top is not flat, the top vertex is exactly
        //     on a right edge and is not drawn
        skip_first = flat_top ? ALG_FALSE : ALG_TRUE;
        // initial pointer for storing scan converted left-edge
        //     coordinates
        edge_point_ptr = working_horz_line_list.horz_line_list_ptr;
        // start from the top of the left edge
        previous_index = minimum_index_right;
        current_index  = minimum_index_right;
        // scan convert each line in the left edge from top to bottom
        do
        {
                if (left_edge_direction == BACKWARD)
                        INDEX_FORWARD( current_index );
                else
                        INDEX_BACKWARD( current_index );
                scan_convert_polygon_edge(vertex_ptr[previous_index],
                                    vertex_ptr[current_index],
                                    ALG_FALSE, skip_first,
                                    &edge_point_ptr);
                previous_index = current_index;
                // now we should scan convert the first point
```

```
            skip_first = ALG_FALSE;
      }
      while (current_index != maximum_index);


      // scan the right edge and store the boundary points in the list


      // skip the first point of the first line unless the top is
      //     flat; if the top is not flat, the top vertex is exactly
      //     on a right edge and is not drawn
      skip_first = flat_top ? ALG_FALSE : ALG_TRUE;
      // initial pointer for storing scan converted right-edge
      //     coordinates
      edge_point_ptr = working_horz_line_list.horz_line_list_ptr;
      // start from the top of the left edge
      previous_index = minimum_index_left;
      current_index  = minimum_index_left;
      // scan convert each line in the right edge from top to bottom.
      do
      {
            if (left_edge_direction == FORWARD)
                  INDEX_FORWARD( current_index );
            else
                  INDEX_BACKWARD( current_index );
            scan_convert_polygon_edge(vertex_ptr[previous_index],
                                    vertex_ptr[current_index],
                                    ALG_TRUE, skip_first,
                                    &edge_point_ptr);
            previous_index = current_index;
            // now we should scan convert the first point
            skip_first = ALG_FALSE;
      }
      while (current_index != maximum_index);


      // draw the horizontal line list that represents the
      //     scan converted polygon to the screen buffer
      alg_draw_horz_line_list_to_screen_buffer(
            &working_horz_line_list, viewport_clipped_polygon->color,
            viewport_clipped_polygon->texture );
```

```
                    // free memory
                    ALG_FREE( working_horz_line_list.horz_line_list_ptr );


                    return;
          }
```

And now a look at the horizontal line list drawing code segment from ALG_SCRN.C (Copyright 1987–1994 Algorithm, Inc.).

```
/*

    +-------------------------------------------------------------------+
    | draw the horizontal line list for a polygon to the screen frame   |
    | buffer                                                            |
    +-------------------------------------------------------------------+
      Code segment from ALG_SCRN.C (Copyright 1987-1994 Algorithm, Inc.).
*/


void alg_draw_horz_line_list_to_screen_buffer(
        alg_horz_line_list_type *horz_line_list_type_ptr,
        alg_byte color, alg_word texture )
{
        alg_horz_line_type    *horz_line_list_ptr;
        alg_int               xs, xe, ys, ye, y, ys_old;
        alg_int               temp;    // for ALG_SWAP

        alg_int                      x,a,b;

        ys = ys_old = horz_line_list_type_ptr->y_start;
        ye = ys + horz_line_list_type_ptr->num_horz_lines;

        if ( (ys < 0) && (ye < 0) )
              return;
        if ( (ys >= ALG_SCREEN_HEIGHT) && (ye >= ALG_SCREEN_HEIGHT) )
              return;
        if (ys > ye)
              ALG_SWAP(ys, ye);
        if (ys < 0)
              ys = 0;
        if (ye >= ALG_SCREEN_HEIGHT)
```

```
        ye = ALG_SCREEN_HEIGHT-1;

// point to the x_start/x_end descriptor for the first
//      horizontal line
horz_line_list_ptr = horz_line_list_type_ptr->horz_line_list_ptr
        + abs(ys - ys_old);

// draw each horizontal line in turn, starting with the top one
//      and advancing one line each time
for (y=ys; y<ye; y++)
{
        xs = horz_line_list_ptr->x_start;
        xe = horz_line_list_ptr->x_end;

        if ( (xs < 0) && (xe < 0) )
            continue;
        if ( (xs >= ALG_SCREEN_WIDTH ) && (xe >=
                    ALG_SCREEN_WIDTH) )
            continue;
        if (xs > xe)
            ALG_SWAP(xs, xe);
        if (xs < 0)
            xs = 0;
        if (xe >= ALG_SCREEN_WIDTH)
            xe = ALG_SCREEN_WIDTH-1;

        switch (texture)
        {
            case TEXTURE_OFF:
                _fmemset( ALG_SCREEN_BUFFER +
                        ALG_Y_PRECALC[y] + xs,
                        color,
                        xe - xs + 1 );
            break;

            case TEXTURE_TRANSPARENT:
                for (x=xs; x<xe; x++)
                {
                    if ( ((x + y) % 2) == 1 )
```

```
                                     ALG_SCREEN_BUFFER[
                                          ALG_Y_PRECALC[y] + x] =
                                               color;
                    }
              break;


              case TEXTURE_CHECKER:
                    for (x=xs; x<xe; x++)
                    {
                          a = (x>>2)%10000;
                          b = (y>>2)%10000;
                          if ( ((a + b) % 2) == 1 )
                                ALG_SCREEN_BUFFER[
                                     ALG_Y_PRECALC[y] + x] =
                                          225;
                          else
                                ALG_SCREEN_BUFFER[
                                     ALG_Y_PRECALC[y] + x] =
                                               color;
                    }
              break;
              }

              horz_line_list_ptr++;
        }

    return;
```

Section 5—Projecting Polygons

You may have remembered from the introduction of this chapter that we needed to get our polygons from the three-dimensional virtual and mathematically defined world onto our very real two-dimensional computer display. Remember that the computer display acts like a window into the virtual world for us, much as the airplane cockpit acts as a window into the real world for the pilot. We see a likeness of the world through the window.

You may also recall that we perform many projections of polygons from the three-dimensional polygonal world onto the two-dimensional screen using geometry and trigonometry and that all of the objects in the world are transformed relative to the viewer, so that only certain objects will be projected onto the screen, the ones that you should see.

Well, this very short section will describe the mathematics required to perform parallel and perspective projections. For our purposes, we want to create a realistic-looking world, and to do that we need perspective.

Parallel Projection

First, let us look at the special case of parallel projection, where the screen, or viewing surface, is parallel to the xy plane. We assume that the computer display is to be parallel to the xy plane, and our viewer is looking along the z axis of the view plane. This is a type of projection where the z coordinate is discarded. As you would expect, the z coordinate is essential for the computation of perspective. A parallel projection is formed when you extend parallel lines from each vertex of the polygon until they intersect the plane of the computer display. See Figure 5.15 for an example of parallel projection. The point of intersection with the computer display is called the projection of the vertex. Project those three-dimensional polygon world coordinate points in the order in which they were defined in the database. We call these projected points vertices and store these two-dimensional coordinates (vertices) in an array. This array is passed to a polygon filling routine for display in a screen buffer, which is subsequently copied to the computer display, Note that in the general case of parallel projection, we may select any direction for the lines of the projection, as long as these lines do not run parallel to the viewing surface. This general case will require the z coordinate.

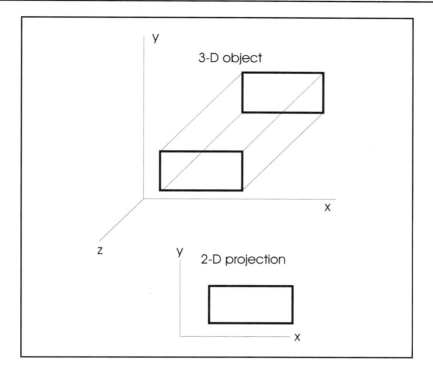

Figure 5.15—Parallel Projection

Perspective Projection

In the case of perspective projection, the z coordinate is very important. The z coordinate gives us a way to taper the scene based on increasing distance from the viewer to the horizon. In perspective projection, the farther away an object is from the viewer, the smaller that object will appear. This size change of an object based on the object's distance from the viewer is a very important depth cue. When many objects are in a scene, the relative sizes of similar objects help cue the brain in on distance. You need this cue, since you have just a single image for both eyes. Without stereo vision for depth cues, you have to have perspective.

In perspective projection, the lines of projection are not parallel lines; they converge at a single point called the *center of projection*, also known as the *vanishing point*. The center of projection is the intersection of all of these converging lines with the plane of the screen that determine the projected image. The projection gives an image that would be seen if the viewer's eye were located at this center of projection. The lines of projection from the object's vertices to the center of projection correspond to the paths of light rays coming from the object to the viewer's eye. See Figure 5.16 for an illustration of perspective projection.

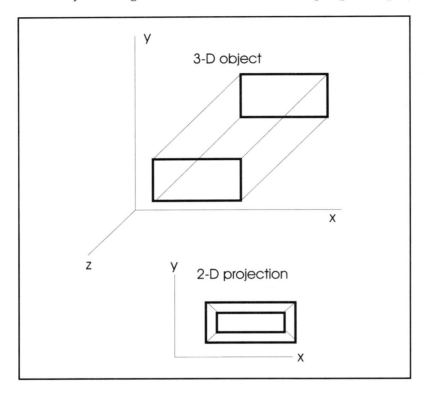

Figure 5.16—Perspective Projection

Remember when, as a kid, you were on a trip with your parents and you were looking out the car windows at layers of trees and mountains, listening to your father speak in colorful metaphors about missing an exit and that he really knew where he was going on that shortcut. Well, you may remember that the mountains usually moved by more slowly than the trees, and the lines in the road and the telephone poles flew past you. Well, this is an example of perspective. Objects that are nearby appear larger and move quickly by you, while objects that are at a a distance move more slowly and appear smaller. As you would expect, we need to create mathematical functions that simulate these effects, and perspective projection gives us that capability.

The way perspective projection works, at least for our simple renderer, is that we perform the projections of the object's polygon vertices as with the parallel projection, with the addition of a z coordinate in the computation. If the z coordinate is small, meaning that the object vertex is nearby, we scale up the xy position of projection, and if the z coordinate is large, meaning that the object vertex is far away, we scale down the xy position of projection. In order to do this, we divide the x and y components of our coodinate with the z coordinate, and scale these new x and y values (our projected values) by a number that represents the distance to the perspective plane. The larger this value, the larger the objects will appear, as the plane will be closer to those objects. Finally, we offset these perspective projected coordinates so that they are in the center of the screen. This completes the perspective projection routine.

PROGRAM LISTINGS:

```
/*

    +------------------------------------------------------------------------+
    |                                                                        |
    |                     Virtual Reality ExCursions                         |
    |                                                                        |
    |          by Christopher D. Watkins and Stephen R. Marenka              |
    |                                                                        |
    |              Copyright 1994 : Academic Press, Inc.                     |
    |                                                                        |
    |------------------------------------------------------------------------|
    |                            ALG_PROJ.C                                  |
    |------------------------------------------------------------------------|
    |                                                                        |
    |                          Software Issues                               |
    |                                                                        |
    |            Copyright 1987-1994 ALGORITHM, Incorporated.                |
    |                                                                        |
    |     ALL RIGHTS RESERVED.   This software is Published, but is NOT      |
    |  Public Domain and remains the property of ALGORITHM, Incorporated and |
    |          Christopher D. Watkins.  This software may not be             |
    |  reproduced or integrated into other packages without the prior written |
    |         consent of Christopher D. Watkins.  Licensing is possible.     |
```

```
        |                                                                    |
    +------------------------------------------------------------------------+
*/

        //      system includes
        #include        <stdlib.h>
        #include        <math.h>

        //      Algorithm, Inc. includes
        #include        "Alg_Defs.H"
        #include        "Alg_Scrn.H"
        #include        "Alg_Proj.H"

        /*
            +----------------------------------------------------------------+
            |            parallel projection of a z-clipped polygon          |
            +----------------------------------------------------------------+
        */

        void parallel_project_z_clipped_polygon( alg_viewer_3D_type *viewer,
                alg_z_clipped_polygon_3D_type *z_clipped_polygon )
        {
                alg_word                vertex_num;
                alg_point_3D_type       *vertex_ptr = z_clipped_polygon-
        >z_clipped_vertex;

                for (vertex_num=0; vertex_num<z_
                        clipped_polygon->num_z_clipped_vertices;
                        vertex_num++)
                {
                        vertex_ptr[vertex_num].x = vertex_ptr[vertex_num].x +
                        (alg_float) ALG_SCREEN_CENTER_X;
                        vertex_ptr[vertex_num].y =
                                vertex_ptr[vertex_num].y +
                                        (alg_float)ALG_SCREEN_CENTER_Y;
                }
        }

        /*
```

```
    +--------------------------------------------------------------+
    |            perspective projection of a z-clipped polygon     |
    +--------------------------------------------------------------+
*/

void perspective_project_z_clipped_polygon( alg_viewer_3D_type *viewer,
        alg_z_clipped_polygon_3D_type *z_clipped_polygon )
{
        alg_word             vertex_num;
        alg_float            inverse_z;
        alg_point_3D_type    *vertex_ptr = z_clipped_polygon-
>z_clipped_vertex;
        alg_float     focal_distance = viewer->focal_distance;

        for (vertex_num=0; vertex_num<
                z_clipped_polygon->num_z_clipped_vertices;
                vertex_num++)
        {
        inverse_z = focal_distance /
                fabs(vertex_ptr[vertex_num].z);
        vertex_ptr[vertex_num].x = vertex_ptr[vertex_num].x *
                inverse_z + (alg_float)ALG_SCREEN_CENTER_X;
        vertex_ptr[vertex_num].y = vertex_ptr[vertex_num].y *
                inverse_z + (alg_float)ALG_SCREEN_CENTER_Y;
        }
```

Section 6—Clipping Polygons

Well, by now, you should have some idea about how polygons that make up our objects are projected and how they are scan-converted for display on your raster computer display. Regarding the projection of those objects, one thing of which you might have thought is what happens when we are sitting within groups of our objects. If we are sitting at a desk in our virtual office, we probably do not see the picture behind us of uncle Bubba on the wall, or even the chair in which we are sitting. If you think about what our equations for perspective projection will do when objects are behind us, you will see that they will basically create a mess on our display. Objects that are behind us will be projected just as the objects in front of us are projected, but with a sort of mirroring effect. You should not see objects behind you, unless you have eyes in the back of your head, and that would be strange, indeed. These projection techniques descibed before are fine, if we are looking at our objects at a distance, but for most virtual reality systems we need to be able to move around throughout the complete virtual world.

Well, there is a solution to this problem, and the solution is called clipping. Clipping will remove polygons or parts of polygons that fall behind us or partially off the sides of the computer display, Clipping is used in conjunction with the perspective projection to project a polygon properly for display on your screen. See Figure 5.17 for a simple example of clipping some lines for display on a compter screen.

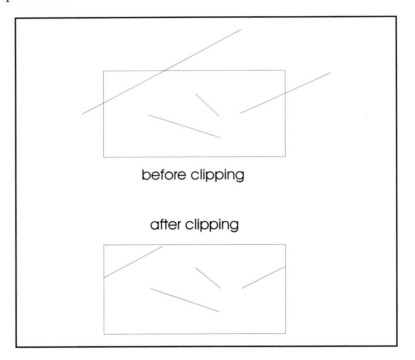

Figure 5.17—Clipping Lines

In a clipping algorithm, it is necessary to determine how a line is positioned relative to some clipping boundary. In Figure 5.17, the rectangle representing the computer display is the boundary, and we want to display any lines or parts of lines that fall within this boundary. In a clipping system, we examine each line scheduled for display to determine whether it lies completely inside the boundary, outside the boundary, or crosses the boundary. If the line is inside, it is displayed. If it is outside, it is trivially clipped and nothing is drawn. If it crosses over the boundary, the point of intersection of the line and boundary must be determined and the portion of the line that lies within the boundary drawn.

The next extension of this concept is to our primitive object, the polygon. Since a polygon is nothing more than a collection of lines called edges, we can apply our algorithm multiple times to clip each edge of the polygon with some boundary. That boundary can be a plane that exists in a three-dimensional world, or it can be a collection of bounding lines that form another polygon. In the preceding example, the edges of the computer display form a rectangle (four-sided polygon). We clip the polygon aginst each of these screen edges individually. See Figure 5.18. This is the Sutherland-Hodgman algorithm applied to clipping a polygon to a screen rectangle. You will see this algorithm again very soon for z-clipping the polygon.

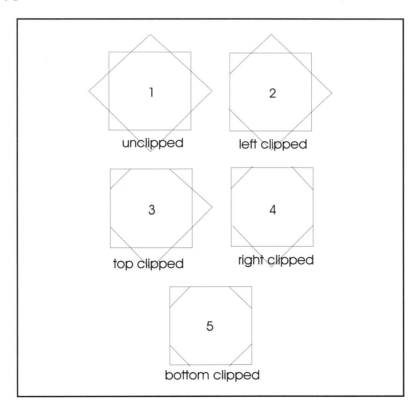

Figure 5.18—Clipping against a Viewport/Screen

As you may have guessed, our virtual reality system needs two types of clipping routines so that we can walk around and through the objects in our virtual world. The first form of clipping is one that clips the polygons in the z dimension (the z dimension represents distance from the viewer along the direction in which the viewer is looking). This is called z-clipping and will effectively remove all of those polygons or parts of polygons that fall behind the viewer. This clipping obviously must be performed before projection, to have any useful effect. The second form of clipping occurs after projection, and it is clipping of the polygons that did not make it fully into the viewable screen area.

We will now look at the two types of clipping that we will use in more detail. We will use the *Sutherland-Hodgman* methodology for clipping polygons in the z dimension before projection. Then we will use another methodology called the *Liang-Barsky* method for clipping polygons. This will be used for the display of those already z-clipped and projected polygons onto the computer screen.

The Sutherland-Hodgman Polygon Algorithm used for Z-Clipping

Up to now, we have discussed the clipping of two-dimensional lines and polygons with a two-dimensional boundary. It is now time to think in three dimensions, where it is not a two-dimensional rectangle that bounds our polygons but some three-dimensional volume. We call this volume a view volume, a clipping volume, or a view frustrum. A view volume is shaped like a box. See Figure 5.19. According to when and how you are clipping, its shape can be that of a rectangular prism (like a cube or cuboid) or some frustrum-shaped volume. Polygons within the view volume are displayed, while those outside it are not. Polygons that cross the boundary of the view volume are cut. Only that portion of the polygon that falls within the view volume is displayed.

All of the edges of a polygon must be tested with each side of the view volume individually. This is similar to testing all of the edges of a two-dimensional polygon with each screen edge, where all edges of the polygon are tested with the left side of the screen, then all edges are tested with the top of the screen, then all edges are tested with the right, and then the bottom of the screen.

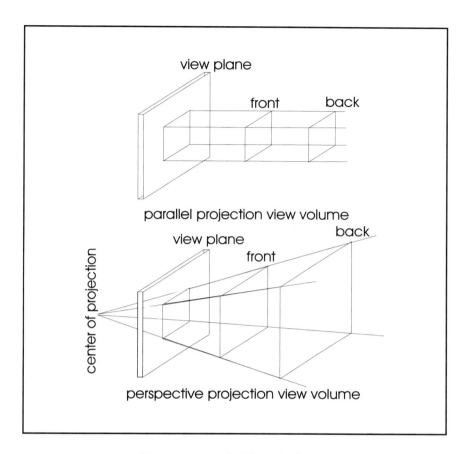

Figure 5.19—A View Volume

With our program, we will use only the front of the view volume (closest plane making the viewing box). We will clip our polygon with this single front plane. We do this in order to remove or clip the polygons that are part of objects that fall behind us. Once again, we do this before projection of the polygon.

For z-clipping a polygon, we test each edge of the polygon with the front clipping plane portion of a view volume. We never actually define a view volume, only the ALG_Z_CLIPPING_PLANE value which defines the z-clipping plane. This value is positive (instead of zero) to guarantee proper calculation of clips. This routine returns a polygon that has been z-clipped and is ready for projection.

Note again that we did not clip against the whole volume (just the front plane), because we will use a clipping routine that is best suited for screen clipping, after we have done the projection of the polygons into two dimensions.

Also note that polygons that have been clipped into non-existence set the trivial_reject flag to ALG_TRUE. This keys in the calling routine that it should not proceed in adding this given polygon to the list of polygons for display.

The Liang-Barsky Polygon Algorithm used for Screen-Clipping

Although multiple applications of the Sutherland-Hodgman method will give you a nicely clipped polygon, when applied to the polygon in three dimensions or when applied to a projected polygon in two dimensions, we chose the Liang-Barsky routine because it is ideal for quickly clipping a two-dimensional polygon with a rectangle. The performance is comparable to and only slightly better than the Sutherland-Hodgman method for the purpose of screen clipping polygons.

For understanding this algorithm, it is best to start with some pseudocode. Below is a listing of the Liang-Barsky polygon clipping algorithm in pseudo-code. See page 930 of *Computer Graphics, Practice and Principles* by Foley, van Dam, Feiner, and Hughes for a detailed description of this algorithm. We will give a brief one in a moment.

```
for (each edge of the polygon)
{
        determine the direction of the given edge

        use this direction to determine which bounding lines for the clip
        region the containing line hits first

        find the t-values for the exit points

        if (t_exit_point2 > 0)
                find t-value for second entry point

        if (t_entry_point2 > t_exit_point1)
        {
                no visible segment
                if (0 < t_exit_point1 <= 1)
                        output_vertex(turning vertex)
        }
        else
```

```
        {
                if ((0 < t_exit_point1) and (1 >= t_entry_point2))
                {
                        there is some visible part
                        if (0 <= t_entry_point2)
                                output_vertex(appropriate side intersection)
                        else
                                output_vertex(starting vertex)

                        if (1 >= t_exit_point1)
                                output_vertex(appropriate side intersection)
                        else
                                output_vertex(ending vertex)
                }
        }

        if (0 < t_exit_point2 <= 1)
                output_vertex(appropriate corner)
}
```

To understand this algorithm, we must think of an edge in parametric form. This means that we call the starting vertex for the edge 0 and the ending vertex for the edge 1. Values between 0 and 1, called t-values, carry us some distance along the edge from the starting vertex. This can be represented in parametric equation form as

$$P(t) = (1 - t)P_0 + tP_1$$

To be precise, we let values $0 < t <= 1$ represent points on the edge, omitting the starting point. As with the polygon filling routine discussed earlier, this guarantees that each vertex of the polygon is contained in exactly one of the two edges that meet there.

We start our discussion with diagonal polygon edges. Such edges must cross each of the lines that determine the boundary of the screen window. If we were to divide the viewing plane into nine regions, where the center region is the screen, you can see that every diagonal line passes from one corner region to the opposite corner region. Each window thus divides the plane into two half-planes. We refer to the region containing the screen the inside half-plane. The regions in Figure 5.20 are labeled by the number of inside half-planes they

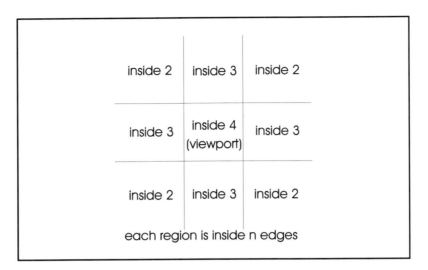

Figure 5.20—Regions for the Liang-Barsky Algorithm

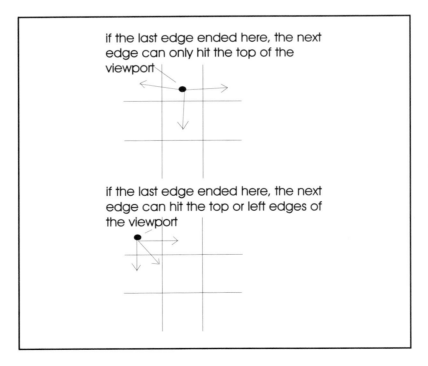

Figure 5.21—The Effects of Totally Outside Edges

lie in. The screen is the only one lying in four. Regions at the corners lie in two and are called corner regions. Regions directly above, below, to the left, and to the right of the screen region lie in three and are called edge regions.

Let us describe the algorithm, using examples. If some part of the edge lies in the screen, that part must be part of the output polygon. The vertices that this edge contributes to the output polygon may be either the ends of the edge (if the edge lies totally inside the screen), or the intersections of the edge with the window edges (if the edge lies totally outside the screen), or there may be one vertex inside the screen and one outside the screen.

Given that both endpoints of an edge lie outside the screen, the next edge may intersect the screen on its journey back into the screen. See Figure 5.21.

If the next edge does intersect the screen, the place where it intersects is determined by its starting point. An edge starting in the upper-edge region can begin its intersection with the screen only by hitting the top edge of the screen, whereas an edge starting in the upper-left corner region can begin its intersection with the screen along either the top boundary or the left boundary.

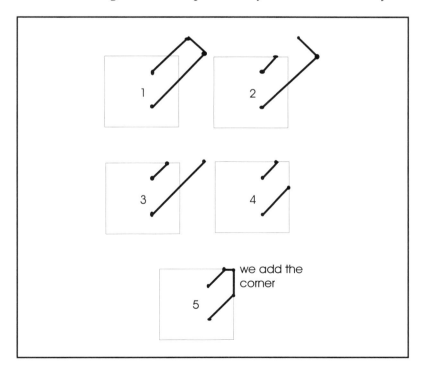

Figure 5.22—Turning Vertex

Imagine that the last edge to intersect the screen generated a vertex at the top of the screen. And the next edge to intersect the screen will do so on the right edge of the screen. The output polygon will then have to contain the upper-right corner of the screen. This means that we must add a vertex for the upper-right corner of the screen. Since we are processing the polygon edge by edge, we must add this corner vertex now (called a turning vertex by the conceptualizers), in anticipation of the next intersection with the screen. See Figure 5.22. If the next edge intersects the top edge of the screen, this additional vertex would be redundant, but we can remove it later (our polygon filling routine will not grok too much if two vertices in a polygon are the same). The reason for adding the vertex is that any intersection point added by the next edge must be able to be reached from the last vertex that we output.

Note that like with our Sutherland-Hodgman implementation, polygons that have been clipped into non-existence will set the trivial_reject flag to ALG_TRUE. This alerts the calling routine that it should not proceed in adding this given polygon to the list of polygons for display. More on this later.

Viewports, Windows, and Screens

One last note on screen displays, windows, and viewports. We refer to viewports in the software comments as those defined rectangular windows that lie somewhere within the boundary of the screen. The viewport is less than or equal to the size of the screen. A window and a viewport are the same, and smaller than the screen, as far as we are concerned with the software.

PROGRAM LISTINGS:

```
/*

      +--------------------------------------------------------------------------+
      |                                                                          |
      |                                                                          |
      |                         Virtual Reality ExCursions                       |
      |                                                                          |
      |                                                                          |
      |           by Christopher D. Watkins and Stephen R. Marenka               |
      |                                                                          |
      |                                                                          |
      |                 Copyright 1994 : Academic Press, Inc.                     |
      |                                                                          |
      |                                                                          |
```

```
|---------------------------------------------------------------------|
|                              ALG_PCLP.H                             |
|---------------------------------------------------------------------|
|                                                                     |
|                           Software Issues                           |
|                                                                     |
|              Copyright 1987-1994 ALGORITHM, Incorporated.           |
|                                                                     |
|       ALL RIGHTS RESERVED.   This software is Published, but is NOT |
|    Public Domain and remains the property of ALGORITHM, Incorporated and |
|           Christopher D. Watkins.  This software may not be        |
|    reproduced or integrated into other packages without the prior written |
|           consent of Christopher D. Watkins.  Licensing is possible. |
|                                                                     |
    +-----------------------------------------------------------------+
*/

    #ifndef __ALG_PCLP__
    #define __ALG_PCLP__

    #define            ALG_Z_CLIPPING_PLANE              0.1

    alg_boolean    z_clip_polygon( alg_polygon_3D_type *polygon,
                       alg_z_clipped_polygon_3D_type *z_clipped_polygon );
    alg_boolean    xy_viewport_clip_z_clipped_polygon(
            alg_z_clipped_polygon_3D_type *z_clipped_polygon,
            alg_viewport_clipped_polygon_2D_type
            *viewport_clipped_polygon );

    #endif // __ALG_PCLP__

/*
    +-----------------------------------------------------------------+
    |                                                                 |
    |                    Virtual Reality ExCursions                   |
    |                                                                 |
    |         by Christopher D. Watkins and Stephen R. Marenka        |
    |                                                                 |
    |                Copyright 1994 : Academic Press, Inc.            |
```

```
|                                                                          |
|--------------------------------------------------------------------------|
|                              ALG_PCLP.C                                  |
|--------------------------------------------------------------------------|
|                                                                          |
|                            Software Issues                               |
|                                                                          |
|                 Copyright 1987-1994 ALGORITHM, Incorporated.             |
|                                                                          |
|      ALL RIGHTS RESERVED.   This software is Published, but is NOT       |
|   Public Domain and remains the property of ALGORITHM, Incorporated and  |
|            Christopher D. Watkins.   This software may not be            |
|  reproduced or integrated into other packages without the prior written  |
|            consent of Christopher D. Watkins.  Licensing is possible.    |
|                                                                          |
+--------------------------------------------------------------------------+
*/


//      Algorithm, Inc. includes
#include      "Alg_Defs.H"
#include      "Alg_Matx.H"
#include      "Alg_Scrn.H"
#include      "Alg_PClp.H"


/*
    +------------------------------------------------------------------+
    |   z-clipping of polygons by the Sutherland-Hodgman method        |
    +------------------------------------------------------------------+
*/


void clip_line_by_z_clipping_plane( alg_point_3D_type vertex1,
alg_point_3D_type vertex2,   alg_point_3D_type *vertex )
{
        alg_float      t;

        t = (ALG_Z_CLIPPING_PLANE - vertex1.z) / (vertex2.z -
             vertex1.z);
        vertex->x = vertex1.x + (vertex2.x - vertex1.x) * t;
        vertex->y = vertex1.y + (vertex2.y - vertex1.y) * t;
```

```
            vertex->z = ALG_Z_CLIPPING_PLANE;
}


// see page 124 of "Computer Graphics, Principles and Practice"
//      by Foley, van Dam, Feiner, and Hughes, 2 ed
alg_boolean z_clip_polygon( alg_polygon_3D_type *polygon,
        alg_z_clipped_polygon_3D_type *z_clipped_polygon )
{
        alg_word                vertex1;
        alg_word                vertex2;
        alg_vertex_3D_type      *vertex1_ptr;
        alg_vertex_3D_type      *vertex2_ptr;


        alg_point_3D_type       *z_clipped_polygon_vertex_ptr =
                z_clipped_polygon-> z_clipped_vertex;
        alg_word                *num_z_clipped_polygon_vertices =
                &z_clipped_polygon-> num_z_clipped_vertices;


        alg_boolean             trivial_reject;



        // initialize z-clipped polygon vertex counter
        *num_z_clipped_polygon_vertices = 0;

        // transfer color from polygon to z-clipped polygon
        z_clipped_polygon->color = polygon->color;

        // make a closed polygon by starting with the edge between the
        //      first and last vertices of the polygon
        vertex1 = polygon->num_vertices - 1;
        vertex1_ptr = polygon->vertex[vertex1];

        // loop through all of the polygon edges
        for (vertex2=0; vertex2<polygon->num_vertices; vertex2++)
        {
                vertex2_ptr = polygon->vertex[vertex2];

                if (vertex1_ptr->viewer.z < ALG_Z_CLIPPING_PLANE)
                {
```

```
            if (vertex2_ptr->viewer.z < ALG_Z_CLIPPING_PLANE)
            {
                    // edge is totally out of "viewable" z
                    //      half-space


            }
            else
            {

                    // edge is entering "viewable" z half-space

                    clip_line_by_z_clipping_plane(
                            vertex1_ptr->viewer,
                            vertex2_ptr->viewer,
                            &z_clipped_polygon_vertex_ptr[
                            *num_z_clipped_polygon_vertices] );
                    (*num_z_clipped_polygon_vertices)++;

                    z_clipped_polygon_vertex_ptr[
                            *num_z_clipped_polygon_vertices] =
                            vertex2_ptr->viewer;
                    (*num_z_clipped_polygon_vertices)++;
            }
    }
    else
    {

            if (vertex2_ptr->viewer.z < ALG_Z_CLIPPING_PLANE)
            {
                    // edge is leaving "viewable" z half-space

                    clip_line_by_z_clipping_plane(
                            vertex1_ptr->viewer,
                            vertex2_ptr->viewer,
                    &z_clipped_polygon_vertex_ptr[
                            *num_z_clipped_polygon_vertices] );
                    (*num_z_clipped_polygon_vertices)++;
            }
            else
            {
                    // edge is totally in "viewable" z
```

```
                                        //      half-space
                                        z_clipped_polygon_vertex_ptr[
                                                *num_z_clipped_polygon_vertices] =
                                                vertex2_ptr->viewer;
                                        (*num_z_clipped_polygon_vertices)++;
                        }
                }

                vertex1_ptr = vertex2_ptr;
        }


        if (*num_z_clipped_polygon_vertices > 0)
                trivial_reject = ALG_FALSE;
        else
                trivial_reject = ALG_TRUE;


        return( trivial_reject );
}


/*

    +-------------------------------------------------------------------+
    |       screen-clipping of polygons by the Liang-Barsky method      |
    +-------------------------------------------------------------------+
*/


// see page 930 of "Computer Graphics, Principles and Practice"
//      by Foley, van Dam, Feiner, and Hughes, 2 ed
alg_boolean xy_viewport_clip_z_clipped_polygon(
        alg_z_clipped_polygon_3D_type *z_clipped_polygon,
        alg_viewport_clipped_polygon_2D_type
        *viewport_clipped_polygon )
{
        alg_point_2D_int_type           entry_point, exit_point;
        // coordinates of entry and exit points
        alg_float               t_exit_point1, t_exit_point2;
        // parameter values of same
        alg_float               t_entry_point2;
        alg_point_2D_type       t_entry_point, t_exit_point;
        // parameter values for intersections
```

```
alg_point_2D_type      delta;           // direction of edge


alg_point_3D_type      *z_clipped_polygon_vertex_ptr =
       z_clipped_polygon-    >z_clipped_vertex;
alg_word               vertex1;
alg_word               vertex2;
alg_point_3D_type      vertex1_ptr;
alg_point_3D_type      vertex2_ptr;


alg_point_2D_int_type       *viewport_clipped_polygon_vertex_ptr
       = viewport_clipped_polygon->viewport_clipped_vertex;
alg_word                 *num_viewport_clipped_polygon_vertices =
                         &viewport_clipped_polygon
                         ->num_viewport_clipped_vertices;


alg_boolean            trivial_reject;

// initialize screen-clipped polygon vertex counter
*num_viewport_clipped_polygon_vertices = 0;

// transfer color from z-clipped polygon to viewport-clipped
//     polygon
viewport_clipped_polygon->color = z_clipped_polygon->color;

// make a closed polygon by starting with the edge between the
//     first and last vertices of the polygon
vertex1 = z_clipped_polygon->num_z_clipped_vertices - 1;
vertex1_ptr = z_clipped_polygon_vertex_ptr[vertex1];

// for each edge
for (vertex2=0; vertex2<
       z_clipped_polygon->num_z_clipped_vertices; vertex2++)
{
       vertex2_ptr = z_clipped_polygon_vertex_ptr[vertex2];

       // determine direction of edge
       ALG_VEC2_SUB( vertex2_ptr, vertex1_ptr, delta );

       // use this to determine which bounding lines for the
```

```
//      clip region the containing line hits first
if ((delta.x > 0.0) || ((delta.x == 0.0) &&
        (vertex1_ptr.x > (alg_float) ALG_WINDOW_MAX_X)))
{
        entry_point.x = ALG_WINDOW_MIN_X;
        exit_point.x  = ALG_WINDOW_MAX_X;
}
else
{
        entry_point.x = ALG_WINDOW_MAX_X;
        exit_point.x  = ALG_WINDOW_MIN_X;
}
if ((delta.y > 0.0) || ((delta.y == 0.0) &&
        (vertex1_ptr.y > (alg_float)ALG_WINDOW_MAX_Y)))
{
        entry_point.y = ALG_WINDOW_MIN_Y;
        exit_point.y  = ALG_WINDOW_MAX_Y;
}
else
{
        entry_point.y = ALG_WINDOW_MAX_Y;
        exit_point.y  = ALG_WINDOW_MIN_Y;
}

// find the t values for the x and y endpoints
if (delta.x != 0.0)
        t_exit_point.x = (exit_point.x - vertex1_ptr.x) /
                delta.x;
else
{
        if ((vertex1_ptr.x <= (alg_float)ALG_WINDOW_MAX_X)
                && ((alg_float)ALG_WINDOW_MIN_X
                        <= vertex1_ptr.x))
                t_exit_point.x = ALG_LARGE;
        else
                t_exit_point.x = -ALG_LARGE;
}

if (delta.y != 0.0)
```

```
                t_exit_point.y = (exit_point.y - vertex1_ptr.y) /
                        delta.y;
        else
        {
                if ((vertex1_ptr.y <= (alg_float)ALG_WINDOW_MAX_Y)
                        && (ALG_WINDOW_MIN_Y <= vertex1_ptr.y))
                        t_exit_point.y = ALG_LARGE;
                else
                        t_exit_point.y = -ALG_LARGE;
        }


        // order the two exit points
        if (t_exit_point.x < t_exit_point.y)
        {
                t_exit_point1 = t_exit_point.x;
                t_exit_point2 = t_exit_point.y;
        }
        else
        {
                t_exit_point1 = t_exit_point.y;
                t_exit_point2 = t_exit_point.x;
        }


        // there could be output - compute t_entry_point2
        if (t_exit_point2 > 0.0)
        {
                if (delta.x != 0.0)
                        t_entry_point.x = (entry_point.x -
                                vertex1_ptr.x) / delta.x;
                else
                        t_entry_point.x = -ALG_LARGE;
                if (delta.y != 0.0)
                        t_entry_point.y = (entry_point.y -
                                vertex1_ptr.y) / delta.y;
                else
                        t_entry_point.y = -ALG_LARGE;


                if (t_entry_point.x < t_entry_point.y)
```

```
            t_entry_point2 = t_entry_point.y;
else
            t_entry_point2 = t_entry_point.x;


// no visible segment
if (t_exit_point1 < t_entry_point2)
{
        // line crosses over immediate corner
        if ((t_exit_point1 > 0.0) &&
                (t_exit_point1 <= 1.0))
        {
                // output turning
                //      clipped_polygon_vertex_ptr
                if (t_entry_point.x
                        < t_entry_point.y)
                {
                        ALG_VEC2_MAKE( exit_point.x,
                                entry_point.y,
                        viewport_clipped_polygon_vertex_ptr[
                *num_viewport_clipped_polygon_vertices]);
                (*num_viewport_clipped_polygon_vertices)++;
                }
                else
                {
                        ALG_VEC2_MAKE(
                                entry_point.x,
                                exit_point.y,
                        viewport_clipped_polygon_vertex_ptr[
                *num_viewport_clipped_polygon_vertices] );
                (*num_viewport_clipped_polygon_vertices)++;
                }
        }
}
else    // line crosses through window
{
        // there is some visible part
        if ((t_exit_point1 > 0.0) &&
                (t_entry_point2 <= 1.0))
        {
```

```
// visible segment
if (t_entry_point2 > 0.0)
{
        // output appropriate side
        //      intersection
        if (t_entry_point.x >
                t_entry_point.y)
        {
                ALG_VEC2_MAKE(
                        entry_point.x,
                        vertex1_ptr.y
                + (t_entry_point.x
                * delta.y),
        viewport_clipped_polygon_vertex_ptr[
*num_viewport_clipped_polygon_vertices] );
(*num_viewport_clipped_polygon_vertices)++;
        }
        else
        {
                ALG_VEC2_MAKE(
                vertex1_ptr.x +
        (t_entry_point.y * delta.x),
                entry_point.y,
        viewport_clipped_polygon_vertex_ptr[
*num_viewport_clipped_polygon_vertices] );
(*num_viewport_clipped_polygon_vertices)++;
        }
}
else
{
        // output starting
        //clipped_polygon_vertex_ptr
        //      (do not include it,
        //      because each
        //clipped_polygon_vertex_ptr
        //      of the polygon should
        //      contain exactly one
        //      of the two edges that
        //      meet there)
```

```
      }

      if (t_exit_point1 < 1.0)
      {
            // output appropriate side
            //      intersection
            if (t_exit_point.x <
                  t_exit_point.y)
            {
                  ALG_VEC2_MAKE(
                        exit_point.x,
                  vertex1_ptr.y +
                  (t_exit_point.x *
                  delta.y),
      viewport_clipped_polygon_vertex_ptr[
*num_viewport_clipped_polygon_vertices] );
(*num_viewport_clipped_polygon_vertices)++;
            }
            else
            {
                  ALG_VEC2_MAKE(
                  vertex1_ptr.x +
                  (t_exit_point.y *
                  delta.x),
                  exit_point.y,
      viewport_clipped_polygon_vertex_ptr[
*num_viewport_clipped_polygon_vertices] );
(*num_viewport_clipped_polygon_vertices)++;
            }
      }
      else
      {
            // output ending
            //clipped_polygon_vertex_ptr
            ALG_VEC2_COPY( vertex2_ptr,
      viewport_clipped_polygon_vertex_ptr[
*num_viewport_clipped_polygon_vertices] );
(*num_viewport_clipped_polygon_vertices)++;
      }
```

```
                              }
                        }

                        // output appropriate corner
                        if ((t_exit_point2 > 0.0) && (t_exit_point2
                              <= 1.0))
                        {
                              ALG_VEC2_COPY( exit_point,
                              viewport_clipped_polygon_vertex_ptr[
                              *num_viewport_clipped_polygon_vertices] );
                              (*num_viewport_clipped_polygon_vertices)++;
                        }
                  }

            vertex1_ptr = vertex2_ptr;
      }


      if (*num_viewport_clipped_polygon_vertices > 0)
            trivial_reject = ALG_FALSE;
      else
            trivial_reject = ALG_TRUE;

      return( trivial_reject );
}
```

Section 7—Removing Hidden Polygons

One of the nastiest problems to solve in computer graphics (in my humble opinion) is the issue of hidden-surface removal. In the real world, for instance, when you look at the front of a building, you see only the front door and windows, you do not see the back of the building, though you know that it is there.

In computer graphics, we need a model that defines all parts of a three-dimensional world. A virtual building would have polygons for the front, back, sides, top, and inside floors of the building. We need this structural detail for a virtual reality system, because we may want to walk through or around that building.

We must find a way to remove those polygons that are out of view. As you would expect, the polygons that we must remove are based on the position and orientation of the viewer, as well as the positions and orientations of the objects in the scene. Remember that the objects may also be moving.

There are many solutions to the hidden-surface problem. None of them (in my humble opinion, again) are very clean. We will discuss many approaches, but only one simple, though incomplete, but efficient approach will be implemented. We start with the backface removal algorithm.

The Backface Removal Algorithm

Since any hidden-surface test can eat up many compute cycles, we must make as many simple tests as possible, in order to quickly reduce the number of polygons that must be processed. A simple test that can do just that for single convex objects is to detect the direction that the polygon is facing, relative to the direction the viewer is facing.

Polygon faces that are facing away from the viewer are considered backfaces. These faces cannot be visible, as the other, closer half of the object is blocking the view. This by no means solves the hidden-surface problem, as we may have another object in front of the first one, or part of the first object may block polygons on itself that are facing us. But this simple test can usually remove about half of the polygons from the scene in one pass.

In order to understand this algorithm, we must look at a polygon as having two sides, like a piece of paper. Our polygon will have one strange characteristic, differing from the sheet of paper, and that is that it will be visible from one side and invisible from the other side. Strange, indeed—the significance will become apparent soon.

We can define which side is which for our polygon by ordering the vertices in a counterclockwise fasion for the visible side. Looking at the polygon from the invisible side, the vertices will appear clockwise, see Figure 5.23.

In order to determine the direction in which the polygon is facing, we must perform a little mathematics. If you remember from the section on the cross-product, the cross-product of two three-dimensional vectors will give you a third three-dimensional vector that is perpendicular to the plane formed by the first two vectors. The formulas for the three-dimensional cross-product of vectors in the right-handed coordinate system that we are using are:

$$\mathbf{v} = \mathbf{v_1} \otimes \mathbf{v_2}$$

$$\mathbf{v_x} = (\mathbf{v_{1y}})(\mathbf{v_{2z}}) - (\mathbf{v_{1z}})(\mathbf{v_{2y}})$$
$$\mathbf{v_y} = (\mathbf{v_{1z}})(\mathbf{v_{2x}}) - (\mathbf{v_{1x}})(\mathbf{v_{2z}})$$
$$\mathbf{v_z} = (\mathbf{v_{1x}})(\mathbf{v_{2y}}) - (\mathbf{v_{1y}})(\mathbf{v_{2x}})$$

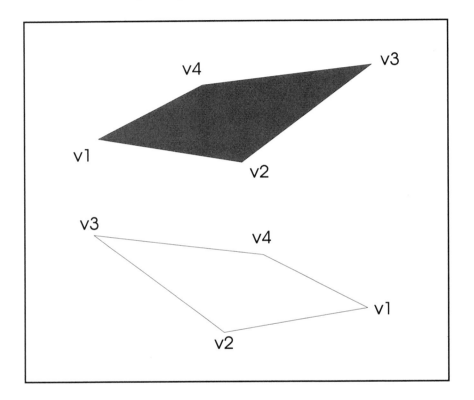

Figure 5.23—Ordering of Vertices for Visible Side of Polygon

Given that two sides of a polygon describe two vectors in the plane of that polygon, the cross-product of those two vectors will give us a normal to the surface of the polygon.

Now that we have a surface normal to the polygon, we just need to know which direction the polygon is facing, toward or away from us. To do that, we need to know if the two sides represented by the two vectors form a convex or concave angle.

If our polygon has two adjacent sides that meet at a convex angle (angle > 180°, meaning that moving one edge to the next turned us slightly to the left, in turn meaning that we are following the vertices in a counterclockwise fashion) at the vertex, the vector cross-product will yield a vector pointing out of the viewable side of the polygon. We call this our surface normal.

Simply stated, this means that the surface normal for a visible polygon should be facing toward us, and the surface normal for an invisible polygon must be facing away from us. This invisible polygon should be removed from the polygon display list in order to save computations later.

In order to determine whether or not the surface normal vector points toward the viewer, we must examine the z coordinate of the surface normal vector. If this z component is positive, the polygon faces the viewer and thus it is not a backface. If this z coordinate is negative, the polygon faces away from the viewer, and this polygon is a backface and should not be added to the polygon display list.

You may remember from the section on dot products of vectors how useful the dot product is for determining whether or not two vectors point in the same direction. The formula for computing the dot product is as follows:

$$\text{dot\_product} = \mathbf{v_1} \bullet \mathbf{v_2}$$

$$\text{dot\_product} = (\mathbf{v_{1x}})(\mathbf{v_{2x}}) + (\mathbf{v_{1y}})(\mathbf{v_{2y}}) + (\mathbf{v_{1z}})(\mathbf{v_{2z}})$$

For the backface check using the dot product, one vector is the normal to the polygon and the other acts as the direction of increasing depth. We can just take another vertex of the polygon for our direction. We can do this because the polygon has been locally transformed, and transformed for viewing, before ever entering this test routine.

We have seen a quick and dirty method for removing some of those backface polygons from our scene. This method is the one that we implemented, and it will work well for single convex objects but may be inadequate for scenes with many objects and objects with concave surfaces.

We will now move on to some other popular methods for properly displaying scenes made of polygons.

The Z Buffer Algorithm [Catmull 1974]

If we are using a frame buffer to compose our images, before they are copied to the computer screen, we can look at the hidden-surface problem as one where we want to arrange the frame buffer so that the color displayed for any given pixel of the buffer is that of the surface that is closest to the viewer from that point. In order to create this, we must compare all of the pixels projected onto that given pixel and sort for the closest one. This sort is called a geometric sort and is essential to most hidden-surface removal algorithms.

A Z buffer is a large frame buffer (array) with a z coordinate entry and color entry for every pixel on your screen. Each z coordinate is set for a very huge number representing the background distance, and each color is set to the background color. As a polygon is transformed and projected for viewing, pixel-by-pixel comparisons are made of the polygon's preprojected z coordinate with the z coordinate sitting in the Z buffer. Note that comparisons are made only for those pixels (elements of the buffer) that the projected polygon could affect. If the polygon's z coordinate is smaller than the one in the Z buffer, the color of the polygon is copied into the Z buffer, and the z coordinate in the Z buffer is updated with the polygon's preprojected z coordinate. If the polygon's z coordinate is larger than the one in the Z buffer, the Z buffer is not updated, as the polygon is not the closest one for that point in the image.

This technique is expensive, regarding memory requirements and processing time. It is, however, a simple method that lends itself to hardware implementation. It is a very good solution to the hidden-surface problem.

Scan Line Algorithms [Carpenter 1976]

Since a Z buffer requires a lot of memory for its implementation, scan line algorithms were developed to collect the polygons and process them together. As each polygon is rasterized in a scan line algorithm, we must be able to store the depth of each of its pixels for recall so that they may be compared against later polygons. Since polygons may vary in size, even as large as the screen, we still need a full-screen Z buffer. We can significantly reduce the memory requirements, though, by processing the polygons together, scan line by scan line. It is like doing the Z buffer processing on a one-pixel height image, image height times. The key point here is that all polygons are processed together, considering all polygons for a scan line before moving to the next scan line, different from the Z buffer in that there we considered all scan lines for a polygon before moving to the next polygon.

The Painter's Algorithm [Newell 1972]

This algorithm is named for the way oil painters create their works of art. An artist begins by painting the background of an image. The artist then paints the objects farthest from the viewer on top of the background. Then the painter adds objects that are closer, painting over parts of the far objects and the background. Fortunately for us, a frame buffer can be used in the same way, with usually efficient results for simple scenes. This is the algorithm that we have implemented with our software.

When we project a polygon into the frame buffer for subsequent display on the computer screen, we may be overwriting pixels in that buffer that we colored with an earlier projected polygon. If you are sure to sort the polygons from farthest to nearest before you project them and write them into the frame buffer, you will correctly create your scene with hidden surfaces removed (overwritten). Code listings for sorting polygons are given at the end of this section. Note that any sort will work—the bubble sort, Hoare's quick-sort, etc.—but we found the insertion sort methodology to work best, as the relative positions of polygons do not change much from image to image.

Note that there are some drawbacks to this technique. Polygons that cut through other polygons will not be displayed properly. The polygon chosen for later display will overwrite the first polygon, producing an incorrect image. We must find a way to break up our polygons into nonintersecting polygons and then sort them for display. This is where our journey leads us to now.

Position Comparison Tests for Polygons

We have several tests at our disposal for determining the relative positions of two polygons. Not all of these tests can be used with all hidden-surface algorithms, and some of the tests are not rigorous and conclusive. The goal is to use simple tests for as many cases as possible and use the more involved costly tests only when absolutely necessary.

A commonly used technique is called the *boxing test*. It is also known as the *cuboid test* and the *minimax test*. This test is useful when we need to know only the orderings of polygons that overlap and not necesarily the orderings of all of the polygons. This test is used to tell us quickly if two polygons do not overlap.

We start our test by placing tight boxes around each polygon so that each box totally encloses its own polygon. Each bounding box is defined by two points: the maximum and minimum points. The minimum point is obtained by looking through the vertices of the polygon and finding the minimum x and y values. The maximum point is obtained by looking through the vertices of the polygon and finding the maximum x and y values.

If the two boxes that are obtained for the two polygons do not overlap, then there is no chance that the two polygons overlap. If the boxes do overlap, then the polygons may or may not overlap and we need to do more testing.

A boxing test applied to the z coordinates of two polygons will often indicate the relative ordering of two polygons that do overlap in x and y. If the smallest z coordinate for polygon A is greater than the largest z coordinate for polygon B, we can assume that polygon A is in front of polygon B.

Another incredibly useful test is one that tells you if all of the vertices of one polygon (A) lie on the same side of the plane containing another polygon (B). If the vertices of polygon A do lie on the same side of polygon B as the viewer, then this polygon A is closer and in front of polygon B. If the vertices of polygon A lie on the other side of the viewer, then polygon B lies in front of polygon A.

But what if the plane of polygon B also intersects polygon A? We can try comparing the vertices of polygon B with the plane of polygon A and make similar deductions as above.

If this test also fails, then we may cut the polygons into pieces so that the preceding tests succeed.

The Binary Space Partitioning Algorithm [Fuchs 1980]

The basic idea of binary space partitioning is to sort the polygons for display from farthest to nearest just as in the Painter's algorithm. Here we use the position comparison test mentioned above that compares the vertices of one polygon with the plane of another polygon. We extend this test so that if the plane intersects the polygon, we will divide the polygon along the plane. Using this test, we can pick one polygon and compare all of the other polygons to it. From the comparisons, we get two groups, the polygons that are in front and those that are behind. For each of these two new groups, we can once again select two polygons and use them to partition the groups, respectively. This process is repeated until all polygons have been sorted. The result of this quick-sort (if you will) is a binary tree, with each node representing a polygon. In one branch are all of the polygons that lie in front of the plane of this polygon, in the other branch are polygons that lie behind the plane of this polygon. An in-order traversal of the tree will give you farthest-to-nearest order of the polygons for display.

See Steven Harrington's most excellent computer graphics text *Computer Graphics, A Programming Approach* for an implementation of this algorithm.

PROGRAM LISTINGS:

```
/*

      +----------------------------------------------------------------------+
      |                                                                      |
      |                    Virtual Reality ExCursions                        |
      |                                                                      |
      |         by Christopher D. Watkins and Stephen R. Marenka             |
      |                                                                      |
      |             Copyright 1994 : Academic Press, Inc.                    |
      |                                                                      |
      |----------------------------------------------------------------------|
      |                                                                      |
      |                            ALG_HIDS.H                                |
      |----------------------------------------------------------------------|
      |                                                                      |
      |                                                                      |
      |                          Software Issues                             |
      |                                                                      |
      |            Copyright 1987-1994 ALGORITHM, Incorporated.              |
      |                                                                      |
      |      ALL RIGHTS RESERVED.   This software is Published, but is NOT   |
      |   Public Domain and remains the property of ALGORITHM, Incorporated and |
      |           Christopher D. Watkins.  This software may not be          |
      |   reproduced or integrated into other packages without the prior written |
      |           consent of Christopher D. Watkins.  Licensing is possible. |
      |                                                                      |
      +----------------------------------------------------------------------+

*/


    #ifndef __ALG_HIDS__
```

```
#define __ALG_HIDS__


//#define      alg_depth_sort_polygon_display_list            \
//                      alg_z_insertion_sort_polygon_display_list
//#define      alg_depth_sort_polygon_display_list            \
//                      alg_z_bubble_sort_polygon_display_list
//#define      alg_depth_sort_polygon_display_list            \
//                      alg_z_heap_sort_polygon_display_list
#define        alg_depth_sort_polygon_display_list            \
                       alg_z_quick_sort_polygon_display_list


alg_boolean    alg_polygon_is_backface( alg_polygon_3D_type polygon );
void           alg_depth_sort_polygon_display_list(
                       alg_polygon_3D_display_list_type
*polygon_display_list );


#endif // __ALG_HIDS__


/*

   +-------------------------------------------------------------------------+
   |                                                                         |
   |                         Virtual Reality ExCursions                      |
   |                                                                         |
   |              by Christopher D. Watkins and Stephen R. Marenka           |
   |                                                                         |
   |                    Copyright 1994 : Academic Press, Inc.                |
   |                                                                         |
   |-------------------------------------------------------------------------|
   |                                 ALG_HIDS.C                              |
   |-------------------------------------------------------------------------|
   |                                                                         |
   |                             Software Issues                             |
   |                                                                         |
   |                 Copyright 1987-1994 ALGORITHM, Incorporated.            |
   |                                                                         |
   |     ALL RIGHTS RESERVED.   This software is Published, but is NOT       |
   |   Public Domain and remains the property of ALGORITHM, Incorporated and |
   |          Christopher D. Watkins.  This software may not be              |
   | reproduced or integrated into other packages without the prior written |
```

```
    |               consent of Christopher D. Watkins.  Licensing is possible.       |

    |                                                                                |

    +--------------------------------------------------------------------------------+
*/


    //      system includes
    #include        <stdlib.h>


    //      Algorithm, Inc. includes
    #include        "Alg_Defs.H"
    #include        "Alg_Matx.H"
    #include        "Alg_HidS.H"


    /*

        +--------------------------------------------------------------------------+
        |      test polygon to determine whether or not it is a backface           |
        +--------------------------------------------------------------------------+
    */


    alg_boolean alg_polygon_is_backface( alg_polygon_3D_type polygon )
    {
            alg_vertex_3D_type      *vertex0 = polygon.vertex[0];
            alg_vertex_3D_type      *vertex1 = polygon.vertex[1];
            alg_vertex_3D_type      *vertex2 = polygon.vertex[2];
            alg_point_3D_type       cross_product;
            alg_float               dot_product;


            // take the cross product to get the surface normal of the plane
            //      made from two of the polygon points and an arbitrary
            //      origin, then take the dot product of the third polygon
            //      point with the earlier cross product result in order to
            //      determine on what side of the plane the third polygon
            //      point lies. This in effect is a convexity test for the
            //      polygon. This gives the direction in which the polygon is
            //      facing relative to the viewer, since we have performed
            //      all local and viewer transformations by this point.
            ALG_VEC3_CROSS( vertex0->viewer, vertex1->viewer,
                    cross_product );
            dot_product = ALG_VEC3_DOT( vertex2->viewer, cross_product );
```

```
        if (dot_product < 0.0)
                return( ALG_FALSE );
        else
                return( ALG_TRUE );
}


/*

   +------------------------------------------------------------------+
   | polygon sorting for farthest-to-nearest display - Painter's      |
   | algorithm                                                        |
   +------------------------------------------------------------------+

*/

// for small polygon counts
void alg_z_insertion_sort_polygon_display_list(
        alg_polygon_3D_display_list_type *polygon_display_list )
{
        // we don't sort the first polygon (ground = polygon_num 0)
        alg_int        first_polygon_num_to_sort = 1;
        alg_int        num_sortable_polygons =
                polygon_display_list->num_polygons -
                first_polygon_num_to_sort;
        alg_int        i, j;
        alg_polygon_3D_type   temp;

        // return if:
        //     only the ground polygon and an assorted polygon
        //     only the ground polygon
        //     only the sky
        if (num_sortable_polygons < 2)
                return;

        for (j=first_polygon_num_to_sort+1; j<=num_sortable_polygons;
                j++)
        {
                // pick out an element
                temp = polygon_display_list->polygon[j];
```

```
                    // look for a place to insert it
                    i = j - 1;
                    while ( (i > (first_polygon_num_to_sort-1)) &&
                            (polygon_display_list->
                                    polygon[i].viewer_to_polygon_distance <
                                    temp.viewer_to_polygon_distance) )
                    {
                            polygon_display_list->polygon[i+1] =
                                    polygon_display_list->polygon[i];
                            i--;
                    }

                    // insert it
                    polygon_display_list->polygon[i+1] = temp;
            }
    }


// for small/medium polygon counts
void alg_z_bubble_sort_polygon_display_list(
        alg_polygon_3D_display_list_type *polygon_display_list )
{
        // we don't sort the first polygon (ground = polygon_num 0)
        alg_int                        first_polygon_num_to_sort = 1;
        alg_int                        num_sortable_polygons =
                                       polygon_display_list->num_polygons -
                                       first_polygon_num_to_sort;
        alg_polygon_3D_type    temp;
        alg_word               polygon_num;
        alg_boolean            swapping;

        // return if:
        //      only the ground polygon and an assorted polygon
        //      only the ground polygon
        //      only the sky
        if (num_sortable_polygons < 2)
                return;
        do
        {
                swapping = ALG_FALSE;
```

```
                for (polygon_num=first_polygon_num_to_sort;
                        polygon_num<num_sortable_polygons; polygon_num++)
                        if (polygon_display_list->
                        polygon[polygon_num].viewer_to_polygon_distance <
                        polygon_display_list->
                        polygon[polygon_num+1].viewer_to_polygon_distance)
                        {
                                ALG_SWAP( polygon_display_list
                                        ->polygon[polygon_num],
                                        polygon_display_list
                                        ->polygon[polygon_num+1] );
                                swapping = ALG_TRUE;
                        }
                }
        while (swapping);
}


// for medium polygon counts
void alg_z_heap_sort_polygon_display_list(
        alg_polygon_3D_display_list_type *polygon_display_list )
{
        // based on the J.W.J. Williams's Heapsort algorithm found on
        //      p.245 Numerical Recipes in C -- The Art of Scientific
        //      Computing (Press, Flannery, Teukolsky, Vetterling)
        //      Cambridge
        // we strongly suggest the purchase of this reference, as it has
        //      many good algorithms and program listings for general,
        //      scientific and engineering use

        // we don't sort the first polygon (ground = polygon_num 0)
        alg_int                         first_polygon_num_to_sort = 1;
        alg_int                         num_sortable_polygons =
                                polygon_display_list->num_polygons -
                                first_polygon_num_to_sort;
        alg_int                         i, j;
        alg_polygon_3D_type     temp;
        alg_int                         r = num_sortable_polygons;
        alg_int                         l = (r >> 1) + 1;
```

```
// return if:
//      only the ground polygon and an assorted polygon
//      only the ground polygon
//      only the sky
if (r < 2)
        return;

for (;;)
{
        if (l > 1)
                temp = polygon_display_list->polygon[--l];
        else
        {
                temp = polygon_display_list->polygon[r];
                polygon_display_list->polygon[r] =
                        polygon_display_list->polygon[1];
                if (--r == 1)
                {
                        polygon_display_list->polygon[1] = temp;
                        return;
                }
        }
        i = l;
        j = l << 1;
        while (j <= r)
        {
                if ( (j < r) &&
                (polygon_display_list
                ->polygon[j].viewer_to_polygon_distance >
                        polygon_display_list->
                        polygon[j+1].viewer_to_polygon_distance) )
                        ++j;
                if (temp.viewer_to_polygon_distance >
                        polygon_display_list
                        ->polygon[j].viewer_to_polygon_distance)
                {
                        polygon_display_list->polygon[i] =
                                polygon_display_list->polygon[j];
                        j += (i = j);
```

```
                    }
                    else
                            j = r + 1;
                }
                polygon_display_list->polygon[i] = temp;
        }
}


// for large polygon counts
void alg_z_quick_sort_polygon_display_list(
        alg_polygon_3D_display_list_type *polygon_display_list )
{

        //based on the C.A.R. Hoare's Quicksort algorithm found on p.251
        //      Numerical Recipes in C -- The Art of Scientific Computing
        //      (Press, Flannery, Teukolsky, Vetterling) Cambridge
        // we strongly suggest the purchase of this reference, as it has
        //      many good algorithms and program listings for general,
        //      scientific and engineering use

        //      size of subarrays when best sorted by insertion sort
        #define             INSERTION_SORT              7
        //      size of auxillary storage for INDEX_STACK polygon indices
        #define             INDEX_STACK        4096
        //      pseudo-random number generator constants
        #define             PRNG_A             211
        #define             PRNG_C             1663
        #define             PRNG_M             7875


        // we don't sort the first polygon (ground = polygon_num 0)
        alg_int                     first_polygon_num_to_sort = 1;
        alg_int                     num_sortable_polygons =
                        polygon_display_list->num_polygons -
                        first_polygon_num_to_sort;
        alg_int                     i, j;
        alg_polygon_3D_type    temp;
        alg_int                     r = num_sortable_polygons;
        alg_int                     l = 1;
        alg_int                     q;
        alg_int                     istack[INDEX_STACK];
```

```
alg_int                        jstack = 0;
alg_long              PRNG = 0L;

// return if:
//      only the ground polygon and an assorted polygon
//      only the ground polygon
//      only the sky
if (r < 2)
        return;

for (;;)
{
        if ((r-l) < INSERTION_SORT)
        {
                // perform insertion sort
                for (j=l+1; j<=r; j++)
                {
                        temp = polygon_display_list->polygon[j];
                        for (i=j-1;
                (polygon_display_list
                        ->polygon[i].viewer_to_polygon_distance <
                        temp.viewer_to_polygon_distance) &&
                        (i > 0); i--)
                                polygon_display_list->polygon[i+1] =
                                polygon_display_list->polygon[i];
                        polygon_display_list->polygon[i+1] = temp;
                }
                if (jstack == 0)
                        return;

                r = istack[jstack--];
                l = istack[jstack--];
        }
        else
        {

                i = l;
                j = r;
```

```
// generate a random integer q with inclusive
//      range (1..r)
PRNG = (PRNG * PRNG_A + PRNG_C) % PRNG_M;
q = 1 + ((r - 1 + 1) * PRNG) / PRNG_M;

temp = polygon_display_list->polygon[q];
polygon_display_list->polygon[q] =
        polygon_display_list->polygon[l];
for (;;)
{
        while ((j > 0) &&
                (temp.viewer_to_polygon_distance >
                        polygon_display_list
        ->polygon[j].viewer_to_polygon_distance))
                j--;
        if (j <= i)
        {
                polygon_display_list->polygon[i] =
                        temp;
                break;
        }
        polygon_display_list->polygon[i++] =
                polygon_display_list->polygon[j];
        while ((temp.viewer_to_polygon_distance <
                                polygon_display_list
        ->polygon[i].viewer_to_polygon_distance)
&& (i <= num_sortable_polygons))
                i++;
        if (j <= i)
        {
                polygon_display_list->polygon[(i=j)]
                        = temp;
                break;
        }
        polygon_display_list->polygon[j--] =
                polygon_display_list->polygon[i];
}
if ((r-i) >= (i-1))
{
```

```
                              istack[++jstack] = i + 1;
                              istack[++jstack] = r;
                              r = i - 1;
                    }
                    else
                    {
                              istack[++jstack] = 1;
                              istack[++jstack] = i - 1;
                              l = i + 1;
                    }
                    if (jstack >= INDEX_STACK)
                    {
                              printf("quick-sort error");
                              exit(0);
                    }
              }
        }
}
```

Section 8—Shading and Texturing Polygons

As mentioned many times throughout this text, it is very important for virtual reality systems to have a graphics engine that can generate images that have a certain degree of realism. Perspective projection is a must for creating depth, but that is not always enough. Without images that effectively fool the sense of vision into thinking that they are real, immersion is not truly possible. The techniques of shading and texturing will help us in our endeavor of photorealism.

A Simple Shading Model

Computer graphics shading models are usually based on simplified physical models of the real world—simplified because complete physical models cannot be computed in a finite amount of time. Additionally, lighting models have generally been "fudged" to create the desired visual effects. However, even with assumptions and approximations, most models produce quite acceptable results. Our model is no different. All of the color terms described below are additive; i.e., we compute each individually and sum the terms to produce the net color. Additionally, we take advantage of the fact that light energy is linear; i.e., we may compute the effects for each light in the scene individually and add the results together. Now let us look at some terminology and definitions. An incident ray of light is a light ray that hits an object. This ray is represented mathematically as a three-dimensional vector. The surface normal, **N**, is a vector that is normal to the surface of the object at the point of intersection of the incident ray with the object. The vectors for reflected rays **R** and the rays to the light sources **L$_n$** are generated using the basic laws of optical reflection. Let us look at some of the shading model mathematical constants and variables.

Ka	ambient coefficient
Kd	diffuse coefficient
Kh	specular highlight
Ns	specular exponent
Ks	specular coefficient
Kt	transmitted coefficient
N	surface normal at intersection point
V	vector of incident ray
R	vector for reflected ray
E	vector from the eyepoint to the intersection point
L$_n$	vector toward nth light source
H$_n$	reflected **L$_n$** vector. This is the direction light reflects directly off the surface.
I	total illumination (the final color)

We mentioned that our process is additive. In order to get the total illumination value, I, we sum together the components:

I = ambient + diffuse + specular + transmitted + specular highlights

Note that in the following discussions, we will be dealing only with a single light source, computing I_n. The I_n are then summed over all light sources to produce the total illumination I.

Background Illumination (Ka)

We begin with the simplest lighting component, the background or ambient lighting. Ambient light is light which comes from all around the environment, points in all directions, and is thus uniformly distributed throughout the scene. We treat this as the light intensity assigned to rays that do not intersect any of the objects or lights in the scene. A daylight scene will have a much brighter ambient component than a nightime one. An object may have an ambient lighting component as well. This is used to model self-luminous objects such as street lamps, fireflies, etc.

Diffuse Illumination (Kd)

The diffuse color of an object is essentially the color of the object under white light. A green ball is green because it reflects the green component of light on the surface and absorbs the others. If you shine a light on a green ball, the light is not reflected as a mirror would reflect, just in one direction, but is instead reflected in all directions. The part of the surface facing the light receives the most intensity per unit area, while the parts facing away receive no light at all. We therefore see the areas facing the light source (surface normal points in the direction of the light source) as the brightest, independent of our viewing direction, since a diffuse surface scatters light equally in all directions. See Figure 5.24. Because of this viewer direction independence, the diffuse intensity is a function of the angle between the surface normal and the light direction, or, equivalently, a function of the dot product of the two:

$$Kd = - \mathbf{N} \bullet \mathbf{L_n}$$

The Lambertian diffuse reflectance model (named after the physicist) tells us that the light intensity is directly proportional to this dot product. If the diffuse value is less than or equal to 0, it is treated as 0. These correspond to the portions of the surface facing away from the light and are thus automatically shadowed from the light source. In the absence of shadows and texture, we can simply multiply the intrinsic diffuse color of the object by the diffuse value to get the net diffuse intensity at this point. But wait—what if we shine a red light on a blue ball? We must take the diffuse color vector and multiply each component (red, green, and blue) by the corresponding light color components. A red light would typically have color (1, 0, 0). Note that the diffuse color would be 0 if the ball were purely blue or green (a most nonphysical situation).

Our model includes a factor for reducing the light intensity as a function of distance from the intersection of the light ray with the object. Physically, light intensity falls off as one over the square of the distance. However, because of the approximations that we have made about the diffuse and ambient light in the environment, a better-looking result is obtained using one over distance intensity scaling. This kind of intensity scaling works for light sources such as light bulbs but is not needed for daylight scenes. The sun intensity does not change appreciably over the distances of your average scene (unless you are viewing the virtual scene from virtual outer space).

Specular Illumination (Kh)

Many surfaces have mirror-like qualities. Metal and plastic surfaces at least partially reflect the light source directly. This is referred to as a specular effect. An image of the light source itself is reflected off the surface. In order for this reflected light to reach our eye, we must be positioned such that the light source reflects in the direction of our eye. The angle between the eyepoint vector and the surface normal must be "close" to the angle between the light vector and surface normal. Unless the surface is a perfect mirror, the light will always be slightly diffused, forming a reflective spot on the surface known as the specular highlight. This spot will be the color of the light source because it is, after all, a distorted reflection of the light source. See Figure 5.25.

The vector $\mathbf{H_n}$ is the direction in which the light would be reflected if the surface were a perfect mirror. As with the diffuse coefficient, the perceived intensity is a function of the angle between the vector $\mathbf{H_n}$ and the eyepoint vector $\mathbf{E}$. Unlike the diffuse component case, we must be facing in the proper direction to perceive the spot. Note that if you are viewing a shiny flat surface, the image of a light source reflected on the surface moves as you do. The model used in virtually every rendering program is the Phong model. The standard equation for computing the specular highlight is

$$Kh = (-\mathbf{H_n} \cdot \mathbf{E})^{Ns}$$

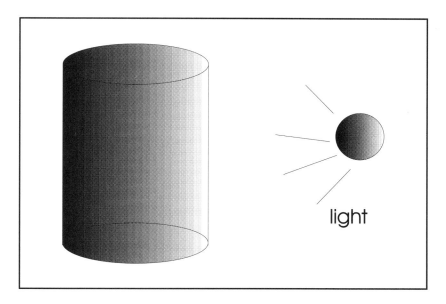

Figure 5.24—Diffuse Reflection

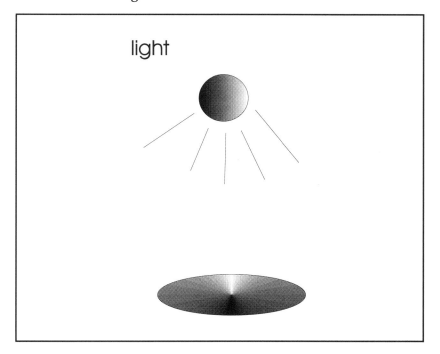

Figure 5.25—Specular Reflection

Note that by introducing the exponent Ns we can control the apparent spot size. The larger Ns is, the tighter the spot size. This is not a particularly physical model but rather one which we can easily control to produce the desired result, namely specular highlights that look as they do in the real world. The computation of diffuse and specular highlights is performed for each light source. As we are talking about light sources, we need to discuss shadows.

Shadows

Shadows are another important cue to the brain, to fool the brain into thinking that a scene is real. There are many methods for computing shadows in computer graphics, but like the hidden-surface problems, the techniques are usually messy. One technique that we will briefly discuss is called ray casting. Shadows are evaluated by casting rays from the intersection point toward each of the light sources. If the ray intersects any opaque objects in between, the light is not visible and thus does not contribute to that lighting computation. If the ray intersects a transparent object, then the light intensity is reduced by the transmissivity of the intervening object. If the ray reaches the light (or equivalently, goes out of the scene), then the light is visible and its full intensity is used, remembering to scale for distance falloff. Point light sources require only a single shadow ray to be cast from the intersection point. Finite-extent light sources, such as spherical light sources, require multiple shadow rays to be cast in order to approximate the effect of the finite size. This can yield soft shadows (penumbra). The ratio of shadow rays that hit the light to the total number of rays determines how far the point is in the shadow. In either case, the shadowing coefficient is used to scale the light intensity used in the calculations. Both the diffuse and specular components will be scaled down in proportion to the shadow coefficient.

The net mathematical effect of shadowing is that we generate an intensity scaling factor which is either 0 (light is blocked), 1 (light is totally unblocked), or between 0 and 1 (intersection point is in shadow penumbra, i.e., can partially see the light). The color is then scaled by the shadow coefficient and added to the ambient lighting terms to produce the total light contribution due to the surface alone. We still, however, must consider the light coming from other surfaces by examining the reflected and refracted rays of light.

Reflection and Refraction

The coefficients **Ks** and **Kt** determine how much of the light is actually reflected and transmitted (refracted), respectively. If **Ks** is 0, then the surface is diffuse and there are no reflected rays. Similarly, if **Kt** is 0, the surface is completely opaque. The reflected ray color is then weighted by **Ks** and the refracted (transmitted) ray is weighted by **Kt**. All contributions are then summed over all light sources and this total color, *I*, is returned as the color of the ray.

Ks and **Kt** are rgb vectors since we may want to weight the color components differently. This allows the simulation of colored glass in which certain colors are transmitted and others reflected. For instance, blue glass might have **Kt** of (.1,.1,.7). Some of you may be interested in how the reflection and refraction of light is modeled mathematically. Modeling reflection is simple. The angle at which a light ray hits an object (the incident light ray) is equal to the ray at which it is reflected (the reflected light ray). See Figure 5.26.

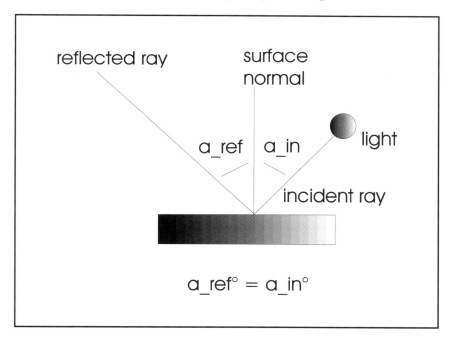

Figure 5.26—Reflection of Light Rays

An equation that models this reflection in vector form is:

reflected_ray_direction = incident_ray_direction + 2 *
(incident_ray_direction • surface_normal) * surface_normal

This equation states that the reflected ray direction is equal to the incident ray direction, plus 2 times the dot product of the incident ray direction with the surface normal, times the surface normal vector. Both reflected ray direction and incident ray direction are three-dimensional vectors (for our purposes). Modeling the transmission and refraction of light rays into materials like glass and water is only a little more complex. You may remember Snell's law from high school physics. It relates the angle of an incident light ray to the angle of a transmitted (refracted) light ray. See Figure 5.27.

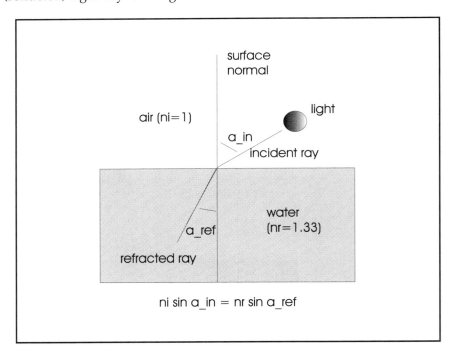

Figure 5.27—Refraction/Transmission of Light Rays

Snell's law models the bending of light when light leaves the material in which it is traveling for another material (i.e., a ray of light is traveling through the air, it intersects a bowl of water and the ray direction bends toward the surface normal when it enters the water, because light travels more slowly in water). The equation that models this phenomenon is

index_of_refraction_for_incident_ray_material *
     sin (incident_ray_angle) =
     index_of_refraction_for_refracted_ray_material *
     sin (refracted_ray_angle)

The index_of_refraction constants are based on the material characteristics. These values are computed as

index_of_refraction = speed_of_light_in_a_vacuum /
     speed_of_light_in_the_given_material.

The index of refraction for air is very close to that of a vacuum. If varies greatly for glass and water. Following is a short table of some indices of refraction for common materials in yellow (600 nm) light.

Gases
    Air   1.0003
    Carbon Dioxide   1.0005

Liquids
    Carbon disulfide   1.64
    Carbon tetrachloride   1.46
    Ethyl Alcohol   1.35
    Water   1.33

Solids
    Diamond   2.42
    Glass   1.50--1.66
    Quartz   1.46

Figure 5.28—Indices of Refraction for Some Common Transparent Materials (table from Physics for Students of Science and Engineering / A.L. Stanford and J.M. Tanner—Georgia Institute of Technology)

Texture Mapping and Textures

The idea of texture mapping, the mapping of an image onto another surface, is conceptually simple. When a point on the surface of an object needs to be rendered, the color for that point is determined by transforming the three-dimensional intersection point to a two-dimensional point in the texture map image. The color of the texture map at that point is input to the shading model to determine the color of the surface at the intersection point. Using this technique, relatively simple geometric models can be rendered with a great amount of apparent complexity. While texture mapping is a very powerful technique, it does have its limitations. The most obvious is the problem of mapping a two-dimensional image onto a three-dimensional object without distorting the texture-mapped image excessively. Flat surfaces are no problem, but surfaces with complex shapes can be difficult to map. Even for a relatively simple surface, such as a sphere, the texture map must be distorted to get it to fit onto the three-dimensional surface. On spheres this results in compression of the texture at the poles.

Peachey[1985] and Perlin[1985] simultaneously developed the idea of solid texturing to solve this problem. The underlying principle of solid texturing is to create a three-dimensional texture map from which the textured object appears to be carved. This texture map may either be explicitly defined as a three-dimensional array of values, consuming huge amounts of memory, or be defined by a procedural function. The procedural function takes an (x,y,z) point and returns the surface characteristics at that point. Perlin introduced the noise() function to generate many of his procedural textures. To this day the images he produced for his SIGGRAPH paper [Perlin 1985] are considered some of the best in computer graphics.

Another useful texturing technique is known as bump mapping. In bump mapping, the surface normal is perturbed to provide the surface with a bumpy or wavy appearance. The idea was originally championed by the guru of computer graphics, Jim Blinn. He was studying the problem of modeling wrinkled surfaces. On a finely wrinkled surface, like an orange, our perception of the wrinkles is due not to being able to see the folds themselves but to how the light bounces off the surface folds. The surface normal is highly variable even though the surface itself is relatively smooth. Thus, he reasoned that you did not have to model the folds but instead could simply vary the surface normal vector in a random fashion across the surface. When this normal is used by the lighting calculations, the variations will cause the surface to appear rough and uneven, when in fact it is still perfectly smooth! Bump mapping is extremely useful in the creation of rough or wavy surfaces for virtual reality systems.

The first, and still most popular, type of texture mapping is the mapping of an image onto a surface. The solid texturing and bump mapping approaches are used for the nonplanar primitives. The basic operation is to convert the three-dimensional intersection point into an index into the texture map. Since the two-dimensional value will normally be floating point, we will interpolate adjacent pixel values in the texture map to get the texture value to use at the intersection point. By default, this texture value is used as the diffuse color at this point, but you can also use it modulate any of the other attributes, most notably the transparency **Kt**.

Noise

The noise() function we have discussed would provide repeatable random numbers which are invariant under rotation and translation and have a narrow limit in frequency. The transformational invariance is required to allow textured models to be moved in space while keeping their surface texture constant. For example, as a chair with a wood texture is moved, its grain pattern should not shift and change as a result of the movement. The narrow frequency band requirement is beneficial because given a noise curve of a known frequency it is fairly easy to create a curve of any desired frequency characteristics by scaling and summing the simpler curve. A narrow frequency range means that, as the fairy tale goes, the function doesn't vary too much and doesn't vary too little but changes just the right amount over space. The noise function is also a continuous function over space.

Totally New Waves

In addition to using stochastic noise to perturb textures, sine waves can give many nice effects. These waves act like compression waves, alternately pushing and pulling the point passed to the texture function along a line from the point of intersection to the source of the wave. Waves should be defined by a source, wavelength, amplitude, phase, and damping factor. The source specifies the point from which the wave emanates, and the wavelength defines the distance between wave peaks. The amplitude determines how far the point is pushed by the wave. The phase is a number which determines the phase of the wave at the source point (whether the wave is up, down, 0, or somewhere in between). The damping factor determines the falloff with distance the wave's amplitude experiences. You should be able to affect a surface by more than one wave source. The offsets generated by the waves are summed to produce the total offset for the intersection point. Waves seem to have limited use in generating interesting solid textures; they are used primarily in procedural bump mapping, described next.

Bump Mapping

The noise and wave functions used by the procedural solid texturing may also be used to provide procedural bump mapping. The results from the functions are used to perturb the surface normal, N, based on the point of intersection. This perturbed normal is then the one used in the shading calculations. Since the surface's brightness, highlights, reflection, and refraction are all dependent on the surface normal, a small change is all that's needed to effect a large difference in the resulting image. It should also be noted that the cost of evaluating the wave function at each intersection point is fairly high, especially if there is more than one set of waves to evaluate.

Atmospheric Effects

The realism of outdoor scenes is greatly enhanced by the addition of atmospheric effects such as fog and haze. In the real world, fog and haze are evident by the scattering of light over a distance, due to what is in the atmosphere. The simplest model of such scattering is that of exponential decay, which assumes a uniform scattering medium. The object color is blended with a background haze color using the equation:

    alpha = exp(- distance / haze_distance);

    color = alpha * object_color + (1-alpha) * haze_color;

where haze_distance is the visibility distance, distance is length of the vector E, and haze_color is normally the background color. As objects get farther away, they will slowly merge into the haze. A fog effect can be achieved by evaluating alpha as a function of the intersection point position as well as the distance. For example, a layered fog effect can be produced by setting alpha = 1.0 if the point is above the top of the fog layer, otherwise evaluating the foregoing equation when it drops below the fog height.

Digital Image Warping

This is our one last note about bitmap image texturing. A method that is of particular use to polygon rendering systems like ours (pending we had the CPU cycles) is to warp an image after projection. When you project the four corners of an image (say that picture of uncle Bob on the wall of your office), you can map the four corners of the rectangular input image to the perspective distorted quadrilateral output image (quadrilateral if you are looking at the picture at an angle). Since you still have your transformation matrix for the projected polygon that represented the image, you can map the pixels of the rectangular image to the quadrilateral projection.

In practice, one should scan the pixels that represent the screen-space projected polygon and compute the texture map (picture) coordinates. This tells you which pixel to grab from the original image. This screen-space pixel takes on this grabbed pixel's color. This is referred to as an inverse sampling.

Below are briefly stated mathematics for performing the forward and inverse functions:

Given the affine transformation:

$$[x,y,1] = [u,v,1] \, \mathbf{M}\text{comp}$$

where $[x,y,1]$ is a pixel in the output image (displayed image), $[u,v,1]$ is a pixel in the input image (original picture), and $\mathbf{M}$ comp is a composite affine transformation matrix holding translation, rotation, and scaling information from the original to the output image,

$$\mathbf{M}\text{comp} = \begin{vmatrix} 1 & 0 & 0 \\ 0 & 1 & 0 \\ T_u & T_v & 1 \end{vmatrix} \begin{vmatrix} \cos t & \sin t & 0 \\ -\sin t & \cos t & 0 \\ 0 & 0 & 1 \end{vmatrix} \begin{vmatrix} S_u & 0 & 0 \\ 0 & S_v & 0 \\ 0 & 0 & 1 \end{vmatrix}$$

$$= \begin{vmatrix} S_u \cos t & S_v \sin t & 0 \\ -S_u \sin t & S_v \cos t & 0 \\ S_u(T_u \cos t - T_v \sin t) & S_v(T_u \sin t - T_v \cos t) & 1 \end{vmatrix}$$

$$= \begin{vmatrix} a_{11} & a_{12} & 0 \\ a_{21} & a_{22} & 0 \\ a_{31} & a_{32} & 1 \end{vmatrix}$$

Computation of the inverse affine transformation matrix gives us:

$$k = \frac{1}{a_{11}a_{22} - a_{21}a_{12}}$$

$$[u, v, 1] =$$
$$k * [x, y, 1] \begin{vmatrix} a_{22} & -a_{12} & 0 \\ -a_{21} & a_{11} & 0 \\ a_{21}a_{32} - a_{31}a_{22} & a_{31}a_{12} - a_{11}a_{32} & a_{11}a_{22} - a_{12}a_{21} \end{vmatrix}$$

So given a point $[x,y,1]$ for the output whose color we want to compute, we have a way of computing the input image (texture map) coordinate that stores our desired color. This also guarantees that we will have all of our output image pixels mapped just once (so no holes and no repeat mappings of the same output pixel).

For those desiring perspective transformation, we need to make the generalization that the affine transformation does not give us, namely:

$$[x', y', w'] = [u, v, w] \ \mathbf{M}\text{comp}$$

and

$$\mathbf{M}\text{comp} = \begin{vmatrix} a_{11} & a_{12} & a_{13} \\ a_{21} & a_{22} & a_{23} \\ a_{31} & a_{32} & a_{33} \end{vmatrix}$$

where our output image coordinate (x,y) is computed as

$$x = \frac{x'}{w'}$$

$$y = \frac{y'}{w'}$$

Once again, the inverse mapping is the most useful, and it is:

```
[u,  v,  w] =

                   |a22a33 - a32a23   a32a13 - a12a33   a12a23 - a13a22|
[x', y', w']       |a23a31 - a33a21   a33a11 - a13a31   a13a21 - a11a23|
                   |a21a32 - a31a22   a31a12 - a11a32   a11a22 - a12a21|
```

See the text *Digital Image Warping* by George Wolberg for an excellent disertation of image warping techniques.

Bubba, Our Shading and Texturing

As you may have guessed, many of the techniques discussed are a bit too computationally expensive for us to deal with on our IBM PCs. Our implementation of shading is nonexistent, and our implementations of texturing that we do have take liberties with proper projection. We resort to techniques for transparency like drawing every other pixel of a polygon (thus you see what was behind this "transparent" polygon—is this cheating???) In any case, we hope that you have a better idea about how shading and texturing work and how they can be important to virtual reality graphics systems. For those interested in the implementation of some of the above shading algorithms, look for the excellent book *Photorealism and Ray Tracing in C* by Christopher D. Watkins, Stephen B. Coy, and Mark Finlay.

Section 9—Motion, Interaction, and Simulation

Modeling and simulating reality is one of the most practical and common uses of the computer for scientists and engineers. Computer simulation of physical laws allows manufacturers and developers to predict how their products and inventions will function out in the real world. Events as complex as space missions can be launched and safely completed in the computer laboratory with no risk to human life (beyond a little eye strain and an occasional reaction to caffeine). Many of the video games that you see are also based on basic computer simulations.

Any virtual reality system must allow the user to interact with a virtual world in a very real way. Controls or input devices are necessary for any interaction to take place. These controls can be basic, like the keyboard, the mouse, or the joystick, or they can be more complex like the six degrees of freedom spaceball, or a yoke and pedals for a flight simulator. Data gloves, human eye position sensors, voice and gesture recognition, and a myriad of other advanced controls are also available.

Interactions with the virtual world can be simple. Grabbing and moving an object in the virtual world is a basic operation. Interaction could be a little more advanced by blocking the user's motion, when the user walks into a wall (referred to as viewer-object collision detection), for instance. Or perhaps the interaction is as complex as a flight simulation, where how the user sets the controls at this instant will affect the feel and response of the same controls in the future. Our virtual reality fellow may be playing "virtual indoor soccer"; he has just kicked the ball, and the ball bounces off of a wall (a form of object-object collision detection is used to detect the ball touching the wall). The system may be even more complex, if he is playing virtual pool with many individual object-object interactions (interactions between the array of pool balls).

These interactions must be modeled mathematically. Kinematics and dynamics are fields of study that allow us to do just that. The results of evaluating the kinematic or dynamical mathematical expressions may affect the view, the positions of objects, or how the controls feel. We call this simulation. If you think of simulation as complex as eye surgery simulation, you will see that the positions and orientations of the controls (a virtual knife, in this case) feed numerical information to mathematical expressions. The mathematically processed information is used by the graphics processors to show you if your knife has contacted tissue. If your virtual knife has contacted tissue, then the mathematical expressions tell the controls (the virtual knife) to be a bit more physically resistive to movement. This tactile/haptic feedback (called force feedback) is essential for realistic simulation.

The mathematics of simulation are usually complex in practice but based on many fundamental physical principles. A bouncing ball, a cannon shot, and the pool balls on a pool table are all affected by gravity, by the frictional surfaces that they contact which apply force, and by their own physical characteristics (mass, surface, etc.). We generally find that we must take liberties with the physics if we want great performance simulating real-world events; i.e., we make approximations. When you are simulating for appearance and not accuracy, even more approximations can be and are commonly made.

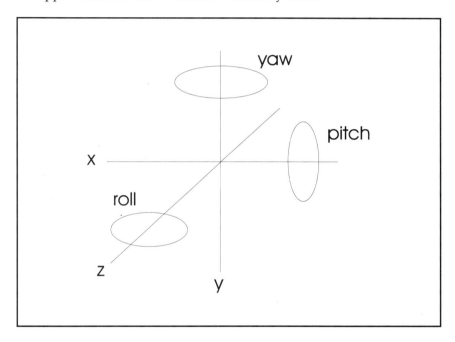

Figure 5.29—Pitch, Yaw and Roll

The Software

The virtual reality software with this book allows full control over viewer pitch, yaw and roll. This means that the viewer can look in any direction and from any position within the virtual world. See Figure 5.29 for an understanding of pitch, yaw, and roll. These are aeronautical terms, referring to control surfaces of an aircraft. The elevator controls aircraft pitch, the rudder controls aircraft yaw, and the ailerons control aircraft roll.

Since for a virtual reality experience, we cannot be static, we have the ability of free dynamical movement. This movement is controlled by the throttle (another airplane part). The viewer is moving in some direction and can change direction by simply changing the view direction to the desired direction of travel.

If you have used the software, you may have noticed that the longer you hold down a key for a given motion (translations or rotations), the more of that movement you will have, up to a maximum limiting value. When you release the key for the given movement, the movement slowly decreases and comes to a rest. The routines found in ALG_CTRL.C govern these control reactions. Basically, by holding down a given key, you are increasing the amount of change for some movement. The longer you hold down the control (key), the more times the control has contributed to some variable that represents the change in movement. When releasing the control, you are no longer contributing to this variable. You might think that the movement would continue forever. Well, that would be true, except that we add a dampening factor for each control that will always try to bring that movement change variable back to zero, stopping any movement after a bit of time. One interesting effect is created by using the roll control keys to "rock" the view from side to side. This motion may remind you of being on a boat. Unfortunately, it reminds me of a certain scuba trip.

In the software, simple interactions with objects like moving and reorienting are handled. Physical stipulations are placed on certain objects to allow them only certain degrees of freedom (i.e., they can move only in certain ways—a door has rotational motion around one axis, and the distance it can swing is usually bound, since it cannot swing through the wall from which it is hanging).

* * *

We have talked about rotations and translations for the viewer and for objects in the virtual world, but up to now we have not really discussed how the program actually performs these functions. Examine the listing in the following program listings section referred to as "transform objects from local and world coordinates to view coordinates." This section of code creates a master transformation matrix by which all polygon vertices will be multiplied in order to transform them for proper viewing. This master transformation matrix is composed from the multiplication of two matrices, the viewer transformation matrix and the object's local transformation matrix.

We first initialize our view matrix to the identity matrix (diagonal elements are 1, all others 0). Then we create a viewer translation matrix and multiply it with our existing view matrix. This in effect will be used to reposition all objects in the virtual world relative to the viewer. Then a viewer rotation matrix is created and multiplied by the existing view matrix in order to rotate our previously shifted (translated) objects around the viewer, so that we see a proper view.

Now that we have the first part of the master transformation matrix under control—i.e., the view matrix that is applied to all of the objects in the virtual world—it is time to perform local transformations on individual objects, based on how each of those objects is positioned, oriented, and scaled in the virtual world. So, for each object, we create a local transformation matrix by first setting the local matrix to the identity matrix. We then simply perform scaling, rotation, and translation of the object by multiplying matrices together that we created for scaling, rotation, and translation.

We now have both the viewer and local object transformation matrices, so to create our master transformation matrix, we simply multiply the two together. Remember always that when multiplying matrices, the order of multiplication is significant.

To finish the transformation routine, we multiply all of the vertices in the virtual world with our master transformation matrix. This multiplication yields vertices for objects that are properly placed for projection from the three-dimensional virtual world to your very real two-dimensional computer display.

After using the software, you will find that performance can be increased by adding a world vertex into the alg_vertex_3D_type structure and transforming vertices from local to world in the conditional statement where the local transformation matrix is built. You would remove the multiply of this local transformation matrix with the viewer transformation matrix, and then transform all vertices from world to viewer. The routine exists the way that it does to show you that you can further transform points by multiplying (concatenating) matrices.

We have also included a simple particle simulation program. Three particles interact in orbital motion, like planets. You could extend the program to control the position of one of the particles and watch how the others interact with it. This program in effect is simulating gravitation attractions and in turn affecting velocities, accelerations, and positions of the particles.

As we have mentioned, mathematics are used to simulate physical events. We will now take a brief look at what some of those mathematical expressions might look like for damped motion, for simple mass-spring systems, and for particle systems. We will cover more information on interaction after our look at these three types of systems.

Any Simple Damped Motion Simulation

As we have mentioned, our controls represent damped motion. The viewer releases the key that he was pressing to cause a roll rotation, and the roll slowly decreases to no roll. You can use a similar idea to simulate frictional surfaces computationally cheaply. The rate of travel of the virtual pool balls on the virtual pool table can be governed by such an algorithm. A quick look at an excerpt from ALG_CTRL.C shows us that damping of the control position toward its initial inactive state (position of control = 0) always happens. Additions are made to the control position only if the key is being held down. These additions should be greater than any damping values; thus the control position (and in turn the roll rate) increases. So, the pool ball's rate is governed by the position of the control, and the force with which it was struck is represented by an initially offset control position. The greater the offset, the greater the force that hits the ball.

```
// control roll with ailerons

if (*aileron_position < -ALG_ZERO)
        *aileron_position += *aileron_dampening;
else
        if (*aileron_position > ALG_ZERO)
                *aileron_position -= *aileron_dampening;

if ((*aileron_left_down) && (*aileron_position
        < *max_aileron_position))
{
        *aileron_position += *delta_aileron_position;
        *aileron_left_down = ALG_FALSE;
}
else
        if ((*aileron_right_down) && (*aileron_position
                > -*max_aileron_position))
```

```
{
        *aileron_position  -=  *delta_aileron_position;
        *aileron_right_down  =  ALG_FALSE;
}
```

Mass-Spring Systems for Simulation

Mass-spring networks are commonly used to define pliable surfaces. Waterbeds to trampolines and any other deformable surface can be modeled with two-dimensional mass-spring networks. Single-dimensional mass-spring systems can model rubber bands and ropes.

You may remember Hooke's law from high school physics:

$$\text{Force} = -kx \qquad\qquad\qquad\qquad\qquad \textbf{(5-14)}$$

where k represents Hooke's spring constant (a positive number) and x is the displacement of the mass. This is the governing fundamental equation of most mass-spring systems.

Let us consider the case shown in Figure 5.30.

Here we have masses m1, m2, ..., m4 connected together with springs. Springs also connect the outside masses to the walls, to make a total count of five springs.

The Hooke's law equation gives us the force exerted by one spring on one mass. Now examine Figure 5.31. If the mass moves to the right, the displacement is considered to be positive, if the mass moves to the left, the displacement is negative.

Looking back at Figure 5.30, let us call x_i the displacement of the ith mass, and let k_i denote the Hooke's constant of the ith spring. The first spring is between the left wall and the first mass. For $i = 2$, 3 and 4, the ith spring connects the $(i\text{-}1)$th mass to the ith mass. The fifth spring connects the last mass to the right wall.

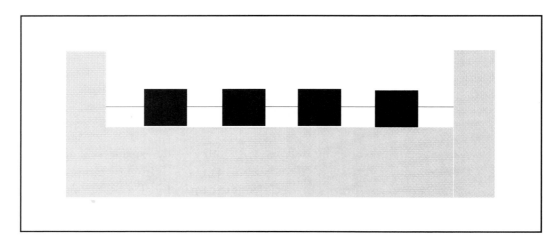

Figure 5.30—A Four-Mass Mass-Spring System

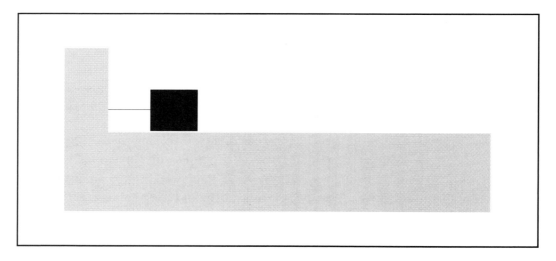

Figure 5.31—One Spring and One Mass

Now for a little mathematics. We will derive differential equations to *mathematically model* the system of masses and springs. For an example, let us look at the forces on the third mass. Say that the spring to the left of the third mass is elongated by x_3-x_2. If this is positive, then the spring pulls to the left, so that the force exerted by the third spring on the third mass is:

$$f_{left} = -k_3(x_3\text{-}x_2) \tag{5-15}$$

The forth spring, the spring to the right of the third mass, also exerts a force on that third mass. A similar analysis shows that this force is:

$$f_{right} = -k_4(x_3\text{-}x_4) \tag{5-16}$$

Using Newton's law, $F = ma$, and the preceding force calculations, we obtain the equation:

$$m_3 \; \frac{d^2x_3}{dt^2} = -(-k_3x_2 + (k_3+k_4)x_3 - k_4x_4) \tag{5-17}$$

For a general ith force-balance equation (excluding the two springs connecting the mass string to the walls), we have:

$$m_i \; \frac{d^2x_i}{dt^2} = -(-k_ix_{(i-1)} + (k_i+k_{(i+1)})x_i - k_{(i+1)}x_{(i+1)}) \tag{5-18}$$

The two end equations are different in that we have walls as fixed boundaries. Given that there are n masses and $n+1$ springs, the equations are:

$$m_1 \; \frac{d^2x_1}{dt^2} = -((k_1+k_2)x_1 - k_2x_2)$$

$$m_n \; \frac{d^2x_n}{dt^2} = -(-k_nx_{(n-1)} + (k_n+k_{(n+1)})x_n) \tag{5-19}$$

As you might have guessed, these equations can be put into matrix form. This matrix would be n-by-n elements. For a four-mass system (where $n = 4$), we have a four-by-four matrix $\mathbf{M}$ with the diagonal elements as the mass values:

$$\mathbf{M} = \begin{array}{cccc} m_1 & 0 & 0 & 0 \\ 0 & m_2 & 0 & 0 \\ 0 & 0 & m_3 & 0 \\ 0 & 0 & 0 & m_4 \end{array} \qquad (5\text{-}20)$$

Let $\mathbf{D}$ be an n-by-n matrix defined by:

$$\begin{aligned} D_{i,i} &= k_i + k_{(i+1)} \\ D_{i,i\text{-}1} &= \text{-}k_i \\ D_{i,i+1} &= \text{-}k_{i+1} \end{aligned} \qquad (5\text{-}21)$$

with all other elements of $\mathbf{D}$ set to 0. If $i=1$ or $i=n$, we ignore the equation, as the index is out of bounds. Our $\mathbf{D}$ matrix looks like:

$$\mathbf{D} = \begin{array}{cccc} k_1+k_2 & -k_2 & 0 & 0 \\ -k_2 & k_2+k_3 & -k_3 & 0 \\ 0 & -k_3 & k_3+k_4 & -k_4 \\ 0 & 0 & -k_4 & k_4+k_5 \end{array} \qquad (5\text{-}22)$$

Let:

$$x = x(t) = \begin{array}{c} x_1 \\ x_2 \\ x_3 \\ x_4 \end{array} \qquad (5\text{-}23)$$

be the vector of displacements. Combining all of this, we get the force-balance equation:

$$\mathbf{M}\, x''(t) = \text{-}\, \mathbf{D}\, x(t) \qquad (5\text{-}24)$$

where $\mathbf{x}''$ is the vector whose components are:

$$\frac{d^2 x_i}{dt^2} \qquad (5\text{-}25)$$

Noting that

$$\mathbf{M}^{-1} = \begin{matrix} 1/m_1 & 0 & 0 & 0 \\ 0 & 1/m_2 & 0 & 0 \\ 0 & 0 & 1/m_3 & 0 \\ 0 & 0 & 0 & 1/m_4 \end{matrix} \qquad (5\text{-}26)$$

and multiplying both sides of the equation by $\mathbf{M}^{-1}$ yields:

$$\mathbf{M}^{-1} \mathbf{M} \, x'' = -\mathbf{M}^{-1} \mathbf{D} \, x \qquad (5\text{-}27)$$

or

$$x'' = \mathbf{M}^{-1} \mathbf{D} \, x \qquad (5\text{-}28)$$

This equation can now be solved. By setting $\mathbf{A} = \mathbf{M}^{-1} \mathbf{D}$, we now guess a solution. It will be in the form of $x(t) = x_0 \sin(\omega t)$. Here x_0 is some unknown fixed vector and ω is some unknown frequency of vibration. Computing yields $x' = \omega \cos (\omega t)$, and $x'' = -\omega^2 x_0 \sin(\omega t)$. Substituting this into the equation yields:

$$-\omega^2 x_0 \sin(\omega t) = \mathbf{A} x_0 \sin(\omega t) \qquad (5\text{-}29)$$

Dividing through by the scalar $\sin(\omega t)$ gives:

$$-\omega^2 x_0 = \mathbf{A} x_0 \qquad (5\text{-}30)$$

This equation possibly triggers the thoughts of eigenvalues and eigenvectors. Examine the following equation:

$$\lambda x_0 = \mathbf{A} x_0 \qquad (5\text{-}31)$$

λ is an eigenvalue of $\mathbf{A}$, if there is a nonzero vector x_0. This vector x_0 is called an eigenvector. We see that $\omega = \upsilon/\lambda$, whenever λ is a negative eigenvalue of $\mathbf{A}$. Simply stated, $x_0 \sin (\omega t)$ is a solution whenever $-\omega^2$ is an eigenvalue of $\mathbf{A}$.

Practical implementation of this would involve computation of the matrix $\mathbf{A}$. We would enter our masses and spring constants and rest positions. The rest positions are used to compute the true positions of the masses for viewing. These values would be added to the x values obtained from our equations, as the x values are just displacements from equilibrium, not real-world positions. Repeated application of the equations, updating the actual positions with the equilibrium offsets, will create the animation of masses moving longitudinally based on spring forces.

This single-dimensional case can be carried to multiple dimensions by creating a two-dimensional array of masses and springs and by adding transverse motion to the system (motion out of the plane of the springs and masses—like waves in a waterbed).

Particle Orbit Models for Simulation

In our simple simulation program, we are going to simulate particle motion in three-dimensional space. Our world will be made of three interacting particles. The particles are given initial positions and velocities, and they are allowed to interact with each other through time. The basic procedure for simulating motion is to erase the current position of the particles, compute their new positions, and then redraw them. If the code that erases the old positions of the particles is commented out, the resulting display will show the particle trails. Notice that the program uses our libraries for three-dimensional transformations, in order to compute the view.

Our program uses a simple physical model of particle motion and mutual interaction. Theoretically, a particle that is in motion will continue to move in the same direction until a force is applied in some other direction. If, instead, the particle is moving along a circular path at a constant velocity, then there is a changing velocity toward the center of the circular path (a force is required to keep the particle moving in a circle). Changing velocity is referred to as acceleration, and this acceleration for circular motion is given by:

$$a = \frac{v^2}{r} \tag{5-32}$$

where a is acceleration, v is velocity, and r is the radius of the circular orbit. By Newton's second law of motion, force equals mass times acceleration. Therefore:

$$F = ma = \frac{mv^2}{r} \tag{5-33}$$

This force is called *centripetal force* and is the force acting toward the center of the circular path. This is the force that keeps the particle orbiting about another particle. In effect, this force is the same as gravity. Let's consider the two-particle case. Each particle in the system is given a position (x_n, y_n, z_n) and a mass (m_n), where n indicates the number of the particle. Particle positions and the distances between them are measured in meters and the masses are in kilograms. The distance between the two particles is the length of the line connecting them. Using the (X, Y, Z) Cartesian coordinate system, the distances are:

$$d_x = |x_2 - x_1|$$
$$d_y = |y_2 - y_1|$$
$$d_z = |z_2 - z_1|$$

(5-34)

The magnitude of the distance vector (dx, dy, dz) is:

$$d = \sqrt{(d_x^2 + d_y^2 + d_z^2)}$$

(5-35)

Now the gravitational force between the particles can be calculated using the law of universal gravitation. This law states that the force due to gravity, F_g, is directly proportional to the product of the masses $(m_1 * m_2)$ and inversely proportional to the distance d between them squared. The gravitational constant of proportionality g has the value of 6.67E-11 (N·m2/kg2). The resulting equation is:

$$F_g = g \frac{m_1 \, m_2}{d^2}$$

(5-36)

This attractive force is along the direction of the line connecting the two particles. The force here is a vector quantity, having both magnitude and direction. Its components are F_x, F_y, and F_z.

Now let's examine some characteristics of systems of particles. Most orbiting patterns generated by the program here will not remain in equilibrium for a long period of time. Sooner or later, a particle will pick up enough momentum to escape the orbiting pattern, or it will be pulled in by another mass (and dividing by a small number will send it flying).

Combination of the equations for acceleration and gravitational force g yields:

$$a_{x1} = \frac{g\ m_2}{d^2} \star \frac{d_x}{d}$$

$$a_{y1} = \frac{g\ m_2}{d^2} \star \frac{d_y}{d} \tag{5-37}$$

$$a_{z1} = \frac{g\ m_2}{d^2} \star \frac{d_z}{d}$$

Since acceleration is the change in velocity with respect to the change in time, the following equations are obtained:

$$\begin{aligned} dv_x &= a_x t \\ dv_y &= a_y t \\ dv_z &= a_z t \end{aligned} \tag{5-38}$$

Given the initial velocity v_0, and traveling through time to time t, we obtain the new vector velocity as:

$$\begin{aligned} v_x &= v_{x0} + a_x t \\ v_y &= v_{y0} + a_y t \\ v_z &= v_{z0} + a_z t \end{aligned} \tag{5-39}$$

Thus, the velocity at the end of the time interval is $v_0 + at$. We can approximate the average velocity throughout the time interval using:

$$v_{avg} = \frac{v_0 + v_0 + at}{2} = v_0 + at \tag{5-40}$$

We want our orbit simulator to show the positions of the particles as the time changes. Therefore we need a set of equations that relate position to time. Since the velocity is the rate of change of position with respect to time, over any time interval, the change in position is the average velocity multiplied by the time. These equations follow:

$$d_x = v_{x0}t + \frac{a_x t^2}{2}$$

$$d_y = v_{y0}t + \frac{a_y t^2}{2} \qquad\qquad \textbf{(5-41)}$$

$$d_z = v_{z0}t + \frac{a_z t^2}{2}$$

Because we know the initial position (x_0, y_0, z_0), the position for any time is:

$$x = x_0 + v_{x0}t + \frac{a_x t^2}{2}$$

$$y = y_0 + v_{y0}t + \frac{a_y t^2}{2} \qquad\qquad \textbf{(5-42)}$$

$$z = z_0 + v_{z0}t + \frac{a_z t^2}{2}$$

Given this mathematical background, we can look at the particle orbit simulation program. We have explored the dynamics of two particles in three-dimensional space. Our program handles three particles in three-dimensional space. Try comparing the preceding discussion with the existing code. You will find that there is only a slight difference in the exponent in the denominator for the calculation of d and that all possible combinations of one particle's effect on another particle are handled (i.e., each particle in the system interacts with and has an effect on every other particle in the system).

The program establishes initial conditions (masses, positions, velocities) for all of the particles. The time step is set to a constant. This step can be any real number greater than zero (moving forward in time). Particles will move faster with a larger step, but the program loses accuracy in position. A loop is now entered that terminates by a keystroke. Within the loop, the particle positions are converted to display coordinates and points are plotted at each particle position. Next, the new position coordinates for each particle after a step in time are computed. The new distance between each set of particles is computed and then used in the gravity equation to compute the effective force on the particle, which in turn generates the new accelerations and velocities. The program continuously loops, plotting positions and leaving particle trails. You may want to remove comment marks to allow erasure of the old particle positions.

More on Interaction

Also included with this book are a couple of simple, yet attractive programs showing you ways of using a mouse as a pointer and as a control for the view of a three-dimensional object. As a pointer, we move the mouse around in one window on the Mandelbrot set, and in another window we see the corresponding Julia set. This is very basic pointing action and an example of how to continue a process while the pointer is moving.

The second, more complex interaction is an intuitive way to deal with a three-dimensional object using a mouse. The left and right mouse motions make the object rotate to the left and to the right, respectively. The up and down mouse motions make the object rotate upward or downward, respectively. Rotation occurs when you hold down the left mouse button. You can make the object continue rotating by releasing the left mouse button while moving the mouse. The faster you are moving when you release the button, the faster the object will rotate. Notice that there is a time delay in the program. This is required in order to determine the speed of the mouse motion (distance mouse traveled per unit time) by allowing the mouse to move some before its position is sampled again.

This second program is located in the section on Stereo Vision and Our Anaglyph Glasses. It is located there, because we have written the program to display stereo pairs for three-dimensional interactive viewing with the anaglyph 3-D glasses included with this book.

Also included at the end of the program listings is a partial listing of a mouse pointer method for snapping onto and selecting a screen point by only being near the point. This routine will snap the mouse to the intersection of displayed spline grid lines that is closest to the mouse position. It is an excerpt from a spline warping program.

One general note: a simple method for selecting a three-dimensional object with a mouse on a two-dimensional screen is to see if the mouse screen position falls within the projected vertices for polygons of that object. That works well for objects with large polygons but not for objects with many small polygons. In order to combat this, project the corners of the bounding volume (box) for the object into screen coordinates, and then see if the mouse screen position falls within these projected bounding box coordinates.

Now, we move on and look at the program listings.

PROGRAM LISTINGS:

```
/*

    +---------------------------------------------------------------------+
    |                                                                     |
    |                      Virtual Reality ExCursions                     |
    |                                                                     |
    |           by Christopher D. Watkins and Stephen R. Marenka          |
    |                                                                     |
    |                 Copyright 1994 : Academic Press, Inc.               |
    |                                                                     |
    |---------------------------------------------------------------------|
    |                                                                     |
    |                              ALG_CTRL.C                             |
    |---------------------------------------------------------------------|
    |                                                                     |
    |                            Software Issues                          |
    |                                                                     |
    |               Copyright 1987-1994 ALGORITHM, Incorporated.          |
    |                                                                     |
    |      ALL RIGHTS RESERVED.   This software is Published, but is NOT  |
    |  Public Domain and remains the property of ALGORITHM, Incorporated and |
    |         Christopher D. Watkins.  This software may not be           |
    |  reproduced or integrated into other packages without the prior written |
    |         consent of Christopher D. Watkins.  Licensing is possible.  |
    |                                                                     |
    +---------------------------------------------------------------------+

*/


//      system includes
#include        <math.h>
```

```c
//      Algorithm, Inc. includes
#include      "Alg_Defs.H"
#include      "Alg_Matx.H"


/*
    +--------------------------------------------------------------------+
    |                 initialize our controls for motion                 |
    +--------------------------------------------------------------------+
*/


void alg_initialize_controls( alg_controls_type *controls )
{
        controls->aileron_left_down          = ALG_FALSE;
        controls->aileron_right_down         = ALG_FALSE;

        controls->aileron_position           = 0.0;
        controls->max_aileron_position       = 0.0;
        controls->delta_aileron_position     = 0.0;
        controls->aileron_dampening          = 0.0;

        controls->elevator_up                = ALG_FALSE;
        controls->elevator_down              = ALG_FALSE;

        controls->elevator_position          = 0.0;
        controls->max_elevator_position      = 0.0;
        controls->delta_elevator_position    = 0.0;
        controls->elevator_dampening         = 0.0;

        controls->rudder_left                = ALG_FALSE;
        controls->rudder_right               = ALG_FALSE;

        controls->rudder_position            = 0.0;
        controls->max_rudder_position        = 0.0;
        controls->delta_rudder_position      = 0.0;
        controls->rudder_dampening           = 0.0;

        controls->throttle_inc               = ALG_FALSE;
        controls->throttle_dec               = ALG_FALSE;
```

```
        controls->throttle_position        = 0.0;
        controls->max_throttle_position    = 0.0;
        controls->delta_throttle_position  = 0.0;
        controls->throttle_dampening       = 0.0;

        controls->halt_translations        = ALG_FALSE;
        controls->halt_rotations           = ALG_FALSE;
}


/*

    +-------------------------------------------------------------------+
    |     interpret the status variables from input for controls status    |
    +-------------------------------------------------------------------+
*/

void alg_interpret_status_variables_for_controls( alg_controls_type
*controls )
{
        alg_boolean   *aileron_left_down  = &controls
              ->aileron_left_down;
        alg_boolean   *aileron_right_down = &controls
              ->aileron_right_down;

        alg_float     *aileron_position       = &controls
              ->aileron_position;
        alg_float     *max_aileron_position   = &controls
              ->max_aileron_position;
        alg_float     *delta_aileron_position = &controls
              ->delta_aileron_position;
        alg_float     *aileron_dampening       = &controls
              ->aileron_dampening;

        alg_boolean   *elevator_up   = &controls->elevator_up;
        alg_boolean   *elevator_down = &controls->elevator_down;

        alg_float     *elevator_position      = &controls
              ->elevator_position;
        alg_float     *max_elevator_position  = &controls
              ->max_elevator_position;
```

```
alg_float      *delta_elevator_position = &controls
     ->delta_elevator_position;
alg_float      *elevator_dampening      = &controls
     ->elevator_dampening;

alg_boolean    *rudder_left  = &controls->rudder_left;
alg_boolean    *rudder_right = &controls->rudder_right;

alg_float      *rudder_position         = &controls
     ->rudder_position;
alg_float      *max_rudder_position     = &controls
     ->max_rudder_position;
alg_float      *delta_rudder_position = &controls
     ->delta_rudder_position;
alg_float      *rudder_dampening        = &controls
     ->rudder_dampening;

alg_boolean    *throttle_inc = &controls->throttle_inc;
alg_boolean    *throttle_dec = &controls->throttle_dec;

alg_float      *throttle_position       = &controls
     ->throttle_position;
alg_float      *max_throttle_position   = &controls
     ->max_throttle_position;
alg_float      *delta_throttle_position = &controls
     ->delta_throttle_position;
alg_float      *throttle_dampening      = &controls
     ->throttle_dampening;

alg_boolean    *halt_translations = &controls->halt_translations;
alg_boolean    *halt_rotations    = &controls->halt_rotations;

// control roll with ailerons

if (*aileron_position < -ALG_ZERO)
     *aileron_position += *aileron_dampening;
else
     if (*aileron_position > ALG_ZERO)
          *aileron_position -= *aileron_dampening;
```

```
if ((*aileron_left_down) && (*aileron_position <
        *max_aileron_position))
{
        *aileron_position += *delta_aileron_position;
        *aileron_left_down = ALG_FALSE;
}
else
        if ((*aileron_right_down) && (*aileron_position >
                -*max_aileron_position))
        {
                *aileron_position -= *delta_aileron_position;
                *aileron_right_down = ALG_FALSE;
        }


// control pitch with elevator

if (*elevator_position < -ALG_ZERO)
        *elevator_position += *elevator_dampening;
else
        if (*elevator_position > ALG_ZERO)
                *elevator_position -= *elevator_dampening;

if ((*elevator_up) && (*elevator_position <
        *max_elevator_position))
{
        *elevator_position += *delta_elevator_position;
        *elevator_up = ALG_FALSE;
}
else
        if ((*elevator_down) && (*elevator_position >
                -*max_elevator_position))
        {
                *elevator_position -= *delta_elevator_position;
                *elevator_down = ALG_FALSE;
        }


// control yaw with rudder
```

```
if (*rudder_position < -ALG_ZERO)
        *rudder_position += *rudder_dampening;
else
        if (*rudder_position > ALG_ZERO)
                *rudder_position -= *rudder_dampening;


if ((*rudder_left) && (*rudder_position < *max_rudder_position))
{
        *rudder_position += *delta_rudder_position;
        *rudder_left = ALG_FALSE;
}
else
        if ((*rudder_right) && (*rudder_position >
                -*max_rudder_position))
        {
                *rudder_position -= *delta_rudder_position;
                *rudder_right = ALG_FALSE;
        }


// control rate of movement with throttle
//      (movement along direction of (roll, pitch, yaw))

if (*throttle_position < -ALG_ZERO)
        *throttle_position += *throttle_dampening;
else
        if (*throttle_position > ALG_ZERO)
                *throttle_position -= *throttle_dampening;


if ((*throttle_inc) && (*throttle_position <
        *max_throttle_position))
{
        *throttle_position += *delta_throttle_position;
        *throttle_inc = ALG_FALSE;
}
else
        if ((*throttle_dec) && (*throttle_position >
                -*max_throttle_position))
        {
                *throttle_position -= *delta_throttle_position;
```

```
                                *throttle_dec = ALG_FALSE;
                    }


            // control halt translations


            if (*halt_translations)
            {
                    *throttle_position   = 0.0;
                    *halt_translations   = ALG_FALSE;
            }


            // control halt rotations


            if (*halt_rotations)
            {
                    *aileron_position    = 0.0;
                    *elevator_position   = 0.0;
                    *rudder_position     = 0.0;
                    *halt_rotations      = ALG_FALSE;
            }
    }


    /*

        +------------------------------------------------------------------+
        |            interpret the controls for motion and view            |
        +------------------------------------------------------------------+
    */


    void alg_interpret_controls_for_motion_and_view( alg_viewer_3D_type
    *viewer,       alg_controls_type *controls )
    {
            static alg_float       lowest_flight_position = 5.0;

            alg_float              *viewer_position_x = &viewer->translate.x;
            alg_float              *viewer_position_y = &viewer->translate.y;
            alg_float              *viewer_position_z = &viewer->translate.z;
            alg_float              *viewer_rotation_x = &viewer->rotate.x;
            alg_float              *viewer_rotation_y = &viewer->rotate.y;
            alg_float              *viewer_rotation_z = &viewer->rotate.z;
```

```
alg_matrix_4x4_type   motion_direction_transformation_matrix;
alg_point_3D_type     rotate;
alg_point_3D_type     base_position;
alg_point_3D_type     delta_position;


// initialize our incremental positional change
ALG_VEC3_MAKE( 0.0, 0.0, controls->throttle_position,
        base_position );

// initialize our incremental directional change
*viewer_rotation_x += controls->elevator_position; // pitch
*viewer_rotation_y += controls->rudder_position;   // yaw
*viewer_rotation_z += controls->aileron_position;  // roll
ALG_VEC3_MAKE( *viewer_rotation_x, *viewer_rotation_y,
        *viewer_rotation_z, rotate );

// initialize motion direction transformation matrix with
//      identity matrix
alg_identity_4x4_matrix(
        motion_direction_transformation_matrix );

// create rotate matrix and multiply it
//      with motion direction transformation matrix
alg_rotate_4x4_matrix( rotate,
        motion_direction_transformation_matrix,
        MOTION_ROTATION );

// transform position with motion direction transformation
//      matrix, thus, viewer is now headed in another direction
alg_transform_4x4_matrix( delta_position,
        motion_direction_transformation_matrix,
        base_position );


// update our viewer position with the incremental positional
//      change
*viewer_position_x += delta_position.x;
```

```
      *viewer_position_y += delta_position.y;
      *viewer_position_z += delta_position.z;

      // do not allow travel below ground, if you hit the ground,
      //     level the viewer
      if (*viewer_position_y < lowest_flight_position)
      {
            *viewer_position_y = lowest_flight_position +
                  controls->delta_rudder_position;
            // note the addition of delta_rudder_position,
            //     this inhibits control oscillation (bounce)
            *viewer_rotation_x = 0.0;
            controls->elevator_position = 0.0;
      }
}
```

Below is the code for a how objects are transformed based on the viewer direction, and any local transformations for objects (i.e., a spinning cube).

```
/*

   +------------------------------------------------------------------+
   | transform objects from local and world coordinates to view       |
   | coordinates                                                       |
   +------------------------------------------------------------------+

      excerpt from ALG_3D.C  Copyright 1987-1994 Algorithm, Inc.
*/

void alg_transform_objects_for_viewing( alg_world_3D_type *world,
      alg_viewer_3D_type *viewer )
{
      alg_word            object_num;
      alg_object_3D_type  *object_ptr;
      alg_word            vertex_num;
      alg_vertex_3D_type  *vertex_ptr;
      alg_point_3D_type   translate;
      alg_point_3D_type   rotate;
      alg_matrix_4x4_type transformation_matrix;
      // compute the viewer transformation matrix
      // initialize viewer transformation matrix with identity matrix
```

```
alg_identity_4x4_matrix( viewer->viewer_transformation_matrix );

// create translate matrix and multiply it with viewer
//      transformation matrix in order to reposition and reorient
//      objects relative to viewer
ALG_VEC3_NEGATE2( viewer->translate, translate );
alg_translate_4x4_matrix( translate, viewer
        ->viewer_transformation_matrix );

// create rotate matrix and multiply it with viewer
//      transformation matrix in order to rotate our shifted
//      objects around the viewer for proper viewing
ALG_VEC3_NEGATE2( viewer->rotate, rotate );
alg_rotate_4x4_matrix( rotate, viewer
        ->viewer_transformation_matrix,
        VIEWER_ROTATION );

// now perform transformations on every object in the world

for (object_num=0; object_num<world->num_objects; object_num++)
{
        object_ptr = &world->object[object_num];

        if (object_ptr->invalid_local_transformation_matrix)
        {
                // compute the object local transformation matrix

                // object local transformation matrix will now be
                //      validated
                object_ptr->invalid_local_transformation_matrix =
                        ALG_FALSE;

                // initialize object local transformation matrix
                //      with identity matrix
                alg_identity_4x4_matrix( object_ptr
                        ->local_transformation_matrix );
                // create scale matrix and multiply it
                //      with object local transformation matrix
                alg_scale_4x4_matrix( object_ptr->scale,
```

```
                               object_ptr->local_transformation_matrix );

               // create rotate matrix and multiply it
               //     with object local transformation matrix
               alg_rotate_4x4_matrix( object_ptr->rotate,
                       object_ptr->local_transformation_matrix,
                       OBJECT_ROTATION );

               // create translate matrix and multiply it
               //     with object local transformation matrix
               alg_translate_4x4_matrix( object_ptr->translate,
                       object_ptr->local_transformation_matrix );
       }

       // create total transformation matrix by multiplying the
       //     viewer transformation matrix by the local
       //     transformation matrix.
       //
       //     Note:  Performance can be increased by adding a
       //     world vertex into the alg_vertex_3D_type sturcture
       //     and transforming vertices from local to world in
       //     the above conditional statement.  You would
       //     remove the multiply below, and then transform all
       //     vertices from world to viewer.  The routine exists
       //     this way to show you that you can further
       //     transform points by multiplying (concatenating)
       //     matrices.
       alg_multiply_4x4_matrix( transformation_matrix,
               viewer->viewer_transformation_matrix,
               object_ptr->local_transformation_matrix );

       // transform object with total transformation matrix
       for (vertex_num=0; vertex_num<object_ptr->num_vertices;
               vertex_num++)
       {
               vertex_ptr = &object_ptr->vertex[vertex_num];
               alg_transform_4x4_matrix( vertex_ptr->viewer,
                                       transformation_matrix,
   vertex_ptr->local );
```

```
            }
        }
    }
```

This is the three-dimensional, three-particle dynamical system simulation, where three particles interact with each other based on gravitational attractions.

```
/*

    +----------------------------------------------------------------------+
    |                                                                      |
    |                     Virtual Reality ExCursions                       |
    |                                                                      |
    |        by Christopher D. Watkins and Stephen R. Marenka              |
    |                                                                      |
    |           Copyright 1994 : Academic Press, Inc.                      |
    |                                                                      |
    |----------------------------------------------------------------------|
    |                            PSYS.C                                    |
    |----------------------------------------------------------------------|
    |                                                                      |
    |                        Software Issues                               |
    |                                                                      |
    |        Copyright 1987-1994 ALGORITHM, Incorporated.                  |
    |                                                                      |
    |    ALL RIGHTS RESERVED.  This software is Published, but is NOT      |
    | Public Domain and remains the property of ALGORITHM, Incorporated and |
    |         Christopher D. Watkins.  This software may not be            |
    | reproduced or integrated into other packages without the prior written |
    |         consent of Christopher D. Watkins.  Licensing is possible.  |
    |                                                                      |
    +----------------------------------------------------------------------+


                    3-D Three-particle Orbit Simulation



        time step "delta_time" should be greater than zero, increasing
            it will increase speed of display, and decrease precision
```

```
            thanks go to Martin Jaspan for some of his ideas about
                the simulation of 2-D particle systems
  */


        //      system includes
        #include        <stdio.h>
        #include        <conio.h>
        #include        <math.h>



        //      Algorithm, Inc. includes
        #include        "Alg_Defs.H"
        #include        "Alg_Math.H"
        #include        "Alg_Matx.H"
        #include        "Alg_Graf.H"


        /*

            +---------------------------------------------------------------+
            |                       variables for projection                |
            +---------------------------------------------------------------+
        */


        // measures in millimeters


        #define         PERSPECTIVE_PLANE_DISTANCE_MM           (3500.0)
        #define         OBJECT_DISTANCE_MM                      (3700.0)


        /*

            +---------------------------------------------------------------+
            |           transformations and projections for points and lines |
            +---------------------------------------------------------------+
        */


        static alg_matrix_4x4_type   transformation_matrix;

        void create_transformation_matrix( alg_point_3D_type scale,
        alg_point_3D_type rotate,     alg_point_3D_type translate )
        {
                alg_identity_4x4_matrix( transformation_matrix );
```

```
        alg_scale_4x4_matrix ( scale, transformation_matrix );
        alg_rotate_4x4_matrix( rotate, transformation_matrix,
              MOTION_ROTATION );
        alg_translate_4x4_matrix ( translate, transformation_matrix );
  }


  void transform_point( alg_point_3D_type pt3D, alg_point_2D_int_type *pt2D
  )
  {
        alg_point_3D_type      pt;
        alg_float              inverse_z;
        alg_float              offset;

        alg_transform_4x4_matrix( pt, transformation_matrix, pt3D );

        inverse_z = PERSPECTIVE_PLANE_DISTANCE_MM / pt.z;
        (*pt2D).x = alg_X_Center + (pt.x * inverse_z);
        (*pt2D).y = alg_Y_Center - (pt.y * inverse_z);
  }


  void point_3D( alg_point_3D_type pt3D, alg_byte color )
  {
        alg_point_2D_int_type          pt2D;

        transform_point( pt3D, &pt2D );
        alg_plot( pt2D.x, pt2D.y, color );
  }


  void line_3D( alg_point_3D_type pt3D1, alg_point_3D_type pt3D2,
        alg_byte color )
  {
        alg_point_2D_int_type pt2D1, pt2D2;

        transform_point( pt3D1, &pt2D1 );
        transform_point( pt3D2, &pt2D2 );
        alg_line( pt2D1.x, pt2D1.y, pt2D2.x, pt2D2.y, color );
  }


  void display_axis( void )
```

```
{
        alg_point_3D_type      pt1, pt2;
        alg_float      len = 0.25 * (alg_float)alg_X_Resolution;

        // draw x axis
        ALG_VEC3_MAKE( -len, 0.0, 0.0, pt1 );
        ALG_VEC3_MAKE(  len, 0.0, 0.0, pt2 );
        line_3D( pt1, pt2, 251 );
        point_3D( pt2, 35 );

        // draw y axis
        ALG_VEC3_MAKE( 0.0, -len, 0.0, pt1 );
        ALG_VEC3_MAKE( 0.0,  len, 0.0, pt2 );
        line_3D( pt1, pt2, 251 );
        point_3D( pt2, 71 );

        // draw z axis
        ALG_VEC3_MAKE( 0.0, 0.0, -len, pt1 );
        ALG_VEC3_MAKE( 0.0, 0.0,  len, pt2 );
        line_3D( pt1, pt2, 251 );
        point_3D( pt2, 107 );
}


/*

    +-------------------------------------------------------------------+
    |                      data-types for particles                     |
    +-------------------------------------------------------------------+
*/

typedef struct
{
        alg_int                      mass;  // mass
        alg_point_3D_type     pos;   // position
        alg_point_3D_type     vel;   // velocity
        alg_point_3D_type     acc;   // acceleration
}
particle_type;


/*
```

```
      +----------------------------------------------------------------+
      |                 three-particle orbital simulation              |
      +----------------------------------------------------------------+
*/


void alg_print_usage( void )
{
printf ("\n\n");
printf ("+----------------------------------------------------------+\n");
printf ("|                                                          |\n");
printf ("|                  3-D Particle Orbit Simulator            |\n");
printf ("|                                                          |\n");
printf ("| Copyright 1987-1994 ALGORITHM, Inc. / Atlanta, Georgia |\n");
printf ("|                     ALL RIGHTS RESERVED                  |\n");
printf ("|                                                          |\n");
printf ("| Software written by Christopher D. Watkins for the book|\n");
printf ("| Virtual Reality ExCursions (1994:Academic Press, Inc.) |\n");
printf ("|     by Christopher D. Watkins and Stephen R. Marenka   |\n");
printf ("|                                                          |\n");
printf ("|                     Usage: psys                          |\n");
printf ("|                                                          |\n")
printf ("|              ALGORITHM, Inc.        (404) 634-0920       |\n");
printf ("| 3776 Lavista Road, Suite 100A, Tucker, Georgia 30084     |\n");
printf ("|                                                          |\n");
printf ( +----------------------------------------------------------+\n");
printf ("\n\n");
}


void main( void )
{
        alg_palette_type        color_palette;

        particle_type           particle1;
        particle_type           particle2;
        particle_type           particle3;

        alg_point_3D_type       Dv12, Dv23, Dv31;
        alg_float               D12, D23, D31;
        alg_point_3D_type       Tv12, Tv23, Tv31;
```

```
alg_float              delta_time;

alg_point_3D_type      scale          = { 1.5, 1.5, 1.5 };
alg_point_3D_type      rotate         = { 80.0, -10.0, 30.0 };
alg_point_3D_type      translate      = { 0.0, 0.0,
       -OBJECT_DISTANCE_MM };


// convert degrees to radians for rotation
ALG_VEC3_SCAL_MULT( ALG_DEG_TO_RAD, rotate, rotate );

// initialize graphics display
alg_set_graphics_mode( 1024, 768 );

// initialize palette
alg_init_palette_2( color_palette );
alg_set_palette( color_palette );

// initialize viewer by creating transformation matrix
create_transformation_matrix( scale, rotate, translate );

// draw axes
display_axis();

// define particles
particle1.mass = 1;
ALG_VEC3_MAKE( -40.0, 0.0, 0.0, particle1.pos );
ALG_VEC3_MAKE( 0.1010, 0.2500, -0.0240, particle1.vel );

particle2.mass = 6;
ALG_VEC3_MAKE( 0.0, 0.0, 0.0, particle2.pos );
ALG_VEC3_MAKE( 0.0010, 0.0010, -0.0440, particle2.vel );

particle3.mass = 4;
ALG_VEC3_MAKE( 90.0, 0.0, 0.0, particle3.pos );
ALG_VEC3_MAKE( -0.0200, -0.1010, 0.1240, particle3.vel );

// set time step
delta_time = 0.1;
```

```
        // particle interactions
        do
        {
                // erase particles (comment out to see particle trails)
//              point_3D( particle1.pos, 0 );
//              point_3D( particle2.pos, 0 );
//              point_3D( particle3.pos, 0 );

                // update particle positions based on velocities and time
                //    increment
                ALG_VEC3_ADD_SCAL_MULT( delta_time, particle1.vel,
                        particle1.pos, particle1.pos );
                ALG_VEC3_ADD_SCAL_MULT( delta_time, particle2.vel,
                        particle2.pos, particle2.pos );
                ALG_VEC3_ADD_SCAL_MULT( delta_time, particle3.vel,
                        particle3.pos, particle3.pos );

                // draw particles
                point_3D( particle1.pos, 143 );
                point_3D( particle2.pos, 169 );
                point_3D( particle3.pos, 205 );

                // compute inter-particle vector distances
                ALG_VEC3_SUB( particle1.pos, particle2.pos, Dv12 );
                ALG_VEC3_SUB( particle2.pos, particle3.pos, Dv23 );
                ALG_VEC3_SUB( particle3.pos, particle1.pos, Dv31 );

                // compute denominators for force contributions
                D12 = 1.0 / ALG_CUBE( ALG_VEC3_LENGTH( Dv12 ) );
                D23 = 1.0 / ALG_CUBE( ALG_VEC3_LENGTH( Dv23 ) );
                D31 = 1.0 / ALG_CUBE( ALG_VEC3_LENGTH( Dv31 ) );

                // compute inter-particle distances divided by
                //    force denominators for force calculation
                ALG_VEC3_SCAL_MULT( D12, Dv12, Tv12 );
                ALG_VEC3_SCAL_MULT( D23, Dv23, Tv23 );
                ALG_VEC3_SCAL_MULT( D31, Dv31, Tv31 );
```

```
              // compute particle accelerations based on masses and
              //      changes in velocities (the existing parts of the
              //      force calculation)
              ALG_VEC3_LIN_COMB( particle3.mass, Tv31, -particle2.mass,
                     Tv12, particle1.acc );
              ALG_VEC3_LIN_COMB( particle1.mass, Tv12, -particle3.mass,
                     Tv23, particle2.acc );
              ALG_VEC3_LIN_COMB( particle2.mass, Tv23, -particle1.mass,
                     Tv31, particle3.acc );

              // update particle velocities based on accelerations and
              //      time increment
              ALG_VEC3_ADD_SCAL_MULT( delta_time, particle1.acc,
                     particle1.vel, particle1.vel );
              ALG_VEC3_ADD_SCAL_MULT( delta_time, particle2.acc,
                     particle2.vel, particle2.vel );
              ALG_VEC3_ADD_SCAL_MULT( delta_time, particle3.acc,
                     particle3.vel, particle3.vel );
       }
   while( !(kbhit()) );

   // exit graphics display
   alg_exit_graphics();

   // exit message
   clrscr();
   alg_print_usage();
}
```

Now, let us look at some simple mouse interaction. Here the mouse is used interactively to select a point on the Mandelbrot set and then draw the corresponding Julia set for that complex plane coordinate.

```
/*

    +-------------------------------------------------------------------------+
    |                                                                         |
    |                      Virtual Reality ExCursions                         |
    |                                                                         |
    |            by Christopher D. Watkins and Stephen R. Marenka             |
    |                                                                         |
    |                  Copyright 1994 : Academic Press, Inc.                  |
    |                                                                         |
    |-------------------------------------------------------------------------|
    |                                MANDJULI.C                               |
    |-------------------------------------------------------------------------|
    |                                                                         |
    |                             Software Issues                             |
    |                                                                         |
    |              Copyright 1987-1994 ALGORITHM, Incorporated.               |
    |                                                                         |
    |        ALL RIGHTS RESERVED.   This software is Published, but is NOT    |
    |    Public Domain and remains the property of ALGORITHM, Incorporated and |
    |             Christopher D. Watkins.  This software may not be           |
    |    reproduced or integrated into other packages without the prior written |
    |           consent of Christopher D. Watkins.  Licensing is possible.    |
    |                                                                         |
    +-------------------------------------------------------------------------+


    Interactive Julia Set Display while Walking on the Mandelbrot Set

*/


    //      system includes
    #include        <stdio.h>
    #include        <conio.h>
    #include        <stdlib.h>
    #include        <string.h>
    #include        <math.h>
    #include        <dos.h>
    #include        <graphics.h>


    //      Algorithm, Inc. includes
    #include        "Alg_Defs.H"
```

```
#include         "Alg_Math.H"
#include         "Alg_Graf.H"
#include         "Alg_Maus.H"


/*

   +------------------------------------------------------------------+
   |                         global variables                         |
   +------------------------------------------------------------------+

*/


// region of Mandelbrot set for display
#define x_min    (-2.2)
#define          x_max    ( 0.6)
#define          y_min    (-1.2)
#define          y_max    ( 1.2)


// special parameters
#define          max_number_of_iterations    (30)
#define          window_res                  (512)
#define          half_window_res             (window_res / 2)
#define          Julia_set_size              (window_res / 4.5)


// mouse parameters
static alg_int       m1, m2, m3, m4;
static alg_int       mx, my, omx, omy;
static alg_boolean   left_pressed_event, left_released_event;
static alg_boolean   right_pressed_event, right_released_event;


/*

   +------------------------------------------------------------------+
   |                        general functions                         |
   +------------------------------------------------------------------+

*/


void draw_window_borders( void )
{
       alg_line( 0, 0, window_res+window_res-2, 0, 250 );
       alg_line( 0, window_res, window_res+window_res-2, window_res,
              250 );
```

```
        alg_line( 0, 0, 0, window_res, 250 );
        alg_line( window_res+window_res-2, 0, window_res+window_res-2,
                window_res, 250 );
        alg_line( window_res, 0, window_res, window_res, 250 );
}


void initialize_cursor( void )
{
        // init the mouse
        alg_init_mouse( &left_pressed_event, &left_released_event,
                        &right_pressed_event, &right_released_event );
        alg_set_mouse_range( 0, window_res-1, 0, window_res-1 );
        alg_set_mouse_rate( 8, 8 );
        alg_position_mouse_cursor( half_window_res, half_window_res );
        mx = half_window_res;
        my = half_window_res;
}


/*

    +----------------------------------------------------------------------+
    |                     iterate the equation z = z2+c                    |
    +----------------------------------------------------------------------+

*/

alg_int iterate( alg_float cx, alg_float cy )
{
        alg_int              number_of_iterations = 0;
        alg_float      x = cx;
        alg_float      y = cy;
        alg_float      x_squared, y_squared;


        x_squared = x * x;
        y_squared = y * y;


        while( (number_of_iterations < max_number_of_iterations) &&
               (x_squared + y_squared < 4.0) )
        {
                y  = cy + 2.0 * x * y;
                x  = cx + x_squared - y_squared;
```

```
            x_squared = x * x;
            y_squared = y * y;
            ++number_of_iterations;
        }

    return( number_of_iterations );
}


/*

    +------------------------------------------------------------------+
    |                   compute the Mandelbrot Set                     |
    +------------------------------------------------------------------+
*/

void compute_Mandelbrot_Set( void )
{
    alg_int              number_of_iterations;
    alg_int              ix, iy;
    alg_float      cx, cy;
    alg_float      dx, dy;
    alg_byte       color;

    dx = (alg_float)(x_max-x_min) / (window_res-1);
    dy = (alg_float)(y_max-y_min) / (window_res-1);

    for (iy=1; iy<=((window_res-1)/2); iy++)
    {
        cy = y_min + iy * dy;
        for (ix=1; ix<(window_res-1); ix++)
        {
            cx = x_min + ix * dx;
            number_of_iterations = iterate( cx, cy );
            if (number_of_iterations ==
                    max_number_of_iterations)
                color = 76;
            else
                if (number_of_iterations <
                        max_number_of_iterations/3)
                    color = 0;
```

```
                              else
                                      color = 192 +
                                      (alg_byte)
                                      (((long)number_of_iterations
                                      * 63) / max_number_of_iterations);
                      alg_plot( ix, iy, color );
                      alg_plot( ix, window_res-1-iy, color );
              }
          }
  }


  /*

      +------------------------------------------------------------------+
      |                       compute the Julia Set                      |
      +------------------------------------------------------------------+
  */


  alg_byte compute_Julia_Set( alg_float cx, alg_float cy )
  {
          alg_boolean            notdone;
          alg_boolean            exiting;
          alg_byte               cnt = 0;
          alg_int                      xp, yp;
          alg_float              x = 0.0;
          alg_float              y = 0.0;
          alg_float              r;
          alg_float              theta;
          alg_point_2D_type      d;


          do
          {
              d.x = x - cx;
              d.y = y - cy;
              if (d.x > 0.0)
                      theta = atan(d.y / d.x) * 0.5;
              else
              {
                  if (d.x < 0.0)
                          theta = (ALG_PI + atan(d.y / d.x)) * 0.5;
```

```
                else
                        theta = ALG_PI * 0.25;
        }
        r = sqrt(cabs(d));
        if (random(100) < 50)     // comment these lines out
                r = -r;           //    for other studies
        x = r * ALG_COS( theta );
        y = r * ALG_SIN( theta );
        xp = half_window_res + (alg_int)(x * Julia_set_size) +
                window_res;
        yp = half_window_res + (alg_int)(y * Julia_set_size);
        alg_plot( xp, yp, 143 );

        // compute at least 150 points before mouse move is
        //     processed allowing the user to see the Julia Set
        //     change shape while moving the mouse
        cnt++;
        cnt %= 150;
        if (cnt == 0)
        {
                // get the mouse statistics
                alg_get_mouse( &m1, &m2, &mx, &my,
                        &left_pressed_event,
                        &left_released_event,
                        &right_pressed_event,
                        &right_released_event );
                exiting = right_pressed_event;
                notdone = !((mx!=omx) || (my!=omy) || exiting);
        }
    }
    while( notdone );

    return( exiting );
}


/*
    +------------------------------------------------------------------+
    |                         go walk-about                            |
    +------------------------------------------------------------------+
```

```c
*/


void erase_Julia_Set_window( void )
{
        setviewport( window_res+1, 1, window_res+window_res-1-1,
window_res-1, 0 );
        clearviewport();
        setviewport( 0, 0, alg_X_Resolution-1, alg_Y_Resolution-1, 0 );
}


void walk_about_on_the_Mandelbrot_Set_and_display_Julia_Set( void )
{
        alg_byte        exiting;
        alg_float       dx, dy;
        alg_float       cx = 0.0, cy = 0.0;
        alg_char        complexposition[14];

        dx = (x_max-x_min) / (window_res-1);
        dy = (y_max-y_min) / (window_res-1);

        do
        {
                alg_show_our_mouse_cursor( mx, my );

                omx = mx;
                omy = my;

                cx = x_min + dx * mx;
                cy = y_min + dy * my;

                erase_Julia_Set_window();

                exiting = compute_Julia_Set( cx, cy );

                alg_hide_our_mouse_cursor( omx, omy );
        }
        while(!exiting);
}
```

```
/*
    +------------------------------------------------------------------+
    |                           main program                           |
    +------------------------------------------------------------------+
*/

printf ("\n\n");
printf ("+----------------------------------------------------------+\n");
printf ("|                                                          |\n");
printf ("| Walk-about on the Mandelbrot Set and see the Julia Set  |\n");
printf ("|                                                          |\n");
printf ("| Copyright 1987-1994 ALGORITHM, Inc. / Atlanta, Georgia  |\n");
printf ("|                     ALL RIGHTS RESERVED                 |\n");
printf ("|                                                          |\n");
printf ("| Software written by Christopher D. Watkins for the book|\n");
printf ("| Virtual Reality ExCursions (1994:Academic Press, Inc.) |\n");
printf ("|     by Christopher D. Watkins and Stephen R. Marenka   |\n");
printf ("|                                                          |\n");
printf ("|                     Usage: mandjuli                     |\n");
printf ("|                                                          |\n")
printf ("|              ALGORITHM, Inc.      (404) 634-0920        |\n");
printf ("|  3776 Lavista Road, Suite 100A, Tucker, Georgia 30084   |\n");
printf ("|                                                          |\n");
printf ( +----------------------------------------------------------+\n");
printf ("\n\n");

void main( void )
{
        alg_palette_type      color_palette;

        // initialize graphics display
        alg_set_graphics_mode( 1024, 768 );
        alg_init_palette_2( color_palette );
        alg_set_palette( color_palette );

        // interact with Mandelbrot Set while displaying
        //     the Julia Set for that coordinate in the complex plane
        draw_window_borders();
        initialize_cursor();
```

```
        compute_Mandelbrot_Set();
        walk_about_on_the_Mandelbrot_Set_and_display_Julia_Set();

        // exit graphics display
        alg_exit_graphics();

        // display exit message
        alg_print_usage();
}
```

And now for a look at the mouse screen-point selecting code. This routine will snap the mouse to the intersection of displayed spline grid lines that is closest to the mouse position. It is an excerpt from a spline warping program (Copyright 1987–1994 Algorithm, Inc.).

```
/*

    +--------------------------------------------------------------------+
    |      edit controls points for warping splines using mouse pointer  |
    +--------------------------------------------------------------------+
        excerpt from CSWARP (Copyright 1987-1994 Algorithm, Inc.).


            warping based on transformation algorithms found in
                    Digital Image Warping, Wolberg 1990 (IEEE)


        Look for the book Modern Computer Animation that will be
        available late Summer 1994, by Christopher D. Watkins and
        Stephen R. Marenka (Academic Press / Cambridge, MA)
*/

alg_int alg_spline_edit_control_points( alg_control_points_type *CP,
alg_image_type *IMG )
{
        alg_int               i, j;
        alg_float     *x_indices, *y_indices;
        alg_float     *x_row, *y_row;
        alg_float     *spline1;

        alg_int               minimum_distance, distance;
        alg_int               point_index_x, point_index_y;
```

```
// mouse parameters
alg_int            m1, m2, mx, my;
alg_int            left_pressed_event, left_released_event;
alg_int            right_pressed_event, right_released_event;


static alg_int            mx_old = 0, my_old = 0;


alg_boolean   done = ALG_FALSE, snapped = ALG_FALSE;


// allocate memory for arrays that store indices used to sample
//      splines
x_indices = ALG_CALLOC( IMG->x_res, alg_float );
y_indices = ALG_CALLOC( IMG->y_res, alg_float );


// allocate memory for arrays to store column data in row order
/       for alg_spline()
x_row = ALG_CALLOC( IMG->y_res, alg_float );
y_row = ALG_CALLOC( IMG->y_res, alg_float );


// allocate memory for arrays to store mapping functions
//      computed in row order in alg_spline()
spline1 = ALG_CALLOC( IMG->x_res, alg_float );


// init arrays that store indices used to sample splines
for (i=0; i<IMG->x_res; i++)
      x_indices[i] = (alg_float)i;
      // indices used to sample horizontal splines
for (j=0; j<IMG->y_res; j++)
      y_indices[j] = (alg_float)j;
      // indices used to sample vertical splines


// all pixel I/O is XOR
setcolor(255);
setwritemode(XOR_PUT);


// initial draw of splines
```

```
// compute vertical splines
for (i=0; i<CP->x_cntr_pnts; i++)
{
        for (j=0; j<CP->y_cntr_pnts; j++)
        {
                x_row[j] = CP->dst_pt[i][j].x;
                y_row[j] = CP->dst_pt[i][j].y;
        }

        alg_spline( CP->y_cntr_pnts, y_row, x_row,
                    IMG->y_res, y_indices, spline1 );

        for (j=0; j<IMG->y_res; j++)
                alg_line( spline1[j], y_indices[j],
                          spline1[j], y_indices[j] );
}


// compute horizontal splines
for (j=0; j<CP->y_cntr_pnts; j++)
{
        for (i=0; i<CP->x_cntr_pnts; i++)
        {
                x_row[i] = CP->dst_pt[i][j].x;
                y_row[i] = CP->dst_pt[i][j].y;
        }

        alg_spline( CP->x_cntr_pnts, x_row, y_row,
                    IMG->x_res, x_indices, spline1 );

        for (i=0; i<IMG->x_res; i++)
                alg_line( x_indices[i], spline1[i],
                          x_indices[i], spline1[i] );
}


// init the mouse
alg_init_mouse(&left_pressed_event, &left_released_event,
               &right_pressed_event, &right_released_event);
```

```
// turn on cursor
alg_show_mouse_cursor();


// edit spline control points with the left mouse button,
//     and exit routine with the right mouse button
while (!done)
{
        alg_get_mouse( &m1, &m2, &mx, &my,
                &left_pressed_event, &left_released_event,
                &right_pressed_event, &right_released_event );


        // exit this routine, so we can see what we have done
        //     so far
        if (right_pressed_event)
                done = ALG_TRUE;


        // exit the whole program
        if (kbhit())
                return( ALG_TRUE );


        // we are editing something
        if (left_pressed_event)
        {
                // snap the cursor to the nearest control point,
                //     if this is the first time through here
                if (!snapped)
                {
                        snapped = ALG_TRUE;


                        // find nearest spline crossing by minimum
                        //     distance search notice we check
                        /// 1..cntr_pnts-1, since edges are frozen
                        minimum_distance = 32767;
                        for (i=1; i<CP->x_cntr_pnts-1; i++)
                                for (j=1; j<CP->y_cntr_pnts-1; j++)
                                {
                                        distance =
                                                (alg_int)ALG_SQRT(
                                ALG_SQR( (alg_float)
```

```
                                    (CP->dst_pt[i][j].x - mx) )
                                + ALG_SQR( (alg_float)
                                    (CP->dst_pt[i][j].y - my) )
                                );
                            if (distance <
                                    minimum_distance)
                            {
                                    minimum_distance =
                                            distance;
                                    point_index_x = i;
                                    point_index_y = j;
                            }
                    }

            mx = CP->dst_pt
                    [point_index_x][point_index_y].x;
            my = CP->dst_pt
                    [point_index_x][point_index_y].y;
            alg_position_mouse_cursor( mx, my );
    }


    // if we have moved the cursor, we must refresh
    //      splines
    if ( (mx != mx_old) || (my != my_old) )
    {
            mx_old = mx;
            my_old = my;

            // turn off the cursor
            alg_hide_mouse_cursor();



            // erase the old horizontal and
            //      vertical splines for the control
            //      point compute vertical spline
            i = point_index_x;

            for (j=0; j<CP->y_cntr_pnts; j++)
            {
```

```
                        x_row[j] = CP->dst_pt[i][j].x;
                        y_row[j] = CP->dst_pt[i][j].y;
                }

                alg_spline( CP->y_cntr_pnts, y_row, x_row,
                        IMG->y_res, y_indices, spline1 );

                for (j=0; j<IMG->y_res; j++)
                        alg_line( spline1[j], y_indices[j],
                                spline1[j], y_indices[j] );

                // compute horizontal spline
                j = point_index_y;

                for (i=0; i<CP->x_cntr_pnts; i++)
                {
                        x_row[i] = CP->dst_pt[i][j].x;
                        y_row[i] = CP->dst_pt[i][j].y;
                }

                alg_spline( CP->x_cntr_pnts, x_row, y_row,
                        IMG->x_res, x_indices, spline1 );

                for (i=0; i<IMG->x_res; i++)
                        alg_line( x_indices[i], spline1[i],
                                x_indices[i], spline1[i] );

                // reassign the control point
                CP->dst_pt[point_index_x]
                        [point_index_y].x = mx;
                CP->dst_pt[point_index_x]
                        [point_index_y].y = my;


                // draw new horizontal and vertical
                //      splines for the control point

                // compute vertical spline
                i = point_index_x;
```

```
                        for (j=0; j<CP->y_cntr_pnts; j++)
                        {
                                x_row[j] = CP->dst_pt[i][j].x;
                                y_row[j] = CP->dst_pt[i][j].y;
                        }

                        alg_spline( CP->y_cntr_pnts, y_row, x_row,
                                IMG->y_res, y_indices, spline1 );

                        for (j=0; j<IMG->y_res; j++)
                                alg_line( spline1[j], y_indices[j],
                                        spline1[j], y_indices[j] );

                        // compute horizontal spline
                        j = point_index_y;

                        for (i=0; i<CP->x_cntr_pnts; i++)
                        {
                                x_row[i] = CP->dst_pt[i][j].x;
                                y_row[i] = CP->dst_pt[i][j].y;
                        }

                        alg_spline( CP->x_cntr_pnts, x_row, y_row,
                                IMG->x_res, x_indices, spline1 );

                        for (i=0; i<IMG->x_res; i++)
                                alg_line( x_indices[i], spline1[i],
                                        x_indices[i], spline1[i] );


                        // turn on the cursor
                        alg_show_mouse_cursor();
                }
                else
                // makes smoother mouse movement
                delay(20);
        }
        else
                snapped = ALG_FALSE;
```

```
      }

      // turn off cursor
      alg_hide_mouse_cursor();

      // free memory
      ALG_FREE( x_indices );
      ALG_FREE( y_indices );
      ALG_FREE( x_row );
      ALG_FREE( y_row );
      ALG_FREE( spline1 );

      return( ALG_FALSE );
}
```

Section 10—Bringing It All Together to Make the Interactive Visualizer Called Bubba

Well, it is now time to bring together all that you have learned so far and apply it to the development of an interactive three-dimensional visualization system called Bubba. Since you are probably familiar with most of the basic concepts by now, we will discuss the functionality of the interactive visualizer using a diagram showing the visualizer's general conceptual flow. Tied to the functional diagram are simple helpful explanations.

Conceptual Program Flow for the Interactive Visualizer

Begin Program

- *Initialization of the control system*—all control surfaces (ailerons, rudder, elevator, and throttle) are set to zero positions. Status variables for control surfaces are set initially to false (status variables indicate whether or not a surface's contribution to the viewer motion is increasing for this program loop).
- *Load the virtual world three-dimensional model into memory*—loads the three-dimensional virtual world model and allocates memory for it and

the polygon display list. **Note that initially for our three-dimensional models, the positive *z* axis comes out of the screen, the positive *y* axis points to the bottom of the screen, and the positive *x* axis points to the left of the screen. Also note that polygons must have counterclockwise vertex ordering for the visible face, as the backface calculation uses these vertices to determine the surface normal; thus ordering is important.**

- *Initialization of the screen frame buffer*—allocates memory for the temporary screen frame buffer. The image is composed here in the memory buffer and subsequently copied to the graphics display.
- *Initialization of the graphics display*—initialize 320 x 200 8-bit color graphics mode.
- *Interaction with the virtual world by looping until an escape keypress*—**THE MAIN LOOP.**

The Main Loop

- *Get any input from the keyboard and set the status variables*—based on a keystroke, we set one of the control surface status variables to true.
- *Process status variables to determine positions for controls*—based on which control surface status variable was set to true, compute the new position for the given control surface.
- *Compute viewing parameters from controls*—based on the positions of controls, modify the three-dimensional viewing parameters in order to move and reorient the viewer.
- *Transform vertices*—transform objects from local coordinates, (into world coordinates) and into viewer coordinates based on viewing parameters.
- *Create the polygon display list*—create a list of polygons for display into the screen frame buffer. Remove all polygons that fall totally behind the viewer (they are totally behind the *z*-clipping plane), and remove all polygons that are backfaces (you should not see these, as they are the other sides of objects, for our purposes). The polygon-viewer distances are computed here for depth sorting later.
- *Perform depth sort on the polygon display list*—the depth sort is performed on the polygon display list to guarantee that the farthest polygons are drawn first and the nearest are drawn last. This is the Painter's polygon display algorithm.

- *Initialization of the screen frame buffer to the background (sky) color*—simply clear the viewport in our temporary screen frame buffer to the sky color. We will build our virtual image on top of it (Painter's algorithm again).
- *Z-clip, project, viewport-clip, (shade) and draw polygons in the polygon display list to the screen frame buffer*—we z-clip the polygon with the z half-plane (the front of the "view volume"), then if the polygon is not totally z-clipped, we project it. Then we viewport-clip the polygon, and if some of the polygon still exists, we draw it into the screen frame buffer. These polygons are flat shaded and can be textured.
- *Draw a viewport border in the screen frame buffer*—draw a three-pixel-width border around the viewport section of the screen frame buffer.
- *Copy the screen frame buffer to the graphics display*—copy the screen frame buffer into the graphics display for viewing.

After Main Loop

- *Exit the graphics display*—exit graphics for text mode.
- *Delete the screen frame buffer*—free memory for the screen frame buffer.
- *Delete the virtual world three-dimensional model from memory*—free memory for the three-dimensional virtual world model and polygon display list.
- *Display the text exit/copyright message*—display copyright notice and exit program for DOS.

Figure 5.32—Conceptual Program Flow for the Interactive Visualizer

PROGRAM LISTINGS:

```
/*

   +--------------------------------------------------------------------------+
   |                                                                          |
   |                      Virtual Reality ExCursions                          |
   |                                                                          |
   |            by Christopher D. Watkins and Stephen R. Marenka              |
   |                                                                          |
   |               Copyright 1994 : Academic Press, Inc.                      |
   |                                                                          |
   |--------------------------------------------------------------------------|
   |                                 VR.C                                     |
   |--------------------------------------------------------------------------|
   |                                                                          |
   |                            Software Issues                               |
   |                                                                          |
   |             Copyright 1987-1994 ALGORITHM, Incorporated.                 |
   |                                                                          |
   |       ALL RIGHTS RESERVED.   This software is Published, but is NOT      |
   |    Public Domain and remains the property of ALGORITHM, Incorporated and |
   |           Christopher D. Watkins.  This software may not be              |
   |   reproduced or integrated into other packages without the prior written |
   |           consent of Christopher D. Watkins.  Licensing is possible.     |
   |                                                                          |
   +--------------------------------------------------------------------------+

*/


   //      system includes
   #include        <conio.h>
   #include        <string.h>
   #include        <stdlib.h>
   #include        <dos.h>


   //      Algorithm, Inc. includes
   #include        "Alg_Defs.H"
   #include        "Alg_Graf.H"
   #include        "Alg_Scrn.H"
```

```c
#include      "Alg_HidS.H"
#include      "Alg_3D.H"
#include      "Alg_Kbd.H"
#include      "Alg_Ctrl.H"
#include      "Alg_Pars.H"

void alg_print_usage( void )
{
printf ("\n\n");
printf ("+---------------------------------------------------------+\n");
printf ("|                                                         |\n");
printf ("|     3-D Interactive Visualizer for Polygonal Models     |\n");
printf ("|                     (Flat Shading)                      |\n");
printf ("|                                                         |\n");
printf ("| Copyright 1987-1994 ALGORITHM, Inc. / Atlanta, Georgia  |\n");
printf ("|                  ALL RIGHTS RESERVED                    |\n");
printf ("|                                                         |\n");
printf ("| Software written by Christopher D. Watkins for the book|\n");
printf ("| Virtual Reality ExCursions (1994:Academic Press, Inc.) |\n");
printf ("|    by Christopher D. Watkins and Stephen R. Marenka     |\n");
printf ("|                                                         |\n");
printf ("|         Usage:  vr <virtual world filename>.vr          |\n");
printf ("|                                                         |\n")
printf ("| Martin - plan to steal and sell this software as well??|\n")
printf ("|                                                         |\n")
printf ("|       Contact Algorithm, Inc. for licensing rights      |\n")
printf ("|                                                         |\n")
printf ("|               ALGORITHM, Inc.      (404) 634-0920       |\n");
printf ("|  3776 Lavista Road, Suite 100A, Tucker, Georgia 30084  |\n");
printf ("|                                                         |\n");
printf ( +---------------------------------------------------------+\n");
printf ("\n\n");
}

void main( alg_int argc, alg_char *argv[] )
{
        alg_palette_type                color_palette;
        alg_controls_type               controls;
        alg_viewer_3D_type              viewer;
```

```
alg_polygon_3D_display_list_type       polygon_display_list;
alg_world_3D_type                      world;
alg_char                               *world_name;
alg_boolean                            world_loaded;

// command-line filename input without extension
if (argc == 2)
{
        world_name = argv[1];
        // we assume the extension to be .vr
        strcat(world_name, ".vr");
}
else
{
        // exit message
        clrscr();
        alg_print_usage();
        exit(0);
}

// initialize the control system
alg_initialize_controls( &controls );

// load the virtual world 3-D model into memory
world_loaded = alg_create_world_model( &controls, &viewer,
        &polygon_display_list, &world, world_name );
if (!world_loaded)
{
        // exit message
        alg_print_usage();
        exit(0);
}

// initialize the screen frame buffer
alg_create_screen_buffer();
alg_clear_screen_buffer();

// initialize the graphics display
alg_set_graphics_mode( ALG_SCREEN_WIDTH, ALG_SCREEN_HEIGHT );
```

```
alg_init_palette_2( color_palette );
alg_set_palette( color_palette );

// interact with the virtual world
do
{
        // get input from the keyboard and set status variables
        alg_update_keyboard_status_variables( &controls );

        // process status variables to determine positions for
        //      controls
        alg_interpret_status_variables_for_controls( &controls );

        // based on positions of controls, modify the 3-D viewing
        //      parameters in order to move and reorient the
        //      viewer
        alg_interpret_controls_for_motion_and_view( &viewer,
                &controls );

        // transform objects from local coordinates, (into world
        //      coordinates) and into viewer coordinates based on
        //      viewing parameters
        alg_transform_objects_for_viewing( &world, &viewer );
        // create the polygon display list, remove polygons that
        //      fall totally behind the viewer, and remove
        //      polygons that are backfaces.  Polygon-Viewer
        //      distances are computed for the following depth
        //      sort.
        alg_create_polygon_display_list( &world,
                &polygon_display_list );

        // perform depth-sort on the polygon display list
        //      for the Painter's display algorithm
        alg_depth_sort_polygon_display_list(
                &polygon_display_list );

        // initialize the screen frame buffer to the background
//      (sky) color
        alg_flood_fill_viewport_in_screen_buffer(
```

```
                        world.background_color );

                // z-clip, project, viewport-clip and draw the
                //      polygon display list to the screen frame buffer
                alg_draw_polygon_display_list_to_screen_buffer(
                        &viewer, &polygon_display_list );

                // draw a viewport border in the screen frame buffer
                alg_draw_viewport_border_to_screen_buffer();

                // copy the screen frame buffer to the graphics display
                alg_copy_screen_buffer_to_screen();
        }
        while ( !alg_exit_program_if_escape() );

        // exit the graphics display
        alg_exit_graphics();

        // delete the screen frame buffer
        alg_delete_screen_buffer();

        // delete the virtual world 3-D model from memory
        alg_delete_world_model( &polygon_display_list, &world );
        // exit message
        clrscr();
        alg_print_usage();
}
```

```
/*

    +----------------------------------------------------------------------+
    |                                                                      |
    |                     Virtual Reality ExCursions                       |
    |                                                                      |
    |          by Christopher D. Watkins and Stephen R. Marenka            |
    |                                                                      |
    |                Copyright 1994 : Academic Press, Inc.                 |
    |                                                                      |
    |----------------------------------------------------------------------|
    |                              ALG_3D.C                                |
    |----------------------------------------------------------------------|
    |                                                                      |
    |                           Software Issues                            |
    |                                                                      |
    |              Copyright 1987-1994 ALGORITHM, Incorporated.            |
    |                                                                      |
    |       ALL RIGHTS RESERVED.   This software is Published, but is NOT  |
    |    Public Domain and remains the property of ALGORITHM, Incorporated and |
    |            Christopher D. Watkins.  This software may not be         |
    |  reproduced or integrated into other packages without the prior written |
    |           consent of Christopher D. Watkins.  Licensing is possible. |
    |                                                                      |
    +----------------------------------------------------------------------+
*/


    //      system includes
    #include        <math.h>
    #include        <mem.h>


    //      Algorithm, Inc. includes
    #include        "Alg_Defs.H"
    #include        "Alg_Matx.H"
    #include        "Alg_Poly.H"
    #include        "Alg_PClp.H"
    #include        "Alg_Proj.H"
    #include        "Alg_HidS.H"
```

```
/*

   +-------------------------------------------------------------------+
   | transform objects from local and world coordinates to view        |
   | coordinates                                                        |
   +-------------------------------------------------------------------+

*/


        See the section on "Motion, Interaction and Simulation" for this
segment of code


/*

   +-------------------------------------------------------------------+
   |                   create the polygon display list                 |
   +-------------------------------------------------------------------+

*/


void alg_create_polygon_display_list( alg_world_3D_type *world,
        alg_polygon_3D_display_list_type *polygon_display_list )
{
        alg_word                        vertex_num;
        alg_point_3D_type               *vertex_ptr;
        alg_word                        object_num;
        alg_object_3D_type              *object_ptr;
        alg_word                        polygon_num;
        alg_polygon_3D_type             *polygon_ptr;
        alg_word                        *num_polygons_for_display =
                                &polygon_display_list->num_polygons;
        alg_point_3D_type               polygon_center;
        alg_point_3D_type               vertex_sum;
        alg_float                       z_coord;
        alg_float                       max_polygon_z_coord;
        alg_boolean                     trivial_reject;
        alg_boolean                     backface_reject;


        // initialize display-list polygon counter
        *num_polygons_for_display = 0;

        // examine all of the polygons that make up the objects found in
```

```
//      the world, create a list of all potentially visible
//      polygons, remove polygons that are backfaces, and remove
//      polygons that are outside of the "viewable" z half-space
//      (i.e. behind viewer)

for (object_num=0; object_num<world->num_objects; object_num++)
{
        object_ptr = &world->object[object_num];


        for (polygon_num=0; polygon_num<object_ptr->num_polygons;
                polygon_num++)
        {
                polygon_ptr = &object_ptr->polygon[polygon_num];


                // if polygon is not a backface, consider it for
                //      display list
                backface_reject = alg_polygon_is_backface(
                        *polygon_ptr );
                if ( !backface_reject )
                {
                        // if part of the polygon is in front of
                        //      the z-clipping plane (z half-space),
                        //      then add the polygon to the
                        //      polygon display list, else the
                        //      polygon is totally behind the
                        //      viewer, and should be trivially
                        //      clipped now by not adding it to the
                        //      polygon display list

                        // compute the maximum z coordinate for the
                        //      polygon
                        max_polygon_z_coord = -ALG_LARGE;
                        for (vertex_num=0; vertex_num<
                                polygon_ptr->num_vertices;
                                vertex_num++)
                        {
                                z_coord = polygon_ptr->
                                vertex[vertex_num]->viewer.z;
                                max_polygon_z_coord = ALG_MAX(
```

```
                                    max_polygon_z_coord,
                                    z_coord );
                }

                // check to see if polygon is behind us
                trivial_reject = (max_polygon_z_coord >
ALG_Z_CLIPPING_PLANE) ? ALG_FALSE : ALG_TRUE;

                // if the polygon is not behind us
                if ( !trivial_reject )
                {
                        // compute the center coordinate of
                        //      the polygon
                        ALG_VEC3_ZERO( vertex_sum );
                        for (vertex_num=0;
                                vertex_num<
                                polygon_ptr->num_vertices;
                                vertex_num++)
                        {
                                vertex_ptr = &polygon_ptr->
                                vertex[vertex_num]->viewer;
                                ALG_VEC3_ADD( vertex_sum,
                                        *vertex_ptr,
                                        vertex_sum );
                        }
                        ALG_VEC3_SCAL_MULT( 1.0 /
                                polygon_ptr->num_vertices,
                        vertex_sum, polygon_center);

                        // compute the distance between the
                        // viewer and the polygon center
                        polygon_ptr->
                                viewer_to_polygon_distance =
                        ALG_VEC3_LENGTH( polygon_center );

                        // add the polygon to the polygon
                        //      display list
                        polygon_display_list->polygon[
                                *num_polygons_for_display] =
```

```
                                         *polygon_ptr;
                             (*num_polygons_for_display)++;
                    }
                }
            }
        }
    }


    /*

        +---------------------------------------------------------------+
        |          draw the polygon display list to the screen buffer   |
        +---------------------------------------------------------------+
    */

    void alg_draw_polygon_display_list_to_screen_buffer( alg_viewer_3D_type
    *viewer,        alg_polygon_3D_display_list_type *polygon_display_list )
    {
            alg_word                              polygon_num;
            alg_z_clipped_polygon_3D_type         z_clipped_polygons;
            alg_viewport_clipped_polygon_2D_type viewport_clipped_polygons;
            alg_boolean                           trivial_reject;

            for (polygon_num=0; polygon_num<polygon_display_list
                    ->num_polygons; polygon_num++)
            {
                    // z-clip polygon with z half-plane (front of view
                    //      frustrum)
                    trivial_reject = z_clip_polygon( &polygon_display_list->
                            polygon[polygon_num], &z_clipped_polygons );

                    // if polygon was not totally z-clipped, then project,
                    //      screen clip and potentially draw it
                    if ( !trivial_reject )
                    {
                            // perform perspective projection
                            perspective_project_z_clipped_polygon(viewer,
                                    &z_clipped_polygons);

                            // screen-clip polygon with viewport (sides of
```

```
//      view frustrum)
trivial_reject =
        xy_viewport_clip_z_clipped_polygon(
            &z_clipped_polygons,
            &viewport_clipped_polygons );


// if polygon was not totally screen-clipped,
//      then draw it to screen buffer
if ( !trivial_reject )
        alg_draw_convex_polygon_to_screen_buffer(
            &viewport_clipped_polygons );
        }
    }
}
```

Section 11—Stereo Vision and Our Anaglyph Glasses

Because, as *Homo sapiens*, our visual fields substantially overlap, we have the possibility of binocular vision: the slightly different shape and angle of the same object seen in the two visual fields enable us to locate that object in 3-space (out to about 100 feet). It is apparent that the visual channels can be fed artificially with different perspectives, in order to produce the sensation of 3-D. In the early 1950s a craze arose for 3-D movies. Although Edwin Land had demonstrated stereo movies with polarizing glasses as early as 1936 (each eye receives an image based on the polarization of light reflecting from each eye's image), the first commercial 3-D movies were shown with red and green projectors, and the audience wore glasses with red and green cellophane lenses—this is called the anaglyphic method for achieving 3-D. To this day, some comic books are sold with stories printed in red and green (or magenta and cyan) inks; the viewing glasses are supplied with the book, just as with ours, but this is no comic book. By the time of such 3-D movie blockbusters as Vincent Price's *House of Wax* (1953), polarized projectors and glasses were universal. Within less than a decade the 3-D movie fad had fizzled; although Alfred Hitchcock's *The Birds* was originally made in 3-D in 1963, it has rarely been shown in that format.

Holograms have now revived interest in 3-D display, but 99.99% of our daily vicarious visual presentation is still tendered in two dimensions. Yet stereo vision is very important in our assessment of how real something is, and this should always be borne in mind in the design of VR systems. A simple example: experiments have shown that babies recognize a rattle and reach for it—when a picture of it is shown stereoscopically. Only many months later will they reach for the same toy shown in flat photos.

Binocular vision can be impaired by stress, something that should be kept in mind when building VR simulators for training people to cope with real-world emergencies. In the naval battle of Jutland in World War I, the British rangefinders—essential for aiming the big battleship guns—were old mechanical clunkers that matched two images with a crank. The Germans had state-of-the-art Zeiss rangefinders based on optical enhancement of the gunners' natural stereo vision, fed into a "heads-up" display. But when the shells started falling, the German gunners lost their stereo perception and were helpless. The Brits, likewise terrified, still had the wits to crank their horribly antiquated coincidence rangefinders and scored hit after hit. (In any case, about 2% of the otherwise normally-sighted are "stereo blind"; for unknown reasons they cannot achieve stereo fusion in artificial situations.)

If you have mastered the trick of fusing adjacent stereo images without glasses, you can make simple stereograms in which print seems to float, just by bumping a line of type in otherwise identical text:

```
              X                           X

        .into the page            into the page
        out of the page           .out of the page
        .into the page            into the page
        out of the page           .out of the page
        .into the page            into the page
        out of the page           .out of the page
        .into the page            into the page
        out of the page           .out of the page

              X                           X
```

Real 3-D

As mentioned, an area of great research these days is the production of stereo images to produce that three-dimensional look for computer simulations. These simulations can be quite impressive—remember how impressed you were looking through your first ViewMaster? We will repeat how it works. The idea is simple: two separate images are generated, each, as mentioned above, with the viewpoint slightly offset to correspond to the separation of your eyes. The set of two images are therefore a *stereo pair*.

An image-rendering program makes this relatively easy to do, at the cost of a little extra computation. The trick is then to present the two images to each eye separately. Your brain does the rest, putting the images together to create the illusion of depth. Do not worry about trying to fuse the above boxes with text in them with just your eyes. The simplest trick has been the use of 3-D glasses with one red lens and one blue lens. That is called the anaglyph technique and is the one we use with our book, which includes 3-D glasses. One stereo image is presented as colored red, the other is presented as colored green. With the glasses on, each eye perceives only one of the images and, voilá!, you have a terribly colored but still three-dimensional effect. In all truth, you will reach a no-color point, where you have looked at the images through the glasses long enough for the brain to learn to process this information properly as three-dimensional. Many other techniques are available for stereo imaging, including the use of polarized lenses (previously mentioned) and LCD lenses that turn one lens on and the other off at 60 frames per second. These techniques all suffer from artifacts of either unacceptable loss of intensity, color, or resolution, or they are too expensive. In either case, this is another area where things will undoubtedly only get better.

In this short section, we will now discuss the anaglyph glasses method for three-dimensional viewing on your PC. Programs are included (like the listing at the end of this section) for viewing objects interactively, and there are even programs that allow you to fly around some virtual terrain.

Our Anaglyph Glasses

Our publisher was kind enough, late in this project, to include three-dimensional anaglyph glasses with this book. We built programs that

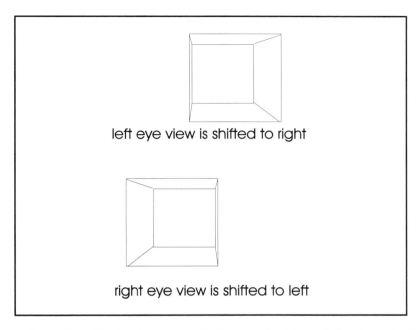

left eye view is shifted to right

right eye view is shifted to left

Figure 5.33—How Two Projections of a Cube are Positioned for Anaglyph Viewing

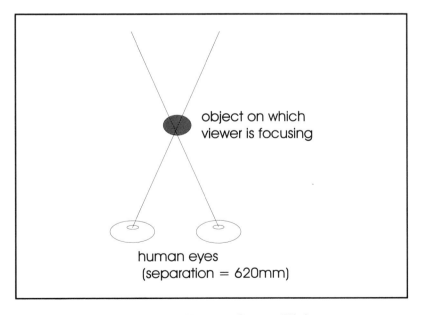

object on which
viewer is focusing

human eyes
(separation = 620mm)

Figure 5.34—Human Stereo Vision

effectively create the sensation of looking at or flying over a three-dimensional terrain. There are a couple of notes about how this was done.

First, our database is different from the one used for the virtual reality solid-object visualizer. There we have objects made of polygons, each made of vertices. Since we are visualizing wire-frames (of single objects)—see Figure 5.33—we can simplify our database by defining vertices, and how lines connect those vertices. The database for a cube looks like that found in Figure 5.34.

```
//************************************************************************
//
//                    Desktop Virtual World Anaglyph Visualizer Database
//
//                    Virtual Reality ExCursions
//                    Copyright 1994 Academic Press, Inc.
//
//                    Software
//                    Copyright 1987-1994 ALGORITHM, Inc.
//                    Christopher D. Watkins
//
//************************************************************************
//
// vertices
//
//      x, y, z
//
//      x positive left
//      y positive down
//      z positive out of screen
//
//
// line-types
//
//      0       - move relative
//      1       - line relative
//      2       - move absolute
//      3       - line absolute
//
//************************************************************************
```

```
alg_vertices
{
    num_vertices      8

    vertex 100.0     100.0    100.0,
    vertex 100.0     100.0   -100.0,
    vertex 100.0    -100.0    100.0,
    vertex 100.0    -100.0   -100.0,
    vertex -100.0    100.0    100.0,
    vertex -100.0    100.0   -100.0,
    vertex -100.0   -100.0    100.0,
    vertex -100.0   -100.0   -100.0,
}
alg_lines
{
    num_vertices 16

    line_type_and_vertex_index   2        0
    line_type_and_vertex_index   3        1
    line_type_and_vertex_index   3        3
    line_type_and_vertex_index   3        2
    line_type_and_vertex_index   3        0
    line_type_and_vertex_index   3        4
    line_type_and_vertex_index   3        5
    line_type_and_vertex_index   3        7
    line_type_and_vertex_index   3        6
    line_type_and_vertex_index   3        4
    line_type_and_vertex_index   2        1
    line_type_and_vertex_index   3        5
    line_type_and_vertex_index   2        2
    line_type_and_vertex_index   3        6
    line_type_and_vertex_index   2        3
    line_type_and_vertex_index   3        7
}
alg_end
```

Figure 5.35—Anaglyph .ANA File for a Cube

Looking at the database, you see a list of vertices followed by a list of line definitions. The line-type variables indicate to the program whether that point should be moved absolutely or relatively to the last point and whether a line should be drawn absolutely or relatively from the last point. The four options are:

```
0        - move relative to last point
1        - line relative to last point
2        - move absolute
3        - line absolute
```

Following this information is the vertex index, which defines the lookup into the vertex list. This point is processed based on the line-type variable for that vertex.

Last, a quick look at the mathematics involved in creating two perspective views is in order. Just as the objects for the solid world visualizer were transformed and projected, we transform and project our object. Here, slight changes have been made in the projection equations, in order to offset the object slightly to the left or to the right. A left rendering of the object will be seen by the right eye, and the right rendering of the object will be seen by the left eye. On a white background, a cyan-colored object will be seen through the red left lens of your glasses. A red-colored object will be seen by the blue/green right lens of your glasses.

The equations for projection look like this:

```
EYE_SEPARATION_MM                =        620.0 mm
HALF_EYE_SEPARATION_MM           =        (EYE_SEPARATION_MM / 2.0) mm
PERSPECTIVE_PLANE_DISTANCE_MM=            3500.0 mm
OBJECT_DISTANCE_MM               =        6000.0 mm
OFFSET_PERCENTAGE                =        0.89

offset = -OFFSET_PERCENTAGE * half_eye_separation_mm /
        OBJECT_DISTANCE_MM;


inverse_z = 1.0 / (OBJECT_DISTANCE_MM + pt.z);


(*pt2D).x = alg_X_Center + PERSPECTIVE_PLANE_DISTANCE_MM *
( ( half_eye_separation_mm + pt.x ) * inverse_z + offset );


(*pt2D).y = alg_Y_Center - PERSPECTIVE_PLANE_DISTANCE_MM
```

```
                     *  (pt.y * inverse_z);
```

where the normal separation of human eyes is 620 mm. Our computations require using half of this value. Notice that in this program the above projection is called twice, where the sign of the constant HALF_EYE_SEPARATION_MM is negative for the red, left-screen side, right-eye image and the sign is positive for the cyan, right-screen side, left-eye image. This value is used to help properly offset the image in the appropriate direction, just before projection.

PROGRAM LISTINGS:

```
/*

     +-----------------------------------------------------------------------+
     |                                                                       |
     |                    Virtual Reality ExCursions                         |
     |                                                                       |
     |           by Christopher D. Watkins and Stephen R. Marenka            |
     |                                                                       |
     |              Copyright 1994 : Academic Press, Inc.                    |
     |                                                                       |
     |-----------------------------------------------------------------------|
     |                            ANAGLYPH.C                                 |
     |-----------------------------------------------------------------------|
     |                                                                       |
     |                          Software Issues                              |
     |                                                                       |
     |             Copyright 1987-1994 ALGORITHM, Incorporated.              |
     |                                                                       |
     |      ALL RIGHTS RESERVED.   This software is Published, but is NOT    |
     |  Public Domain and remains the property of ALGORITHM, Incorporated and |
     |         Christopher D. Watkins.  This software may not be             |
     | reproduced or integrated into other packages without the prior written |
     |         consent of Christopher D. Watkins.  Licensing is possible.    |
     |                                                                       |
     +-----------------------------------------------------------------------+

*/
```

```
/*

        ideas for how a mouse control should interact with a
                three-dimensional object came from Stephen B. Coy
*/


//      system includes
#include        <math.h>
#include        <graphics.h>


//      Algorithm, Inc. includes
#include        "Alg_Defs.H"
#include        "Alg_Math.H"
#include        "Alg_Matx.H"
#include        "Alg_Graf.H"
#include        "Alg_Maus.H"


/*

    +-------------------------------------------------------------------+
    |                      variables for projection                     |
    +-------------------------------------------------------------------+
*/


// measures in millimeters

#define         EYE_SEPARATION_MM               (620.0)
#define         HALF_EYE_SEPARATION_MM          (EYE_SEPARATION_MM / 2.0)
#define         PERSPECTIVE_PLANE_DISTANCE_MM       (3500.0)
#define         OBJECT_DISTANCE_MM              (6000.0)
#define         OFFSET_PERCENTAGE               (0.89)


/*

    +-------------------------------------------------------------------+
    |                     variables for mouse control                   |
    +-------------------------------------------------------------------+
*/


#define         DELTA_ROTATE_ANGLE              (0.001)


/*
```

```
    +------------------------------------------------------------------+
    |                object transformations and projections            |
    +------------------------------------------------------------------+
*/
static alg_matrix_4x4_type   transformation_matrix;

void create_transformation_matrix( alg_point_3D_type scale,
alg_point_3D_type rotate,     alg_point_3D_type translate )
{
        alg_identity_4x4_matrix( transformation_matrix );
        alg_scale_4x4_matrix ( scale, transformation_matrix );
        alg_rotate_4x4_matrix( rotate, transformation_matrix,
                MOTION_ROTATION );
        alg_translate_4x4_matrix ( translate, transformation_matrix );
}


void transform_point( alg_point_3D_type pt3D, alg_float
        half_eye_separation_mm, alg_point_2D_int_type *pt2D )
{
        alg_point_3D_type       pt;
        alg_float               inverse_z;
        alg_float               offset;

        alg_transform_4x4_matrix( pt, transformation_matrix, pt3D );

        offset = -OFFSET_PERCENTAGE * half_eye_separation_mm /
                OBJECT_DISTANCE_MM;
        inverse_z = 1.0 / (OBJECT_DISTANCE_MM + pt.z);
        (*pt2D).x = alg_X_Center + PERSPECTIVE_PLANE_DISTANCE_MM *
                ( ( half_eye_separation_mm + pt.x ) * inverse_z +
                offset );
        (*pt2D).y = alg_Y_Center - PERSPECTIVE_PLANE_DISTANCE_MM *
                (pt.y * inverse_z);
}


/*
    +------------------------------------------------------------------+
    |                         drawing object                           |
    +------------------------------------------------------------------+
```

```
*/

#define                NUM_CUBE_VERTICES      8

// measures in millimeters
alg_point_3D_type        cube[NUM_CUBE_VERTICES] = {

                                        { 100.0,   100.0,   100.0},
                                        { 100.0,   100.0,  -100.0},
                                        { 100.0,  -100.0,   100.0},
                                        { 100.0,  -100.0,  -100.0},
                                        {-100.0,   100.0,   100.0},
                                        {-100.0,   100.0,  -100.0},
                                        {-100.0,  -100.0,   100.0},
                                        {-100.0,  -100.0,  -100.0}

                                                                };

#define                DRAW_CUBE                      \
{                                                      \
        moveto(pnts[0].x, pnts[0].y);          \
        lineto(pnts[1].x, pnts[1].y);          \
        lineto(pnts[3].x, pnts[3].y);          \
        lineto(pnts[2].x, pnts[2].y);          \
        lineto(pnts[0].x, pnts[0].y);          \
        lineto(pnts[4].x, pnts[4].y);          \
        lineto(pnts[5].x, pnts[5].y);          \
        lineto(pnts[7].x, pnts[7].y);          \
        lineto(pnts[6].x, pnts[6].y);          \
        lineto(pnts[4].x, pnts[4].y);          \
        moveto(pnts[1].x, pnts[1].y);          \
        lineto(pnts[5].x, pnts[5].y);          \
        moveto(pnts[2].x, pnts[2].y);          \
        lineto(pnts[6].x, pnts[6].y);          \
        moveto(pnts[3].x, pnts[3].y);          \
        lineto(pnts[7].x, pnts[7].y);          \
}

void draw_cube( alg_point_3D_type scale, alg_point_3D_type rotate,
```

```
        alg_point_3D_type translate, alg_boolean *firstdraw )
{

        static alg_point_3D_type    old_rotate = { 0.0, 0.0, 0.0 };
        alg_word                    point_number;
        alg_point_2D_int_type           pnts[NUM_CUBE_VERTICES];
        alg_boolean                 same;

        if (*firstdraw)
                *firstdraw = ALG_FALSE;
        else
        {
                // return if the same, object not rotating, do not erase
                ALG_VEC3_COMPARE( old_rotate, rotate, same );
                if (same)
                        return;

                // clear red left cube for right-eye image
                for (point_number=0; point_number<NUM_CUBE_VERTICES;
                            point_number++)
                        transform_point( cube[point_number],
                                -HALF_EYE_SEPARATION_MM,
                                &pnts[point_number] );

                setcolor(2);
                DRAW_CUBE;

                // clear cyan right cube for left-eye image
                for (point_number=0; point_number<NUM_CUBE_VERTICES;
                            point_number++)
                        transform_point( cube[point_number],
                                HALF_EYE_SEPARATION_MM,
                                &pnts[point_number] );

                setcolor(1);
                DRAW_CUBE;
        }

        // create transformation matrix for new rotation
        create_transformation_matrix( scale, rotate, translate );
```

```
        // update old rotation
        old_rotate = rotate;

        // draw red left cube for right-eye image
        for (point_number=0; point_number<NUM_CUBE_VERTICES;
                    point_number++)
            transform_point( cube[point_number],
                    -HALF_EYE_SEPARATION_MM,
                    &pnts[point_number] );

        setcolor(2);
        DRAW_CUBE;

        // draw cyan right cube for left-eye image
        for (point_number=0; point_number<NUM_CUBE_VERTICES;
                    point_number++)
            transform_point( cube[point_number],
                    HALF_EYE_SEPARATION_MM,
                    &pnts[point_number] );

        setcolor(1);
        DRAW_CUBE;
}


/*

    +------------------------------------------------------------------+
    |         anaglyph glasses demo - mouse control in main program    |
    +------------------------------------------------------------------+
*/

void alg_print_usage( void )
{
printf ("\n\n");
printf ("+-----------------------------------------------------------+\n");
printf ("|                                                           |\n");
printf ("|  3-D Interactive Visualizer for Anaglyph Line Models      |\n");
printf ("|                      (Wireframe)                          |\n");
printf ("|                                                           |\n");
```

```c
printf ("| Copyright 1987-1994 ALGORITHM, Inc. / Atlanta, Georgia |\n");
printf ("|                     ALL RIGHTS RESERVED                 |\n");
printf ("|                                                         |\n");
printf ("| Software written by Christopher D. Watkins for the book|\n");
printf ("| Virtual Reality ExCursions (1994:Academic Press, Inc.) |\n");
printf ("|      by Christopher D. Watkins and Stephen R. Marenka   |\n");
printf ("|                                                         |\n");
printf ("|        Usage: anaglyph <virtual world filename>.ana     |\n");
printf ("|                                                         |\n")
printf ("|                 ALGORITHM, Inc.       (404) 634-0920    |\n");
printf ("| 3776 Lavista Road, Suite 100A, Tucker, Georgia 30084    |\n");
printf ("|                                                         |\n");
printf ( +-------------------------------------------------------+\n");
printf ("\n\n");
}


void main( alg_int argc, alg_char *argv[] )
{
        alg_palette_type        color_palette;


        // mouse parameters
        alg_int                 m1, m2, mx, my;
        alg_point_2D_type       mouse;
        alg_boolean             left_pressed_event, left_released_event;
        alg_boolean             right_pressed_event, right_released_event;


        alg_point_2D_type       mouse_position;
        alg_point_2D_type       mouse_position_change;


        alg_boolean             done = ALG_FALSE;
        alg_boolean             firstdraw = ALG_TRUE;


        alg_point_3D_type       scale       = { 1.8, 1.8, 1.8 };
        alg_point_3D_type       rotate      = { 0.0, 0.0, 0.0 };
        alg_point_3D_type       translate   = { 0.0, 0.0, 0.0 };


        alg_point_3D_type       rotate_rate = { 0.0, 0.0, 0.0 };


        // initialize the graphics display
```

```
alg_set_graphics_mode( 640, 480 );

// use XOR_PUT so that drawing the same line twice will erase it
setwritemode( XOR_PUT );
// initialize the graphics display palette
      // background color is white
alg_set_palette_entry( 63, 63, 63, color_palette, 0 );
      // left eye sees cyan against white
alg_set_palette_entry(  0, 63, 63, color_palette, 1 );
      // right eye sees red against white
alg_set_palette_entry( 63,  0,  0, color_palette, 2 );
      // left and right eye overlap color is black
alg_set_palette_entry(  0,  0,  0, color_palette, 3 );

// initialize the mouse control
alg_init_mouse( &left_pressed_event, &left_released_event,
             &right_pressed_event, &right_released_event );

alg_show_mouse_cursor();

// interact with the object using the mouse
//      holding left mouse button while moving will rotate the
//              object around its x or y axis
//      releasing the left mouse button while still moving will
//              cause the object to remain in rotational motion
//      the right mouse button exits program
while (!done)
{
      // keep image on screen longer, and allow enough time for
      //      the user to move the mouse so that releasing the
      //      left mouse button while still moving will cause
      //      the object to remain in rotational motion
      delay(30);

      // get the mouse
      alg_get_mouse( &m1, &m2, &mx, &my,
              &left_pressed_event, &left_released_event,
              &right_pressed_event, &right_released_event );
```

```
        ALG_VEC2_MAKE( mx, my, mouse );

        // update any rotational information based on mouse
        //     status
        if ( left_released_event )
                mouse_position = mouse;
        else
        {
                ALG_VEC2_SUB( mouse, mouse_position,
                        mouse_position_change );
                rotate_rate.x = -mouse_position_change.y *
                        DELTA_ROTATE_ANGLE;
                rotate_rate.y = -mouse_position_change.x *
                        DELTA_ROTATE_ANGLE;
                mouse_position = mouse;
        }

        // exit on right mouse button
        if ( right_pressed_event )
                done = ALG_TRUE;

        // update the rotation
        ALG_VEC3_ADD( rotate, rotate_rate, rotate );

        alg_hide_mouse_cursor();

        // transform and draw object
        draw_cube( scale, rotate, translate, &firstdraw );

        alg_show_mouse_cursor();
    }

    alg_hide_mouse_cursor();

    // terminate the graphics display
    alg_exit_graphics();
}
```

Section 12—Other Rendering Methodologies

Our primary goal in the production of computer-generated imagery is to create images that can pass for photographs of real or imagined objects. Many techniques are used to render three-dimensional scenes, each with its own set of good and bad points. Computer graphics has expanded in many directions with great numbers of people researching various techniques for improving image quality, fidelity with the real world, and visualization of complex data sets. Many problems, such as realistic human animation, have yet to be solved.

Realistic models require a sophistication and complexity which bring many high-powered computing systems to a screeching halt. High polygon counts and complex textures for detail and complex mathematical models for accurately simulating the environment and object-object interactions make virtual reality simulations impossible on many generic computing systems. Silicon Graphics have the right approach with their high-speed graphics engines and environment texture mapping (mapping a bitmap image of the environment to the surface of an object).

In this section, we take a look at two other rendering technologies that get us closer to photorealism: ray tracing and radiosity. But, as mentioned before, each has its good points and its bad points.

RAY TRACING

Ray tracing is an excellent technique for rendering worlds that contain specularly reflective objects. The ray tracing technique offers an approach that can truly simulate how a camera (or human eye) might see a scene. The concept is actually quite sraightforward: namely, we simulate how light interacts with objects by tracing light rays through a scene to see what objects they interact with. With this approach, we are modeling how light interacts physically with objects. Since we are concerned only with the light rays that eventually reach our eye (or pass through the computer screen), we follow the light rays in reverse. Rays are followed from the eye, through the "screen," and out into the scene. The rays are traced as they are reflected, refracted, diffracted, and focused following the basic laws of optics.

The ray tracing algorithm is quite simple. The screen is defined as an array of pixels, set up in a viewing geometry as shown in Figure 5.36. For each screen pixel, we generate an initial ray starting at the eyepoint, passing through the screen, and out into some environment we have already defined. The environment consists of three-dimensional objects, lights, and background models. The ray tracing algorithm then proceeds as follows:

- Find the nearest object that the ray intersects (if any) and determine the point of intersection, as shown in Figure 5.37.
- Calculate the ambient color of the object surface at the point of intersection based on the object's characteristics and the light sources.
- Cast "shadow" rays from the point of intersection to each light source in the scene, as shown in Figure 5.38. These are used to generate the diffuse and specular lighting of the surface. The shadow rays also determine whether the point of intersection is shadowed from a light source by another obstructing object, either wholly or partially.
- If the object surface is reflective, compute a new ray starting at the intersection point and pointing in the "reflected" direction. Find the effective color of this ray by recursively calling the very same procedure.
- If the object surface is transparent, compute a new transmitted ray, again starting from the intersection point. Find the color of this ray and add it to the color of the other rays.
- Add the object color to the color of the reflected and transmitted rays, and then return this as the color of the pixel.

This procedure has several interesting properties:

- It is inherently recursive, which makes C and other such languages ideally suited. Each time a ray is cast, we simply call the procedure again with the new ray.
- It is based on a model of light interacting with objects. We can accurately model how light is reflected and refracted through the scene in ways that more traditional methods simply cannot handle.
- It is very amenable to parallel processing (having multiple CPUs work on different parts of a picture). Each pixel can be processed independently of the other pixels in the scene.

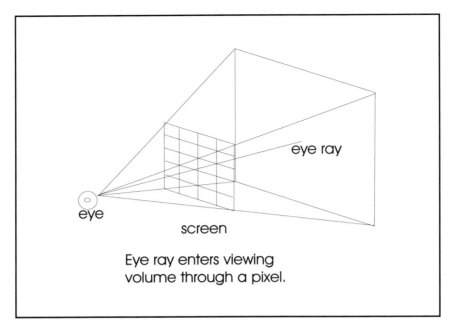

eye ray

eye

screen

Eye ray enters viewing
volume through a pixel.

Figure 5.36—Ray Tracing Viewing Geometry

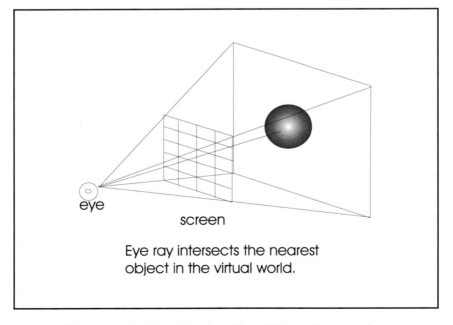

eye

screen

Eye ray intersects the nearest
object in the virtual world.

Figure 5.37—Ray Tracing Ray-Object Intersection

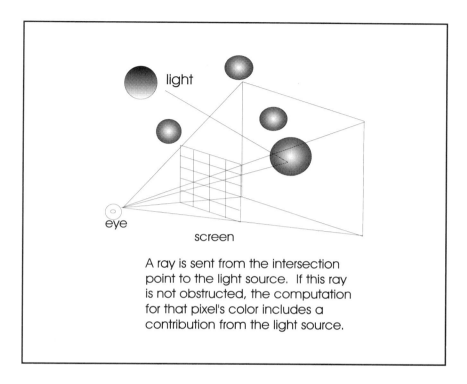

light

eye

screen

A ray is sent from the intersection
point to the light source. If this ray
is not obstructed, the computation
for that pixel's color includes a
contribution from the light source.

Figure 5.38—Ray Tracing for Shadows

While ray tracing satisfies our main goal of producing high-quality imagery, it also provides another important tool in computer graphics. Namely, it gives us a method for testing our understanding of how light interacts with an environment. Many researchers have adapted their physical models of the interaction of light with matter to ray tracing programs to see if they produce images that look like the real thing. If so, then we have greatly increased our confidence that our theoretical model is an accurate description of the processes that are taking place. This is especially true in modeling very complex phenomena such as waves, clouds, and terrain. Thus, the tools provided here allow you not only to produce high-quality imagery but also to test even more complex models of light.

Having waxed eloquent about the virtues of ray tracing, let's explore in more detail the elements of the basic algorithm.

Ray Tracing Theory

The following is a pseudocode representation of the basic ray tracing algorithm as we have described it.

```
main()
{
        Ray     *ray;
        long    x, y;
        long    pixel;
        Color   color;
        Point   screen_point;

        init_global_variables();    // basic initialization
        define_environment();       // where are our objects and where
                                    //     are we ?
        do_precalculations();       // set up for rendering

        for(y=0; y < yscreen; y++)
        {
                for(x=0; x < xscreen; x++)
                {
                        // make first ray from the eye to the position x,y
                        //     on the screen
                        screen_point = make_vector_from_screen(x, y);
                        ray = new_ray(screen_point, eyepoint);
                        trace(ray, &color);
                        pixel = color_composite(color);
                        output[x, y] = pixel;

                } // end of row
        } // end of image

        write_image_to_output_file();
        exit(0);
} // end of main()

void    trace(ray, colorp)
```

```
    Vector3D      *ray;
    Color         *colorp;
{
    Isect  *intersect;
    Color  color, refl_color, trans_color;
    Ray    *shadow_ray, *refl_ray, *trans_ray;
    int    l;

    intersect = find_intersection(ray);
    if(intersect)
    {
         // we intersected an object, so process it
        curobject = intersect->object;

        // first color is the "intrinsic" object color
        color = curobject->ambient_color +
                (diffuse(curobject, intersection->point) *
                ambient_light);

        for(l = 0; l < numlights; l++)
        {
                // for each light, determine if it shadows the
                //     object, and if so, whether we are
                //     completely blocked, or only partially
                curlight = lights[i];
                shadow_ray = new_ray(curlight->position,
                        intersect->position);
                shade = shadow(shadow_ray);
                color += (curlight->color * shade) *
                        curobject->diffuse_color;
                spec_color = compute_specular(intersect->point,
                        curlight);
                color += spec_color;
                free(shadow_ray);
        } // end of loop for all lights

    if(curobject->reflective)
    {
        // surface is reflective, so generate a new ray
```

```
            refl_ray = compute_reflected(ray, curobject,
                    intersect->point,
                    intersect->normal);
        trace(refl_ray, &refl_color);
        color += refl_color * curobject->specular;
        free(refl_ray);
    }


    if(curobject->transparent)
    {
        // surface is, at least slightly, transparent
        trans_ray = compute_transmitted(ray, curobject,
                intersect->point,
                intersect->normal);
        trace(trans_ray, &trans_color);
        color += trans_color * curobject->transparency;
        free(trans_ray);
    }
    *colorp = color;
    }
    else
    {
        // no intersections were found, so use background
        get_background(ray, colorp);
    }


    return;
    // done - *colorp now contains our color
}
```

Examine *trace*. It takes an input ray and a color pointer (for returning color) as arguments. Note that it is called recursively, if the surface is reflective or at least partially transparent. This is the essence of the ray tracing approach: we follow a light ray through the environment until it moves out of the environment into the background, or it strikes a light source. The process is inherently recursive as rays are traced from one surface to another. The effective color of each ray is summed at the intersection point to find the color of the surface at that point.

Interactive-Rate Ray Tracing?

Ray tracing algorithms have never really been used in any type of real time visualization system because today the computer horsepower simply isn't available to perform the sorting operations (building the heirarchical tree and determining the nearest object for each ray) quickly enough. The standard projective rendering programs (like the software with this book) have the advantage that they need only sort the object lists, from farthest to nearest, one time per frame. If you use only one level of recursion, then a ray tracer could do the same thing, but then you lose the improved image quality and realism of ray tracing. One of the real hopes for ever achieving this goal is in parallel computing. Remember that each pixel is processed independently, and thus the image calculation can be spread across several processors that have access to the same scene description. As the cost of these types of machines decreases, we can expect to see more people attempting to run ray tracing in near real time. It should be noted, however, that we can always saturate any ray tracing computation by increasing the recursion level, computing depth-of-field effects, and adding more complicated shadow and lighting computations.

Radiosity

Radiosity is an excellent technique for rendering worlds that contain many diffusely reflecting objects like interior walls and ceilings. The entire subject of the physical modeling of the interaction of light and surfaces within a scene is called *radiosity*. This type of modeling tries to create a complete physical model of how light reflects throughout a scene. It is based on the theory of radiative heat transfer between surfaces. An object surface receives light not only from the light sources and specularly reflective objects but also from the diffuse illumination of surfaces.

Imagine an interior wall. A radiosity model would actually compute the entire diffuse light contribution from the entire wall reflecting onto the surface of some object. Compare this with modeling a mirrored surface. With a mirror, we looked only for specular reflections and needed to cast only a single ray. With a radiosity solution, we must integrate the contributions from all of the diffuse surfaces within a scene. Additionally, a radiosity approach makes no particular assumption about the ambient and diffuse lighting of a scene. All of the light contributions are computed as integrated contributions rather than single point evaluations. This applies to specular as well as diffuse components. Recall that in ray tracing the specular contribution came from the light sources only. A full radiosity solution also includes specular effects of diffuse surfaces. For even a simple scene, such as a typical office, these are very extensive computations.

Approximations for Radiosity

Because of the long compute times, even purists have been driven to develop approximations and shortcuts for radiosity solutions. The key to using these heuristics is that for a static scene with no highly reflective objects, we need only compute the diffuse contributions of the surfaces once. The contribution depends only on the geometry of the objects, not on the particular lighting within the scene. This contribution is expressed in terms of effective light intensity from the surfaces involved and so can be used for the diffuse contribution directly. This is ideal for a z-buffered ray tracing approach in that the diffuse contribution can be computed and stored at the same time as the z-buffering occurs. Once this diffuse intensity map is created, we may add new light sources to the scene with much less difficulty. Only the contributions due to this light source need be considered; all of the others have been accounted for. It is still time-consuming but much less so than recomputing the entire scene.

Advantages of Radiosity

The advantage of a radiosity solution is that it can make a scene appear much more like its real-life counterpart, providing more details in shadowed areas and correctly depicting the effects of indirect lighting. This is particularly useful to an architect who wants to know what type of lighting and what intensity to use in designing a new office building. A radiosity solution provides the flexibility of being able to add new light sources at will, such as a desk lamp, and literally being able to turn it on and off and see the effect. Shadowing effects are more accurate in a radiosity solution as well. The real advantage, however, is that it provides a test bed for fully understanding and testing our theories of how light propagates through a scene.

THE IDEAL GRAPHICS CARD

To this point, we have talked about rendering algorithms that were implemented in software. Most of these algorithms can be implemented in hardware with many orders of magnitude performance increase. Now it is time to define quickly what would make the "ideal" graphics hardware complement to a computer system. Here, some of the software algorithms like anti-aliasing and projections are implemented in hardware, so they execute much faster. The added performance buys the time needed to increase the polygon count and add complex texturing. With greater polygon count and better textures, your virtual world can approach photorealism. Let us look at an outline for such graphics hardware.

Features:

- High-speed, geometry processor on board (e.g., Motorola 88110)
- Default, manufacturer-provided driver ROM'd. TIGA compatible? Custom drivers can be downloaded for optimum performance on an application-by-application basis.
- Eyepoint/object coordinate transformations
- FOV (field-of-view)/perspective calculation
- Texture coordinate calculations
- Clipping
- Collision detection

Custom hardware render processor performs:

- Pixel fill
- Anti-aliasing
- Interpolation calculation (e.g., for Gouraud shading)

Additional features:

- 32-bit color frame buffer
- 32-bit Z buffer

- 1280 x 1024 maximum resolution
- 32 color tables for "color-table-per-window" operation
- Integrated pointer (mouse) interface
- GL 3-D Library

Optional feature modules:

- Image manipulation (warp, scale, rotate, translate)
- Colorspace conversion
- Double buffer
- Image compression/decompression

Performance Specs for a PC:

- 25,000 flat-shaded, anti-aliased traingles per second
- 15,000 Gouraud-shaded, anti-aliased triangles per second
- 5000 textured, shaded, anti-aliased triangles per second

Conclusion

Well, you have made it to this point, the end of the technical section, and the end of this book. Perhaps you were a bit suprised about just how many of the technical concepts you understood and just how much you learned about virtual reality and human perception.

In any case, let us create a little déjà vu and review conceptually the workings of the virtual reality graphics system that we have developed. Then we will define a visual system in outline form.

Imagine that you are back in that airplane from the beginning of this section. A window exists at the front of the cockpit which allows you to see the world in front of you. The world outside is made of three-dimensional objects like trees and houses. If you had never been outside your airplane before, the two-dimensional image that you see through the cockpit window would be all that you know. Your computer screen is now that cockpit window.

Also imagine that all of the surfaces of the three-dimensional objects in your real world are made up of tiny polygonal patches. That simple house (Figure 5.39) in your view could be made of four rectangles for walls, two rectangles for a roof, two triangles to fill in the ends of the roof, and assorted rectangles for windows and doors. The more polygons you have and the smaller the polygons are, the more precisely you can define curved surfaces for your objects.

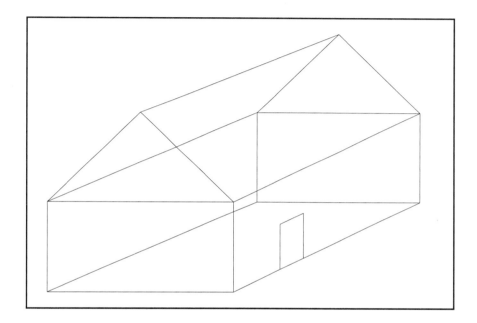

Figure 5.39—House Constructed of Polygons

Now visualize how your very complex three-dimensional surroundings might look if they were made up only of flat shaded triangles and rectangles. Coloring, shading, and texturing those polygons will help. You can make smooth objects, rough objects, highly reflective or transparent objects. Your objects can have textures like wood and marble. Just use mathematics to define the way light reflects from an object into your eyes. Apply these mathematics to each individual polygon, and you obtain objects that have varying shade across their surfaces. This creates a sense of realism.

So we now have a three-dimensional world whose objects are constructed of shaded polygons. We also have a computer display that acts like a window into that world. Given that our computer display can assume any position and orientation in our virtual three-dimensional world, we can perform perspective projection on all of the three-dimensional polygons onto the two-dimensional display and, thus, view our virtual world.

As time passes, our computer "window" can be repositioned and reoriented in space, just like the airplane cockpit window, based on the positions of the controllers (keyboard, mouse, yoke, etc.).

Given stereo vision, force feedback (dynamic resistance) to the controllers, and good mathematical models for how the viewer position and orientation would change based on changes in controller position, we have a simulator. Add sound and smell, humidity and temperature effects, and you have the beginnings of a total immersion system.

Now let us look at the makings of a desktop virtual reality visual system. By no means is this complete; it is a good start, though.

Modules for a Desktop Virtual Reality Software Development

Materials Factory

All objects have to be made of something. This module defines what the somethings are and their physical properties (e.g., intrinsic color, surface texture, deformability, reflectivity).

Laws of Nature Maker

It seems that a world not only has objects but also has universal rules for object-object interactions and object-world environment interactions. This module helps define those rules.

Object Builder

This is a tool for creating object descriptions and databases. It deals with paradigms for object construction/description including the facet/vertex list like the one we used, and others like an approach that better handles active (e.g., light source) as well as passive objects. Here we also define object mechanics.

World Builder

A tool for defining the extent and contents of the virtual world. Placing objects within the world, establishing an "initial condition", since you expect that objects will be manipulated in time. Of interest is a means for defining what happens at the "edge" of the world: reflected world? truncated world? This would includes an interactive rate viewer. Manipulation of objects within the world will occur at real-time rates.

Stimulus/Response Linker

Links a certain stimulus from the environment to a particular action based on object mechanics perviously defined.

Involver

The interactive rate viewer.

File Converter

Allows import of many 3-D model formats (e.g., DXF conversion for object builder).

Remote VR

VR through telephone lines using data compression and tokens to represent positions and orientations of objects. Here the scene is rendered on both ends simultaneously.

Control VR

Process control using VR. Basic control systems and monitoring of processes could be handled by the software.

Immersion VR

The extension from the desktop to datagloves and headsets/headphones including sound support.

Closing Comments

Well, there you have it, virtual reality in a nutshell. By no means have we totally covered the technical and physiological aspects, psychological aspects, historical and application aspects, or any other aspect of the field. But we do hope that we have given you enough information for you to feel as though you know what virtual reality really is and that it is not something threatening or mystic, or even some "buzz" word. The main point was to show you that, in reality, the field is a collection of many diverse technologies, and that it represents intellegent ways for humans to interact with computers for a variety of purposes.

As with all good things, this too must come to an end. We really hope that you enjoyed your reading, as well as working and playing with the software. Many seemimingly endless hours and bottles of Jolt Cola went into its development, so now it is time for you (and us) to have fun with it.

If you found the section on human perception particulary interesting, you can contact Vincent Mallette at the Georgia Institute of Technology, or Christopher D. Watkins at Algorithm, Inc. in Atlanta, Georgia. Vincent Mallette is an expert in the human visual system. If you found the sections on computer graphics interesting and you would like to know more about computer graphics, virtual reality, image processing, or other computer-related technologies, look for the following excellent books and organizations.

BOOKS:

- *Programming in 3 Dimensions, Ray Tracing and Animation*—a simple graphics text including diskette with a ray tracer, renderers, and an animator (includes all source code), by Christopher D. Watkins and Larry Sharp, M&T Publishing, San Mateo, CA (Henry Holt, New York)
- *Photorealism and Ray Tracing in C*—a most excellent general to technical graphics text including diskettes with very useful photorealistic ray tracer and fractal database generators (includes all source code and three-dimensional models), by Christopher D. Watkins, Stephen B. Coy and Mark Finlay, M&T Publishing, San Mateo, CA (Henry Holt, New York)
- *Computer Graphics, a Programming Approach*—an excellent general graphics discussion, by Steven Harrington, McGraw Hill, New York
- *Computer Graphics, Principles and Practice*—an excellent, more technical graphics text, by James Foley, Addison Wesley, Reading, MA
- *Modern Image Processing, Warping, Morphing and Classical Techniques*—a simple image processing text including diskette (includes all source code), by Christopher D. Watkins, Alberto Sadun, and Stephen R. Marenka, Academic Press, Inc., Cambridge, MA
- *Modern Computer Animation* (tentatively titled)—a most excellent general computer graphics text including diskette (and maybe CD) with full warping, morphing, scanline rendering and PC animation software (includes all source code), by Christopher D. Watkins and Stephen R. Marenka, Academic Press, Inc., Cambridge, MA (available summer 1994)

ORGANIZATIONS:

- Association of Computing Machinery (ACM), 11 West 42nd Street New York, NY 10036; ACM/SIGGRAPH (Special Interest Group on computer GRAPHics)
- IEEE *Computer Graphics and Applications* (magazine) 10662 Los Vaqueros Circle, Los Alamitos, CA 90720

REFERENCES

Network Reference List

The newsgroup is Sci.virtual-worlds maintained by the Human Interfaces Technology Lab in Seattle Washington. Archives are at ftp.u.washington.edu (128.95.136.1).

Much of the following is a list found on the Internet compiled by Bill Cockayne, who wishes updates to be sent to him at billc@apple.com.

FTP sites:

avalon.chinalake.navy.mil (129.131.31.11)
        —huge repository of 3D objects in all types of formats
        /pub

ftp.apple.com (130.43.2.3)
        —sites list, Macintosh vr, CAD projects info
        /pub/VR

karazm.math.uh.edu (129.7.128.1)
    —home of the glove list, nice code
    /pub/VR

src.doc.ic.ac.uk (146.169.2.1)
    —great usenet archives including stuff from sci.v-w, also
        has info on ISIS and a VR app for ISIS
    /usenet/comp.archives/auto/comp.sys.isis
    /usenet/comp.archives/auto/sci.virtual-worlds

stein.u.washington.edu (140.142.56.1)
    —home of sci.virtual—worlds, huge faq w/ great info!
    —if unable to use try ftp.u.washington.edu
    /public/virtual-worlds
sunee.uwaterloo.ca (129.97.50.50)
    —home of REND386 (freeware VR library/package)
    /pub (misc directories on pglove, raytracing, et al.)
    /pub/vr

sunsite.unc.edu (152.2.22.81)
    —virtual reality demos, iris info, glasses, mirrors some of
    milton.u.washington.edu, uforce info
    /pub/academic/computer-science/virtual-reality

wuarchive.wustl.edu (128.252.135.4)
    —complete mirror of milton.u.washington.edu VR archive
    —docs for sega glasses —> RS232 iface, nintendo glove stuff
    —wuarchive is also a graphics archive with over 500 megs of
        graphics related info and source (/graphics)

TELNET sites:

phantom.com (38.145.218.228)
    —home of the MindVox system. telnet to and log in as guest.
        (you will be charged an access fee if you decide to become a
    user)

Discussions/Newsgroups:

Internet

—sci.virtual-worlds and sci.virtual-worlds-apps, moderated by Bob Jacobson and Mark A. DeLoura, are the main online VR discussions.

—alt.cyberpunk and alt.cyberpunk.tech often concerns topics related to VR, though that is not the focus of the discussions themselves.

America Online

The VR discussion on AOL is sponsored by Virtus Corporation and can be found in their directory. To get to the discussion, use the keyword VIRTUS, and look in the "Let's Discuss" folder.

The Well

Telnet 192.132.30.2 or dial up and type "go vr"

BIX

BIX's Virtual World Conference hosts extended discussions of all aspects of the field

Bulletin Boards

Diaspar Virtual Reality Network
(714) 376-1200 2400 bps
(714) 376-1234 9600 bps

SENSE/NET
(801) 364-6227

Reference List of Companies

This is a list of companies and institutions involved in developing products or in research related to virtual reality. It is intended to be utilized as a starting point, certainly not as a comprehensive listing. Names of companies, addresses, and telephone numbers listed are current at the time this work is going to press.

An excellent reference is the latest *Virtual Reality Special Report* available from *AI Expert*.

Advanced Robotics Research Centre
University Rd.
Salford, England M5 4PP
Voice (4461) 745 7384
Fax (4461) 745 8264

Advanced Technology Systems
800 Follin Lane, Ste. 270
Vienna, VA 22180
Voice (703) 242 0030
Fax (703) 242 5220

AICOM Corp.
1590 Oakland Rd., Ste. B112
San Jose, CA 95131
Voice (408) 453 8251
Fax (408) 453 8255

Algorithm, Inc.
3776 Lavista Rd., Ste. 100A
Atlanta, GA 30084
Voice (404) 634 0920
Fax (404) 998 7934

Artificial Reality Corp.
55 Edith Road
Vernon, CT 06066
Voice (203) 871 1375
Fax (203) 871 7738

Ascension Technology Corp.
P.O. Box 527
Burlington, VT 05402
Voice (802) 860 6440

Autodesk, Inc.
Advanced Technology Department
2320 Marinship Way
Sausalito, CA 94965
Voice (415) 332 2344

BioControl Systems, Inc.
430 Cowper St.
Palo Alto, CA 94301
Voice (415) 329 8494
Fax (415) 321 5973

CIS Graphics, Inc.
1 Stiles Rd., Ste. 305
Salem, NH 03079
Voice (603) 894 5999

Covox Inc.
675 Conger St.
Eugene, OR 97402
Voice (503) 342 1271
Fax (503) 342 1283

Crystal River Engineering
12350 Wards Ferry Rd.
Groveland, CA 95321
Voice (209) 962 6382
Fax (209) 962 4873

CyberEdge Journal
#1 Gate Six Rd., Ste. G
Sausolito, CA 94965
Voice (415) 331 3343

CyberSense
169 S. Main St.
Oregon, WI 53575
Voice (608) 835 2115

CyberStudio
2061 Challenger Dr.
Almeda, CA 94501
Voice (510) 522 3584
Fax (510) 522 3587

Digital Image Design Inc.
170 Claremont Ave., Ste. 6
New York City, NY 10027
Voice (212) 222 5236
Fax (212) 864 1189

Division, Inc. (USA)
400 Seaport Ct., Ste. 101
Redwood City, CA 94063
Voice (415) 306 1521

Division Ltd. (UK)
19 Apex Court
Woodlands, Almondsbury
Bristol, England
BS12 4JT
Voice (44 454) 615554
Fax (44 454) 615532

Electronic Design Laboratories
Bristol, England
Voice (44 272) 741918
Fax (44 272) 741861

Evans & Sutherland
600 Komas Dr.
P.O. Box 59700
Salt Lake City UT 94158
Voice (801) 582 5847
Fax (801) 582 5848

EXOS, Inc.
2A Gill St.
Wolburn, MA 01801
Voice (617) 933 0022
Fax (617) 270 5901

Fake Space Labs
935 Hamilton Ave.
Menlo Park, CA 94025
Voice (415) 688 1940
Fax (415) 688 1949

Focal Point 3 D Audio
1402 Pine Ave., Ste. 127
Niagra Falls, NY 14301
Voice (416) 963 9188
Fax (416) 963 9188

General Electric
Simulation & Control
Systems Dept.
P.O. Box 2825
Daytona Beach, FL 32115
Voice (904) 239 2906

Gyration, Inc.
12930 Saratoga Ave., Bldg C
Saratoga, CA 95070
Voice (408) 255 3016
Fax (408) 255 9075
(see Horizon Entertainment)

Horizon Entertainment
(Distributor for W Industries)
501 North Broadway
St. Louis, MO 63102
Voice (314) 331 6051
Fax (314) 331 6002

Institute for Simulation and
Training
Univ. of Central Florida
12434 Research Parkway, Suite 300
Orlando, FL 32826
Voice (407) 658 5074
Fax (407) 658 5059

Latent Image Dev. Corp.
Two Lincoln Square
New York City, NY 10023
Voice (212) 873 5487

LEEP Systems, Inc.
241 Crescent St.
Waltham, MA 02154
Voice (617) 647 1395
Fax (617) 899 9602

Logitech Inc.
6505 Kaiser Dr.
Fremont, CA 94555
Voice (510) 795 8500
Fax (510) 792 8901

MULTIPOINT Tech. Corp.
319 Littleton Rd, Ste. 201
Westford, MA 01886
Voice (508) 692 0689
Fax (508) 692 2653

NASA Ames Research Center
Moffett Field, CA 94035
Voice (415) 604 3937
Fax(508) 604 3953

Paracomp, Inc.
1725 Montgomery Street, 2nd Fl.
San Francisco, CA 94111
Voice (415) 956 4091

Polhemus Incorporated
1 Hercules Drive
P.O. Box 560
Colchester, VT 05466
Voice (802) 655 3159
Fax(802) 655 1439

Polhemus Laboratories, Inc.
P.O. Box 9
Cambridge, VT 05446
Voice (802) 644 5569
Fax (802) 644 2943

Sense8 Corp.
1001 Bridgeway, Ste.477
Sausalito, Ca 94965
Voice (415) 331 6318
Fax (415) 331 9148

Shooting Star Technology
1921 Holdom Ave.
Burnaby, BC Canada
V5B 3W4
Voice (604) 298 8574
Fax (604) 298 8580

Silicon Graphics, Inc.
2011 N. Shoreline Blvd.
Mountain View, CA 94039
Voice (415) 335 1293
Fax (415) 968 3579

SimGraphics Engineering Corp.
1137 Huntington Drive
South Pasadena, CA 91030
Voice (213) 255 0900
Fax (213) 255 0987

Spaceball Technologies, Inc.
600 Suffolk St.
Lowell, MA 01854
Voice (508) 970 0330
Fax (508) 970 0199

StereoGraphics Corp.
2171 H E. Fransico Blvd.
San Rafael, CA 94901
Voice (415) 459 4500
Fax(415) 459 3020

StereoMed Inc.
724 S. Victory Blvd.
Burbank, CA 91502
Voice (818) 559 6515
Fax(818) 761 4971

StrayLight Corp.
150 Mt. Bethel Rd.
Warren, NJ 07059
Voice (908) 580 0086
Fax (908) 580 0092

Teleprescence Research
635 High St.
Palo Alto, CA 94301
Voice (415) 325 8951
Fax (415) 325 8952

The Vivid Group
317 Adelaide St. W., Ste. 302
Toronto Ontario
Canada M5V 1P9
Voice (416) 340 9299
Fax (416) 348 9809

Virtual 'S' Ltd.
The Limes
123 Mortlake High St.
London SW14 8SN, England
Voice (44 81) 3929000
Fax (44 81) 3922424

Virtual Research
1313 Socorro Ave.
Sunnyvale, CA 94089
Voice (408) 739 7114
Fax (408) 739 8586

Virtual Technologies
P.O. Box 5984
Stanford, CA 94309
Voice (415) 599 2331

Virtus Corp.
117 Edinburgh S., Ste. 204
Cary, NC 27511
Voice (919) 467 9700

Visual Synthesis, Inc.
4126 Addison Rd.
Fairfax, VA 22030
Voice (703) 352 0258

VPL Research
656 Bair Island Rd., 3rd Fl.
Redwood City, CA 94063
Voice (415) 361 1710
Fax (415) 361 1875

VR News
Cydata Ltd.
P.O. Box 2515
London, N4 4JW
England
Voice (44 81) 292 1498
Fax (44 81) 292 1346

VREAM Inc.
2568 N. Clark St., Suite 250
Chicago, IL 60614
Voice (312) 477 0425
Fax (312) 477 9702

W Industries Ltd.(UK)
Virtuality House
3 Oswin Rd.
Brailsford Industrial Park
Leicester LE3 lHR England
Voice (44) 533 542127
Fax (44) 533 471855

Xtensory Inc.
140 Sunridge Drive
Scotts Valley, CA 95066
Voice (408) 439 0600

Color Inserts

Plate Data1   Interaction with a three-dimensional visualization of molecular
                     data.
                     Glyph binder interface for mapping data variables onto
                     graphical elements in the virtual environment. The data is
                     classified by types, and here the user chooses the type
                     associated with a NaCl cluster.
                     Data Credits: David Luedtke and Uzi Landman.
                     Photo Credits: Ron van Teylingen/Bill Ribarsky
                     GVU Lab Project: SV—Georgia Institute of Technology
                     (data1.tif)

Plate Olytorch   Georgia Tech's 1996 Atlanta Torch Carrier used in City
                     Demonstration
                     3-D Model Credit: Kleizer-Walczak
                     Photo Credit: Michael Sinclair/Frank Witz
                     Multimedia Technology Lab Project—Georgia Institute of
                     Technology
                     (olytorch.tif)

Plate Shrine2   Side View of a Japanese temple
                     1991 Competition Winner—Lucas Santosa
                     College of Architecture, Imagine Group
                     Photo Credits: Thomas Meyer/Lucas Santosa/Tolek
                     Lesniewski
                     GVU Lab Project: DVE—Georgia Institute of Technology
                     (shrine2.tif)

Plate Hmd   HMD, DataGlove, and Elevator (worn by Thomas Meyer)
                     Photo Credits: Thomas Meyer/Rob Kooper
                     GVU Lab Project: ICV—Georgia Institute of Technology
                     (hmd.tif)

Plate Ivex1   IVEX Corporation Flight Simulator
                     Image showing light points on runway
                     (ivex1.tif)

Plate Ivex2   IVEX Corporation Flight Simulator
Image showing light points and fog on runway
(ivex2.tif)

Plate Ivex4   IVEX Corporation Flight Simulator
Image showing 3-D models of buildings in scene
(ivex4.tif)

Plate Ivex7   IVEX Corporation Flight Simulator
Image showing tank simulation
(ivex7.tif)

Plate Ivex10   IVEX Corporation Flight Simulator
Image showing incredible textured mountains and terrain
(ivex10.tif)

Plate Balcony1   View from a balcony
Photo Credits: Rob Kooper/Larry Hodges
GVU Lab Project: Phobia—Georgia Institute of Technology
(balcony1.tif)

Plate Bridge1   View from a bridge over a river
Photo Credits: Rob Kooper/Larry Hodges
GVU Lab Project: Phobia—Georgia Institute of Technology
(bridge1.tif)

Plate Eyes2   Ocular Surgery Simulator—Fusable Stereo Pair
In conjunction with the Medical College of Georgia
Photo Credit: Michael Sinclair
Multimedia Technology Lab Project—Georgia Institute of
Technology
(eyes2.tif)

Plate Eyes   Ocular Surgery Simulator
In conjunction with the Medical College of Georgia
Photo Credit: Michael Sinclair
Multimedia Technology Lab Project—Georgia Institute of
Technology
(eyes.tif)

Gray-Scale Inserts

Figure 1. 1   Left: Virtual Research HMD (640 x 480 x 55° version) worn by Tom Meyer
Right: Virtual Research HMD (320 x 240 x 80° version) worn by E. J. Lee
Photo Credits: Thomas Meyer/Rob Kooper
GVU Lab Project: ICV—Georgia Institute of Technology
(hmd1.tif)

Figure 1. 2   VR Aerial View of GVU Center Lab
Photo Credits: Augusto Op den Bosch/Walter Patterson
GVU Lab Project: ICV—Georgia Institute of Technology
(lab1.tif)

Figure 1. 3   View of VR Man in HMD in the Virtual Environments Area of GVU Lab
Photo Credits: Augusto Op den Bosch/Walter Patterson
GVU Lab Project: ICV—Georgia Institute of Technology
(lab2.tif)

Figure 1. 4   View of Tech Campus and downtown Atlanta from the North
Photo Credits: Thomas Meyer/Larry Hodges
GVU Lab Project: DVE—Georgia Institute of Technology
(gatech1.tif)

Figure 1. 5   View over Tech Tower and Tech Campus
Photo Credits: Thomas Meyer/Larry Hodges
GVU Lab Project: DVE—Georgia Institute of Technology
(gatech2.tif)

Figure 1. 6   View over Tech Coliseum and Tech Campus
Photo Credits: Thomas Meyer/Larry Hodges
GVU Lab Project: DVE—Georgia Institute of Technology
(gatech3.tif)

Figure 1. 7   View above GSU Urban Life/Law Building and downtown Atlanta
Photo Credits: Thomas Meyer/Brian Wills/Tolek Lesniewski
GVU Lab Project: DVE—Georgia Institute of Technology
(gastate1.tif)

Figure 1. 8   View from street of GSU Law Building and downtown Atlanta
Photo Credits: Thomas Meyer/Brian Wills/Tolek Lesniewski
GVU Lab Project: DVE—Georgia Institute of Technology
(gastate2.tif)

Figure 1. 9   Interaction with a 3-D widget using gesture recognition for data visualization. A time step in molecular dynamics simulation as seen in the virtual environment. Here a NaCl cluster is smashing into a Ne surface with temperature mapped onto atom color. In the foreground one can see how color is attached, by direct manipulation, to the temperature property of the glyph.
Data Credits: David Luedtke and Uzi Landman.
Photo Credits: Ron van Teylingen/Bill Ribarsky
GVU Lab Project: SV—Georgia Institute of Technology
(data2.tif)

Figure 1.10   IVEX Corporation Flight Simulator
Image showing simulator cockpit and view
(ivex11.tif)

Figure 1.11   IVEX Corporation Flight Simulator
Image showing running simulation system behind the scenes
(ivex12.tif)

Figure 1.12   IVEX Corporation Flight Simulator
Image showing helicopter cockpit connected to simulator system
(ivex13.tif)

Figure 1.13   Motion Interactive of a Diver through Sequence
                   Photo Credit: Michael Sinclair
                   Multimedia Technology Lab Project—Georgia Institute of
                   Technology
                   (diverseq.tif)

Figure 1.14   View from a balcony over the Georgia Tech campus
                   Photo Credits: Rob Kooper/Thomas Meyer/Larry Hodges
                   GVU Lab Project: Phobia—Georgia Institute of Technology
                   (balcony2.tif)

Figure 1.15   View from the glass elevator over a lobby
                   Photo Credits: Rob Kooper/Thomas Meyer/Drew
                   Kessler/Larry Hodges
                   GVU Lab Project: Phobia—Georgia Institute of Technology
                   (elevator.tif)

Figure 1.16   Motion Interactive of a Diver
                   Photo Credit: Michael Sinclair
                   Multimedia Technology Lab Project—Georgia Institute of
                   Technology
                   (diver.tif)

Figure 1.17   Motion Interactive of an Athelete
                   Photo Credit: Michael Sinclair
                   Multimedia Technology Lab Project—Georgia Institute of
                   Technology
                   (mint.tif)

Figure 1.18   Ocular Surgery Simulator
                   In conjunction with the Medical College of Georgia
                   Photo Credit: Michael Sinclair
                   Multimedia Technology Lab Project—Georgia Institute of
                   Technology
                   (eye.tif)

Figure 1.19   Ocular Surgery Simulator
                   — Mike Sinclair using simulator
                   In conjunction with the Medical College of Georgia
                   Photo Credit: Michael Sinclair
                   Multimedia Technology Lab Project—Georgia Institute of
                   Technology
                   (eyesurg.tif)

Figure 1.20   Ocular Surgery Simulator—Fusable Stereo Pair—inner features
                   In conjunction with the Medical College of Georgia
                   Photo Credit: Michael Sinclair
                   Multimedia Technology Lab Project—Georgia Institute of
                   Technology
                   (eyes3.tif)

Figure 1.21   Ocular Surgery Simulator—Fusable Stereo Pair
                   In conjunction with the Medical College of Georgia
                   Photo Credit: Michael Sinclair
                   Multimedia Technology Lab Project—Georgia Institute of
                   Technology
                   (eyes4.tif)

Figure 2.1   Front View of a Japanese temple
                   1991 Competition Winner—Lucas Santosa
                   College of Architecture, Imagine Group
                   Photo Credits: Thomas Meyer/Lucas Santosa/Tolek
                   Lesniewski
                   GVU Lab Project: DVE—Georgia Institute of Technology
                   (shrine1.tif)

Figure 3. 1   "An anatomical look at the arrangement of the visual
                   projection system in humans. Information from each visual
                   half-field is projected directly to the visual cortex of the
                   contralateral hemisphere."
                   Illustration modeled after: *Science*, 24 Sept 1993, p. 1755, from
                   Hemispheric Asymmetry
                   (viscor.tif)

Figure 3. 2   The impression of a flying bird is built up in the brain from
                     color, motion, form, and depth
                     Illustration modeled after: Fig. 5, *National Geographic*, Nov. 92
                     (build.tif)

Figure 3. 3   Filling in the blind spot with a pattern—close your left eye,
                     stare at the cross, and slowly move the page closer and farther
                     until you notice the disk filled in by slanted lines.
                     Illustration modeled after: Fig. 1, *National Geographic*, Nov. 92
                     (build1.tif)

Figure 3. 4   Filling the blind spot with background
                     Illustrations modeled after: *Scientific American*, May 1992, pp.
                     86ff
                     (blind2.tif)

Figure 3. 5   Beauty is in the pupil of the beholder: pupil shapes in
                     vertebrates
                     Illustration modeled after: Fig. 4 on p. 584 of the *McGraw-Hill
                     Encyclopedia of Science and Technology*
                     (pupil.tif)

Figure 3. 6   Roger Hayward's pattern for a Prevost-Fechner-Benham disk
                     Illustration modeled after: *Scientific American*, March 1971, p.
                     111
                     (pfb.tif)

Figure 3. 7   The Necker cube
                     Illustration modeled after: *Scientific American*, May 1970, p. 127
                     (top)
                     (necker.tif)

Figure 3. 8   Thiéry's figure
                     Illustration modeled after: *Physics Today*, Dec. 1992, p. 27
                     (thiery.tif)

Figure 3. 9   The Gibson after-effect
                     Illustration modeled after: *Science Digest*, Feb. 1971, p. 14
                     (right)
                     (gibson.tif)

Figure 3.10   Here about 80% of the white triangle <u>is not present</u>, but is
                     synthesized in toto by the brain, and appears as convincing, if
                     not more so, than the line triangle, which is 80% explicitly
                     drawn.
                     Illustration modeled after: Fig. 5 on p. 217 of McGraw-Hill
                     (triangle.tif)

Figure 3.11   What do you see?
                     Illustration modeled after: Figure in Mathematical Games
                     chapter on p. 126 of *Scientific American*
                     (what.tif)

Figure 3.12   "perverted signature"
                     (sig.tif)

Figure 3.13   The ototconia crystals
                     Illustration modeled after: *Scientific American*, Nov. 1980, the
                     otoconia crystals on p. 119
                     (crystal.tif)

Figure 3.14   The vestibular apparatus and the semi-circular canal
                     Illustration modeled after: *Scientific American*, Nov. 1980, the
                     diagram on p. 120
                     (sccanal.tif)

Figure 3.15   The human inner ear
                     Illustration modeled after: *Scientific American*, Jan. 1983, at the
                     bottom of p. 59
                     (ear.tif)

Figure 3.16   Hair bundle displacement
                     Illustration modeled after: *Scientific American*, Jan. 1983, at the
                     bottom of p. 60
                     (hairbund.tif)

Figure 3.17   Here is a modern update, for motor and sensory cortex, of the famous "homunculi" diagrams of Wilder Penfield and others. Illustration modeled after: *Scientific American*, Sept. 1979, p. 182 (homun.tif)

Figure 4.1   Stereo VR Glasses in the GVU Lab (worn by Rob Kooper)
                Photo Credits: Thomas Meyer/Rob Kooper
                GVU Lab Project: ICV—Georgia Institute of Technology
                (glasses.tif)

Figure 4.2   View of downtown Atlanta over Peachtree Plaza
                Photo Credits: Thomas Meyer/Larry Hodges
                GVU Lab Project: DVE—Georgia Institute of Technology
                (atlanta1.tif)

Figure 4.3   "A Virtual Party"
                Left: Virtual Research HMD (320 x 240 x 80° version) and a CyberGlove Data Glove worn by Tom Meyer
                Middle: StereoGraphics StereoEyes Stereo Glasses
                Right: Virtual Research HMD (640x480x55° version) worn by E. J. Lee
                Photo Credits: Thomas Meyer/Rob Kooper
                GVU Lab Project: ICV—Georgia Institute of Technology
                (hmd2.tif)

Figure 4.4   3-D Scanner
                Photo Credit: Michael Sinclair
                Multimedia Technology Lab Project—Georgia Institute of Technology
                (mattclr.tif)

MULTIMEDIA TECHNOLOGY LABORATORY

Michael Sinclair, Director
Georgia Institute of Technology
Atlanta, GA 30332
(404) 894-4195

Overview and Projects

Virtual reality of social significance is being investigated at the Multimedia Technology Laboratory of Georgia Tech. Surgical simulation with photo-realistic imagery, real time tool-tissue interaction, and tactile feedback is now possible with recent improvements in fast and affordable graphic workstations.

OCULAR SURGERY SIMULATOR

Ocular surgeons and commercial airline pilots share a common problem: they may encounter certain unusual or emergency situations for which they have not been trained or cannot practically be trained. During surgery, the physician may be presented with a complication that requires quick and accurate decision making, but in which he or she has had little or no experience. One example might be the rare occurrence of an expulsive choroidal hemorrhage during cataract surgery. For the commercial airline pilot, computer-driven flight simulators have been developed to give the pilot an interactive, real time experience that realistically simulates the emergency. Until recently, however, the technology required to produce realistic visual simulation has been extremely expensive or nonexistent. The current development in graphic computers makes the generation and real time presentation of medical imagery economically approachable.

Through a collaborative effort with the Medical College of Georgia, the Georgia Institute of Technology has developed a prototype ocular surgery simulator utilizing such computer-driven real time and realistic visual simulation technology. This device is capable of demonstrating photorealistic stereo images of the anterior ocular structures of the human eye with real time surgical instrument manipulation and elementary tactile feedback. Georgia Tech has developed near-realistic tissue manipulation for the ocular structures being cut with a knife and an early simulation for lens phakoemulsification—a process for removing a problem lens.

With the present simulator prototype, the physician views the simulated surgery through a stereo eyepiece, similar to an operating microscope. The three-dimensional image viewed by the surgeon is generated on a Silicon Graphics ONYX computer graphics workstation. The hand-tool interaction area (which the surgeon does not actually see) is occupied by the surgeon holding a 3-D Polhemus digitizing stylus (simulating the surgical instrument). With a real time position-sensing stylus and appropriate image generation, the view of the simulated interaction area appears as if it were the surgeon's own. The eye's anterior segment structures, viewed by the surgeon and generated by computer, appear in three-dimensional reality with sufficient detail and resolution (for example, blood vessels, texture of the iris and sclera, and transparency of the cornea) so that the surgeon, we believe, is not significantly distracted by the simulation appearance. The system is presently designed for one-handed surgery with future improvements planned for two-handed techniques.

We have created two simulated instruments: a scalpel and a phakoemulsifier. The knife is always "on" and cuts when it encounters tissue, but the surgeon must activate the selected phakoemulsifier by pressing a button on the side of the stylus. We have developed near-realistic tool-tissue interaction algorithms for the knife intersecting with cornea or sclera and interactions for the phakoemulsification of the lens.

Another medical VR area being pursued is the simulation of catheter insertion and arterial navigation. Under normal conditions, a physician will attempt to feed a long catheter into a patient's heart, inserting it through an artery in the leg. The physician, while observing a fluoroscope, twists, pulls, and pushes the catheter, attempting navigation through the complex maze of arterial branches. This is done while the beating heart causes the structures to move, making it difficult to navigate along the correct arterial route. A simulator is being devised to allow a student to practice this technique over and over again without endangering the patient.

MOTION INTERACTIVE

In the area of kinematics, VR is playing a role in the capture and analysis of human motion. Georgia Tech is using this technology to try to improve the understanding and performance in sports and human rehabilitation. Motion-tracking systems use active or passive optical targets placed on the joints of a body. These targets are tracked automatically by computer cameras, where the 3-D position data is processed and can be used to drive an animation or gesture recognition system or give the observer some insight into human motion dynamics. Tracking targets can be worn on the hand and track hand and finger movements, similar to the operation of a data glove. Targets worn on all articulated parts of the body can be used as the whole-body input device to a VR environment.

3-D SCANNER

To enable the rapid capture of a 3-D object for use in VR animation, Georgia Tech has developed a low-cost PC-based scanner that can generate a 20,000-polygon version of a real object in a few minutes. It is based on off-the-shelf components and calibration and contour extracting algorithms executing on a PC.

GRAPHICS, VISUALIZATION & USABILITY CENTER

James D. Foley, Director
College of Computing, 0280
Georgia Institute of Technology
Atlanta, GA 30332
(404) 853-0672

Overview of the GVU Center

The Graphics, Visualization & Usability Center was established at the Georgia Institute of Technology in 1991 in recognition of the central importance of these three disciplines to the future growth of computing.

Making computers usable by every person is the next and perhaps greatest frontier in the computer and information revolution which has swept the world during the last few decades. Hardware has become inexpensive; software is increasingly easier to produce; only the challenge of bringing the power of computing to every person remains. The GVU Center's vision is a world in which individuals are empowered in their everyday pursuits by the use of computers, a world in which computers are used as easily and effectively as televisions, telephones, and automobiles.

The GVU Center, located at Georgia Tech's College of Computing, provides an environment which promotes education, research, and service in ways which allow us to move toward this frontier. In our education role, we provide courses, seminars, and lectures on the principles and methods of computer graphics, scientific visualization, and human-computer interaction to members of the academic community ranging from students to researchers to faculty. Our research spans the areas of computer graphics animation, virtual environments, user interfaces, medical informatics, software visualization, image understanding, and computer-supported collaborative education.

Our service mission is carried out jointly with the Georgia Tech Information Technology department to provide state-of-the-art computing hardware and software to the entire Georgia Tech community, including over 150 faculty, researchers, and student users.

Overview of Virtual Environments at the GVU Center

Larry F. Hodges, Associate Director

Human-computer interaction has historically consisted of limited interaction with virtual displays of iconic character data on a two-dimensional screen. A virtual environment (VE) offers an alternative interaction paradigm in which users are no longer simple external observers of data but are active participants with their data and designs in the three-dimensional world of virtual reality.

The Virtual Environments group in the Graphics, Visualization & Usability Center at Georgia Tech conducts an ongoing research program that involves experimental verification of virtual reality hardware and software interaction techniques, development of software to make virtual environments better, and application of virtual environments to problems in visualization, design, and training.

Hardware equipment currently being used by the virtual environments include:

Workstations: Silicon Graphics Reality Engine/Crimson, Silicon Graphics Reality Engine II/Onyx, Silcon Graphics Indigo Elan.

Devices: Virtual Research Head Mounted Displays (2), Ascension Bird Flock System tracking equipment, Virtual Technologies CyberGlove, StereoGraphics CrystalEyes Stereo Glasses (3), SpaceBall 6D input device, and our own internally designed input devices.

Current Projects of the Virtual Environments Group at the GVU Center

THE PHOBIA PROJECT

The goal of this study is to assess the effectiveness of virtual reality graded exposure in the treatment of acrophobia, the fear of heights. A person with acrophobia experiences substantial difficulty in height situations, which are prevalent within a large metropolitan city. Imaginal exposure and in vivo graded exposure have been effective in the treatment of acrophobia. Current virtual reality technology allows us to create virtual enviroments that we are using to provide an intermediate step between imaginal and in vivo graded exposure.
PROJECT MEMBERS:
    Larry Hodges (GVU Center Asst. Professor)
    Barbara Rothbaum (Emory University Psychologist)
    Dan Opdyke (Georgia State University Psychology student)
    Rob Kooper, Drew Kessler, Thomas Meyer, E.J. Lee (College of Computing
        students)

THE DESIGN VIRTUAL ENVIRONMENT

We are building a virtual reality system, the Design Virtual Environment (DVE), as a tool for communication of design ideas and as a teaching tool for design education. DVE allows us to experiment with immersive instructional concepts that are not currently possible with either traditional or CAD-based computer graphics design tools. In particular, DVE allows a student to get inside designed structures and visually fly through and inspect the design in a visually immersive environment. Additionally, DVE provides features for a multiparticipant virtual environment including voice annotation tools.
PROJECT MEMBERS:

Thomas Meyer, Rob Kooper, Drew Kessler (GVU Center Researchers)
Brian Wills, Lucas Santosa, Eric Zundel (College of Architecture Researchers)
Larry Hodges (GVU Center Asst. Professor)
Tolek Lesniewski (College of Architecture Research Scientist)

SVE LIBRARY

We are working on a software application library that provides a system within which a virtual environment application can easily be developed. The goal of the Simple Virtual Environment (SVE) system is to perform most of the work needed for a virtual environment application, including storing and rendering a hierarchy of graphical objects, navigation, manipulation, and annotation. SVE also provides an environment where new input and output devices can be easily added to the system as needed.
PROJECT MEMBERS:
Drew Kessler, Rob Kooper, E.J. Lee, Thomas Meyer (GVU Center
Researchers)
Larry Hodges (GVU Center Asst. Professor)

Other VR Projects at the GVU Center

INTERACTIVE CONSTRUCTION VISUALIZER

We are developing the Interactive Construction Visualizer (ICV) as a visual simulation system that considers the dynamic nature of construction processes. Unlike conventional computer-aided design and animation systems, ICV generates a virtual environment which can more accurately account for the actual time and the behavioral and geometrical constraints of the people, materials, and equipment used during construction. Furthermore, ICV explores methods for effective communication between the parties involved such design and construction processes.
PROJECT MEMBERS:
Augusto Op den Bosch, Walter Patterson (Civil Engineering Students)

SCIENTIFIC VISUALIZATION IN VIRTUAL ENVIRONMENTS

Our research involves the development of data visualization environments in order to represent accurately and efficienty, interact with, and analyze data. We are working on the visual representation of discrete objects and the dynamic variables attached to these objects during simulations. The methods we are developing use attributes such as shape, color, and position of discrete, three-dimensional objects to convey behavior of several variables at once. Symbols such as "glyphs" and other iconic widgets are used to interact with and display the full information content of data.
PROJECT MEMBERS:

Ron van Teylingen (Visiting Research Scientist from T. U. Delft, Netherlands)
Bill Ribarsky (GVU Center Research Scientist)

Members of the GVU Center Virtual Environments Group

The following selected members of the VE Group can all be contacted at the GVU Center, College of Computing 0280, Georgia Institute of Technology, Atlanta, GA 30332.

Larry F. Hodges is an Assistant Professor at Georgia Tech's College of Computing and Associate Director for Education at the GVU Center. He received his Ph.D. in Computer Engineering in 1988 from North Carolina State University. He also holds an M.S. in Computer Science and Computer Engineering and a B.A. in Mathematics and Physics. His research and consulting interests include virtual environments, stereoscopic computer graphics, and scientific visualization.
Internet E-mail: hodges@cc.gatech.edu

Drew Kessler is a 1992 Computer Science graduate of the University of Virginia. He is a Ph.D. student and Graduate Research Assistant at the GVU Center whose research areas include virtual reality and human-computer interaction.
Internet E-mail: drew@cc.gatech.edu

Thomas C. Meyer is a 1993 Computer Science graduate of the Georgia Tech College of Computing. He is a Ph.D. Student and Graduate Research Assistant at

the GVU Center whose research include virtual reality and computer graphics modeling and rendering.
Internet E-mail: tom@cc.gatech.edu

Eun Jae (E.J.) Lee is a 1993 Computer Science graduate of the Georgia Tech College of Computing. He is a Master's student and Graduate Research Assistant at the GVU Center whose research areas includes virtual reality and computer graphics rendering techniques.
Internet E-mail: gt0054b@gvu.gatech.edu

Robert J. Kooper is a 1992 Computer Science graduate of the Technical University of Delft, Netherlands. He is a visiting Research Scientist who is completing his Master's thesis at the GVU Center. His research interests includes virtual reality and multimedia.
Internet E-mail: kooper@cc.gatech.edu

APPENDIX C

GLOSSARY OF TERMS AND PEOPLE

Ames Human Factors Reserach Division/NASA—created VR testbed using off-the-shelf components; first to combine a data glove (built by VPL) and an HMD; the system eventually included a suit, voice input with speech recognition, and three-dimensional sound.

ARC—Augmentation Research Center at Stanford Research Institute, founded by Engelbart (and Licklider); pioneered the mouse, hypertext, multiple windows, multiple document views (outline processing), video imagery in conjunction with computer graphics to convey info, text, and graphics in the same document; a working version was demonstrated in 1968 at the Fall Joint Computer Conference by Engelbart.

Arch-Mac—Architecture Machine Group at MIT in the 1970s, led by Nicholas Negroponte and Richard Bolt; predecessor to the MIT Media Lab; had strong backing from ARPA, virtual environments, virtual desktop workspace, visualization of data.

ARPA—Advanced Research Projects Agency; funded ARC, responsible for ARPAnet, the forerunner of the Internet, funded projects around the U.S. to help the U.S. regain predominance in the space race.

ARPAnet—The forerunner of the Internet, designed to allow researchers at disparate sites to share information and send mail.

Aspen Movie Map—Arch-Mac, Lippman, and Fisher; could walk around Aspen, Colorado, go inside buildings, explore streets, etc., a room with a photographics map all around, and used hand-gestures, used videodisk maps.

Atari Research Sunnyvale Labs—in the early 1980s the place to be, saw the creation (and extension of the Arch-Mac) framework for VR.

ATR—Advanced Telecommunications Research Institute, Kansai Science City, Japan; Japanese VR research center, near Kyoto, backed by MITI, NTT, NEC, Toshiba, Hitachi, and others.

Batch computing—Method of "interacting" with a computer that involves specifying all the possible run-time parameters beforehand, then receiving a response at the program's completion, typically associated with batch (IBM or punch) cards or paper tape.

Bolt, Richard—human interface researcher at Arch-Mac; gaze direction is important in human communications.

Brooks, Frederick Jr.—A legend in the computer field, directed the IBM team that developed the IBM 360 series operating system software (the largest programming feat of its time); author of The Mythical Man-Month, director of the Computer Science Department at the University of North Carolina in Chapel Hill, which supports one of the longest on-going virtual environments research projects in the world; proponent of intelligence amplification and the driving problem philosophy.

Cinerama—A multiple-projector, multiple-screen system designed by Fred Waller, expanded the peripheral vision available to the moviegoer; inspired Morton Heilig.

Consensus reality—tThe "real" world, the world that most humans agree to be the physical world.

Cyberspace—Coined by William Gibson in *Neuromancer* (1984)—"A consensual hallucination experienced daily by billions of legitimate operators, in every nation, by children being taught mathematical concepts. ... A graphic representation of data abstracted from the banks of every computer in the human system. Unthinkable complexity. Lines of light ranged in the nonspace of the mind, clusters and constellations of data. Like city lights, receding."

DataGlove—Invented by Thomas Zimmerman, adopted by Jaron Lanier and "mass produced" by VPL Research; used with HMDs and other VR equipment; first used at NASA/Ames.

Dataland—Part of SDMS, a visual window into the operator's personal data set, programs, files, etc.

Display—A device that gives information in communications

Driving problem philosophy—Frederick Brooks' philosophy for furthering computer science, involves choosing a sufficiently technical and appropriate real-world problem to give direction to computer science research.

Engelbart, Doug—WW II radar operator and Electrical Engineer, in 1950 had the idea to use computers to help people think (mind amplifier, augmentation), wrote a conceptual framework, founded ARC at Stanford Research Institute under the auspices of ARPA in the 1960s.

Environment—The conditions, circumstances, and influences surrounding and affecting an organism.

Experience theater—Morton Heilig, Sensorama.

Fisher, Scott—NASA Ames, lectured and researched at the MIT Center for Advanced Visual Studies, Arch-Mac, HMDs—PLZT displays, strong interest in using technology for artistic representation, surrogate travel, worked on Aspen Movie Map, student of Negroponte, founded Telepresence Research with Laurel (after NASA Ames).

FLOPS—Floating point operations per second; a measure of the speed of a computer's computational power.

Foster, Scott—Crystal River Engineering president, help invented three-dimensional sound system called the Convolvotron with Dr. Wenzel.

Fuchs, Henry—Student of Alan Kay's at the University of Utah, Principal Investigator at UNC Chapel Hill

Furness, Thomas III—Former director of the USAF's VR Supercockpit program, former director and chief of the Visual Systems Branch of Armstrong Aerospace Medical Research Lab at Wright-Patterson AFB, founded the Human Interface Technology Lab, the "HIT" Lab, in Seattle, WA.

Gibson, William—Author of *Neuromancer*, one of the founders of cyberpunk, coined the term matrix.

Goertz, Armond—Designed the remote manipulator arm for Argonne National Labs (ARM, Argonne Remove Manipulator), provided an ARM to UNC Chapel Hill.

Haptic—Relating to or based on the sense of touch.

Haptic perception—the touch senses, tactile, proprioception (informs us about the position of our limbs relative to us and the space around us), internal sensors at joints and in muscles which sense changes in pressure and position, the effectors for transmitting commands from the sensing and sense-making systems to muscles.

Heilig, Morton—Sensorama Simulator (patent in 1962, as early as 1955); but for backing, bad luck, and other people's foresight, might have started VR from arcades in Hollywood; cinematographer and multisensory media specialist.

HIT Lab—See Human Interface Technology Lab.

Hulteen, Eric—Atari Research, MIT Media Lab, gestural input and other human factors research at Apple.

Human Interface Technology Lab—HIT Lab, run by Thomas Furness III, in conjunction with the University of Washington; acts as a clearinghouse for virtual environments research.

Intelligence amplification—Humans do pattern recognition, evaluation, and sense of context; computers do evaluations of computations, storing massive amounts of data, and remembering things without forgetting.

Interactive computing—style of using a computer that involves some sort of near-real time interface to the computer, typically a terminal of some sort; replaced batch computing as the standard interface to computers.

Internet—an outgrowth of the former ARPAnet, used by academic and business researchers around the world to exchange information and ideas, it is currently expanding at an incredible rate.

IPTO—Information Processing Techniques Office; funded technology that led to today's computers, input devices, and display devices for VR.

Kay, Alan—junior ARPA researcher, MIT AI Lab; one of the key architects of personal computers, psychology and computer interface design, learning process modeled on "exploration," Dynabook creator.

Krueger, Myron—Artist and technologist, "Responsive Environments", coined the term artificial reality, creator of GLOWFLOW, METAPLAY, PSYCHIC SPACE, and VIDEOPLACE.

Lag problem—Time lag.

Lanier, Jaron—created "Moondust," worked at Atari Research, founder of VPL Research and coinventor of the DataGlove (with Zimmerman), creator of Mandala

Laurel, Brenda—Atari Research, MIT Media Lab, founded Telepresence Research with Fisher (after NASA Ames).

Licklider, J. C. R.—(ARPA), MIT psychoacoustician; did a study on how scientists spend their time—85% getting ready to "think"; also studied how to use computers in modeling, SAGE, interactive computing, IPTO director 1962, "discovered" Ivan Sutherland.

Lincoln Labs—Prestigious lab assicated with MIT and a classified military research center.

Link, Edwin—Inventor of the first flight simulators which were based on player piano technology.

Mandala—Jaron Lanier; a programming language for nonprogrammers involving symbols such as a music staff, kangaroos, and ice cubes; the input system is the DataGlove, also known as "Grasp" and "Embrace."

Matrix—Coined by William Gibson in *Neuromancer*, the future's version of the Internet, an all-encompassing interconnected network.

McGreevey, Michael—NASA Ames, graduate student of Stephen Ellis; cognitive engineering, three-dimensional displays, created an off-the-shelf HMD for NASA.

Media Lab—MIT; goal was to look at what media might look like in the future, "Put That There" experiment using Polyhemus cubes and a wall-size display, 3-D displays.

Minsky, Marvin—Leader of the Artificial Intelligence Lab at MIT; created AI (1950s); coined the term "artificial intelligence" (with John McCarthy, now of Stanford); coined the term "telepresence" (1979).

MIPS—Million instructions per second, a measure of the speed of a computer's computational power.

Movie map—See Aspen Movie Map.

Negroponte, Nicholas—Arch-Mac; "combine the presentation powers of cinema with the power of computers"—1970; computers/VR as a medium for communications, transmission of presence.

Nelson, Ted—"The Home Computer Revolution"—1977; hypertext, Xanadu, prophetic and provocative, coined "teledildonics."

NTT—Nippon Telephone and Telegraph, Human Interface Lab, Visual Media Lab.

Parallel processing—Multiple computer processors working together to solve a problem, implies a particular series of processor architectures.

PARC—Palo Alto Research Center, Xerox (and Stanford); pioneered "bit-mapped graphics," interactive computer graphics, and the Alto (forerunner of the Macintosh).

Polyhemus Navigation Systems—Created small, expensive magnetic position-sensing cubes.

Reality—Of or related to practical or everyday concerns or activites.

Robinett, Warren—Part of the NASA Ames VR team; UNC Chapel Hill (until 1993); creator of *Rocky's Boots*, a computer game that taught Boole's algebraic logic to ten-year-olds; a game programmer at Atari during their height (*Adventure*); "interactive graphical simulations."

Ruina, Jack—Director of ARPA, established Licklider as the IPTO director (1962).

SAGE—Semi-Automatic Ground Environment, 1960s project at Lincoln Labs to protect U.S.A. from nuclear attack; Licklider worked on helping with human perception clues.

SDMS—Spatial Data Management System, Media Lab, MIT; a system for visually navigating through databases, of which Dataland was a part.

Sketchpad—Ivan Sutherland's thesis, first truly interactive computer program; operators could use a light pen to change things on the display screen directly (1962).

Sutherland, Ivan—Created the first head-mounted display (1965); interactive computing; "found" by Licklider at MIT Lincoln Labs; thesis was Sketchpad; Ph.D. student of Claude Shannon (inventor of information theory); succeeded Licklider as IPTO director in 1964, cofounded Evans and Sutherland.

Taylor, Bob—NASA research administrator who funded Engelbart, became one of Licklider's converts, succeeded Sutherland as IPTO director in 1965, assembled PARC's research team.

Telepresence—The idea of using a human to control a "remote" robot or robotic arm (or whatever), especially in hazardous environments, coined by Marvin Minsky; the idea is first found in Robert Heinlein's *Waldo* (1940).

Tesla, Nikola—Creator of remote-controlled robots, radio, and bunches of other things; responsible for much of the fundamental theories of electromagnetics, among other fields.

Time lag—In general terms, a problem in which the hardware is incapable of processing information fast enough, for instance, when an image cannot be updated fast enough to fool the eye.

Todd, Mike—Producer of Cinerama (created by Fred Waller).

UNC Chapel Hill—University of North Carolina in Chapel Hill, North Carolina; U.S.A. The Computer Science Department and Virtual Environments research are led by Frederick Brooks, Jr.

Virtual—Being in effect but not in actual fact.

VPL Research—Founded by Jaron Lanier; developed the DataGlove under the auspices of NASA Ames, made off-the-shelf VR research possible; "lost" basic VR patents to Thompsom-CSF for failure to repay loan.

Waller, Fred—Experimented with multiple display screens, after World War II used this knowledge to create Cinerama.

Wenzel, Elizabeth—3-D sound, with Professor Frederick Wightman of the Univ. of Wisconsin and Scott Foster, research psychologist at NASA Ames.

World of Windows—MIT Media Lab; large windows of information would open on a wall-sized screen, under eye-tracking control.

Zimmerman, Thomas—Atari Research, VPL Research, inventor of the glove.

A Complete Virtual Reality Glossary

This is so good and so complete, I want ya'll to see it in all of its glory. It's from the sci.virtual-worlds newsgroup.

From prism!gatech!news-feed-2.peachnet.edu!darwin.sura.net!math.ohio-state.edu!usc!elroy.jpl.nasa.gov!decwrl!usenet.coe.montana.edu!netnews.nwnet.net!news.u.washington.edu!stein.u.washington.edu!scivw Fri Aug 6 19:26:07 EDT 1993
Article: 9372 of sci.virtual-worlds
Path: prism!gatech!news-feed-2.peachnet.edu!darwin.sura.net!math.ohio-state.edu!usc!elroy.jpl.nasa.gov!decwrl!usenet.coe.montana.edu!netnews.nwnet.net!news.u.washington.edu!stein.u.washington.edu!scivw
From: GBNEWBY@VMD.CSO.UIUC.EDU (Greg Newby)
Newsgroups: sci.virtual-worlds
Subject: TERMS: A Complete Virtual Reality Glossary
Message-ID: <23q5lu$1tv@news.u.washington.edu>
Date: 4 Aug 93 19:16:08 GMT
Organization: University of Washington
Lines: 695
Approved: scivw@u.washington.edu
NNTP-Posting-Host: stein.u.washington.edu
Originator: scivw@stein.u.washington.edu

VIRTU-L

VIRTUAL REALITY TERMS
Joe Psotka and Sharon Davison

6DOF—Six degrees of freedom: yaw, pitch, roll, up-down, left-right, front-back (or pan, zoom, swivel).

A-Buffering—Keeping track of the Z-depth of pixels to cull them before rendering.

Accelerator—Specialized hardware to increase speed of graphics manipulation.

Accommodation—Change in the focal length of the eye's lens.

Actors—CAD representations of players performing actions for them, as in the Mandala system (see Agent, Character).

Affine—Any transformation composed from rotations, translations, dilatations (expansions and contractions), and shears.

Agents—CAD representations of human forms capable of guiding (Guides) navigators through a VR (see Actor, Character).

Aliasing—An undesirable jagged edge on many 3-D renderings on bitmapped displays. Creates jaggies along the sides of objects and flickering of objects smaller than a pixel (see Anti-Aliasing).

Allocentric—Other than egocentric, such as a bird's-eye view, or adopting another person's viewpoint.

Ambient light—General nondirectional illumination.

Anti-Aliasing—Removing jagged edges on bitmapped displays by interpolating neutral colors or intermediate intensities.

Articulation—Objects composed of several parts that are separably movable.

Artificial Intelligence—The attempt to mimic and automate human cognitive skills through rules and knowledge representation techniques (e.g., understanding visual images, recognizing speech and written text, solving problems, making medical diagnoses, heuristic knowledge).

Artificial Reality—Introduced by arts and computer visualization scholar Myron Krueger in the mid-1970s to describe his computer-generated responsive environments. Krueger has emphasized the nonintrusive (Second-person VR) systems that track people with pattern recognition techniques and display them and the surround on projection systems (see CAVE). As realized in his VIDEOPLACE and the Vivid Group's Mandala system, it is a computer display system that perceives and captures "a participant's action in terms of the body's relationship to a graphic world and generates responses (usually imagery) that maintain the illusion that his actions are taking place within that world." (M. Krueger, Artificial Reality, 1992) (See Virtual Reality and Cyberspace).

Aspect ratio—Ratio of width to height of the field of view.

Augmented Reality—The use of transparent displays worn as glasses on which data can be projected. This allows someone to repair a radar, for example, and have the needed data displayed on the glasses while walking around the radar.

Back clipping plane—A distance beyond which objects are not shown.

Backface Removal—The elimination of those polygons that are facing away from the viewer.

Backward raytracing—From the eye to the object (currently how most raytracing is done).

Binaural—Stereo sound incorporating information about the shadows at human ears and heads.

Biosensors—Special glasses or bracelets containing electrodes to monitor muscle electrical activity. One interesting VR use is for tracking eye movements by measuring muscle movements.

BOOM—A 3-D display device suspended from a weighted boom that can swivel freely about so the viewer doesn't have to wear an HMD; instead, it steps up to the viewer like a pair of binoculars. The boom's position communicates the user's point of view to the computer.

Browser—Overviews such as indexes, lists, or animated maps to provide a means of navigating through the physical, temporal, and conceptual elements of a VR.

CAVE—A VR using projection devices on the walls and ceiling to give the illusion of immersion.

Character—A being with a virtual body in virtual reality (Walser, 1991) (see Agents, Actor).

Concept Map—A browser or terms, definitions, or icons arranged in semantic proximity.

Consensual Reality—The world, or a simulation of a world, as viewed and comprehended by a society (Walser, 1991).

Convergence—The angle between the two eyes at a fixation point. This changes for objects at varying depths in the real world and on 3-D displays.

Convolvotron—A system for controlling binaural sound production in a VR.

Culling—Removing invisible pieces of geometry and only sending potentially visible geometry to the graphics subsystem. Simple culling involves rejecting objects not in the view frustum. More complex systems take into account occlusion of some objects by others, e.g., a building hiding trees behind it.

Cyberia—See Cyberspace and a pun on Siberia; an Autodesk project and the first VR project by a CAD company.

Cybernetic Simulation—Dynamic model of a world filled with objects that exhibit lesser or greater degrees of intelligence.

Cyberspace playhouse—Social center or place where people go to play roles in simulations (Walser, 1991).

Cyberspace—1. A place filled with virtual "stuff" populated by people with virtual bodies. A special kind of virtual space which promotes experiences involving the whole body (Walser, 1991). 2. A term coined by William Gibson in his book *Neuromancer* (1984, a coincidental date!) to describe a shared virtual universe operating within the sum total of all the world's computer networks. (See Artificial Reality and Virtual Reality.)

DataGlove—A glove wired with sensors and connected to a computer system for gesture recognition. It is used for tactile feedback and it often enables navigation through a virtual environment and interaction with 3-D objects within it.

DataSpace—A visualized representation of complex information.

DataSuit—Same as a DataGlove, but designed for the entire body. Only one DataSuit has yet been built, with limited capabilities.

De-rez—Techniques to make pixels less visible in a display.

Deck—A physical space containing an array of instruments which enable a player to act within, and feel a part of, a virtual space (Walser, 1991).

Depth cuing—Using shading, texture, color, interposition (or many other visual characteristics) to provide a cue for the z-coordinates or distance of an object.

Direct manipulation—A term coined by Shneiderman to reflect the use of computer icons or text as if they were real objects.

Disorientation—Confusion about distances and directions for navigation.

Dreaming—A state of mind during sleep where vivid colored imagery becomes realistic and immersive. A natural counterpart to VR.

Droid—Puppet that embodies a human intellect (as in android) (Walser, 1991).

Dynamic lighting—Changes in lighting effects on objects as they and the observer move.

Dynamics—The way that objects interact and move. The rules that govern all actions and behaviors within the environment.

Effectors—The output techniques that communicate a user's movements or commands to the computer and to the VR.

Egocenter—The sense of self and personal viewpoint that determines one's location in a VR. See Projection point.

Electromagnetic forces—Effects of emf on human tissues are poorly understood and may constitute an important hazard from tracking and display devices.

Endoscopic—Part of a family of new surgical procedures that avoid cutting open major portions of the patient in favor of making small holes through which tools and sensors are inserted and the surgery performed. In a VR or telepresence application, the surgeon manipulates the tools by observing the surgery site on a monitor via optical fibers and a tiny video camera.

Environment—This a computer-generated model that can be experienced from the "inside" as if it were a place.

Exoskeletal devices—In order to provide force feedback designers have added rigid external supports to gloves and arm motion systems.

Eye Tracking—Devices that measure direction of gaze. Most HMDs do not currently support eye tracking directly.

Eyeball in the Hand—A metaphor for visualized tracking where the tracker is held in the hand and is connected to motion of the projection point of the display.

Eyephone—A HMD made by VPL that combines visual and auditory displays.

Field of view—The angle in degrees of the visual field. Most HMDs offer 60 to 90 degrees FOV. Since our two eyes have overlapping 140 degree FOV, binocular or total FOV is roughly 180 degrees in most people. A feeling of immersion seems to arise with FOV greater than 60 degrees.

Finite element modeling—Decomposition of complex structures into small, simple elements so that engineering computations are manageable.

Fish Tank VR—With stereographic display systems attached to a monitor and the scene's virtual image behind the screen, the egocentric projection is called a fish tank.

Flat shading—A uniform shading in which one value is applied to each facet of a polygon.

Force Feedback—Representations of the inertia or resistance objects have when they are moved or touched. The computer guides a machine to offer just the degree of resistance to motion or pressure a situation would offer in real life.

Fractal—Any function that contains elements of self-similarity (after the work of Benoit Mandelbrot).

Frustum of Vision—3-D field of view in which all modeled objects are visible.

Gesture—Hand motion that can be interpreted as a sign or signal or symbol.

Goggles—Often used to refer to HMD or other displays.

Gouraud—Shading polygons smoothly with bilinear interpolation.

Haptic interfaces—Interfaces that use all the physical sensors that provide us with a sense of touch at the skin level and force feedback information from our muscles and joints.

Head tracking—Monitoring the position of the head through various devices.

Head-coupled—Displays or robotic actions that are activated by head motion through a head tracking device.

Head-related transfer function—A mathematical transformation of sound spectrum that modifies the amplitude and phase of acoustic signals to take into account the shape effects of the listener's head.

Heads up display (HUD)—A display device that lets users see graphics superimposed on their view of the world. (Created for aviators to see symbols and dials while looking out the window.)

Hidden surface—Parts of a graphics object occluded by intervening objects.

HMD (head-mounted display)—A set of goggles or a helmet with tiny monitors in front of each eye that generate images, seen by the wearer as being 3-D. VPL Research refers to the HMDs they sell as Eyephones.

Holodeck—Virtual reality simulation system and place used primarily for entertainment by the crew of the Enterprise in Star Trek: The Next Generation television series.

Hypermedia—The combination of digital text, video, and sound with navigation techniques like buttons, links, and hotspots into one system.

HyperSpace—The space of hypertext or hypermedia documents.

Immersion—The feeling of presence, of "being there," surrounded by space and capable of interacting with all available objects that is the hallmark of good VR.

Impressionists—A 19th century group of artists whose paintings were directed at capturing color and mood, rather than exact perspective outlines.

Interactive fiction—Dramatic creations that encourage user and viewer participation through computer technology, e.g., hypertext, group feedback, or VR.

Interaural amplitude—Differences between a person's two ears in the intensity of sound.

Interaural time—Differences between a person's two ears in the phase of sound.

Interface—A set of devices, software, and techniques that connect computers with people to make it easier to perform useful activities.

Internet—A worldwide digital network.

Inverse kinematics—A specification of the motion of dynamic systems from properties of their joints and extensions.

Jack—To connect to the matrix of virtual space (see Gibson).

Joysticks—Graphic interface devices.

Kinaesthetic dissonance—Mismatch between feedback or its absence from touch or motion during VR experiences..

Lag—Delay between an action and its visual, acoustic, or other sensory feedback, often because of inherent delays in the tracking devices or in the computation of the scene.

Laparoscopy (also laparoscopic surgery)—Less invasive forms of surgery that operate through small optics and instruments, lending themselves to robotic manipulation and VR training.

LBE (location-based entertainment)—A VR game that involves a scenario based on another time and place; filling a studio or space with VR games.

LCD (liquid crystal display)—Display devices that use bipolar films sandwiched between thin panes of glass. They are lightweight and transmissive or reflective, and ideal for HMD.

LOD (level of detail)—A model of a particular resolution among a series of models of the same object. Multiple LODs are used to increase graphics performance by drawing simpler geometry when the object occupies fewer pixels on the screen. LOD selection can also be driven by graphics load, area-of-interest, gaze direction.

Magic wand—A 3-D interface device used for pointing and interaction; an elongated 3-D mouse.

Metaball—A kind of "equipotential surface" around a point. You specify a point, a radius, and an "intensity" for each ball; when balls come close, their shapes blend to form a smooth equipotential surface. They seem to be very useful for modeling shapes like animals and humans. They can be rendered by most raytracing packages (also "blobs" or "soft spheres" or "fuzzy spheres").

Microsurgery—A form of surgery that lends itself to robotics and VR. See also Laparoscopy.

MIDI—A digital sound standard for music.

Monitor—Display, HMD, goggles, HUD, LCD.

MOO—A MUD, object-oriented.

Motion parallax—Objects at different distance and fixation points move different amounts when the viewpoint is dollied along the x axis (left—right).

Motion platform—A controlled system that provides real motion to simulate the displayed motion in a VR.

Motivation—A psychological need, drive, or feeling that raises the intensity of an action.

MRI—Magnetic resonance imaging; a way of making internal organs and structures visible by analyzing radio frequency emissions of atoms in a strong magnetic field. Can be made 3-D with rendering of large amounts of data.

MUD—A multiuser dungeon; a place on the Internet where people can meet and browse (also a MOO).

Multiperson space—1. Multiplayer space involving two or more human players. 2. A type of interactive simulation which gives every user a sense that he/she, personally, has a body in a virtual space (Walser, 1991).

Multiplayer space—Cyberspace that emerges from simulation that is generated simultaneously by two or more decks. Players can be made up of one human and the rest AI (Walser, 1991).

Nanomanipulation—Ability to visualize and affect objects in the nanometer range.

Navigation—Moving through virtual space without losing one's way.

Objects—Graphical entities that can be dynamically created or loaded from model files. Many functions act upon them:

Tasks:	each object performs a task per frame
Hierarchies:	objects can be "linked" together
Sensors:	objects can be connected to sensors
Modify:	color, texture, scale, etc.
Collision Detection:	between objects and polygons
Vertices:	these can be dynamically created along with the definition of a vector normal for Gouraud shading.

Occipital cortex—The back of the brain receiving retinotopic projections of visual displays.

Occlusion—Hiding objects from sight by interposition of other objects.

Pan—The angular displacement of a view along any axis or direction in a 3-D world; or a move through translation in a 2-D world.

Parietal cortex—An area of the brain adjacent and above the occipital cortex, thought to process spatial location and direction.

Paths—Objects or viewpoints can follow predefined paths that can be dynamically created and interpolated.

Perspective—The rules that determine the relative size of objects on a flat page to give the impression of 3-D distance.

Phong shading—A method for calculating the brightness of a surface pixel by linearly interpolating points on a polygon and using the cosine of the viewing angle. Produces realistic shading.

Photorealism—An attempt to create realistic appearing images with much detail and texture.

Pitch—The angular displacement of a view along the lateral axis (front--back).

Pixel—The smallest element of a display that can be adjusted in intensity.

Polygons—An ordered set of vertices connected by sides: these can be dynamically created and texture-mapped using various sources of image data. Various hardware platforms support different texturing methods and quantities. Rendering is performed in either wire-frame, smooth-shaded, or textured modes.

Pop—When an object's visible appearance suddenly changes or an object appears out of nowhere. Usually an undesired artifact of poor LOD.

Portals—Polygons that, once passed through, automatically load a new world or execute a user-defined function.

Position trigger—A hotspot, or sensitive spot or button, that begins a computation when touched in some way.

Presence—A defining characteristic of a good VR system, a feeling of being there, immersed in the environment, able to interact with other objects there.

Projected reality—A VR system that uses projection screens rather than HMDs or personal display monitors.

Radiosity—A diffuse illumination calculation system for graphics based on energy balancing that takes into account the multiple reflectances off many walls.

Raytracing—A rendering system that traces the path of light from objects to light sources (see Backward raytracing).

Real projection—A VR projection system (a pun on rear projection).

Real-time—Appearing to be without lag or flicker (e.g., 60 cps displays; highly interactive computation).

Renaissance—A period of art dominated by the exploration of perspective.

Render—Convert a graphics object into pixels.

Resolution—Usually the number of lines or pixels in a display; e.g., a VGA display has 640 by 480 pixels.

Roll—The angular displacement of a view along the longitudinal axis (left—right).

Scan conversion—The change of video signals from one form (e.g., RGB) to another (e.g., NTSC).

Scintillation—The "sparkling" of textures or small objects. Usually undesirable and caused by aliasing.

Second person VR—The use of a computational medium to portray a representation of you that is not realistic, but still identifiable. For example, in the Mandala system a video camera allows you to see yourself as another object over which you have control by your own bodily movement.

Sensor Lagtime—Delays in the feedback or representation of your actions caused by computation in the tracker or sensor.

Sensors—Mechanisms or functions that act to change objects in response to multiple devices connected to lights, objects, viewpoints, etc. in the real world.

Sensory substitution—The conversion of sensory information from one sense to another; e.g., the use of auditory echoes and cues to "see" the shape of your surroundings.

Sequence (keyframe animation)—Interpolate images between stored frames (tweening).

Shared worlds—Virtual environments that are shared by multiple participants at the same location or across long-distance networks.

Shutter glasses—LCD screens or physically rotating shutters used to see stereoscopically when linked to the frame rate of a monitor.

Simnet—A prototype networked simulation system built by BBN for training military skills in tanks, helicopters, and other vehicles. Using networked graphics and displays built into physical mock-ups, it has been called a vehicle-based VR or synthetic environment.

Simulator sickness—The disturbances produced by simulators, ranging in degree from a feeling of unpleasantness, disorientation, and headaches to nausea and vomiting. Many factors may be involved, including sensory distortions such as abnormal movement of arms and heads because of the weight of equipment, long delays or lags in feedback, and missing visual cues from convergence and accommodation. Simulator sickness rarely occurs with displays of less than 60 degrees visual angle.

Sound—Accurate localization of sounds without individualized head transfer functions remains a problem.

Spatial navigation—Accurate self-localization and orientation in virtual spaces is not as easy as real-world navigation. Techniques for embedding navigational assists in complex dataspaces remain important research goals.

Spatial representation system—The cortical structures and functions that maintain spatial orientation and recognition.

Spatial superposition—In augmented reality displays, accurate spatial registration of real and virtual images remains difficult.

Spreadsheets—Early spreadsheets made the computer a valuable tool for accounting and helped spread computers throughout industry. What is the "spreadsheet" or commercial application that will make VR a success?

Star Trek—The fantasy rich series offers a widely known example of a VR in its Holodeck. Plans are also under way to use VR in a Star Trek LBE (location-based entertainment).

Stereopsis—Binocular vision of images with horizontal disparities. The importance of stereopsis for immersion is not established.

Striate cortex—Visual cortex (see Occipital, Parietal).

Supercockpit—An Air Force project led by Tom Furness that advanced the engineering and human factors of HMDs and VR. It used digital displays of instruments and terrain.

Synthetic environments—VR displays used for simulation.

Tactile displays—Devices like force feedback gloves, buzzers, and exoskeletons that provide tactile, kinaesthetic, and joint sensations.

Tactile stimulation—Devices like force feedback gloves, buzzers, and exoskeletons that provide tactile, kinaesthetic, and joint sensations.

Tele-existence—Remote VR.

Telemanipulation—Robotic control of distant objects.

Teleoperation—see Telemanipulation.

Telepresence—VR with displays of real, remote scenes.

Telerobotic—Robotic control of distant objects (see Telemanipulation, Teleoperation).

Telesurgery—Surgery using Teleoperation.

Terrain—Geographic information and models that can be either randomly generated or based on actual data. Dynamic terrain is an important goal for current SIMNET applications.

Texture mapping—A bitmap added to an object to give added realism. Detail texture. A texture superimposed on another texture to increase the apparent resolution of the original texture image. Used when the eyepoint is so close to the textured object that the base texture is being magnified (i.e., one texel in the texture image being mapped to many pixels on the screen). A detail texture, typically a noise image, is blended into the image at a higher resolution, adding a gritty realism to the appearance of the object.

Texture swimming—Unnatural motion of static textures on the surfaces of objects as they are rotated. Caused by quick and dirty texture interpolation in screen coordinates. Correctable by subdividing polygons sufficiently or by doing perspective correction.

Theater—VR opens new metaphors to explore with interactive theater.

Tracker—A device that emits numeric coordinates for its changing position in space.

Transparency—How invisible and unobtrusive a VR system is.

Trompe l'oeil—Perspective paintings that deceive viewers into believing they are real (e.g., a painting of the sky and clouds on the inside of a dome).

Universe—This is the "container" of all entities in a VR. Entities can be temporarily added or removed from consideration by the simulation manager. The sequence of events in the simulation loop can be user-defined.

Viewpoints—Points from which raytracing and geometry creation occurs. The geometric eye point of the simulation. You can have multiple viewpoints. They can be attached to multiple sensors.

Virtual cadaver—A current NIH project to slice and digitize a complete human body.

Virtual Environments—Realistic simulations of interactive scenes.

Virtual patient—Telerobotic or digitized animations of humans with accurate disease models.

Virtual prototyping—The use of VR for design and evaluation of new models.

Virtual Reality—An immersive, interactive simulation of realistic or imaginary environments (Jaron Lanier)

Visualization—Use of computer graphics to make visible numeric or other quantifiable relationships.

Voxel—A cubic volume pixel for quantizing 3-D space.

VRactors—Virtual actors, either autonomous or telerobotic in a VR theater.

Waldo—A remotely controlled mechanical puppet (Robert Heinlein).

Windows—On some hardware platforms, you can have multiple windows and viewpoints into the same virtual world.

Wire-Frame outlines—Displays of the outlines of polygons, not filled in.

World in the hand—A metaphor for visualized tracking where the tracker is held in the hand and is connected to motion of the object located at that position in the display.

World—Whole environment or universe.

Yaw—The angular displacement of a view around the vertical, y axis (up—down).

We thank many people for their help and input, particularly all the users of virtu-l and sci.virtual.worlds. Latham's dictionary was particularly useful.

Latham, R. (1991) The Dictionary of Computer Graphics Technology and Applications. New York: Springer-Verlag.

Benedikt, M. (Ed.), (1991) Cyberspace: First Steps. Cambridge, MA: The MIT Press.

Earnshaw, R. A., Gigante, M. A., Jones, H. Virtual Reality Systems. New York: Academic Press.

Ellis, S. R. (Ed.), (1991) Pictorial Communication in Virtual and Real Environments. London: Taylor and Francis.

Kalawsky , R. (1993) The Science of Virtual Reality and Virtual Environments. New York: Addison-Wesley.

Laurel, B. (1991) Computers as Theater. New York: Addison-Wesley.

Pimentel, K. and Teixeira, K. (1992) Through the Looking Glass. New York: Intel.

Rheingold, H. (1991) Virtual Reality. New York: Simon & Schuster.

We thank many people for their help and input, particularly all the users of virtu-l and sci.virtual.worlds.

THE C LANGUAGE AND OUR CONVENTIONS

Introduction

This appendix is intended both as an introduction to the C programming language and as a description of the kind of programming style that we adhere to in the programs accompanying this book.

Since the code was developed primarily by one person over a year or so, the style changes just a little from module to module. This is inevitable in any creative and time consuming project. We wanted to develop certain programming practices to make the project go more smoothly. We do not intend to lecture you on what our idea of good programming style is. Rather, we merely want to give you the benefit of our experience of which techniques do and do not work.

The Benefits of C

The C language has become the language of choice for the development of most complex modern sofware, like programs for interactive computer graphics and scientific simulations. Though classified as a high-level language, it allows the scientist and engineer to produce code whose efficiency approaches that of assembly language for real time applications. It was initially available only on larger machines and certain operating systems but is now available on just about every system around, including IBM compatibles.

The C language has many advantages over FORTRAN and Pascal. C's portability between machines of both the UNIX (a trademark of AT&T) and MS-DOS (a trademark of IBM Corporation) platforms makes it quite appealing to those who have little choice of which machines to use. The C data structures are well suited for graphics programming, due to their inherent modularity. Fast, efficient compilers, debuggers, and other tools are now available, which makes using C the attractive choice for large projects. The C language is most appropriate for the development of general library routines, which can be used as the building blocks for many graphics programs.

Naturally, the C code is much quicker and easier to develop than its equivalent assembly code. Without too much effort, the C code efficiency can approach that of assembly code. What may take days to program in assembly can take as little as half an hour in C. The added performance that assembly might provide is not worth the effort in developing it. It is often the case (such as in using Borland C++) that C and assembly can be mixed together in the same program. Such a hybrid can have a main program and human interface written in C, and other routines that are computationally intensive (such as mathematics and graphics modules) would be written in assembly. Now that we have established that C is the program language of choice for our purposes, let's see how it is used in the development of graphics applications.

Concepts of a Programming Language

The main purpose of a programming language is to provide a means of expressing an algorithm that can then be executed by a computer. A programming language should have five basic elements in order to conform to this definition:

1. a methodology for organizing data (*data* refers to data types and variables)

2. a methodology for describing operations (these are *operators*)

3. a methodology for controlling operations based on previous operations (this is called *program control*)

4. a methodology for structuring the data and operations so that a sequence of program statements can be executed from any location within the program (these are *data structures* and *functions*)

5. a methodology for moving data between the program and the outside world (referred to as *I/O*—input/output)

How these goals are achieved in C makes up the remainder of this chapter. The following program is an example of some of the points mentioned.

```
main()
{
    float       add_nums();                   // declare functions
    int         added,numbs_to_add;           // declare variables
    int         index, i;
    float       num_array[50];
    float       total;

    printf("\n\nNumber of numbers to add? ");
    scanf("%d", &numbs_to_add);

    printf("\n\nEnter numbers to add?\n ");
    for(index=0; index<numbs_to_add; index++)
    {
        i = scanf("%f", &num_array[index]);
        if (i != 1) break;
    }

    total = add_nums(num_array, numbs_to_add);

        printf("\n\nTotal is %f", total);
}


float add_nums(array, array_size)
    float array[], int array_size
{
    int i;
    float sum=0.0;

    for(i=0;i<array_size;i++)
        sum=sum+array[i];
    return(sum);
}
```

(Listing AD-1) A simple C program to add numbers

Listing AD-1 is of a sample C program that sums numbers and contains each of the elements mentioned above. The first line is *main*(). This declares that a program which has no arguments will be defined after the left brace ({ found on the next line) and up to the line just before the next function called *add_nums*. The main program is the main control of the program. This is the first executed part of the program .

The next line declares the functions that are called throughout the main program. The function addnums will sum the elements of an *array* called array of length *array_size* and return this value. This corresponds to goal 1, providing a means to organize data—in this case, using the array data construct. The term // is used for comments at the end of a line (on many compilers). /* and */ can be used to define multiple line comments on all compilers. Notice next that we declare variables like "added" and "numbs_to_add."

Input is then taken regarding the number of numbers that you wish to add together (goal 5, interaction with the outside world). The program then prompts you to enter the actual numbers into an array for later addition. The function add_nums is then called to add the numbers found in the array and return the value to a variable called "total." The provision for functions and operators satisfies goal 4. Within addnums, a *for loop* is used to cycle through the array and add all of the elements together. This corresponds to goal 3, program execution control. The provision of operators like + and - satisfies goal 2. The result from add_nums() is subsequently displayed on the terminal.

Variables and Data Types

It is in the nature of computer programs that they operate by the manipulation of information represented in some digital format. A variable in C is defined by a declaration of an alphanumeric group of characters which, for all references to that variable, will recall the number assigned to it. This variable name (*identifier*) must start with a letter or an underscore and cannot be the same as the standard or compiler-specific C key words. Note that C is a case-sensitive language—numbs_to_add is different from Numbs_To_Add and Numbs_to_add, for instance.

There are many different number types in C. Table AD-1 shows some of the standard types and how they are represented internally.

Variable declaration	Number of bits	32-bit range
char	8	-128 -> 127
unsigned char	8	0 -> 255
short	16	-32768 - > 32767
unsigned short	16	0 -> 65535
int	32 (16)	-2.1e9 -> 2.1e9
unsigned int	32 (16)	0 -> 4.3e9
long	32	-2.1e9 -> 2.1e9
unsigned long	32	0 -> 4.3e9
float	32	-1e-38 -> 1e38
double	64	-1e-308 -> 1e308

(Table AD-1) Variables declarations in C

Most high-level languages allow for the definition of indexed lists, more commonly referred to as *arrays*. Arrays can also be multidimensional. Such multidimensional arrays are implemented in C as an array of arrays. An element of such an array can be accessed in the following way:

```
type name_of_array[size1][size2]...[sizeN]
```

This example shows an N-dimensional array of a generic type. The specific types available are those listed in Table AD-1 (such as *int* and *double*). In C the size for each dimension is held in brackets, whereas in many languages the sizes of each dimension are separated by commas.

Text data types like *char* actually define 8-bit numbers that represent an alphanumeric character (i.e., ASCII). Note that strings in C are terminated with a NULL (ASCII 0) character. So a 35-character message will actually occupy 36 bytes (characters) of data. Some particularly useful characters are:

\\   - defines a backslash

\'   - defines an apostrophe

\"   - defines a quote

\n   - defines a charriage return line feed

\xhhh   - defines a hexadecimal ASCII character

The Operators

Here we are referring to the methods used to manipulate variables and actually produce some sort of useful result. The C language seems to have a nearly endless set of operators to perform both mathematical and logical operations. C++ compounds this tremendously by allowing you to define your own operators on your very own data types. Some of the more common types of operators are presented below.

- Assignment operators assign a value to a variable. The equal sign is the assignment operator.
- Arithmetic and bitwise operators are used to perform multiplication, division, addition, subtraction, and modulus (integer remainder after division). The modulus operator works only on integer-type variables, whereas all of the other operators will work with all variable types. In C, there are three unary arithmetic operators, the unary minus (-), an increment (++), and a decrement (--). The increment and decrement are usually used with pointers (data addresses).
- Binary bitwise operations are performed on integer operands using the & symbol for AND, the | symbol for OR, the ^ symbol for bitwise exclusive OR (XOR), the << symbol for the arithmetic shift left, and the >> symbol for the arithmetic shift right. The number of bits is the operand for the arithmetic shifts. The unary bitwise NOT operator will invert all of the bits in the operand. The symbol for this is ~.

Operators can be combined using the assignment operator and any of the arithmetic operators. A few examples are listed below.

```
a = a+b        a += b
a = a-b        a -= b
a = a*b        a *= b
a = a/b        a /= b
a = a%b        a %= b
a = a&b        a &= b
a = a|b        a |= b
a = a^b        a ^= b
a = a<<b       a <<= b
a = a>>b       a >>= b
```

For readibility of code during development, many programmers do not use the combined operators. They can be very useful, though, if instead of the variable *a*, you have some kind of complicated pointer expression. In this way, you don't have to enter it on both sides of the expression, and the meaning is a little clearer. That is, you want to modify the value and store it back in the same location.

Logical operators are operators that yield an absolute, true or false response. They are commonly used to control loops and to perform machine level coding. The == operator is used to determine the equality of two arguments. Do not confuse this with the = assignment operator. < is the less than comparison operator. <= is the less than or equal comparison operator. The >= and > logical operators are greater than or equal to, and greater than logical comparisons, respectively. != is the not equal to logical operator. And the last three logical operators are && for AND, | | for OR, and ! for NOT.

Our last glance at operators takes us into the subject of operator precedence (the order in which multiple operations will be performed in the absence of () to clarify it) and type conversion. Here is a list of operators in decreasing precedence:

++ --	increment, decrement
-	unary minus
* / %	multiplication, division, modulus
+ -	addition, subtraction
<< >>	shift left, shift right
< <= >= >	comparison with less than or greater than
== !=	equal, not equal
& ^ |	bitwise AND, XOR, OR
&& | |	logical AND, OR

A few rules regarding C and the conversion of types must be taken to heart. First, if an operation involves two types, the one of higher rank takes precedence. The ranking from highest to lowest is *double, float, long, int, short*, and *char*. Unsigned outranks signed. For example, if you add a float and a double together, the float is promoted to type double and then added to the double variable. The result is then converted to the type of variable on the left-hand side of the assignment. In an assignment statement, the result is converted to the type of the variable being assigned.

Program Control

Our next discussion involves the ability to control the conditional execution or repetition of certain statements based on the results of certain expressions. We start with conditional execution. The If-Else statement is used to execute conditionally a series of statements based on the results of some expression. Its format is as follows:

```
if (integer_value)
{
    first set of statements
}
else
{
    second set of statements
}
```

If integer_value is nonzero, then the first set of statements are executed, else the second set of statements are executed. Note that compound statements can be created with the if-else statement by use of brackets enclosing certain statements.

The switch statement is another useful statement when more than four alternatives are chosen for a situation. The statement reads as follows:

```
switch(integer_expression)
{
    case constant1:
            statements;
            break;

    case constant2:
            statements;
            break;

    case constant3:
            statements;
            break;

    case constant4:
            statements;
```

```
        break;

   default:
           statements;
}
```

C also supports a strange kind of single-line conditional expression that lets you express a single if-else statement in one line. The form for such an expression is:

```
expression1 ? expression2 : expression3.
```

If expression1 is nonzero, then the whole conditional expression has the value of expression2. If expression1 is zero, then the whole expression has the value of expression3. This type of expression should never be used directly in your code. However, it can be used to define a macro that will be very efficient to execute. For example, we can define a macro to find the maximum of two variables as :

```
#define MAX(a,b) ( (a) > (b) ? (a) : (b) )
```

C supports this type of expression because it can usually be implemented very efficiently by the compiler. Since macros are usually in-line substitutions, the MAX function above will be performed efficiently.

The next basic program control construct is the loop. C has three loop types: the while loop, the do-while loop, and the for loop. The while loop takes the form :

```
while(expression)
       statements;
```

The while loop will repeat the statements until the expression becomes zero. The decision to pass through the loop is made at the beginning, so we may never pass through it. The format for the do-while loop is as follows :

```
do
{
       statements;
} while(expression);
```

The do-while loop will repeat the statements until the expression becomes zero. Note that the decision to pass through this loop is made at the end of the loop; therefore we will always pass through this loop at least once. Finally, we have the for loop, which is a more general form of a FORTRAN do loop. The for loop looks as follows:

```
for(initial condition; test condition; modify)
        statements;
```

The for loop is commonly used for indexing arrays. It is an infinite loop if no bounds are set, that is, if you leave out the test condition all together. The initial condition is the initial value for a variable. The test condition may be any logical expression but is usually a comparision of the loop variable to some ending value like i < 10. The loop variable is usually altered by the modify expression, such as i++.

Now we jump into other program control issues. C provides three additional control statements: break, continue, and goto. Note that these statements can make a complex program difficult to follow but are often quite handy. As shown earlier, the break statement can be used to exit a switch statement or any other type of loop. The continue statement, on the other hand, tells the program to skip to end of the loop and proceed with the next iteration. Goto is just that, a statement that will carry you to any other place in the program, exiting out of any loop that you might be in at the time.

Functions

Now that we know a little more about variables, data types, and program control, let's move our focus to the all important function. All C programs consist of one or more functions; even main() is considered a function. A function has a type, a name, a pair of parentheses containing an optional argument list, and a pair of braces containing an optional list of executable statements. The format is as follows:

```
type name(argument list)
        declarations for arguments in argument list
{
        body of function (statements)
}
```

The type is that of the value the function returns. C provides a special data type of *void* for functions that do not return a value. The types for the arguments in the argument list are located in the second line of the function. Within the function body, the return statement is used to return a number back as the value of the function. Many of the more recent batch of compilers allow the declarations for the arguments in the argument list to be included in the parentheses. This type of declaration corresponds to the ANSI standard version of C as well as to C++.

C makes extensive use of header files, traditionally having the extension of .h, to define data structures and to declare functions. The ANSI standard supports the use of function prototypes to define not only the return value of a function but also the data types of its arguments. Note that for C, *function prototypes* are optional, whereas C++ requires them. Function prototypes allow the compiler to do much more extensive error checking of your code at compile time. Calling a function with the wrong number and/or type of argument is very common. If the function has a prototype, the compiler can check each of the calls to see that the correct number and type of variables are passed to the function. This can greatly reduce the number of mystifying bugs in a program. A typical prototype in a header file looks like:

```
extern void thefunction(int)
```

Macros

Macros and the C preprocessor make up some of the most appealing aspects of C. The ability to conditionally compile program segments, create aliases of any text in the program, and create user-defined macros makes C a very powerful language indeed. Very powerful, however, can also be translated as *very confusing*. One short example of a macro is one that finds the greater value of two numbers. When using a macro that has arguments, ***always*** put the arguments in parentheses as we did in the MAX macro above. This is to ensure that if an expression is passed to the macro, the expression is evaluated before the rest of the macro is processed. Without this convention, you can create some of the most irritating and subtle bugs imaginable.

Pointers and Arrays

Pointers are variables that hold addresses of the data, rather than the data itself. Pointers are primarily used to access different data elements within an array, to allow for dynamic memory allocation, and to access different locations in a data structure. They are also used to pass structures as arguments. C uses the call-by-value convention for argument passing. This means that it passes a *copy* of the data to the function, not the data itself. If you want the function to be able to modify the actual variable, you must pass a pointer to that variable. If you want to pass some huge structure to a function, you pass the pointer; otherwise the program will copy the entire structure each time the function is called. This would be most inefficient.

There are three pointer operators: *, &, and ->. The first is called the *indirection operator*. The indirection operator is used whenever the data stored at the address pointed to by a pointer is required (thus, indirect addressing). The second pointer operator fetches the address of the variable to which it is applied. For example, &a is the address of a. The third pointer operator is the *member access operator*. If s is a pointer to a structure, then s->member is the element member of that particular structure.

Memory

Unlike FORTRAN, C fully supports dynamic memory allocation. There are four standard functions used to manipulate memory in C. The first function is *malloc*. malloc() allocates a chunk of memory of whatever size (in bytes) which you pass to it. It returns a pointer to this newly allocated memory. *calloc*() does the same thing except that it sets all of the memory to 0 as well. *free*() returns the memory allocated by malloc() or calloc() back to the system, making it available for other uses. *realloc*() essentially performs a free() followed by another malloc(). It recognizes the case that you may want less memory than was already allocated, so it would give you back only the memory you already had. It is more efficient in some cases than using free() and malloc() separately.

Example uses of these functions are:

malloc

```
int *pointer;     pointer = (int *) malloc(sizeof(int));
```

calloc

    int *array;   array = (int *) calloc(100, sizeof(int));

Note the use of the *sizeof()* function. This function returns the size of data types in bytes. This makes your code system independent. For example, an *int* on a PC is usually 16 bits long, whereas on a workstation it may be 32 bits long.

Structures

One of the most useful features of C is the *structure* data type. Structures allow you to group together data types into a manageable packet. Unlike arrays, you may freely mix and match data types in whatever fashion you need. For example, we might want to define an image as:

```
struct texture_map_image
{
    int xres;
    int yres;
    int pixres;
}
```

Now let's declare a structure called *ourimage*:

```
struct texture_map_image ourimage;
```

ourimage is now a structure of type *texture_map_image*. We can now initialize and access the data in the structure as follows:

```
ourimage.xres = 1280;
ourimage.yres = 1024;
ourimage.pixres = 32;
```

We can also declare a pointer to such a structure as:

```
struct texture_map_image *image_ptr;
```

```
image_ptr = &ourimage;
image_ptr->xres = 1280;
image_ptr->yres = 1024;
image_ptr->pixres = 32;
```

Now all of the data for an image can be passed around in one easy-to-use package, rather than as separate arrays with confusing and complicated indices.

Typedef

C provides the capability essentially to define your own data types via the *typedef* statement. Basically, you declare one name to be equivalent to some other name, usually a structure definition. You may then use this equivalent name just as any other data type declaration like *int* or *char*. For instance, if we want another way to express our texture_map_image structure template, we can create the TEXTURE_MAP_IMAGE type.

```
typedef   struct texture_map_image   TEXTURE_MAP_IMAGE;
```

This statement replaces all occurrences of TEXTURE_MAP_IMAGE with the struct texture_map_image definition. We can now declare our image to be :

```
TEXTURE_MAP_IMAGE          ourimage;
```

which looks much cleaner than

```
struct texture_map_image          ourimage;
```

Input and Output

Two of the fundamental I/O functions in the C programming language are *scanf* and *printf*. Scanf parses a line entered by the user and places this data into a variable (or variables), much like the FORTRAN read statment. *printf* displays variables on the console in a program-specified format using a format string. A *printf* statement might look something like this:

```
printf("\nImage X Resolution = %d", ImageResX);
```

And some of the format specifiers are the following:

%5d   signed integer with width 5
%16p   pointer value with width 16
%5.4f   floating point number with width 5 and 4 places past the
        decimal point
%5.4e   floating point number in exponential format with width 5
        and 4 places past the decimal point
%c   single character
%s   string
%8x   integer in hexadecimal format with width 8

A few of the special escape sequences in the format string are:

\\   print a single backslash
%%   print a single percent sign
\n   carriage return and line feed

The scanf function is very similar to the printf function. For example:

scanf("%d %f", integernumber, floatingpointnumber);

File I/O

There are many standard C disk I/O functions, so we'll just look at the basics. Most C file access is sequential. That is, the file is read until you reach the end of the file. A file may be read character-by-character using the functions *getc()* and *putc()*. The functions *fprintf()*, *fsanf()*, *fgets()*, *fputs()* allow you to treat a file as a buffered stream of text. To randomly access a binary file, use *fread()*, *fwrite()*, and *fseek()*. A conventional way of handling a file might look like this:

FILE *file_pointer;

file_pointer = fopen("the_filename","the_filetype_string")

fclose(file_pointer);

First we must open a file called the_filename, using the options specified in "the_filetype_string." The available filetype strings are:

"r"	open file for reading
"w"	create new file or overwrite old file
"a"	append existing file or create new file
"r+"	open existing file for reading and writing
"w+"	create a new file for reading and writing
"a+"	append an existing file for reading and writing

Also, an "t" or a "b" can be appended to the strings listed above to select either ASCII file format or Binary. You will find that most UNIX systems will not require this distinction, but our MS-DOS based PCs will.

Programming Style

C programming, like any other art form, requires a great deal of practice, patience, and understanding. Many subtle tricks and nuances must be seen and tried before they can be used effectively. While pointers allow great program flexibility, they may also cause no end of grief. Typical examples are use of uninitialized global pointers or freeing the wrong portion of memory. These kinds of problems are difficult to track down as well. So, be careful and let your experience be your guide!

We have tried to make the included code fairly modular and straightforward. Modular code means keeping such things as file I/O limited to one small set of routines. Try not to put disk I/O calls throughout your code. Instead, make one set of routines to read and write each file type you support. This is only one tenet of modularity. There are a plethora of others that are beyond the scope of the present discussion. You may wish to examine the visualizer code to see both where we have tried to modularize things and where we failed to do so for the sake of expediency.

Our Software Conventions

The easiest way to convey the software conventions used is to show examples of pseudocode. For functions, the lowercase name of the file where the function is located becomes the first part of the function, and this is followed by an underscore:

alg_math_AddMatrices()

The remainder of the function's name is uppercase and follows the underscore. Global variables are indicated by a 'g' preceding the first letter of the variable. Global variables and local variables are both lowercase, where local variables receive no special treatment or marking. Macros are always uppercase, and look like the following:

```
#define        DAMPING_FACTOR = 3;
#define        ROUND(a)      (int)((a)+0.5)
```

Data types are always uppercase; for example,

Alg_Math_Matrix

References

We strongly recommend that you peruse some of the references in the bibliography for further information. In particular, Kernighan and Ritchie's *The C Programming Language* is the virtual bible of C programming style and convention. There is also a wealth of other books at your local technical bookstore that can assist you.

Having ever so briefly described the C language and some of the conventions we use, let's proceed to some of the supporting code itself. In the following appendix we will describe some of the libraries and utility modules used by the image processor for vector manipulation, three-dimensional projections, and other low-level graphics routines. We describe how to compile the source code and proceed to do so for the modules that we use in the software.

APPLICATION SOFTWARE

Program Bubba—the Interactive 3-D Virtual World Visualizer

Bubba is the three-dimensional virtual world polygon visualizer for which we provide the executables and all source code. Bubba is the basis for any virtual reality graphics engine.

USING BUBBA—THE CONTROLS

Using Bubba is easy; there are 4 template *.vr* files that contain three-dimensional worlds with which to work and modify. These files are

AlgorWld.vr
CrazyWld.vr
WallyWld.vr
WayneWld.vr

EschrWld.vr
TorusWld.vr
XYZZYWld.vr

At the DOS prompt, type

    bubba algorwld

to visualize the *algorwld.vr* virtual world. With a skillful hand, a few little gray cells, and some patience, you can use the keyboard controls to interact with the virtual world. Your direction of travel will be the direction that you the viewer are facing at that moment. Use the *throttle* to increase (+ key) or to decrease (− key) your *rate* of travel. The *ailerons* (left and right arrows on keypad) control your *roll*, the *elevator* (up and down arrows on keypad) control your *pitch* (up-down motion), and the *rudder* (home and pg up keys) control your *yaw* (left-to-right motion). You can brake your translational motion by hitting the (ins) key. You can stop your rotational motion by hitting the center of the keypad (5). A summary of commands is as follows:

```
+-------------------------------------------------------------------+
|                                                                   |
|                                                                   |
|                         ----- yaw -----                           |
|                            |          |                           |
|                            |       -------|-----------            |
|                            |      |       |          |            |
|                            7      8       9          p            |
|                                                      i            |
|                        -- 4      5       6 --        t            |
|                       |                     |        c            |
|                       |  1      2       3   |        h            |
|                       |         |           |   |                 |
|                       |      ----------|-------                   |
|                       |                |                          |
|                        --------- roll --------                    |
|                                                                   |
| Ins  -  brake                    5    -  brake roll, pitch and yaw |
| +/-  -  accelerate/decelerate   Esc  -  exit program              |
|                                                                   |
+-------------------------------------------------------------------+
```

    The controls mentioned above respond to your key presses based on a set of parameters fixed in the .vr file. A section of a .vr file showing these parameters is given below. This section shows how the positions, limits on positions, and dampening of certain controls are set to create the feel of the controls (i.e., how the displayed scene responds to your control input).

```
alg_controls
{
        max_aileron_position        18.0
        delta_aileron_position      1.0
        aileron_dampening           0.2
        max_elevator_position       18.0
        delta_elevator_position     1.0
        elevator_dampening          0.2
        max_rudder_position         18.0
        delta_rudder_position       1.0
        rudder_dampening            0.2
        max_throttle_position       250.0
        delta_throttle_position     10.0
        throttle_dampening          1.5
}
```

Note: you must make sure that there are no extra characters on any of the lines, and that there are no extra blank lines inside of the *alg_controls* structure.

THE VIEWER

Below is a section from the *algorwld.vr* file defining the initial position and orientation (viewing direction) of the viewer.

```
alg_viewer
{
        translate        0.0      500.0    14000.0
        rotate           0.0      0.0      0.0
        perspective_plane_distance        350.0
}
```

Note: you must make sure that there are no extra characters on any of the lines, and that there are no extra blank lines inside of the *alg_viewer* structure.

THE WORLD

Below is a section from the *algorwld.vr* file defining the virtual world sky color and intensity, and the maximum number of objects that can be found in the virtual world. This statement must come before any object definitions in a .vr file.

```
alg_world
{
        background_color       cyan
        background_intensity   23
        num_objects            18
}
```

Note: you must make sure that there are no extra characters on any of the lines, and that there are no extra blank lines inside of the *alg_world* structure.

VIEWER-OBJECT COLLISIONS

The *algorwld.vr* virtual world model is set up to allow you to fly through the virtual world and interact (collide) with some of its objects. Some objects (like the main building) are *permeable*, thus they allow you to fly in and out of them. Other objects (like the cars) are *pushable_and_rotatable*, thus if you hit them, they will fly off into space, assuming your traveling direction before the collision, and also assuming any rotation (like roll) that you, the viewer, had before collision. Some objects are only *pushable* and can only be moved, while others are just *rotatable* and can just be rotated based on the viewer rotation. Other objects (like the monolith) are *solid*, and cannot be moved; you the viewer will bounce off of these objects, if you hit them. Objects can be *manipulatable* and simply be pushed and rotated without flying into space.

A skillful hand on the controls can have objects flying off into all directions with any rotations that you can imagine (hit the car while moving fast, while you are in a roll and a yaw rotation, and watch it fly—note that this should only be tried in virtual environments; in the real world, hitting cars at high rates of speed with a swerve can ruin your whole day!) .

A brief list of collision types is as follows:

solid
pushable
rotatable
pushable_and_rotatable
permeable
manipulatable

OBJECT ORIENTATIONS

Objects can assume any position, orientation, and scaling in a virtual world. These parameters have components in all three dimensions. Below is the format of the world position, orientation and scaling parameters for an object.

translate	x	y	z
rotate	x	y	z
scale	x	y	z

OBJECT MOTIONS

As described above, objects can be in motion. Motions have components in all three dimensions. Motions can take the form of changing position (translation), orientation (rotation), and scale. An object can be either *static* or *active*. Note that a collision may override the motion status (*static* or *active*) parameter for an object, if that object is *pushable*, *rotatable*, or *pushable_and_rotatable*. Below is the format of the motion parameters for an object.

```
motion
{
        static or active
        translate      x      y      z
        rotate         x      y      z
        scale          x      y      z
}
```

OBJECT SURFACES

You may remember that a polygon is only visible from one side; this aids in polygon backface removal for increased performance. Our vertex ordering scheme for polygons states that counterclockwise ordering of vertices gives the visible side. Some objects (like far away mountains, or like non-penetrable *solid* objects) are likely to be represented by an *outside* surface only. Other objects may be *permeable*, and thus we need to have two polygons produced—one for the inside and one for the outside. Thus we have *inside_and_outside* surfaces. An *inside* surface is just an *outside* surface with the vertices in clockwise order. The following is a list of the surface types:

    inside_and_outside
    inside
    outside

OBJECT COLORS

Each polygon that makes up any object in the scene can have its own color. There are seven colors from which to choose. Each color can have 36 different intensity levels, from black to that color, saturated (see the following list). Note that each polygon must have an intensity value associated with its color, and that polygons that are inside and outside surfaces must have colors and intensities defined for both the inside and outside polygon (as a polygon that is an *inside_and_outside* surface is actually two separate polygons facing in opposite directions—as defined by our vertex ordering scheme mentioned earlier in Chapter 5). Here is the list of colors:

    blue
    green
    cyan
    red
    magenta
    yellow
    gray or gray

* each color has intensities of 0 to 35 (black to saturation)

OBJECT TEXTURES

No virtual world would be acceptable without a little texturing to help fool the sense of vision. We really want to create a suspension of disbelief (mind you, we will not create this effectively on a PC). The following is a list of polygon texture types. The *flat* shading provides the basic polygon solid color fill. The four transparent textures, *transparent_hatch*, *transparent_diagonal_stripe*, *transparent_vertical_stripe*, *transparent_horizontal_stripe*, give us a means by which to see through polygons by drawing only certain pixels of those polygons into the screen buffer. Since we are using the Painter's algorithm for display, polygons that were drawn before the transparent polygon will only be partially covered with the sparse pixels of our transparent polygon. We therefore see both polygons. The *checkerboard* texture is a computed texture, producing a checkerboard pattern on an object.

The *map* textures are used to create fast, complex surface textures. In that these textures are precomputed into memory arrays, you have no control from the .vr file over their color (the color and intensity inputs are thrown away—perhaps a future modification will be some palette manipulation to allow control). The *checkerboard_map* texture produces a black-and-white checkerboard pattern. The *grit_map* texture produces a gray grit/sand texture. The *marble_map* and *wood_map* textures use the Perlin noise function to create black-and-white marble and light brown wood textures, respectively. The *waves_map* texture produces a wicked wavy blue texture. And finally, the *image_map1* and *image_map2* textures are used to load 8-bit color (gray-scale) .PCX image files defined in the ALG_TEX.H file into memory for display. A list of the textures is as follows:

```
flat
transparent_hatch
transparent_diagonal_stripe
transparent_vertical_stripe
transparent_horizontal_stripe
checkerboard
checkerboard_map
grit_map
marble_map
wood_map
waves_map
```

image_map1
image_map2

SOME OBJECT DEFINITIONS

Now that we know a little about how objects work in a .vr file, let us take a quick
look at the actual format for an object in a .vr file. Notice that the ground (our
first example object) that runs out to the horizon line of the world is nothing
more than a huge square polygon. Also note that the minimum height of flight is
5 (as hard-coded in ALG_CTRL.C). All objects below this point (like the ground
and roadways) can be permeable, as they are never reached by the viewer.
Various object generators for terrain, equations, spheres, cones, cylinders, and
tori are included. Three objects from *algorwld.vr* are as follows:

THE GROUND:

```
alg_object
{
        name            ground
        surface         outside
        collision       permeable
        translate       0.0        0.0        0.0
        rotate          0.0        0.0        0.0
        scale           10000000.0     10000000.0     10000000.0
        motion
        {
                status          static
                translate       0.0        0.0        0.0
                rotate          0.0        0.0        0.0
                scale           0.0        0.0        0.0
        }
        vertex_list
        {
                num_vertices    4
                vertex  -1.0       0.0        -1.0
                vertex   1.0       0.0        -1.0
                vertex   1.0       0.0         1.0
```

```
                        vertex  -1.0      0.0       1.0
                }
        polygon_list
        {
                num_polygons 1
                polygon
                {
                        GRASS
                        num_vertices    4
                        vertex_index    0
                        vertex_index    1
                        vertex_index    2
                        vertex_index    3
                        color           green
                        intensity       12
                        texture  flat
                }
        }
}

THE ROADWAYS:

alg_object
{
        name            roadways
        surface         outside
        collision       permeable
        translate       0.0     1.0     7000.0
        rotate          0.0     0.0     0.0
        scale           150.0   150.0   150.0
        motion
        {
                status          static
                translate       0.0     0.0     0.0
                rotate          0.0     0.0     0.0
                scale           0.0     0.0     0.0
        }
        vertex_list
        {
```

```
        num_vertices   8
        vertex  50.0              0.0        25000.0
        vertex  50.0              0.0        -6000.0
        vertex  90.0              0.0        -6000.0
        vertex  90.0              0.0        25000.0
        vertex  -6000.0 0.0       10.0
        vertex  -6000.0 0.0       -30.0
        vertex  25000.0           0.0        -30.0
        vertex  25000.0           0.0        10.0
}
polygon_list
{
        num_polygons 2
        polygon
        {
                ROAD
                num_vertices   4
                vertex_index   0
                vertex_index   1
                vertex_index   2
                vertex_index   3
                color          gray
                intensity      15
                texture grit_map
        }
        polygon
        {
                ROAD
                num_vertices   4
                vertex_index   4
                vertex_index   5
                vertex_index   6
                vertex_index   7
                color          gray
                intensity      15
                texture grit_map
        }
}
```

```
        }

THE BUILDING ROOF:

alg_object
{
        name            building_roof
        surface         inside_and_outside
        collision       permeable
        translate       0.0       1000.0    0.0
        rotate          0.0       0.0       0.0
        scale           250.0     50.0      250.0
        motion
        {
                status          static
                translate       0.0       0.0       0.0
                rotate          0.0       0.0       0.0
                scale           0.0       0.0       0.0
        }
        vertex_list
        {
                num_vertices    5
                vertex  -10.0     -20.0     -10.0
                vertex  10.0      -20.0     -10.0
                vertex  10.0      -20.0     10.0
                vertex  -10.0     -20.0     10.0
                vertex  0.0       -45.0     0.0
        }
        polygon_list
        {
                num_polygons 4
                polygon
                {
                        ROOF
                        num_vertices    3
                        vertex_index    0
                        vertex_index    1
                        vertex_index    4
                        out_color       gray
```

```
          out_intensity    12
          out_texture      flat
          in_color         gray
          in_intensity     12
          in_texture       flat
}
polygon
{
      ROOF
      num_vertices     3
      vertex_index     1
      vertex_index     2
      vertex_index     4
      out_color        gray
      out_intensity    14
      out_texture      flat
      in_color         gray
      in_intensity     14
      in_texture       flat
}
polygon
{
      ROOF
      num_vertices     3
      vertex_index     2
      vertex_index     3
      vertex_index     4
      out_color        gray
      out_intensity    16
      out_texture      flat
      in_color         gray
      in_intensity     16
      in_texture       flat
}
polygon
{
      ROOF
      num_vertices     3
```

```
                              vertex_index    3
                              vertex_index    0
                              vertex_index    4
                              out_color       gray
                              out_intensity   18
                              out_texture     flat
                              in_color        gray
                              in_intensity    18
                              in_texture      flat
                      }
              }
      }
```

Note: you must make sure that there are no extra characters on any of the lines, and that there are no extra blank lines inside of the *alg_object* structure.

Programs for the Anaglyph Glasses

Along with the 3-D virtual world visualizer, we include some simple programs that allow you to use your anaglyph glasses that you get for free with the book. Hopefully these programs will act as an introduction to three-dimensional viewing technologies. The sensation of 3-D created when the brain finally fuses the two different colored wire-frames into one "no-color" image is still fascinating to me.

FLYING

A program (ANA_FLY.C) for which we give you executables and all source code for the visualization of the .vr worlds using the anaglyph glasses.

VIEWING 3-D SHAPES

A simple program for which we give you executables and all source code for the visualization of simple 3-D shapes with the anaglyph glasses (ANAGLYPH.C).

The mouse is used to manipulate the three-dimensional shape. Releasing the mouse button while moving the mouse will leave the object in rotation. Eight .ANA objects are included.

VIEWING STEREO PAIRS AS A SINGLE IMAGE

A program for which we give you executables and all source code (ANA_IMG.C) that will take two image files that form a stereo pair, and convert them into a single image that can be viewed with the anaglyph glasses. Three sample outputs and a stereo pair are included.

MISCELLANEOUS

We also include assorted other programs for visualizing particle systems (PSYS_ANA.C) and a field or stars (STAR_ANA.C) with the anaglyph glasses.

Programs Files And Directories

Installation from the 3.5″ diskette will create the following directory structure. It is suggested that you work the compiler from the C:\VRBOOK\SOURCE\BIN directory. The project files call on program modules found in the C:\VRBOOK\SOURCE\LIB directory. Copying compiled programs into the C:\VRBOOK\SOURCE directory and running them from there is suggested, as that is where the .PCX files and the .BGI file are kept. If you have screen problems running the software, look for the latest .BGI driver on your local BBS. Enjoy!

C:\VRBOOK\SOURCE\LIB

ALG_3D.C   — creation of polygon display list
ALG_3D.H

ALG_ANA.H   — anaglyph color table

ALG_COLL.C — viewer-object collision detection
ALG_COLL.H

ALG_CTRL.C — interpreting keyboard input for control
ALG_CTRL.H

ALG_DEFS.H — miscellaneous definitions

ALG_GRAF.C — PC graphics
ALG_GRAF.H

ALG_HIDS.C — hidden-surface and sorting
ALG_HIDS.H

ALG_KBD.C — keyboard input
ALG_KBD.H

ALG_MATH.C — mathematics function
ALG_MATH.H

ALG_MATX.C — matrix and vector functions
ALG_MATX.H

ALG_MAUS.C — mouse input
ALG_MAUS.H

ALG_MEM.C — memory allocation/deallocation
ALG_MEM.H

ALG_MOTN.C — object motion
ALG_MOTN.H

ALG_OBJ.C — object database maker
ALG_OBJ.H

ALG_PARS.C — parse the .vr file and create world
ALG_PARS.H

ALG_PCLP.C   — Sutherland-Hodgman and Liang-Barsky polygon
ALG_PCLP.H   clipping

ALG_PCX.C   — load .PCX image file into image texture buffers
ALG_PCX.H

ALG_POLY.C   — convex polygon drawing
ALG_POLY.H

ALG_PROJ.C   — 3-D to 2-D projection
ALG_PROJ.H

ALG_SCRN.C   — screen-buffer and screen routines
ALG_SCRN.H

ALG_SHAD.C   — object polygon shading routine
ALG_SHAD.H

ALG_TEX.C   — procedural and image textures
ALG_TEX.H

ALG_VR.C   — .vr file info writing
ALG_VR.H

\VRBOOK\SOURCE\BIN

ANAGLYPH.C   — anaglyph glasses shape visualizer
ANAGLYPH.DSK
ANAGLYPH.PRJ

ANA_FLY.C   — anaglyph glasses flying simulation
ANA_FLY.PRJ   (actually found in its own directory)

ANA_IMG.C   — anaglyph glasses convert stereo pair to viewable image
ANA_IMG.PRJ

BUBBA.C   — 3-D virtual world visualizer
BUBBA.PRJ

MANDJULI.C   — walk on Mandelbrot set and see the Julia set for that
MANDJULI.PRJ   complex location

PSYS.C   — three-particle orbital simulation
PSYS.PRJ

PSYS_ANA.C   — anaglyph glasses three-particle orbital simulation
PSYS_ANA.PRJ

STAR_ANA.C   — anaglyph glasses field of stars simulation
STAR_ANA.PRJ

\VRBOOK\SOURCE

SVGA256.BGI   — Borland graphics driver by Jordan Hargrave

ANAGLYPH.EXE— anaglyph glasses shape visualizer (with 8 .ANA models)

ANA_FLY.EXE   — anaglyph glasses flying simulation

ANA_IMG.EXE   — anaglyph glasses convert stereo pair to viewable image
POOL.GIF   (the GIF files can be viewed with VPIC. These were
STACK.GIF   generated by ANA_IMG and IMG2GIF. The left and
STACK_L.GIF   right images for the 3-D STACK are included)
STACK_R.GIF
GIF2IMG.EXE
IMG2GIF.EXE

BUBBA.EXE   — 3-D virtual world visualizer with .vr world models and
BUBBA.DOC   .PCX image texture maps (DOCK.PCX, HOUSE.PCX,
                     RINGNEB3.PCX, SATRN.PCX, TESLA.PCX)

ALGORWLD.VR   (also including TERRAIN, EQUATION, CONE, CYLINDER, SPHERE, and TORUS object database generators).

CRAZYWLD.VR
ESCHRWLD.VR
TORUSWLD.VR
WALLYWLD.VR
WAYNEWLD.VR
XYZZYWLD.VR

MANDJULI.EXE   — walk on Mandelbrot set and see Julia set for that complex location

PSYS.EXE   — three-particle orbital simulation

PSYS_ANA.EXE   — anaglyph glasses three-particle orbital simulation

STAR_ANA.EXE   — anaglyph glasses field of stars simulation

DEMO_ANA.BAT, DEMO_BUB.BAT, DEMO_AF.BAT, DEMO_MSC.BAT, DEMO_.BAT   — miscellaneous demo batch files

\VRBOOK\SOURCE\ANA_IMG

The following modules are used by the ray tracer Bob found in the book *Photorealism and Ray Tracing in C* written by Christopher D. Watkins, Stephen B. Coy, and Mark Finlay. The book can be obtained from M&T Publishing (San Mateo, CA) now Henry Holt (NY, NY). These modules cause the ray tracer in that book to generate stereo pairs that the program ANA_IMG.C in this book will convert to a single Anaglyph glasses viewable file. This file can be converted to .GIF for viewing with VPIC.

POOL.BAT   STACK_BAT
POOLBALL.BO   STACK_L.B
STICK.BO   STACK_R.B
POOL_L.B   ANA_IMG.DOC
POOL_R.B

APPENDIX F

BIBLIOGRAPHY

VR References

Adam, John A. "Virtual Reality Is for Real." *IEEE Spectrum.* Oct. 1993: 22–29.

Airey, John M., John H. Rohlf, and Frederick P. Brooks, Jr. "Towards Image Realism with Interactive Update Rates in Complex Virtual Building Environments." Department of Computer Science, University of North Carolina, Chapel Hill, N.C.

Amato, Ivan. "In Search of the Human Touch." *Science* 258. 27 Nov. 1992: 1436–1437.

Antonoff, Michael. "Living in a Virtual World." *Popular Science.* July 1992: 83–86, 124–125.

Baecker, Ronald and Ian Small. "Animation at the Interface." *The Art of Human-Computer Interface Design.* Ed. Laurel, Brenda. Reading, Mass.: Addison-Wesley, 1990.

Benedikt, Michael. *Cyberspace: First Steps.* Cambridge Mass.: MIT Press, 1993.

Brennan, Susan. "Conversation as Direct Manipulation: An Iconoclastic View." *The Art of Human-Computer Interface Design.* Ed. Laurel, Brenda Reading, Mass.: Addison-Wesley, 1990.

Brooks, Frederick P. Jr. "Grasping Reality Through Illusions–Interactive Graphics Serving Science" TR88–007. *Proceedings of the Fifth Conference on Computers and Human*

Interaction. 1–11. Eds. E. Soloway, D. Frye, and S. Sheppard. Reading, Mass.: Addison-Wesley, 1988.

Brooks, Frederick P. Jr. et al. "Six Generations of Building Walkthroughs—Final Technical Report to the National Science Foundation." Department of Computer Science, University of North Carolina, Chapel Hill, N.C., June 1992.

Brooks, Frederick P. Jr. and William V. Wright. "Nineteenth Annual Progress Report Interactive Graphics for Molecular Studies." TR92-014. Department of Computer Science, University of North Carolina, Chapel Hill, N.C., April 1993.

Brooks, Frederick P. Jr., Ming Ouh—Young, James J. Batter, and P. Jerome Kilpatrick. "Project GROPE—Haptic Displays for Scientific Visualization." *ACM SIGGRAPH— Computer Graphics.*ACM-0-89791-344-2/90/8/177: 177–185. 1990.

Butterworth, Andrew Davidson, Stephen Hench, and T. Marc Olano. "3DM: A Three-dimensional Modeler Using a Head-Mounted Display." *ACM SIGGRAPH— Computer Graphics.*ACM-0-89791-471-6/92/3/135: 135–138, 226. 1992.

Campbell, Joseph. "Day of the Dead." 1988. as quoted in Rheingold, *Virtual Reality.*

Cheney, Margaret. *Tesla, Man Out of Time.* New York: Dorset Press, 1989.

Cobb, Nathan. "Cyberpunk: Terminal Chic." *The Boston Globe* 24 Nov. 1992. Living Arts: 29, 32. (as found on the Internet)

Cockayne, William. "On Law Enforcement Agencies in Cyberspace." billc@apple.com.

Cook, David A. *A History of Narrative Film.* New York: Summit Books, 1981. as quoted in Pimentel.

Coull, Tom and Peter Rothman. "Virtual Reality for Decision Support Systems." *AI Expert.* Aug. 1993: 22–25.

Cramblitt, Bob. "World's Fastest Graphics Computer." *Computer Graphics World.* PennWell, 1993.

DeFanti, Thomas A., Daniel J. Sandin, and Carolina Cruz—Neira. "A 'room' with a 'view.'" *IEEE Spectrum.* Oct. 1993: 30–33.

Delaney, Ben. "Big Brother Is Watching." *AI Expert Virtual Reality Special Report.* July 1992: 35–38.

Department of Computer Science, University of North Carolina, Chapel Hill, N.C. "Head—Tracker Project Summary." Oct. 1993.

Department of Computer Science, University of North Carolina, Chapel Hill, N.C. "Pixel-Planes 5 Project Summary." Jul. 1993.

Dunn, Frank ed. *VR Monitor* 2:1 Jan./Feb. 1993.

Edupage 8/10/93 quotes *New York Times.* 9 August 93, C2

Eisenberg, Bart, Butler Hine, and Daryl Rasmussen. "Telerobotic Vehicle Control: NASA Preps for Mars." *AI Expert*. Aug. 1993: 19–21.

Fisher, Scott. "Virtual Interface Environments." *The Art of Human-Computer Interface Design*. Ed. Laurel, Brenda Reading, Mass.: Addison-Wesley, 1990.

Fuchs, Henry, Gary Bishop, and et al. "Research Directions in Virtual Environments." TR92–027 *ACM SIGGRAPH—Computer Graphics*. 26-3: 153–177. August 1992.

Georgia Institute of Technology's Graphics, Visualization, and Usability Center Literature. (GVU)

Gottschalk, Stefan and John Hughes. "Autocalibration for Virtual Environments Tracking Hardware." *ACM SIGGRAPH—Computer Graphics*. ACM-0-89791-601-8/93/8/65: 65–72. 1993.

Graff, Gordon. "Virtual Acoustics Puts Sound in Its Place." Science 256. 1 May. 1992: 616–617.

Hamilton, Joan, et al. "Virtual Reality: How a Computer-generated World Could Change the Real World." *Business Week*. Oct. 5, 1992: 97–105.

Hancock, Dennis. "'Prototyping' the Hubble fix." *IEEE Spectrum*. Oct. 1993: 34–35.

Holloway, Richard, Henry Fuchs, and Warren Robinett. "Virtual—Worlds Research at the University of North Carolina at Chapel Hill as of February 1992." Department of Computer Science, University of North Carolina, Chapel Hill, N.C., Feb. 1992 .

IVEX Press Releases and Literature.

Jacobson, Linda. "The Business of Selling Virtual Reality." *AI Expert Virtual Reality Special Report*. July 1992: 39–41.

Kay, Alan. "User Interface: A Personal View." *The Art of Human-Computer Interface Design*. Ed. Laurel, Brenda Reading, Mass.: Addison-Wesley, 1990.

Kerris, Richard. "Virtual Performers." *IRIS Universe* 20. Spring 1992: 12–13.

Krueger, Myron. "VIDEOPLACE and the Interface of the Future." *The Art of Human-Computer Interface Design*. Ed. Laurel, Brenda. Reading, Mass.: Addison-Wesley, 1990.

Lanier, Jaron. "A Brave New World: Virtual Reality Today." *AI Expert Virtual Reality Special Report*. July 1992: 11–17.

Latta, John. "The Business of Cyberspace." *AI Expert Virtual Reality Special Report*. July 1992: 27–33.

Laurel, Brenda, ed. *The Art of Human-Computer Interface Design*. Reading, Mass.: Addison-Wesley, 1990.

Laurel, Brenda. "A New Opposable Thumb." *AI Expert Virtual Reality Special Report*. July 1992: 23–26.

Laurel, Brenda. "Interface Agents: Metaphors with Character." *The Art of Human-Computer Interface Design.* Ed. Laurel, Brenda Reading, Mass.: Addison-Wesley, 1990.

Maddox, Tom. "After the Deluge: Cyberpunk in the '80s and '90s." newsgroup alt.cyberpunk. tmaddox@netcom.com.

Molendi, Gloria and Matteo Patriarca. "Virtual Reality: Medical Researches." Technical Report 1/92 *Universita' degli Studi di Milano Dipartimento di Scienze della Informazione.*

Naimark, Michael. "Realness and Interactivity." *The Art of Human-Computer Interface Design.* Ed. Laurel, Brenda. Reading, Mass.: Addison-Wesley, 1990.

Naj, A. K. *Wall Street Journal.* 3 March 93. B1, B8.

Negroponte, Nicholas. "Hospital Corners." *The Art of Human-Computer Interface Design.* Ed. Laurel, Brenda Reading, Mass.: Addison-Wesley, 1990.

Negroponte, Nicholas. "The Noticeable Difference." *The Art of Human-Computer Interface Design.* Ed. Laurel, Brenda. Reading, Mass.: Addison-Wesley, 1990.

Newquist, Harvey P. III. "Reach Out and Touch Someone." *AI Expert.* Aug. 1993: 44–45.

Oren, Tim. "Designing a New Medium." *The Art of Human-Computer Interface Design.* Ed. Laurel, Brenda. Reading, Mass.: Addison-Wesley, 1990.

Park, Brian V. "The Cyberfactory: View of the Future." *AI Expert Virtual Reality Special Report.* July 1992: 59–64.

Parsons, Donald F. "History and Research on the Reliability of Telemedicine Diagnosis." Article 520 of newsgroups sci.med.telemedicine.

Peterson, Ivars. "Looking—Glass Worlds." *Science News* 141. Jan. 4, 1992: 8–10, 15.

Pfeiffer, John. *The Creative Explosions.* 1982. as quoted in Rheingold, *Virtual Reality.*

Pimentel, Ken and Kevin Teixeira. *Virtual Reality: Through the new Looking Glass.* New York: Windcrest, 1993.

Reid, Elizabeth. "Electropolis: Communication and Community on Internet Relay Chat." Honours Thesis. University of Melbourne, 1991.

Rettig, Marc. "Virtual Reality and Artificial Life." *AI Expert.* Aug. 1993: 15–17.

Rheingold, Howard. "A Slice of Life in My Virtual Community." hlr@well.sf.ca.us. June 1992.

Rheingold, Howard. "What's the Big Deal about Cyberspace?" *The Art of Human-Computer Interface Design.* Ed. Laurel, Brenda. Reading, Mass.: Addison-Wesley, 1990.

Rheingold, Howard. *Virtual Reality.* New York: Summit, 1991.

Robinett, Warren and Jannick Rolland. "A Computational Model for the Stereoscopic Optics of a Head-Mounted Display." *Presence.* 1:1 (Winter 1992): 45–62.

Robinett, Warren and Richard Holloway. "Implementation of Flying, Scaling, and Grabbing in Virtual Worlds." *ACM SIGGRAPH—Computer Graphics.* ACM-0-89791-471-6/92/3/189: 189–192. 1992.

Robinett, Warren. "Electronic Expansion of Human Perception." *Whole Earth Review.* Fall 1991.

Rogoff, Leonard. "Virtual Reality." *The University Alumni Report.* University of North Carolina, Chapel Hill, N.C., Oct. 1991.

Sense 8 Corporation. *Universe.* 1:1 July 1992.

Simgraphics Press Releases.

Smith, Norris Parker. "Virtual Illusions." 9 July 1987. Daily news item from somewhere on the Internet.

Stix, Gary. "See-Through View." *Scientific American.* Sept. 1992: 166.

Sutherland, Ivan. "The Ultimate Display." *Proceedings of the IFIP Congress.* 1965: 506–508.

Swaine, Michael. "Psychedelic Technology." *Dr. Dobb's Journal.* April 1993: 99–102.

Taylor, Russell, Warren Robinett, et al. "The Nanomanipulator: A Virtual—Reality Interface for a Scanning Tunneling Microscope." *ACM SIGGRAPH—Computer Graphics.* ACM-0-89791-601-8/93/8/127: 127–134. 1993.

University of North Carolina's Department of Computer Science Literature.

VPL Research, Inc.. *Virtual World News.* 3:1 U.S. edition. Summer/Siggraph 1991.

VR World. 1:1 Jan./Feb. 1992.

Ward, Mark, Ronald Azuma, et al. "A Demonstrated Optical Tracker With Scalable Work Area for Head-Mounted Display Systems." Department of Computer Science, University of North Carolina, Chapel Hill, N.C.

Warner, Dave. "Medical Rehabilitation, Cyber-Style." *AI Expert Virtual Reality Special Report.* July 1992: 19–22.

Woolley, Benjamin. *Virtual Worlds: A Journey in Hype and Hyperreality.* Cambridge, Mass.: Blackwell, 1992.

Technical References

Abrash, Michael. "Fast Convex Polygons." *Dr. Dobb's Journal.* Mar. 1991: 129.

Abrash, Michael. "The Polygon Primeval." *Dr. Dobb's Journal.* Feb. 1991: 153.

Arbib, Michael A., and Allen R. Hanson. *Vision, Brain, and Cooperative Computation.* Cambridge, Mass.: The MIT Press, 1987.

Arvo, James. *Graphics Gems II*. Academic Press. 1991.

Blanton, Keith. "Image Extrapolation for Flight Simulator Visual Systems." *AIAA Conference*. 1988.

Carpenter, L. "A New Hidden Surface Algorithm," *Proceedings of NW76*, ACM, Seattle, WA, 1976.

Catmull, E., "A Subdivision Algorithm for Computer Display of Curved Surfaces," University of Utah, Salt Lake City, December 1974.

Embree, Paul M. and Bruce Kimble. *C Language Algorithms for Digital Signal Processing*. Englewood Cliffs, N.J.: Prentice Hall, 1991.

Escher, M.C. *The World of M. C. Escher*. New York: H.N. Abrams, 1971.

Finlay, Mark. "Fractal Terrain Image Synthesis for Simulation Using Defense Mapping Agency Data," SPIE Technical Symposium on Optics, Electro-Optics, & Sensors. Orlando, FL, 1987.

Foley, James., Andries van Dam, Steven Feiner, and John Hughes. *Computer Graphics Principles and Practice*. Reading, Mass.: Addison-Wesley, 2nd ed., 1990.

Fuchs, H., Kadem, Z., "On Visible Surface Generation by a Priori Tree Structures," *Computer Graphics*, vol. 14, no. 3, pp. 124–133, 1980.

Glassner, Andrew S. *An Introduction to Ray Tracing*. Academic Press, 1989.

Glassner, Andrew S. *Graphics Gems*. Academic Press, 1990.

Harrington, Stephen, *Computer Graphics, A Programming Approach*, McGraw-Hill Book Company, New York, 1987.

Heckbert, P. S., "Survey of Texture Mapping," *IEEE Computer Graphics and Applications*, 6 (11), pp. 56–67, 1986.

Kirk, David. *Graphics Gems III*. Academic Press, 1992.

Morley, T. D., and A. D. Andrew. *Linear Algebra Projects Using Mathematica*. McGraw-Hill, Inc., 1993.

Newell, M. E., Newell, R. G., Sancha, T. L., "A New Approach to the Shaded Picture Problem," *Proceedings of the ACM National Conference*, 1972.

Newman, W. M., and Sproull, R. F., *Principles of Interactive Computer Graphics*, McGraw-Hill, New York, 1981.

Pavlidis, Theo, *Algorithms for Graphics and Image Processing*. Rockville, MD.: Computer Science Press, 1982.

Peachy D. R., "Solid Texturing of Complex Surfaces," *Computer Graphics*, 19 (3), pp. 253–259, 1985.

Perlin, K., "An Image Synthesizer," *Computer Graphics*, 19 (3), pp. 287–296, 1985.

Press, William H., Brian P. Flannery, Saul A. Teukolsky, and William T. Vetterling, *Numerical Recipes in C: The Art of Scientific Computing.* Cambridge University Press, 1988.

Sutherland, I. E., Sproull, R. F., and Schumacker, R., "A Characterization of Ten Hidden-Surface Algorithms," Computing Surveys, 6 (1), pp. 1–55, 1974.

Watkins, Christopher D., Alberto Sadun, and Stephen R. Marenka. *Modern Image Processing: Warping, Morphing and Classical Techniques.* Cambridge, Mass.: Academic Press, Inc., 1993.

Watkins, Christopher D., and Larry E. Sharp. *Programming in 3 Dimensions: Ray Tracing and Animation.* San Mateo, CA.: M&T Publishing, Inc., 1992.

Watkins, Christopher D., and Roger T. Stevens. *Advanced Graphics Programming in C and C++.* San Mateo, CA.: M&T Publishing, Inc., 1991.

Watkins, Christopher D., and Roger T. Stevens. *Advanced Graphics Programming in Turbo Pascal.* San Mateo, CA.: M&T Publishing, Inc., 1990.

Watkins, Christopher D., Stephen B. Coy, and Mark Finlay. *Photorealism and Ray Tracing.* San Mateo, CA.: M&T Publishing, Inc., 1992.

Watt, Alan. Fundamentals of Three–Dimensional Computer Graphics. Addison-Wesley, 1989.

Wolberg, George. *Digital Image Warping.* IEEE Computer Society Press Monograph, 1990.

Index

A

Abrams-Gentile Entertainment (AGE), 75
Advanced Research Projects Agency (ARPA), 6, 19,
    52–60, 61, 66, 82
    Information Processing Techniques Office (IPTO),
    54, 57, 58, 60, 61
Advanced Robotics Research, Ltd., 28
affine transformations, 166, 181–187, 220, 304–306
agents, 135
algorithm, xix, xxi, 32, 39, 77, 104, 105, 153, 231, 255,
    260, 262, 279, 280, 281, 306, 311, 358, 394,
    399
    backface removal (*see* polygon, hidden surface,
        backface removal)
    binary space paritioning (*see* polygon, hidden
        surface, binary space partitioning)
    Blinn (*see* polygon, texturing, bump mapping)
    Carpenter (*see* polygon, hidden surface, scan line)
    Catmull (*see* polygon, hidden surface, Z buffer)
    color filling (*see* polygon, color filling)
    Fuchs (*see* polygon, hidden surface, binary space
        partitioning)
    hidden removal (*see* polygon, hidden removal)
    Liang–Barsky, 259–263
    Newell's (*see* polygon, hidden surface, painter's)
    Painter's (*see* polygong, hidden surface,
        painter's)
    Peachey's (*see* polygon, texturing)
    Perlin's (*see* polygon, texturing, noise)
    position comparison (*see* polygon, position
        comparison)
    ray tracing (*see* rendering, ray tracing)
    Sutherland–Hodgman, 255–258
alias (*see* anti-alias)
amniocentesis, 82
anaglyph, 106, 321, 369–376, 384, 485, 486, 488, 489,
    490
Anastazi, 45
Anatomist, Digital, 40
anti-alias, 228, 232, 233, 234–235, 394, 395
    motion blur, 235
    progressive refinement, 235
    spatial alias, 233
    temporal alias, 234
    texture, 235
Apple Computer, Inc., 23, 62, 70, 74

ARC (*see* Augmentation Research Center)
Arch-Mac (*see* MIT, Architecture Machine Group)
architectural walkthroughs, 1, 2–11, 80–81, 129–130
Argonne National Laboratories, 15, 78
Argonne Remote Manipulator (ARM), 15, 78
Aristotle, 46, 93, 115
ARPA (*see* Advanced Research Projects Agency)
ARPAnet, 60
ARRC Teletact Glove, 28
Art+Com, 6
arterial navigation, 39
Artificial Realities Systems, 33
Aspen Movie Map, 67–69
Atari Research, 69–70, 71, 73
atomic bomb, 50
augmentation, 1, 11–12, 25, 54–55, 76–78, 130–131,
    132, 147, (*see also* medicine, augmentation)
Augmentation Research Center (ARC), 55, 61, 83

B

background illumination (*see* polygon, shading,
    background illumination)
Barlow, John Perry, 141
BattleMech, 23
BattleTech, 23
Berkeley, Bishop, 97
Berlin, Germany, 6
Binary space partitioning (*see* polygon, hidden
    surface, binary space partitioning)
BioControl Systems, 28
BioMuse, 27, 28
bit-mapped graphics, 61
blind spot, 95–98, 115
Blinn's algorithm (*see* polygon, texturing, bump
    mapping)
Boeing Co., 6, 12
Bolt, Richard, 66
boxing test (*see* polygon, position comparison)
Boyle, Robert, 47
Bradbury Ray, 145
Brennan, Susan, 69
Brigham and Women's Hospital, 35
Brooks, Frederick P. Jr., xxiii, xxiv, 3, 14–16, 22, 25,
    76, 80–82
Brushnell, Nolan, 69
Bush, Vannevar, 84

T